CHIVALRY

ALLEGORICAL REPRESENTATION OF CHIVALRY.   [*Frontispiece.*]

DEDICATION.

I dedicate this work to the memory of MIGUEL CERVANTES SAAVEDRA *who laughed at Chivalry in his books and was a true "Chevalier" in his life.   I dedicate it to the greatest of Spanish authors and to one of the most valiant soldiers of Spain—the author of " Don Quixote "—the wounded Knight of Lepanto !*

CHIVALRY

LÉON GAUTIER

CRESCENT BOOKS
NEW YORK

This 1989 edition published by Crescent Books,
distributed by Crown Publishers, Inc., 225 Park Avenue South,
New York, New York 10003.

Printed and bound in Finland

ISBN 0-517-68635-X

h g f e d c b a

CONTENTS.

CONTENTS.

The Knight.

LIST OF ILLUSTRATIONS.

CAROLVS·IMPERATOR

PREFACE.

OUR first intention was to give this volume the more expanded title of "Chivalry, according to the Epic Poems," but we have been compelled to consult so many other authorities that we feel obliged to adopt a more general and shorter title.

The Epic Poems (*Chansons de Geste*) do not the less remain as the principal and the best of all our sources of information; for in them (in our own opinion) we find the truest pictures of Chivalry itself, and the most exact representations of the days of Chivalry. The authors of these popular poems, whose sincerity is unquestionable, only depicted what they actually witnessed. No other writers have so minutely described the costumes, armour, habitations, furniture, the private lives and the manners of the Feudal nobility. Good judges are not easily deceived. There is perhaps not a page of the admirable Glossary of Ducange, or of the Memoirs of Saint Palaye, which does not bear witness to the truthfulness of our songs. Nor does Jules Quicherat hold them in less esteem; he declares in round terms that "their heroes are creations modelled on Feudal seignors." Viollet le Duc quotes them as frequently as Ducange. They complete the Annals and the Chronicles, filling in lapses, and adding force to the cases recorded. It is, besides, very easy to assure one's self that the poets spoke the same language as our historians. This can be substantiated by reading alternately such a Chronicle as that of Lambert d'Ardre and a poem like *Ogier*.

It will appear to many good souls that our enterprise is rather a rash one, if we reflect how many volumes have been inspired by Chivalry. But we have chosen to produce our book on a new plan, and this view may commend it to competent judges. We have devoted a large portion of the volume to the private life of the period : and have enshrined it in a chronological frame which is not very elastic. We have seldom gone farther back than the time of Philip Augustus, and rarely go lower than his death. Within these limits, as has been truly said, lies the golden epoch of the Middle Ages—and to it we have confined ourselves. The chief fault of works which have preceded this is, in our opinion, the long period included in them, and they do not sufficiently draw the distinction between the Chivalry of the twelfth and of the thirteenth centuries. We hope we have avoided this confusion.

The result of many years of application, this volume has been from all points of view the object of conscientious preparation. The writer has above all things striven to be perfectly impartial, and would be the very last person to deliberately lay on colour too thickly or to embellish his models. His confessed aim is to bring out the glories of old France, to compel affection by making her known; and, as Guizot says, "to bring her back to the memory, and into the intelligence, of her generations."

But we conceived another idea, which may appear more daring still : this was to enlarge the mind, to check the mercantile spirit which abases, and the egotism which is killing it : to convey to it some of the enthusiasm for the Beautiful, which is menaced; and for the Truth, which seems to us to be dying out.

There is more than one kind of Chivalry, and lance thrusts are not everything ! In default of the sword we have the pen : failing the pen, speech : and in default of speech, honour, in our lives !

The Author of Chivalry will esteem himself happy if he has created some "knights."

LÉON GAUTIER.

CHIVALRY.

CHAPTER I.

THE ORIGIN OF CHIVALRY.

I.

CHIVALRY is not one of those official institutions which make their appearance suddenly in history, promulgated by a Pope and decreed by a Sovereign.

Religious as it might have been, it had nothing in its origin that reminded one of the foundation of a religious order. One may in fact declare, that every single monastic order has been conceived in the mind of an individual. The grand Benedictine order arose out of the intelligence of Saint Benedict, and the Franciscan order from the heart of Saint Francis. There is no parallel to this in the case of chivalry, and it would be useless to search for the place of its birth or for the name of its founder. What a great archæologist of our day has said of the Romance Architecture is scientifically applicable to the birth of chivalry. It was born everywhere at once, and has been everywhere at the same time the natural effect of the same aspirations and the same needs. There was a moment when the Christians in the East experienced the necessity of sheltering themselves at prayers in churches built of stone which could not be burned ; and then, to use the graceful terms of Raoul Glaber, the Christian soil was everywhere covered with the white robes of new churches.

Hence the Romance architecture. There was another moment when people everywhere felt the necessity of tempering the ardour of old German blood, and of giving to their ill-regulated passions an ideal. Hence chivalry !

Chivalry, as we shall presently show, arose from a German custom which has been idealized by the Church.

It is less an institution than an ideal.

Many volumes have been written upon this noble subject, and a few words will be sufficient to define clearly chivalry and the knight. "Chivalry is the Christian form of the military profession: the knight is the Christian soldier."

II.

One has hardly arrived at this conclusion when a great problem arises quickly in our minds. "Did the Church sanction war?" We know of no more important question, nor one more intimately connected with our subject.

The Church's theory is well known: in three words—*She hates war!* Vainly have certain sophists endeavoured to tone down the grand words of the Saviour, "They who take the sword shall perish with the sword." After much hesitation and the inevitable searchings out, the true thought of the Church was magnificently formulated by Saint Augustine when he said:

"He who can think of war and can support it without great sorrow, is truly dead to human feelings;" and when he laid down the grand principle—this fertilizing principle, "It is necessary to submit to war—but to wish for peace."

Another axiom, again, is that of which the Fathers of the Council of Kiersy, in 858, threw at the heads of the feudal system, then in its wild youth. "We ought," they said, "to war against our vices, and make peace with our brethren." So, from axiom to axiom we pass on to the celebrated proclamation which Leo X. made to the Lateran Council in 1514: "Nothing is more pernicious, nothing is more disastrous to the Christian Republic than the inhuman rage for war."

The Church hated war, but it was forced, alas! to acknowledge its existence in the New World as in the Old, and we are led to give a philosophical explanation of it, which we must here make known with rigorous impartiality and in no apologetic tone. War, then, presents to the eyes of the Church the triple character of being at once a righteous punishment, a useful expiation, a Providential preparation. As soon as a nation ceases to be manly and self-sacrificing, as soon as it enters into its era of decadence, and becomes capable of rendering other nations effeminate; or again when in the midst of its prosperity and splendour it becomes tyrannical; oppresses the human conscience, and threatens the free destiny of the truth on the earth—God makes use of another people to chastise this corrupt, haughty, and dangerous nation.

The Church and Chivalry.

These are the righteous punishments of which we speak: these are the redoubtable executions of Divine Justice. But nevertheless they do not explain all wars, and it is beyond doubt that there are many instances in history in which they have assisted in the downfall of nations both pure and noble, which deserved well of God and the Truth: it happens that these faithful nations are unfortunately conquered and on the point of succumbing beneath the efforts of a people who are far inferior. The Catholic philosophy of war is not embarrassed by this view. "These nations," says she, "are punished for themselves or for others," and this noble doctrine is easily applicable to individuals, and to the last of the soldiers who take part in the struggle. War is, in fact, a great means of expiation. "Cruel separations: a home quitted in tears; a family which no longer thinks of the absent ones; many physical ills; hunger, thirst, fatigue, and mortal wounds from which one dies by inches on the field of battle: death at length: death alone a hundred leagues from one's home and friends: death unconsoled:" the soldier who wishes to make expiation for himself or for others has only to choose, amid so many sufferings, that which he can efficaciously offer to Heaven, and it is by such means that he merits so well the noble title of expiator which we need not comment on any further. As for war considered as the terrestrial preparation for the kingdom of God, we must refer to Bossuet and show, with him, how empires fall one upon another to form a foundation whereon to build the Church. But after Bossuet we must be silent.

Such is the "Catholic theory of war and of the soldier." It was necessary to examine it plainly in the first pages of a volume dedicated to chivalry. We shall have no occasion to return to it.

III.

The Church tolerates war, but it only authorises righteous war. "It is righteous war," says Saint Augustine, "when one proposes to punish a violation of law: when it has become necessary to chastise a people who refuse to repair a wrong, or who refuse to restore property unjustly acquired." We may add, with Raban Maur, the odious and alas too frequent cases of invasion, which it is always legitimate to resist. Vincent de Beauvais, the greatest encyclopædist of the middle ages, develops the doctrine in the reign of Saint Louis, at the time when all France was listening to the "chansons de geste," from which we have borrowed the chief elements of our work. "There are," he says, "three conditions under which a war may be just and lawful: the authority of the prince who commands the war—a just cause, and lastly a lawful intention." But let us harken to the illustrious thirteenth century compiler when he adds—"By just cause we mean one in which we do not march against our brothers save when they have deserved chastisement for some infraction of duty: and the lawful intention

consists in making war to avoid evil, and to advance well being."
As for unjust war the great Bishop of Hipponus long since charac-
terized it in a single sentence, but one which is immortal : " It is
brigandage on a large scale." That feudal wars deserved this
definition we shall have occasion, and be obliged, to maintain more
than once. Compelled to tolerate the war which it abhorred, the
Church organized against it, throughout all history, a whole series
of grand and often successfully opposed obstacles. The " Peace "
and the " Truce of God " are perhaps the most widely known :
Chivalry is the most beautiful. Nevertheless the Church after all
was unable to achieve its generous purpose, and was constrained in
practice not only to permit war but even to encourage it ! She did
not descend to this save in two cases easy to determine : when it
became a question of subduing and crushing out advancing barbarism and triumphant evil, and when it was necessary in the limits
of duty that the Catholics should conform to the injunctions of the
civil authority. Such, since the earliest times, has been the conduct of the Church *vis-à-vis* with war. We can easily adduce proofs
of this.

That the Church authorized her children to serve in the armies
of the Roman Emperor : that military service was permitted to the
first Christians, no one can doubt who has read the beautiful Dis-
sertation of the Bollandists. The light has come.

It is important nevertheless to distinguish here between the
epoch of persecution and the centuries which followed the peace of
the Church.

During the period of persecution the doctors and martyrs were
not unanimous upon the question of military service. Grand and
noble spirits had misgivings on the subject. Origen, whose teaching is not always certain, declares in set terms that military service
is incompatible with the Christian profession. Lactantius is not
less precise in proclaiming that there exists no objection to the
divine decree—" Thou shalt not kill." Man is a sacred being, and
it is always a crime to kill him. But the great enemy to the service was the fiery, the incomparable Tertullian ; and I do not think
he ever wrote more eloquently than when declaiming against the
profession of arms. " So," he says, " you would permit people to
live while practising the profession of a soldier, when the Saviour

declared that 'he that takes the sword shall perish by the sword.' He to whom such means are forbidden, the son of peace, would be doing the work of battle. He to whom it is forbidden to revenge his own injuries would inflict upon others fetters, imprisonment, torture, death.'' The appeal is long, and it must be allowed that it touches the sublime. But, with orators, one must be on one's guard; and the greater part of Tertullian's reasonings will not stand the test of rigorous philosophic examination. Let us confess at once that they are less arguments than images.

Notwithstanding all this, such an appeal found a loud echo in the breasts of youthful Christendom, and the Tertullian doctrine found defenders who stood by it to the death. A certain number of martyrs preferred death to military service; the most illustrious of these was Saint Maximilian, who, in the year 295, at Thevestis in Numidia, refused to serve the emperor to whom he was bound as the son of a veteran soldier. "I am a Christian," he cried, "and I cannot do this evil." Saint Theogenes at Cyzie made the same resistance, and it was in vain that the tribune pointed out to him all the other soldiers, saying, " They also are Christians." Others who had accepted service renounced it under circumstances which demanded from them idolatrous practices. But these are only the exceptions; and one may truthfully affirm that there was a considerable number of Christians in the legions. Tertullian himself admits as much : " We are but of yesterday, and lo ! we fill your *castella* and your *castra*." Besides, nothing was more able than the Roman policy. With a view to retain their good soldiers the emperors took care not to impose anything upon Christians that would trouble their consciences. The military oath itself was deprived of all that might give umbrage to the spirit of their faith, and they were only obliged to swear *per salutem imperatorum, per caput imperatoris, per pietatem et victoriam imperatorum.* In fact it was only in the year 298 that the mask of Roman policy was permitted to fall, and that Galerius attempted to snatch away the souls of the Christian soldiers from the Church. Up to that time they had not been seriously alarmed : each one had said that in serving the empire he was serving God and the Church; " for I am fighting against the barbarians and opening the way to the truth." And the great majority of the doctors and the fathers en-

couraged them in this view. The doubts which seized upon some
scrupulous minds only arose, as we have said, from the idolatrous
practices to which the soldiers of the pagan emperors *could* be subjected. These doubts had no more excuse for existence when
peace had been made with the Church, and the Council of Arles in
314—a council which was attended by all the Western bishops—
separated from the communion those who refused or abandoned
military service. The cause was understood, and military service
finally permitted.

The idea of the legitimacy of certain wars and the glorification
of the Christian soldier, the idea which had aroused the soul of a
Tertullian and that of an Origen, made very decided progress in the
Western world between the fourth and the tenth centuries, during
which period it was full of invasions, barbarity, and mortal struggles
between religions and races. Certainly it was permitted to the
Apostolic fathers to dream of a new land where the peace of the
Gospel flourished, where the sword had been sheathed, where the
violence of the soldier had been replaced by the gentleness of the
priest. But these admirable theories must in some degree give
way before stern facts, and it came to pass that the Church, without
ceasing to detest war, tolerated the thought of it, and even went
farther than that. Saint Augustine, the lofty genius who had the
misfortune to live in terrible times, and to be the contemporary of
Vandals, was one of the first teachers to formulate, so to speak, the
Christian theories concerning war and warriors. "What is there
to be condemned in war? Is it the death of men who must die
sooner or later? Such a reproach should be in the mouths of
cowards, and not in use amongst truly religious men! No, no!
what is blamable in it is the desire to hurt other men : the cruel
love of vengeance : it is this implacable spirit, this enemy of peace,
this savagery of revolt, this passion for domination and for empire !
It is certain that crimes shall be punished, and this is precisely
why according to God's ordinance, or by legitimate authority, good
people are sometimes compelled to undertake wars."

"If every war were to be condemned," says the great theologian
in another passage, "the Gospel would have said as much. It
would have said to the soldier, 'Throw down your arms—give up
your profession.' But the Lord did not say that : He contented

himself with recommending them to exercise moderation and justice."

Elsewhere the voice of the eloquent apologist is heard with more vigour. "Let those who pretend that the teaching of Christ is contrary to the interests of the common weal, let them give the state an army composed of soldiers modelled upon those of the Gospel; they are a fine race indeed, those true and faithful warriors, who, amid a thousand dangers, and by the aid of Heaven, triumph over enemies reputed invincible, and bring peace to the empire. When they are victors, these champions of a just cause, I say it is right to congratulate them upon their victory, and the most desirable peace that succeeds it : I say that in this we must see a gift of God."

Such is the language of Saint Augustine, who detested war, and the Middle Ages have hardly done anything but repeat it, or stammer over it. For it is the destiny of great thinkers to impose upon many centuries the domination of their doctrines and the echo of their words.

During the centuries which separated those two giants of the Christian ages, St. Augustine and St. Thomas, one is witness of acts which may appear strange to an impartial observer. The Church, in its canons issued by its councils, continued to manifest at intervals its profound horror of war, while in the writings of its teachers it encourages soldiers who are really Christians. Nothing is more logical nor more consistent than this, and no one has ever known how better to reconcile the interests of the absolute and those of the relative. "War is bad: but since it is inevitable, one must justify those who make war honestly, and simply for the advancement of the right." In the fifth century St. Maximus, of Turin, did not hesitate to break away from his former hesitancy, and declare that there was nothing blamable in military service. A deacon who was an ornament to the Church at Carthage in the sixth century, Fulgentius Ferrandus, permits himself to lay down this rule for a Christian general: "Love the Commonwealth as thyself, and let thy life be as a mirror in which thy soldiers can see their duty clearly." St. Gregory the Great, who died at the commencement of the seventh century, addressed one of his beautiful epistles to the soldiers at Naples, and told them their principal virtue should be obedience. It was to the most military and the most manly nation of its age—to the Franks—that St. Leo IV. addressed in the ninth century, this most manly and military language directed against the enemies of the Christian faith: "Have no fear : think of your fathers. Whatever the number of their enemies, those warriors were always victorious." And the Pope added, "To him who dies in such a battle God will open the gates of Heaven." Does not one seem to hear in advance a couplet of Roland? Some years later, in 865, the Bulgarians consulted St. Nicholas I. on the disputed question, "Is it lawful to make war during Lent?" And the sovereign pontiff replied in words which might serve as the motto of our book, "War is always devilish in its origin, and we should always abstain from it ; but if we cannot avoid it, if we must wage it in self-defence, in defence of our country and of our laws, no doubt we may make preparations for it, even in Lent." Pierre Damien is scarcely less decided in his language ; for about the time when an unknown poet was dedicating our most ancient epic poem to the memory of the glorious disaster of Roncevaux, he branded with infamy all refugees and deserters. At the Lateran council in 1139, the Church, which still detests war and endeavours to mitigate it, forbade the too murderous use of the bow and the arbalast in all battle between Christians ; but she cannot kill war itself, and so endeavours in every way to impart to the combatants a high and proper spirit.

"In the eyes of a soldier," says Hildebert, "it is not death which is terrible, but dishonour!" Observe that the Christian theory of war becomes more precise from day to day, and calculate, if you can, the progress it has made since the Council of Arles. The features of chivalry are becoming more distinct. The outline has become a drawing with accentuated lines, and this will in time become a richly coloured picture. In fact, the day is breaking in which we shall see suddenly founded those grand orders, at once religious and military. And to whom do they go for advice regarding the management of the most celebrated of these orders? To a monk, to a cenobite, to a saint who has left his name upon the age in which he lived, St. Bernard! The great Cistercian, the White Friar, at once set to work and wrote his famous letter to the Knights of the Temple, which may pass for the most daring contribution to the subject:

"They can fight the battles of the Lord, and can be of a surety the soldiers of Christ. Let them kill the enemy or die: they need have no fear! To submit to die for Christ or to cause His enemies to submit to death, is nought but glory, it is no crime! Besides, it is not without a reason that the soldier of Christ carries a sword: it is for the chastisement of the wicked, and for the glory of the good. If it bring death to the malefactor, the soldier is not a homicide, but—excuse the word—a malicide! And we must recognise in him the avenger who is in the service of Christ, and the liberator of the Christian people."

One can scarcely go beyond this, and Joseph de Maistre himself does not appear more audacious if we compare him to the preacher of the first crusade. But John of Salisbury, about the same time, condenses this doctrine into a typical sentence which has often been repeated—sometimes exaggerated: "The military profession, as praiseworthy as it is necessary, was instituted by God himself." This is the end of our journey across the centuries: and we may believe that John of Salisbury has overshot the mark. "Instituted" may seem to be too strong a term, and war is after all only an evil; an evil which the Church is forced to tolerate, and which God ordains shall swell the triumph of the Good.

If one wishes to reduce it to the proportions which Saint Augustine gave it, such a doctrine is a truly wise one: for, as a matter of fact, from the termination of the persecution to the epoch of the Crusades, the Church has never believed in its right to cry "halt" to war. During those iron ages she was not able to, and she did not, condemn any but intestine struggles and private wars. Could she—ought she—to have prevented Clovis from founding, by his heroic struggles against the Alemanni and the Goths, that grand Frankish unity which was to be so favourable to the great Christian unity? Could she—ought she—to have detained Charles Martel when he was hurrying to Poitiers to preserve not only France, but all the Christian Western world from the Eastern barbarian? Could she—ought she—to have strangled the ardour of Pepin, who so energetically prepared all his son's wars; and should she have stopped him on the road to Italy, whither he was proceeding to give to the throne of St. Peter the temporal support of which it had need? Could she—ought she—to have bound down the two powerful arms of Charlemagne, who with one hand hurled back the Mussulmans across the Ebro, and with the other strangled German paganism? Could she—ought she—in face of the incessant menaces of Islam, advocate the insensate doctrine of those Albigenses, who declared that they would consider as homicides all preachers of the Crusade against the Saracens?

I appeal to the most determined advocates of peace, and I beg them to reply honestly to these questions. Is it not true that without all the wars favoured by the Church, we would be to-day Mussulmans, pagans, barbarians? Is it not true that, without them, France would not even have had the liberty to gain its existence?

Not being able to prevent war, the Church has christianised the soldier. And so we are logically led to elucidate the origin of this chivalry, which on a former page we have termed "a German custom idealised by the Church."

IV.

There is a sentence of Tacitus which here comes to the front and which illustrious scholars have brought out before us; this is the celebrated passage from the *Germania* which refers to a German rite in which we really find all the military elements of our future chivalry. The scene took place beneath the shade of an old forest. The barbarous tribe is assembled, and one feels that a solemn ceremony is in preparation. Into the midst of the assembly advances a very young man, whom you can picture to yourself with sea-green eyes and long fair hair and perhaps some tattooing. A chief of the tribe is present, who without delay places gravely in the hands of the young man a *framea* and a buckler. Failing a sovereign ruler, it is the father of the youth—who presently will be a man—it is his father or some relative who undertakes this delivery of weapons. "Such is the 'virile robe' of these people," as Tacitus well puts it :—" such is the first honour of their youth. Till then the young man was only one in a family; he becomes by this rite a member of the Republic. *Ante hoc domûs pars videtur:*

mox rei publicæ. This sword and buckler he will never abandon, for the Germans in all their acts, whether public or private, are always armed. So, the ceremony finished, the assembly separates, and the tribe reckons a *miles*—a warrior—the more. That is all!"

The solemn handing of arms to the young German—such is the first germ of chivalry which Christianity was one day to animate into life. "*Vestigium vetus creandi equites seu milites.*" It is with reason that Sainte-Palaye comments in the very same way upon the text of the *Germania,* and that a scholar of our own days exclaims with more than scientific exactness—"The true origin of *miles* is this bestowal of arms which amongst the Germans marks the entry into civil life."

No other origin will support the scrutiny of the critic, and he will not find anyone now to support the theory of Roman origin with Père Honoré de Sainte-Marie, or that of the Arabian origin with M. de Beaumont. There only remains to explain in this place the term knight (*chevalier*) but it is well known to be derived from *caballus* which, primarily, signifies a beast of burthen—or packhorse;—and has ended by signifying a war-horse. The knight, also, has always preserved the name of *miles* in the Latin tongue of the middle ages, in which chivalry is always called *militia.* Nothing can be clearer than this.

We do not intend to go farther, however, without replying to two objections, which are not without weight, and which we do not wish to leave behind us unanswered.

V.

In a certain number of Latin books of the middle ages we find, to describe chivalry, an expression which the "Romanists" oppose triumphantly to us, and of which the Romish origin cannot seriously be doubted. When it is intended to signify that a knight has been created, it is stated that the individual has been girt with the *cingulum militare.* Here we find ourselves in full Roman parlance, and the word signified certain terms which described admission into military service, the release from this service, and the degradation of the legionary. When St. Martin left the militia, his action was qualified as *solutio cinguli*, and at all those who act like him the insulting expression *militaribus zonis discincti* is cast. The girdle which sustains the sword of the Roman officer (*cingulum —zona*—or rather, *cinctorium*) as also of the baldric, from *balteus*, passed over the shoulder, and was intended to support the weapon of the common soldier. "You perceive quite well," say our adversaries, "that we have to do with a Roman costume." Two very simple observations will, perhaps, suffice to get to the bottom of such a specious argument :—The former is that the Germans in early times wore, in imitation of the Romans, "a wide belt ornamented with bosses of metal," a baldric, by which their swords were suspended on the left side ; and the second is that the chroniclers of old days, who wrote in Latin and affected the classic style, very naturally adopted the word *cingulum* in all its accepta- tions, and made use of this Latin paraphrasis—*cingulo militari decorare*—to express this solemn adoption of the sword : this evidently German custom was always one of the principal rites of the collation of chivalry. There is then nothing more in it than a somewhat vague reminiscence of a Roman custom with a very natural conjunction of terms which has always been the habit of literary people. To sum up—the word is Roman, but the thing itself is German. Between the *militia* of the Romans and the chivalry of the middle ages there is really nothing in common but the military profession considered generally. The official admittance of the Roman soldier to an army hierarchically organised, in no way resembled the admission of a new knight into a sort of military college, and the "pink of society." As we read further the singularly primitive and barbarous ritual of the service of knightly reception in the twelfth century, one is persuaded that the words exhale a German odour, and have nothing Roman about them. But here is another argument, and one which would appear decisive. The Roman legionary could not, as a rule, with- draw from the service ; he could not avoid the baldric. The youthful knight of the middle ages, on the contrary, was always free to arm himself or not as he pleased, just as other cavaliers are at liberty to leave or join their ranks. The principal characteristic of the knightly service, and one which separates it most decidedly from the Roman *militia*, was its freedom of action.

VI.

One very specious objection is made as regards feudalism
which some clear-minded people obstinately confound with
chivalry.   This was, I remember, the favourite theory of M. de
Montalembert, and he took a delight in explaining it to us on
his death-bed.

Now there are, as everyone is aware, two kinds of feudalism,
which the old feudalists put down very clearly in two words now
out of date—"fiefs of dignity" and "fiefs simple."

About the middle of the ninth century, the dukes and counts,
who were functionaries of the empire similar to our *préfets*, made
themselves independent of the central power; and declared that
people owed the same allegiance to them as they did to the emperor
or the kings.   Fancy the *préfets* of 1884 breaking away from all
allegiance and relations with ministers, and saying, " 'Tis to us the
taxes shall be paid ; in our names shall justice be done ; to us you
owe military service ! "   Such, however, were the acts of the "fiefs
of dignity ; " and we may at once allow that they had nothing in
common with chivalry.

The "fiefs simple," then, remained.

In the Merovingian period we find a certain number of small
proprietors, called *vassi*, commending themselves to other men
more powerful and more rich, who were called *seniores*.   To his
senior who made him a present of land the *vassus* owed assistance
and fidelity.   It is true that as early as the reign of Charlemagne
he followed him to war, but it must be noted that it was to the
emperor, to the central power, that he actually rendered military
service.   There was nothing very particular in this, but the time
was approaching when things would be altered.   Towards the
middle of the ninth century we find a large number of men falling
" on their knees " before other men !   What are they about ?
They are " recommending " themselves still, but in plainer terms,
"Protect us and we will be your men ; " and they added, " It is to
you and to you only that we intend in future to render military
service ; but in exchange you must protect the land we possess—
defend what you will in time concede to us ; and defend *us* ourselves."   These people on their knees were " vassals " at the feet

of their "lords : " and the *fief* was generally only a grant of land conceded in exchange for military service.

Feudalism of this nature has nothing in common with chivalry.

If we consider chivalry in fact as a kind of privileged body into which men were received on certain conditions, and with a certain ritual which we shall soon investigate, it is important to observe that every vassal is not necessarily a cavalier. There were vassals who, with the object of averting the cost of initiation or for other reasons, remained *damoiseaux*, or pages, all their lives. The majority, of course, did nothing of the kind ; but all could do so, and a great many did.

On the other hand we see conferred the dignity of chivalry upon insignificant people who had never held fiefs and who owed to no one any fealty and to whom no one owed any.

We cannot repeat too often that it was not the cavalier (or knight), it was the *vassal* who owed military service or *ost* to the *seigneur* or lord ; and the service *in curte* or *court:* it was the vassal, not the knight, who owed " assistance" and " counsel"; it was the vassal, not the knight, who owed to the " lord" relief, " aid," homage !

One word more : the feudal system soon became hereditary. Chivalry, on the contrary, has never been hereditary, and a special rite has always been necessary to create a knight. In default of all other arguments this would be sufficient.

But if, instead of regarding chivalry as an institution, we consider it as an ideal, the doubt is not really more admissible. It is here that in the eyes of a philosophic historian chivalry is clearly distinct from feudalism. If the Western world in the ninth century had *not* been feudalised, chivalry would nevertheless have come into existence ; and, notwithstanding everything, it would have come to light in Christendom ; for chivalry is, as we have already said, nothing more than the Christianised form of military service, the armed *force* in the service of the unarmed Truth ; and it was inevitable that at some time or other it must have sprung, living and fully armed, from the brain of the Church, as Minerva did from the brain of Jupiter.

Feudalism, on the contrary, is not of Christian origin at all. It is a particular form of government, and of society, which has scarcely been less rigorous for the Church than other forms of society and government. Feudalism has disputed with the Church over and over again, while chivalry has protected her a hundred times. Feudalism is force—chivalry is the break.

Let us look at Godfrey de Bouillon. The fact that he owed homage to any suzerain; the fact that he exacted service from such and such vassals, are questions which concern feudal rights, and have nothing to do with chivalry. But if I contemplate him in battle beneath the walls of Jerusalem; if I am a spectator of his entry into the Holy City; if I see him ardent, brave; powerful and pure; valiant and gentle; humble and proud, refusing to wear the golden crown in the Holy City where Jesus wore the crown of thorns, I am not then anxious—I am not curious—to learn from whom he holds his fief, or to know the names of his vassals; and I exclaim, " There is the knight ! " And how many knights, what chivalrous virtues have existed in the Christian world since feudalism has ceased to exist !

VII.

To sum up. The adoption of arms in the German fashion remains the true origin of chivalry; and the Franks have handed down this custom to us—a custom perpetuated to a comparatively modern period. This simple, almost rude rite so decidedly marked the line of civil life in the code of manners of people of German origin, that under the Carlovingians we still find numerous traces of it. In 791 Louis, eldest son of Charlemagne, was only thirteen years old, and yet he had worn the crown of Aquitaine for three years upon his " baby brow." The king of the Franks felt that it was time to bestow upon this child the military consecration which would more quickly assure him of the respect of his people. He summoned him to Ingelheim, then to Ratisbon, and solemnly girded him with the sword which " makes men." He did not trouble himself about the *framea* or the buckler—the sword occupied the first place. It will retain it for a long time.

In 838 at Kiersy we have a similar scene. This time it is old Louis who, full of sadness and nigh to death, bestows upon his son Charles, whom he loved so well, the "virile arms "—that is to say,

the sword. Then immediately afterwards he put upon his brow the
crown of "Neustria." Charles was fifteen years old.

These examples are not numerous but their importance is
decisive, and they carry us to the time when the Church came to
intervene positively in the education of the German *miles*. The
time was rough, and it is not easy to picture a more distracted
period than that in the ninth and tenth centuries. The great idea

Charlemagne stopping the Sun!

of the Roman Empire no longer, in the minds of the people,
coincided with the idea of the Frankish kingdom, but rather
inclined, so to speak, to the side of Germany, where it tended to fix
itself. Countries were on the way to be formed, and people were
asking to which country they could best belong. Independent
kingdoms were founded which had no precedents, and were not
destined to have a long life. The Saracens were for the last time
harassing the Southern French coasts, but it was not so with the
Norman pirates, for they did not cease for a single year to ravage
the littoral which is now represented by our Picardy and Normandy

coasts, until the day it became necessary to cede the greater part of the coast to them. People were fighting everywhere more or less —family against family—man to man. No road was safe, the churches were burned, there was universal terror, and everyone sought protection. The king had no longer strength to resist any-one, and the counts made themselves kings. The sun of the realm was set, and one had to look to the stars for light. As soon as the people perceived a strong man-at-arms, resolute, defiant, well established in his wooden keep, well fortified within the lines of his hedge, behind his palisade of dead branches, or within his barriers of planks; well posted on his hill, against his rock, or on his hillock, and dominating all the surrounding country, as soon as they saw this each said to him, "I am your man;" and all these weak ones grouped themselves around the strong one, who next day proceeded to wage war with his neighbours. Thence super-vened a terrible series of private wars. Everyone was fighting, or thinking of fighting.

In addition to this, the still green memory of the grand figure of Charlemagne and the old empire, and I can't tell what imperial splendours, were still felt in the air of great cities: all hearts throbbed at the mere thought of the Saracens and the Holy Sepulchre: the crusade gathered strength of preparation far in advance, in the rage and indignation of all the Christian race: all eyes were turned towards Jerusalem, and in the midst of so many disbandments and so much darkness, the unity of the Church survived fallen majesty! What a time!

It was then, it was in that terrible hour—the decisive epoch in our history—that the Church undertook the education of the Christian soldier; and it was at that time by a resolute step she found the feudal baron in his rude wooden citadel, and proposed to him an ideal.

This ideal was chivalry!

VIII.

Chivalry may be considered as an eighth sacrament, and this is perhaps the name that suits it best, which describes it most accurately. It is the sacrament, it is the baptism of the warrior.

But we must also regard it as a corporation, like a college, of which every member is a responsible individual.

It is true that this last idea is not of very ancient date, that it has taken a long time to shape itself, and has only at a comparatively late period reached its normal development. But, at any rate, amongst the formulas which were customary in the reception of a knight, there was one which from this point of view is very significant, "I receive thee willingly into our college." A curious confraternity, too, one of which all the members were every day exposed to do battle, to fight with, and to massacre each other, as a matter of course.

Yet it was necessary, in order to kill each other in this fashion, that these adversaries should entertain a real esteem one for the other, and consider themselves as equals. The very poorest, the most humble of the knights was the equal of a knightly-king—of an emperor.

They had all been baptised in the same way—with the same baptism.

IX.

That chivalry may be considered a great military confraternity as well as an eighth sacrament will be conceded after a careful perusal of the text. But, before familiarising themselves with these ideas, the rough spirits of the ninth, tenth, and eleventh centuries had to learn the principles of them. The chivalrous ideal was not conceived " all of a piece," and certainly it did not triumph without sustained effort ; so it was by degrees, and very slowly, that the Church succeeded in inoculating the almost animal intelligence and the untrained minds of our ancestors with so many virtues. Nothing is improvised—such is the law of history. Whoever cannot see it is blind. This same Church which we have to thank for the best elements of our chivalry has scarcely put down slavery in eight or nine hundred years. It cannot, as a matter of fact, march with a more rapid step.

It is the fashion of the day to fancy that everything comes of its own accord. Contemporary reformers persuade themselves that a decree or a vote is sufficient to efface the work of twenty centuries :

to create a new army, a new legislation, a new phase of society, all of a sudden. We all know what comes of such efforts : the past does not die and the innovations crumble to pieces. Then the reformers dash themselves against the obstacle. Not being able to effect reforms by legal process, they call force to their aid. Nothing comes of it, and everything falls to pieces. Time must be taken into consideration !

In the hands of the Church which wished to mould him into a Christian knight, the feudal baron was a very intractable individual. No one could be more brutal or more barbarous than he. Our more ancient ballads—those which are founded on the traditions of the ninth and tenth centuries—supply us with a portrait which does not appear exaggerated. I know nothing in this sense more terrible than " *Raoul de Cambrai*," and the hero of this old poem would pass for a type of a half-civilized savage. This Raoul was a species of Sioux or Red-Skin, who only wanted tattoo and feathers in his hair to be complete. Even a Red-Skin is a believer, or superstitious, to some extent, while Raoul defied the Deity Himself. The savage respects his mother as a rule ; but Raoul laughed at his mother who cursed him. Behold him as he invaded the Vermandois contrary to all the rights of legitimate heirs. He pillaged, burned, and slew in all directions : he was everywhere pitiless, cruel, horrible. But at Origni he appears in all his ferocity. " You will erect my tent in the church, you will make my bed before the altar, and put my hawks on the golden crucifix." Now that church belonged to a convent. What did that signify to him ? He burned the convent, he burned the church, he burned the nuns ! Amongst them was the mother of his most faithful servitor, Bernier—his most devoted companion and friend—almost his brother ! but he burned her with the others. Then, when the flames were still burning, he sat himself down, on a fast day, to feast amid the scenes of his sanguinary exploits ; defying God and man, his hands steeped in blood, his face lifted to heaven. That was the kind of soldier, the savage of the tenth century, whom the Church had to educate !

Unfortunately this Raoul de Cambrai is not an unique speci-men ; he was not the only one who had uttered this ferocious speech : " I shall not be happy until I see your heart cut out of your body." Aubri de Bourguignon was not less cruel, and took no trouble to curb his passions. Had he the right to massacre? He knew nothing about that, but meanwhile he continued to kill. "Bah!" he would say, "it is always an enemy the less." On one occasion he slew his four cousins. He was as sensual as cruel. His thick-skinned savagery did not appear to feel either shame or remorse; he was strong and had a weighty hand—that was sufficient. Ogier was scarcely any better, but notwithstanding all the glory attaching to his name, I know nothing more saddening than the final episode of the rude poem attributed to Raimbert of Paris. The son of Ogier, Baudouinet, had been slain by the son of Charlemagne, who called himself Charlot! Ogier did nothing but breathe vengeance, and would not agree to assist Christendom against the Saracen invaders unless the unfortunate Charlot was delivered to him. He wanted to kill him, he determined to kill him, and he rejoiced over it in anticipation. In vain did Charlot humble himself before this brute, and endeavour to pacify him by the sincerity of his repentance; in vain the old emperor himself prayed most earnestly to God; in vain the venerable Naimes, the Nestor of our ballads, offered to serve Ogier all the rest of his life, and begged the Dane "not to forget the Saviour who was born of the Virgin at Bethlehem." All their devotion and prayers were unavailing. Ogier, pitiless, placed one of his heavy hands upon the youthful head, and with the other drew his sword, his terrible sword "Courtain." Nothing less than the intervention of an angel from heaven could have put an end to this terrible scene in which all the savagery of the German forests was displayed.

The majority of these early heroes had no other shibboleth than, "I am going to separate the head from the trunk!" It was their war-cry. But if you desire something more frightful still, something more "primitive," you have only to open the "*Loherains*" at hazard, and read a few stanzas of that raging ballad of "derring do," and you will almost fancy you are perusing one of those pages in which Livingstone describes in such indignant terms the manners of some tribe in Central Africa. Read this: "Begue struck Isore upon his black helmet through the golden circlet, cutting him to the chine; then he plunged into the body his sword Flamberge with the golden hilt; took the heart out with both hands, and threw it, still warm, at the head of William, saying, ' There is your cousin's heart, you can salt and roast it.'" Here words fail us; it would be too tame to say with Gœdecke, "These heroes act like the forces of nature, in the manner of the hurricane which knows not pity." We must use more indignant terms than these, for we are truly amid cannibals. Once again we say, there was the warrior, there was the savage whom the Church had to elevate and educate!

Such is the point of departure of this wonderful progress in which we have the pleasure to assist : such are the refractory elements out of which chivalry and the knight have been fashioned.

The point of departure is Raoul of Cambrai burning Origni. The point of arrival is Girard of Roussillon falling one day at the feet of an old priest and expiating his former pride by twenty-two years of penitence. These two episodes embrace many centuries between them.

A very interesting study might be made of the gradual transformation from the "Redskin" to the knight; it might be shown how, and at what period of history, each of the virtues of chivalry penetrated victoriously into the undisciplined souls of these brutal warriors who were our ancestors : it might be determined at what moment the Church became strong enough to impose upon our knights the great duties of defending it, and of loving one another.

This victory was attained in a certain number of cases undoubtedly towards the end of the eleventh century : and the knight appears to us perfected, finished, radiant, in the most ancient edition of "the Chanson of Roland," which we consider was produced between 1066 and 1095, A.D.

It is scarcely necessary to observe that chivalry was no longer in course of establishment when Pope Urban II. threw with a powerful hand the whole of the Christian West upon the East where the Tomb of Christ was in possession of the Infidel.

In legendary lore the embodiment of chivalry is Roland: in history it is Godfrey de Bouillon. There are no more worthy names than these.

X.

"*Ordena questo amore*" exclaims the Redeemer in one of the most beautiful canticles attributed to Saint Francis d'Assisi, and it is to Saint Francis himself that he addresses the astonishing words —"Moderate your love." The Church said the same to the barbarous warriors of the ninth century. "Moderate your courage," she said. They did moderate it, and their savagery by degrees became their prowess. We use the word designedly, and we may quote in relation to the subject these excellent proverbs. "In the result one recognises the workman, in prowess the knight;" and, "No knight without prowess." All other virtues follow hand in hand as the angels crowned with roses give their hands to the Elect in the "Paradise" of Fra Angelico. First loyalty, then *largesse*, then moderation, and finally that perfection of civilised chivalry which we call courtesy. Honour crowns them all. "Death rather than dishonour:" the whole code of chivalry is contained in these four words, which, by the grace of God, have become a commonplace term with us. It is the grand saying of Hue le Maine, brother of the King of France, before Antioch: "Who does not prefer death to dishonour has no right in *seignorie*." And throughout the middle ages this motto was preserved.

No matter in what sequence the Church bestowed these virtues upon the warrior, she gave him a definite aim and object—a precise law.

The law was the Decalogue, the Ten Commandments of chivalry, which we purpose to illustrate.

The object was to enlarge the Kingdom of God on earth.

When our knights attended mass one might have seen them, before the reading of the second lesson, draw their swords and hold them unsheathed in their hands until the reading of the lesson was finished. This defiant attitude seemed to imply their readiness to defend the Gospel. "If the Word is to be defended, we are ready."

This is the whole spirit of chivalry.

CHAPTER II.

THE CODE OF CHIVALRY.—THE FIRST THREE COMMANDMENTS.

I.

SAINTE PALAYE, in his "Memoirs of Ancient Chivalry," observes that "the laws of chivalry might have been adopted by the wisest legislators and by the most virtuous philosophers of all nations, and of all epochs." We can only take exception to this for its slight flavour of the eighteenth century. It is in other respects perfectly correct.

This highly praised code has unfortunately never been formulated with sufficient clearness, and it is too true that the pure gold of ancient chivalry was very quickly alloyed. In the twelfth century—one is too apt to forget the date—the romance of the Round Table spread amongst us the taste for a less wild but also a less manly chivalry. The elegancies of love in them occupied the place formerly reserved for the brutality of war : and the spirit of adventure in them extinguished the spirit of the crusades. One will never know how much harm this cycle of the "Round Table" inflicted on us. It civilised us no doubt; but effeminated us. It took away from us our old aim, which was the tomb of Christ gained by blood and battle. For the austerities of the Supernatural it substituted the tinsel of the Marvellous. It is to this dangerous but charming literature that we owe the theatrical, the boastful, rash chivalry which proved so fatal during the Thirty Years War. It was against it and not against our old Epopœia that Cervantes pointed his pencil, and we must confess that some complaints of the great satirist were not without foundation. Thanks to this regrettable encroachment we now entertain a false idea of the true chivalry, which we confuse with a certain delicate and sometimes an excessive gallantry. The time has arrived to protest against such an error.

The chivalry, of which we are about to examine the code, is that of the eleventh and twelfth centuries—that of the crusades, that of our national epopœia. It will appear rude and barbarous to some people, but in truth it is strong and healthy, and has formed for us the powerful race whose glory has filled the world. Despite the invasion of the Breton Romances the twelfth century remains, as Jules Quicherat has said, the great century of the middle ages ;

The Crusaders' first sight of Jerusalem.

and it is to the most vigorous works of that period that we are indebted for the best elements of our work in these pages.

We may reduce the ancient code of chivalry into ten "Commandments," and we wish to express them here in a popular form so that they may be the more easily understood. It was in such a form that it pleased the Creator to set forth the Decalogue on Sinai, so as to engrave it in all its meanings in all hearts.

The following are the Ten Commandments of the code of chivalry—

I. Thou shalt believe all that the Church teaches, and shalt observe all its directions.

II. Thou shalt defend the Church.

III. Thou shalt respect all weaknesses, and shalt constitute thyself the defender of them.

IV. Thou shalt love the country in the which thou wast born.

V. Thou shalt not recoil before thine enemy.

VI. Thou shalt make war against the Infidel without cessation, and without mercy.

VII. Thou shalt perform scrupulously thy feudal duties, if they be not contrary to the laws of God.

VIII. Thou shalt never lie, and shalt remain faithful to thy pledged word.

IX. Thou shalt be generous, and give *largesse* to everyone.

X. Thou shalt be everywhere and always the champion of the Right and the Good against Injustice and Evil.

II.

The first commandment of this almost unknown code is the most important and the most sacred of all. No one could become a knight without first becoming a Christian, without having been baptized. That was a *sine quâ non*, officially requisite and necessary.* This act of faith was, in the eyes of our forefathers, the absolute equivalent of genuineness; it was the *certain law.* The thought of God then filled and animated all, and it was as the breath of their nostrils in those believing centuries. The Deity was present with them even physically, and at every breath they drew they believed they could feel His presence as behind a curtain.

This idea of the Deity had nothing vague about it, and it was accentuated by the affirmation of the divinity of Christ. " He loved us so much that he gave us his name, and we are called

---

* "Sainte ordene de Chevalrie seroit en vous mal emploie, se n'avez batesme en foi." " L'ordene de Chevalrie, Lausanne, 1259."

Christians." Before the celebrated battle of Aliscans, which was destined to be so disastrous for the whole race of Christians, young Vivien, who was so soon to perish, addressed his knights in a short speech. " These pagans," he said, " only believe in Antichrist, and all their gods are wretched and miserable things ! But we ourselves believe in the King of Paradise who died and rose again." Then he added, raising his eyes to Heaven, " Think of our souls, O God, and reunite them on high. As for our bodies, do as Thou wilt with them."

Then he rushed—what do I say—they all rushed to meet death : a martyrdom ! The faith of these rude warriors, that faith which was so precise, had nothing namby-pamby in it : nothing *dilettante* or effeminate. We have not to do with the little sugar-plums of certain contemporary devotion—but with a good and frank wild-honey. It is a grosser but a loyal Catholicism. One is not astonished to find that these knights were rigorously logical. They knew too much to stand upon the sterile heights of theory : they knew that they ought to practise their faith. " Listen to my song," said one of our latter-day poets to his auditors. " You will learn how to suffer here below to accomplish the law of God ; that law which all honest men obey. ' *Essanplir la loi Deu.*'" It is all contained in that.

The spirit of atheism was not fitted, as we may see, to enter into the mind of the feudal baron who was being transformed more and more into the Christian knight : and we meet with few instances of atheism in all our epic poetry. That ferocious Raoul of Cambrai— a kind of savage who was only a Christian outwardly—had moments of fierce atheism. In the primitive poem which is dedicated to him, and in which we find in full the tradition of the tenth century, there is one very solemn moment described : it was when Raoul in battle found himself face to face with Ernaut Count of Douai, whose nephew he had just slain, and whose two sons he had formerly killed, or caused to be killed. To this duel, in which Ernaut represented Right, and Raoul Force, the poet does not hesitate to devote many pages. The poor Count of Douai was not in form to struggle long against such an opponent, and so he fled across the fields, his hand cut off, losing blood fast, and more than half dead. All his pride had deserted him, he felt himself lost, and begged for mercy in touching accents, which Chenier in after times put in the mouth of his young captive : " *Jeunes hom sui, ne vuel encor morir.*" " I am still a young man, and have no wish to die yet ! " He added, that if spared, he would become a monk and leave his territory to his conquerer.

But nothing could soften Raoul, and the name of God threw him into a paroxysm of rage.

" I deny God," he exclaimed ; " I deny His existence."

. " Since that be so," replied Ernaut, " I consider you no better than a mad dog. The earth and grass themselves will come to my assistance, and so will the God of glory, if He will have mercy on me ! "

It is Raoul, however, now, and not Ernaut who is about to die, and in that supreme moment the Count of Cambrai suddenly recovered his childhood's faith.

" Glorious Father—universal Judge—and you, sweet Queen of Heaven, come to my aid."

These were his last words, and it is evident that he was only a pretended atheist.

A thorough atheist was Gaumadras in " *Garin de Mont-glane :* " we may look upon him as a type of the lost soul. If the name of the Deity were pronounced in his presence, he incontinently went into convulsions. In his struggle against Garin he had demons for his allies, with whom he contracted a feudal pact. He belonged to them entirely, and he gloried in this possession. When the hour of his death arrived, he made up his mind to die a rebel, in Satan, as he had lived. No one killed him : he killed himself. Moreover, he chose a theatrical, nay, a spectacular death ! He embarked with his relatives in a vessel which he steered in the direction of a rock. The fated bark was dragged to destruction. The unfortunate passengers perceived their danger, and, overcome by terror, called upon the Deity to succour them.

" No, no," cried Gaumadras, " you must invoke the devil." So this man, possessed, killed them. Then he make the sign of the cross backwards, and standing upright in the vessel which was about to be wrecked, his face turned defiantly to Heaven, and implacable, horrible, heard unmoved the crash with which the vessel dashed against the rock, and was broken up.

"Run; come hither, you demons; I am your man; I am yours; I am—— ! "

Here the waves closed his blaspheming mouth and he died. He was the most brutal and most cynical atheist of all our epic literature. But he was not the only one !

Yet we need not attach too much importance to a few sacrilegious sallies of some of our heroes, to whom we may apply the beautiful words of Lamartine :—"These are exclamations which escape the lips, but after which the soul rushes very quickly, before God has heard them."

When Froumondin understood that his enemy was laying hands on his fiefs, he said, "Well, though I were already in Paradise with the angels, I would rather descend into hell than abandon my territory thus." That is, after all, only a foolish remark, an oath long drawn out, and cannot be compared to the Satanic rebellious-ness of the traitor Herchambaut, whom the author of *Doon de Maience* has painted in such lurid colours. This prototype of Gaumadras denied the Deity again and again, and spit against Heaven.

"Yes, I deny you," he exclaimed. "I deny you and all your benefits. Neither you nor your belongings shall I ever care for."

This is another degree of atheism which bears little resemblance to the former, and appears a thousand times more detestable. But there is a lower depth still, and atheism in our poems finishes by condensing itself into a kind of secret society and of remarkable institution. The famous "Words and deeds of traitors" becomes the atheistic record; and Hardré, in "Amis and Amiles," clearly exposes the tenets of the sect. "Never think of serving God," said he to his god-son Alori, "and never tell the truth. If you meet an honest man dishonour him. Burn towns, villages, and houses; overthrow the altars, and break the crucifixes." We are only too well accustomed to such language, but who would have expected to find such an explosion of Nihilism in the twelfth century ?

But such exceptions only prove the rule, and the greater number of our heroes believed devoutly in the personality of the Creator. The knights were more than once called " Men of God." "It is for God that you support so many misfortunes. Yes, you are really men of God, and your reward is in Paradise." * So said at Aliscans the youthful Vivien whose death was so soon to be as glorious as that of Oliver or Roland. In the " Song of Antioch " —in that poem which is as good as a chronicle—our barons are called " *Li Jhesu chevalier,*" and the old troubadour completes his definition by adding, " *Cil qui Damedieu servent de loial cuer entier.*" † In every circumstance of their lives, amid all their joys and troubles, when in the great halls of their castles they petted their children and listened to the jongleurs singing ; or when in the midst of the *mêlée,* stained with blood up to their horses' breast-plates, everywhere, in all circumstances, they lifted up their hearts to the God who created " the Heaven and the dew, who created worlds and established laws, who caused all the good things of the earth to flourish, who formed us in his own image : who is ever true, born of a Virgin, and permitted himself to be crucified for us, who has redeemed us all, and in whose name, lastly, are made and created all the knights of Christendom."

Never, no never has any race on earth been more profoundly imbued with the idea of the Deity.

Our knights did not remain content with the mere belief in God: they considered it their duty to abandon themselves wholly to Him and not to limit their trust in Him. This faith (or trust) was an integral portion of the Code of Chivalry. " *Qui en Dieu a fiance il ne doit estre mas,*" ("He who has faith in God shall not be confounded,") says the author of " Jerusalem ; " and so in other passages. One day some Greek fire was thrown into the camp of the Christians, and some of the proudest barons lost their heads.

"Decidedly," said they, "we cannot fight against such an enemy as this ; " and they wept !

But the Bishop of Mautran renewed their courage. " It is God," said he, " who permits these trials : but be assured that, on the day He has appointed, you will be in Jerusalem."

These simple words served to re-animate the drooping courage of our crusaders : their souls grew strong again, and their faces were lifted up once more.

* " *Amis et Amiles.*"   † " *Covenans Vivien.*"

Judas Maccabeus even found himself one day with only one hundred men opposed by twenty thousand foes : his faith never flinched—and Heaven assisted him—"*fiance a que Dex li aidera*" (Auberon). But it was not only on the field of battle that the knight thus yielded to the will of Providence.

"You are as poor as proud," said Charlemagne to Almeri of Narbonne.

"Nothing can be more true," replied the page ; "but is there not a God in Heaven?"

To some who were jestingly remarking upon his poverty, Aïöl replied with the same proud utterance—

"If I am poor, God has sufficient!" and in this speech he but echoes the reply of his father, Elias, who as he bestowed upon him fourpence on the day of his leaving home, added to that poor gift the noble words—"When those are expended, God is in Heaven."

Nevertheless I prefer the simple yet profound expression of Fromondin in "*Garin de Loherain.*" Guillaume de Monclin was, as tutor, putting his nephew Fromondin through a strict course of chivalry. "If you follow my counsels," said he, "you will rise to a high position;" and the youth contented himself by replying, "Everything is in the hands of God."

It is not surprising that such soldiers knew how to pray, and that they were religiously compelled to prayer by the code which they had freely accepted. Moreover it was a practice common to heroes of all human epopees, and one may say that the epopee excluded atheism. One cannot figure the epic poems without gods or the Deity. In every clime, in every time, true epic characters raised their eyes to Heaven and waited the assistance from it which would give the victory to their insufficiency, to their failing forces. Our French heroes never were wanting in this respect, and their prayers were no less natural nor less noble than those of the heroes of antiquity, Greek or Latin. The best prayer, says a poet of the middle ages, is that which "the heart puts into the mouth," such ought to have been, such indeed were, the prayers of our knights. It would not have been reasonable to demand from them the fervour of mystic prayer. Facts, not reasonings, most forcibly struck these ignorant and simple natures : we shall presently see that their form of prayer everywhere presents this characteristic.

They delighted to recall the miracles of the Old and New Testaments, and particularly delighted in those miracles which appealed most to their somewhat gross and material imaginations: such, for instance, as the narrative of Jonah in the whale's belly; the miracle of the children singing in the midst of the burning fiery furnace, unharmed; Daniel in the den of the lions, which licked his feet in the dark; the raising of Lazarus; above all, the saving of Peter on the lake, by our Saviour, who led him victoriously to Rome and placed him on the throne of the world.

After the enumeration of these Biblical facts which—and this is noteworthy—correspond exactly with the paintings in the catacombs, and with the sculptures of the first Christian sarcophagi; after this military summary of the Old and New Testaments, our heroes considered it always necessary to affirm distinctly their faith in all these miracles, *Si com c'est voirs, et nos bien le creons.*

The miracles were " plain to them, and they entirely believed in them," and they considered themselves authorised to pass to the special object of their prayer. But here they were brief—a few words were sufficient; and thus, in these curious orisons, the preface occupies more space than the book.

When it happened that they had committed some crime or some fault of which they earnestly repented, the knights would suddenly bethink themselves of the consolitory face of Mary Magdalen, who throughout the middle ages was the most popular type of penitence blessed by God. And we can, as it were, hear all the sinners crying out to Heaven, "Thou who hast fully pardoned Mary Magdalen have mercy on us." The best of them believed themselves always guilty, and invoked this image of the Magdalen in the time of danger or in the hour of death. The best knight of all, Godfrey de Bouillon, who has the good fortune to be as great in history as in legend, was the first to recall this Gospel reminiscence when, beneath the walls of Antioch, dangerously wounded, *blecies el' foie et el' pomon,* and in fear of death, he said—

" Glorious Lord and Father, who by thy word caused Lazarus to arise from the dead: Mary Magdalen, the beautiful one, came nigh to thee in the house of Simon, and there, Lord, wept so copiously all the tears of her heart that she washed Thy feet with those tears, and then, with good intent, anointed them with spikenard.

She did wisely, and was fully recompensed, for she received from Thee pardon of all her sins. If this is true, Lord, and if it is true that we believe it, preserve my body from prison and from death."

Thus prayed, thus ought to pray, the knight.

We have not yet spoken of the adoration of the Virgin, but in reality she animates, she enlightens all our old romances, and the name of Mary is in them repeated as many times as is that of her Son.

This devotion has not in our truly epic poems the graceful character which it presents in the works of the thirteenth century.

It is all manly and of a military character. It was in after years that the charming legend was conceived—a somewhat far-fetched and puerile one—of the Virgin taking the place of a knight at a tourney, and other tales of an equally frivolous character, and which cannot add to the majesty of the Mother of our Lord. Here, as elsewhere, our poets of the eleventh and twelfth centuries are more simple and more pious. With these primitive writers, we gain in nobleness what we lose in grace, and there is nothing in the devout recitals of Gautier de Coincy which can be compared with the following scene in the " *Chanson d'Antioche:*" " The whole French army fell upon their knees to implore God to show them the true way to Jerusalem ; " or with that other episode, in a poem of the same period, in which we read that when the crusaders perceived the Holy City for the first time, they suddenly burst into tears. One verse of manly and dignified nature, is worth the whole of a puny and insipid poem.

The knight was trained to observe other religious laws as well as the practice of prayer. He was bound to share in the sacramental lives of other Christians, but with certain privileges which appear strange, and of which it is difficult to fix the origin with exactness.

One may say that the daily attendance at Mass was, if not a duty, at least a habit of all the barons, and it does not appear that in this respect they made any difference between Sundays and week-days. Every morning, and often before daylight while all the other inmates of the castle were asleep, the knight arose, and generally fasting, proceeded to hear Mass with his chaplain. If we turn to the King of France, we find the same devotion, and the awakening was not less early : the rite was only the more solemn, and a bishop took the place of the chaplain.   On *fête* days the Pope officiated—the Pope, whose sovereign magistracy our old poets did not altogether comprehend, and whom they transformed quite voluntarily into an almoner of the moneys of the emperor.

Writers have frequently described the grandeur of military Masses, and more than one artist has been happily inspired by them.   But what are we to say concerning those services of the twelfth century—those Masses sung in front of a Christian army on the morning of the day of battle, at daybreak, in the midst of some extensive plain, amid the terrible uproar of an army of Saracens who were pressing on with shouts and cries of victory ?   What can we say to those mail-clad soldiers who prostrated themselves before an improvised altar, and in silence offered their lives to Him who had died on the Cross ?   A rite as austere—but more singular—had to precede, and always did precede, the judicial encounter or duel : both champions were legally compelled to hear Mass before meeting in deadly combat.   They approached the altar, knelt down and received the sacrament.   One of the two was actually the guilty one they were seeking, and of the two communicants— horrible thing !—one only could be pure and innocent.

This duel, besides, was a brutal custom, a gross, superstitious, observance, against which at one time the voice of Agobard, and those of many other priests were uplifted.   What matter ?   Those barbarians pretended to sanctify their barbarisms, and mixed up the Deity with the interest of their anger : a strange mixture of savagery and faith, which the Church was compelled to tolerate, and on which she could only confer a more elevated character.   It is needless to add that this duel came to us from the Germans, and we may perceive once again, that that violent race has decidedly cut out too much work for the Church.

Confession also was demanded from the knights equally as from the lowest of the serfs.   Besides, those knights reckoned amongst them some grand and simple souls to whom a rigorous avowal of their faults would not cost any great effort.   They confessed themselves before performing any solemn act of their lives, and most particularly before going to battle.   " Let each one of you confess himself, and let no one hide a single sin. Then let us rush into the struggle, and let each one kill a pagan.

Peter the Hermit also did not think it out of place to relate to the Crusaders, that Saint Andrew had appeared to him in daytime, to recommend them to be really confessed. They always confessed before the judiciary duel. Before undertaking a long journey they also confessed themselves. When Begue crossed France to see his brother Garin whom he loved so dearly, once again he did not fail to halt at Grandmont to confess his sins to a hermit there. This confession was the great pre-occupation of the knights when about to die.

Richard, the son of Aymon, was at the foot of the gibbet, the rope around his neck, and the emperor insisted that this young baron should be put to death in the same way as a common male-factor. To be sure, Richard had no fear, and so much was evident; but in the supreme agony of imminent death he never ceased to repeat, "I wish to confess," and he only became composed when Bishop Daniel had heard his confession.

It will be understood that I am not speaking in this place of the phenomenon of conversion—of the thunderclaps on the road to Damascus—which cast our worst knights at the feet of the priest. "You have greatly offended God, but if you wish it you may still continue His friend." "Oh, I wish it very much."

Such was the dialogue one reads in more than one passage in our "*Chansons de geste*," and which will be heard, I think, until the end of this sad world. Nevertheless, even the best knights some-times postponed the sacrament ; and such delays even in the present day are only too easy to verify. But on the eve of battle, reddened with blood, pierced by lances in twenty places, and feeling as if their souls were escaping from their bodies, the barons would repent themselves of forgetfulness, and search eagerly around for a priest. If they could not find one, they went, if able, in search of their nearest relative, and drawing him aside, made their con-fession to him. Failing an ecclesiastic, a friend, a companion in arms, was sufficient.

By the voice of its most influential doctors, the Church has at least not disapproved of this practice, and Peter Lombard, in his "Book of Sentences," which has been the theological manual, and, so to speak, the great "classic" of the Middle Ages, does not hesitate to affirm that one ought to confess first to God, to the priest afterwards, and, failing a priest, to a relative or a friend ; *proximo vel socio,* he says.

Both history and tradition agree in presenting us with such confessions to laymen, a custom which obtained to a late date. Bayard, when dying, confessed humbly to the keeper of his inn, "in default of a priest." And nothing is more noble, nothing is more touching, than this historical scene—unless it be the legend which we read in the beginning of our "*Aliscans,*" and in which the youthful Vivien plays the principal part. On the eve of that famous battle "*ou la dolor fu grant,*" this hero of fifteen years old, made, ere he died, a supreme and affecting attempt to confess to his uncle, the old Count Guillaume, and confided to him in a low tone his sins. "I retreated one day before the infidels," said he. But he could not remember any more offences !

This confession was not the only sacrament in vogue amongst the knights which presents some obscurity to us, and we feel the same when considering the curious symbolical communion "with the three blades of grass and the three leaves of the tree," of which we could easily quote twenty examples culled from our best and most ancient poems. All our barons did not precisely resemble Count William, who took care to furnish himself with a consecrated wafer when he fought with the Saracens at Aliscans, where the greater number of men, as we read, contented themselves with leaves or blades of grass.

But how far back amid the ages can we trace this curious symbol, and what is its origin ? Those are questions which we are unable to answer, notwithstanding all our research. Other people, perchance, may be more successful than we.

Amongst the obligations which belonged to this first commandment of chivalry, is another, the last, "to die in the faith and for the faith." It is not our purpose here to set forth the death of our barons, and to point out how their death partook of martyrdom; but we must conclude that such an end was regarded by them as a duty.

> " Chevalier en ce monde-ci
> Ne peuvent vivre sans souci
> Ils doivent le peuple defendre,
> Et leur sanc pour la foi espandre."

THE DEATH OF ORRI, KING OF BAVARIA, MADE PRISONER BY THE SARACENS. [p. 37.

They *must* notice the word. It was thus in obedience to the call of duty that Roland died on the summit of the cliff at Roncesvalles, resting on Durandal: his victorious gaze turned from Spain—surrounded by angels.

In obedience to the voice of duty, King Orri, in the "*Auberi le Bourgoing,*" died as Regulus died, a thousand times more gloriously than the hero of antiquity, exclaiming in his terrible agony, "God forbid that I should betray my king and my God!"

It was in obedience to the voice of duty solely, that in another of our poems (one little known) the aged Ameri of Narbonne, who had lived a hundred years, spotless and fearless, stood boldly up before the Moslem and refused to acknowledge Mahomet. They beat the aged man with briars and rods, they cut into his living flesh, they prepared the wood-pile to burn him, and the Narbonnais could hear the crackling of the flames which were so soon to devour him. Nothing daunted him; and perceiving on the ramparts his wife, Ermengart, who was a weeping spectator of this horrible punishment, he cried to her—

"Let me die; but for the love of God, the son of Saint Mary, do not surrender the town.'

But why quote these instances in preference to so many others? It was only in obedience to the call of duty that the legendary heroes of our poems died; and in the same manner died the historical heroes of the crusades. For in these cases, as everywhere historical, fact is as strange as or stranger than fiction.

Such is the first commandment of chivalry, and those who practised it on earth are recompensed in Heaven by the possession of the absolute glory—*la glorie asolue*—and by the perfume of the holy flowers of Paradise.

III.

The second commandment details the first, and the Christian soldier was compelled to have always before him these words, which were to serve with him for the battle-cry, "Defend the Church!" We abstain from quoting too often here the little thirteenth century poem, entitled "*L'Ordene de Chevalrie,*" which we consider as a document drawn too late, far-fetched and subtilised.

Our old poems are better and prove more. Nevertheless the author of the "*Ordene*" possesses in part the merit of condensing successfully all the doctrine scattered throughout our old poems, and it is from this point of view that we must estimate the two verses—so characteristic as they are addressed to the knights themselves :—

> " Tout votre sanc derez espandre
> Pour la sainte Eglise deffendre." *

This is as concise as an article of the Creed.

It is convenient to distinguish in this place two currents.

The author of the "*Ordene*" is a cleric who speaks and writes clerically, and he represents a whole family of theologians, who must not be confounded with our old national poets, who were much more military, much less pious.

Would you know the true thoughts of the Church? Open the official book where it is carefully formulated—open the "*Pontifical*" and read :—

" Receive this sword in the name of the Father, the Son and the Holy Ghost ; use it for your own defence, for that of the holy Church of God, and for the confusion of the enemies of the Cross of Christ. Go: and remember that the Saints did not conquer kingdoms by the sword but by faith."

To sum up in a few words, chivalry has never been, is not, and never will be anything but armed force in the service of the unarmed truth : and I am not aware that anyone has ever given a higher or more exact definition of it.

The knight in any case, however he might regard it, was bound to hold himself in armed readiness at the gate of the yet threatened palace whence the Papacy delivered the truth to men : he was bound to hold himself in readiness, sword in hand, behind the throne of the Sovereign Pontiffs, whose independence was necessary to the world. He was bound to be at the door of our council chambers mounting guard—if I may use such a common-place expression—to secure the liberty of those Assemblies in which the greatest, the most momentous, and the most serious questions were discussed. It was he, again, who was looked for as the protector of the thousands of temples of the true God, of those baptismal

---

* All your blood should be poured out in defence of the Holy Church.

fonts from which emanate generations of Christians, of the altars where is renewed the immortal sacrifice which serves them at once for expiation and example, and of the pulpit from which all errors are denounced, all vices attacked, from which the greatest truths are proclaimed, and whence all virtues are inculcated.

It was he—it was once more he—who was born protector of all religious orders, and who was bound to say " Evangelise, teach, baptize, convert, expiate ; I am present to defend you : go on." Thanks to him the Benedictine could freely clear so much waste land, instruct so many ignorant people, undertake so many distant missions with so many powerful volumes. Thanks to him the Dominican possesses the freedom of speech and the Franciscan the liberty of poverty. Works of charity, too, owe to him something of their utility and beauty : they increased under his care, and that is why the hospitals receive everywhere thousands of sick, the infirmaries thousands of lepers, the monasteries thousands of hungry people. Wherever the Church was, there the knight also was to be found to accompany and to protect this holy mother, *ubi Ecclesia ubi miles.*

It is not necessary to pause and seek in our epic poetry for a doctrine so elevated and so profound as this, but in place of these ideas which remain too often mere theories, we meet therein with a popular and outspoken notion of the duties of the knight with regard to the Church.

"In all his acts," says the author of the *Entry into Spain,* "the knight is bound to propose to himself a double aim—the safety of his own soul, and the honour of the Church of which he is the guardian." To maintain Christianity : this is a sentence often repeated in our old poems, and it well expresses the idea. When the young pages left the paternal roof the last word of their mothers was to exhort them to this high duty. Serve Jesus Christ and holy Church. But this is not the end of the matter. Here is the sum of it : in the eyes of all our epic poets Christian humanity was an immense crowd of feeble people for whom it was necessary to pray and fight. Above this multitude who had the right to prayer and protection were two chosen families, two aristocracies, two distinct and powerful groups. The one was composed of the clergy, whom Providence had created for prayer ; the other the knights, whom God had made to protect those who prayed, and those for whom they interceded. Such is the theory which the Archbishop of Rheims promulgates in set terms in the opening pages of " *Garin de Loherain*," and we cannot do better than quote it. He says,

"We are clerics, and our duty is to serve God while we pray for our friends. But as for you knights, do not forget that God has called you to be the rampart of the Church." It was this same sentiment which inspired those quaint designs in the past centuries representing a priest, a soldier, and a labourer, who were clasping hands and saying, " I pray for France, I defend her, and I support her." * Has any one found aught better ?

IV.

The Church is here below a weakness, but it is not the only one, and the knight's mission was to defend all weaknesses. Now notwithstanding the charming satire of Cervantes, it is a mission which one must highly esteem, it is an ideal which we must admire, and we are persuaded that some pages, such as "*L'Ordene de Chevalerie*" do more honour and have been more useful to humanity, than that Don Quixote of which some enthusiastic admirers exaggerate both the philosophic value and the moral force. However this may be, the knight was bound to defend in this world all that was defenceless, and particularly the priests and monks "who serve God;" the women and children, widows and orphans. The origin of these precepts is not doubtful : it is entirely Christian, and there is in it no mixture of Roman, Celtic, or German elements. It is pure and without alloy.

This commandment, which resembles an article of faith, was not always so easy in practice. But commonly enough it was the devotion to the priesthood which sometimes cost our knights the most difficult and cruel efforts. It is quite certain that between the soldier and the priest there has always been a singular *modus*

* This is a parallel to the " Five Alls " formerly on old inn signs in England : " I pray for all, I fight for all, I work for all," &c.—*Trans.*

vivendi. In time of war they love and esteem each other, holding hand to hand, but in time of peace they are visibly antagonistic. The cruelties of the soldier disgust the priest, the placidity of the priest irritates the soldier. Our old songs are filled with references to this unlooked for antagonism, and we shall see elsewhere in what savage form the author of " *Garin le Loherain* " has painted this hatred which the baron entertained for the churchman. The secular clergy, whom the metrical romances of the Trouvères have so ridiculed, come scarcely within the scope of our epic poetry—it is to the monks that they address themselves. These monks in their eyes are too rich and too fat. They laugh at them with gross ante-Rabelaisian laughter ; they quiz them, they rally them, and nothing resembles the vulgar pleasantry of the *Marriage Renouart* and of the *Marriage Guillaume* so much as certain gross caricatures of our own day. It is more than Gallican.

Notwithstanding all this, the precept is there and it must be obeyed. Thou shalt honour the clergy. One may chafe at the bridle, but one ends by submitting to it. When King Charles espoused the charming woman who had been destined for Gerard de Roussillon and whom Gerard loved, the Count got very angry and was on the point of hurling a fierce defiance at Charles : but *respect for the clergy* restrained him. That monster whom people call Raoul of Cambrai took it into his head one day to destroy the convent of Origni, and as a matter of fact he did so, and burned the nuns with it. But this was a really exceptional, unprecedented crime, which the records of the Middle Ages have preserved as an unparalleled scandal. The knights of Raoul's force were the very first to be horrified at such horrible sacrilege. " We are not tyrants who fall upon holy bodies," they said, and the firm friend of the Count of Cambrai, Gueri le Sor, a man of savage and violent temperament, did not hesitate to hurl at his chief the most sanguinary reproaches.

" You go a great deal too far," he said, " and if God hate you, you have only yourself to thank for it. *Par les frans homes est cil lius honorés ; ne doit pas estre li cor sains vergondez.*" *

We know the rest, and how Origni was burned. The nuns came

---

* By Frenchmen is this place respected. It must not be defamed.

out calmly from their convent, psalter in hand and chanting in
composed tones the monastic office.   They begged Raoul to consider that all the country would suffer with them.   Vain were
their efforts and their prayers, they were soon seized and
devoured by the flames.   A poet of our own time, M. Coppée,
has related in flowing verse a similar legend to which he has given
a much happier ending.   His "*Liseron*" recalls our "*Raoul of
Cambrai.*"

No condition of life before the advent of the Saviour was more
sad than that of widows, and the Jews themselves regarded widowhood as a reproach.   The primitive Church enlarged hitherto
narrow ideas, and widows were considered by her as the "Altar of
the Lord."   They occupied almost the very first place in the
hierarchy of the poor as detailed by Christ, and they eventually
formed on order of their own.   St. Chrysostom did not shrink from
declaring that "without them the plenitude of the Church would
not have attained its entire perfection."

As regards orphans, the Church was equally concerned with
them.   She gave them occupations, brought them up, married
them, and finally opened wide for them the gates of *Orphano-
trophia.*   All these Christian traditions were absorbed into chivalry,
and no two things bear more resemblance to one another than do
the precepts of the *Apostolic Constitutions*, and the most beautiful
pages of our old romances.   But here again we must be careful to
guard against exaggeration.   In face of a society so gross, and so
armed as was feudal society, it was not expedient to proceed after
the manner of the primitive Church.   Instead of saying to our
barons, "You must defend the widow and the orphan," it was
necessary to begin by saying, "You shall do them no wrong;"
then a little later, "You shall not permit any one to do them
harm."   That was the order which was followed or encouraged by
the Church.

In the "*Chanson d'Aspremont*," Naimes, is considered as the
type of the all-accomplished knight, and of him were written these
beautiful words—"*Tel conseiller n'orent onques le Franc.*"   Such
an adviser the Frank never had.   Naimes was the object of this
eulogy by the poet by which all knights might have profited.
"He never betrayed confidence, he never deserted a good and true

man ; nor the starving widow and little child," or in the old French—

> " Il ne donna conseil petit ne grant
> Par coi preudome deserité faissant
> Les veves fames ne li petit enfant."

Animated by the same spirit, and feeling the approach of death, Charlemagne charged his son not to deprive orphans of their fiefs, nor widows of their little remaining money. But the son was, alas ! too quickly unmindful of his father's injunctions, and in the " *Charroi de Nîmes* " we have him cynically suggesting to Count William to bestow upon him the fiefs of such and such a baron who was about to die. But Count William was not one of those persons who listen patiently to such propositions as these. He revolted at the idea, and was very much enraged. He bounded up—

" And their widows, and their orphans," he cried—" what will become of them ? "

The king grew pale, and trembled beneath the contempt of William, when he exclaimed—

" If anyone injures those little ones or their land, here is my sword that shall cut off the head of any such traitor or robber." So said this true knight.

And no one dared to face that vengeful sword, nor him who bore it.*

So far we have only been concerned with negative precepts—we will now soar to higher summits.

In the " *Entrée en Espagne* " it is clearly laid down that the knight is bound before all things to assist and succour the widow and the orphan. It was not a certain category of wretched ones nor a certain class of human weakness that the knight was bound to defend ; it was, *all* the weak, *all* the poor, *all* the little ones, who had a prescriptive right to his protection. Charlemagne, on his death-bed, bade his son humiliate himself before the poor. " Before them be of no reputation. Give them help and counsel." The " *Ordene de Chevalerie,*" which we quote here for the last time, is naturally much more precise and more fully expressed.

" The duty of the knight is to constitute himself the guardian,

---

* Charroi de Nîmes, v. 312, 322, 366—376.

the protector, of the poor, so that the rich shall never injure them."
And the poet adds, "The duty of the knight is to sustain the weak
so that the strong shall never oppress them." Whenever he perceives a poor man or a stranger, "every gentleman, every knight,
is bound to accompany him, so that no one molest him or strike
him, for he is poor who has a haughty courage."

> " Que quant on voit un povre home estraingier,
> Tuit gentil home ti doient acointer.
> Ains qu'on le doie ne ferir ne tochier
> Car telz est povers qui a coraige fier."—*Girars de Viane.*

So wrote one of our poets who most deserves the epithet of
haughty, so little sought for in these days; and the author of
" *Girars de Viane* " has only crystallized in a few lines a correct
and universal precept.

Besides, the Church had anticipated him. In the most ancient
mass-book, in which one can read the prayers composed for the
benediction of a knight used in a ceremonial in the opening years
of the eleventh century, the Christian soldier is invited " to be the
living protection of all weaknesses ; " and in the thirteenth century,
at the consecration of a knight in the basilica of Saint Peter's, the
Arch-Priest said solemnly to him—

"Be thou the defender and the bold champion of the Church,
the widow, and the orphan ! "

And we have the pleasure to find to-day in the " *Roman
Pontifical* " the expression of the same doctrine, which the pagan
world never knew, and which will stand as an eternal honour to the
Christian race.

Here, as everywhere, the thought of the Church is more elevated
than that of our military epic poetry.

We venture to express the hope that no one will be surprised at it.

CHAPTER III.

THE CODE OF CHIVALRY.—THE FOURTH, FIFTH, AND SIXTH COMMANDMENTS.

I.

"Thou shalt love the country in which thou wast born." It is not surely in this dogmatic form that our old poets promulgated the noble precept to the ears and to the hearts of their popular auditory. They were better inspired, and have put on their pages Frenchmen who loved France!

France beloved eight hundred years ago! That is a fact which astonishes some minds now-a-days, and nine Frenchmen out of ten, in fact, persuade themselves that their France has only been beloved a hundred years. We remember having read a certain "Speech" delivered at a distribution of prizes countenanced by the Directory, in which we find word for word this candid paradox—

"Dear children, you have only had a country during the last five or six years!"

If we may believe the defenders of this *naïve* system, there was in France, before 1789, neither government, unity nor industry; art, intelligence, nor life! Before the Fourteenth of July, which is the exact date of the birth of France, nothing existed! since then, everything! *

We are the only nation in the whole world which thus despises its past, and takes a real pleasure in dating itself only from yesterday. Our powerful neighbours, the Germans and the English, persist in tracing their origins as far back as possible, and love them with ardent affection. Those are traditional nations, and possess in their traditions the best elements of their unity, and

* This is contrary to M. Rénan, who has protested against such a system in one of his later speeches at the French Academy, when he spoke of France built up at the price of a thousand years of heroism and patience, by the bravery of some, by the intelligence of others, by the sufferings of all.

their strength. Nevertheless they are very far from possessing annals at all comparable to our history, and no country ever deserved to be loved so greatly as does ours!

But we do not mean to say that this love can be arrived at at a bound.

The ancient Celtic country, formerly so much loved, ended, thanks to the violence and the skilfulness of Roman politics, by being fused with the Empire itself, and we have every authority for believing that in the Fifth Century of our era the cult of the Gaul included few of the faithful. On the other hand, we cannot call by the beautiful name of "love of country" the coarse attachment which the mighty and powerful Frankish warrior—this semi-savage with long hair in German forests, felt for his nomad tribe or his clan. One day, however, this tribe set out on the march, attracted by the West as the iron is to the magnet, and reached the territory which was one day ceded to it by Provus. They bestowed on this territory the name—the cherished name—of *Francia*, which was given successively to all the countries inhabited by the Frankish Confederation: but it was not yet a true country. At length these wanderers halted and installed themselves as victors in the grand country which is bound to preserve their name—Salians on one side, Ripuarians on the other.

Each tribe at first retained its independence and its code of laws, but these are now innumerable fragments and endless tatters. New kingdoms were created and even made—by chance, by the force of circumstances, and by the fancy of the Merovingian Princes, who desired to have an extensive kingdom in the North, and some sunny cities in the South. Thus there is still the great division in Austrasia and in Neustria which has nothing factitious about it, and represents two civilizations, two tendencies, and so to speak two different races. Who can find the "love of country" in all this scattering of badly-disposed forces without a common aim, or unity? Wait a little!

The Carlovingians appeared above the horizon and hastened the blessed hour in which we should possess a "native country." To tell the truth they were Teutons (Goths), those Carlovingians, but Goths also had the appreciation of unity, and knew how to sacrifice their German ideas to the Latin idea of which the Church was in their eyes the best incarnation and the last refuge. They bowed themselves before her and set themselves bravely to work to rebuild the old Roman Empire. It appears at first sight that nothing could be more antagonistic to this love of country, of which we are seeking, not without some pain, to determine the sources, but this " country " and this " love " were decidedly impossible amid all the Merovingian string-pulling, and it was necessary—most

The first King of France crowned by Angels.

necessary—that a powerful unity should be newly founded in our Western world. This unity no doubt was not of long duration, but it gave to modern nations the power and the time to recognise themselves.

The century in which Charlemagne died is the same that witnessed the clear separation of the Germans, Italians, and French. The Duchy of France became with us the nucleus of a country; but this glorious name was extended with the progress—the slow but sure progress—of the first Capets. They were French, and that dynasty was truly national. So it became national to call all the dominions of the King of France, France; and this territory, thank Heaven, has continually increased! One cannot help loving it.

To the somewhat insecure monarchs of the tenth and eleventh centuries succeeded the kings on horseback, the kings militant of the twelfth century, of whom Louis VI. is the first and not the least noble specimen. But there is no need to come so far down to have the pleasure of saluting the " native country " definitively constituted and dearly loved. In the " *Chanson de Roland* "—which was composed between the years 1066 and 1095, the country beloved of the nephew of Charlemagne " is our Northern France with its natural boundaries on the east and having all Southern France for its tributary." The country which Roland loved is then the country which we love; and the France for which he died, is the same France for which our soldiers died in 1884. The country—there is the " Patrie." She has taken centuries to build up, *to form herself;* but in the beating of our hearts we feel that she lives, and that she is beloved!

Such is the nation which our poets have celebrated; such is the country which the code of chivalry commands our heroes to cherish to the death; such is the country they have loved!

And there is no necessity to confuse with this great love the slighter attachment which we feel for the town or the village in which we were born. Nothing is more natural, more human, more laudable than this feeling of the second order, and it is not unusual to meet with the expression of it in our epics of the Middle Ages. When the bishop of Mautran offered successively the kingdom of Jerusalem to all the commanders of the First Crusade, they in turn declined the offer. And what reasons did they allege for refusing so distinguished a crown? Amongst so many illustrious barons Godfrey was truly humble; the others were simply fatigued, and desirous to return to their castles, to their native lands.

" Would to God and St. Simon that I were now at Arras in my dear home, and that I could put the arms of my son Baudouin around my neck."

Thus spoke Robert le Frison, and the others thought so.

The last wish of these iron-clad knights was often for their little native place. When Aleaume in *Raoul de Cambrai* is mortally wounded by Gueri le Sor, he exclaims, sobbing—

"Sainte Marie! I shall never see Saint-Quentin or Nesle again."

This native land, besides, seemed to them more beautiful than any other, and the Count of Flanders gave vent to this feeling very plainly as he contemplated the arid solitudes which surrounded Jerusalem. He said—

"I am astonished to think that Jesus Christ, the son of Mary, could have lived in such a desert as this! Ah, I far prefer the big castle of my district of Arras."

Evidently the good knight regretted the fact that the Saviour had not been born in Arras. Human nature again, but narrow-minded in its application. It was not the native country, it was the homestead.

It was the whole country which our knights were bound to love : the true France which extends "from Seint Michiel del' Peril as far as Seinz, and from Besançon to the port of Guitsand.*" The France which "lies extended to the sun from Saint Michel on the Sea to Germaise † on the Rhine," and from "Huiscent on the Sea to Saint Gille." This is the noble and extensive country which our poets unceasingly praise to the detriment of the Lombards (that is to say, the Italians), and the Tiois (that is to say, the Germans), so as to mark the exact boundaries of our nationality and to divide it clearly from the two great countries with which it might possibly be confounded. It is this incomparable territory—"the finest in the world"—which is as beautiful to the eye as acceptable to the heart. This is the charming country "which abounds in woods, in rivers, in meadows, in virgins and beautiful women, in good wines and in brave knights." This is the splendidly endowed country in which people are so open-handed. France is a country in which one surely finds "honour and loyalty and all good things;" and besides, "in no country is there a greater or a truer people." This is indeed the native land of proud hearts. "This people is prouder than leopard or lion." It is a people who during many centuries has had the incontestable honour to be united with the Christian race itself in all the Mussulman world where the word

* S. Michiel del' Peril is St. Michael's Mount. Seinz is Cologne (Xanten). Guitsand is Wissant (Pas de Calais).
† Germaise is Worms.

"Frank" is the glorious synonym of Christian, and to such an extent that it is not the Latin East but the French East that one should speak of. It is the soil blessed of God from which such a fine race has emanated. We must not confound France with mediocre peoples "where they take care of hunting-birds and where every knight has his female companion." No, the memory of the true Cross is there cherished for ever and that of the Holy Sepulchre. Spain struggles for its existence against the African enemies of her faith; Italy is bled by hostile factions; Germany is French in her court, her nobles, her tribunals, her books; under the vain title of the Holy Empire, Germany is an encampment of barbarians; but France, ever since the eleventh and twelfth centuries, has been really a nation.

The love of this country which is at length conscious of itself, lights up all the pages of our old poems. Listen again:—"When Providence founded one hundred kingdoms the best was fair France, and the first king whom God sent there was crowned by the hands of His angels. Since the time of Charlemagne all nations have sprung up from France—Bavaria, Germany, Burgundy, Lorraine, Tuscany, Poitou, Gascony, to the borders of Spain. But the King who wears the gold crown of France upon his brow must be a warrior, and be able to lead an army of one hundred thousand men, even to the ports of Spain. If he is not thus capable then France is dishonoured and we make a mistake in crowning him."

These ideas are repeated almost word for word at the commencement of another of our poems, as follows:—

"The chief of all crowns is that of France, and the first king of France was crowned by angels singing, 'Thou shalt be,' saith God, 'My representative on earth, where thou shalt cause Law and Justice to triumph.'"

Our forefathers spoke of their country with great pride. These verses, no doubt, excited tumultuous applause every time a *Jongleur* chanted them, and they chanted them pretty often. They were a kind of national anthem which only required a popular and catching tune. The *Marseillaise* is not more beautiful.

Such accents are significant, such poetry eloquent. But in fact we are a concrete race, and it became necessary one day to crystallise, as it were, the French native land into a man. This living

THE DEATH OF ROLAND. [p. 51.

epitome of " Patrie " was Roland. Roland without any exaggeration was France made man. Nothing could happen to Roland which did not at the same time happen to France. When he made ready for the combat a wave of hope thrilled France ; if he were victorious France shook with joy ; if he were vanquished France mourned and wept. At the very time when the disastrous engagement at Roncesvalles was about to commence, there occurred in France phenomena analogous to those which actually happened throughout the whole world at the crucifixion of the Man-God. The poet, who certainly was a profound Christian, has not hesitated to imagine, or rather to state, for he believes in the prodigy, all that concatenation of supernatural presages. " In France," he says, " there was a terrible tempest, an earthquake from Saint Michel del' Peril to Xanten ; from Besançon to Wissant. At midday the earth was shrouded in darkness." Might not we believe that he was referring to the phenomena of Calvary ? No, no ; do not be deceived. It was the great grief for the demise of Roland. " *C'est li granz doels pur la mort de Rollant !* "

That illustrious personage thought of nothing but the emperor and France. Every time he wielded his great sword he would ask himself, " What would they say in France ? " and the honour of his family engaged his mind less than the honour of his country. If he refused so obstinately to sound the horn to call his uncle to his assistance, if he committed that admirable imprudence from which Oliver sought in vain to dissuade him, it was entirely because of his native land. " God forbid," he cried on two occasions, " that France should be abased because of me. God, His saints, and angels forbid that fair France should lose her honour on my account ! " Then he launched into the midst of the battle—a lost man !

During the continuance of this " Waterloo," the one word, continually in his mouth, was " France." When the Christian barons were all slain a touching sentence uprose to his lips. " Land of France," he exclaimed, " *mult estez dulz pais* " (What a sweet land thou art) !

At length the hour of his own death approached. He died as he had lived—a Frenchman, and beaming with pride exclaimed, " There shall never again be in France such another as Roland."

Then when he felt darkness falling upon his eyes announcing the inevitable approach of death, one of his last looks was for France.[*] "*Et dulces moriens reminiscitur Argos.*"

No nation can, even in the latest age of ours, offer such a type, a more glorious ideal of the love of country; but Roland is not the only one who has been burned in this purifying fire. All the French of our "Chansons" are so many Charlemagnes and Rolands. They are represented as a chosen nation, and a special race. The author of our Roland enumerates somewhere the different *corps* of the Christian army, in the same way as Homer catalogued the ships of the Grecian fleet. In the *ost* of Charles, three *échelles*—three army corps—out of ten were composed of Frenchmen; but we must peruse the description which the old Trouvère has given us.

"The tenth *échelle*," said he, "is composed of the barons of France; there are one hundred thousand of them, of our best captains. They are of stout frame and haughty demeanour, their heads all white, and their beards grizzled. They mount on horseback and demand battle! 'Montjoie, Montjoie,' they cry. Charlemagne is with them." And wishing to paint them in a single verse, which one may easily remember, the poet adds—

"These are those Frenchmen who conquer Kingdoms."

Roland was proud of his Frenchmen, and halted to inspect them, "Not one of you," he exclaimed, "would fail even to the death," and full of admiration for the men of the "great land," the nephew of Charles cried out, "Frenchmen are good, they fight like gallant soldiers."

The other "Chansons du Geste" present our countrymen in an equally good aspect. Everywhere they bear witness to their, often desperate, courage; and their somewhat lengthy speeches preserve their cheerfulness, which is rather noisy. The national character has not changed. Our poets, in order to depict our heroes, used a term which describes them accurately, "Gay Knights." Beneath their helmets we perceive fine features, ready to smile, full of pleasant raillery. They joke and exchange some pleasantry even over the bodies of their dying enemy. They move forward to battle grand, superb, terrible in aspect, always wearing that mocking

---

[*] De pluseurs choses à remembrer lui prist, de dulce France ("Roland," 2375, 81).

smile, and that proud appearance. Their advance to the field was the same at Roncesvalles as at Waterloo. Even the Saracens themselves, like the English in after years, could not help admiring them. " Of a surety, whoever could be constituted like these Frenchmen, whoever could resemble them and possess their stability, would live all the longer." The terms are strong and the poet puts them in the mouth of a pagan.

They are so attached to this beautiful land of France, that they are unable to leave it. With what delight do they return thither, and how regretful they are when they are forced to leave it. " Sweet mother," said Bertha to her mother, when they were about to part for a long while, " I feel as if I were being cut to the heart with a knife." " Daughter," replied the mother, " be happy and joyous, you are going into France."

Aye d'Avignon, when a prisoner amongst the Saracens, begged Garnier her husband not to recognize her. " I was born in France ; speak to me only of France, speak only to me of my country, and give me some news of my sweet native land."

Strangers, pagans, experienced the same regret. The ambassador of the Saracens, Balan, when he was quitting Charles' Court turned round many times to look at the French people once again. He regretted Charles, " his rich baronage," and the Frenchmen " who were so fine." The regret of William of Orange is still more touching. " Towards rich France he turned, and the breeze from France blew in his face. He opened his dress so as to permit the breeze to play upon him more fully. Facing the wind he kneeled down and cried, ' O sweet wind that blows from France ! There are all those whom I love. I commit thee to the care of God, for I have no hope of ever seeing thee again.' Then from his beautiful eyes tears rained down. They trickled down his face in streams."

It is the same sentiment so well expressed by the Troubadour in the verses which we ourselves have so frequently quoted when far away from France. " When the soft wind blows from the direction of my native land I fancy I can perceive the fragrance of Paradise."

It is not then surprising that France should be so dearly loved ; and such a country well merits such a love !

France is like a queen seated on a throne at the base of which

two oceans unite.   Beneath a sky of a delightful and charming
equability it displays the beauty of its fine rivers, the fertility of its
immense plains, the majesty of its Alps, of its Cevennes and its
Pyrenees.   It contains every tree, every vine, every fruit.   A fine
people in truth : youthful and vivacious ; and one is tempted to enquire how they can ever grow old ; possessing an intelligence which
nothing can cloud, a devotion which nothing can upset, in the will
an energy which is too easily extinguished, but which is still more
readily re-illumined.   Talking well and fond of speaking for a long
time, listening with less willingness and not troubling itself with
much temporising, it astonishes the world by the disinterestedness
of its sacrifices, the rapidity of its resolves, and the fervour of its
enterprises.   It possesses a sprightly courage and a courageous spirit,
but of all things it possesses *dash* (*élan*,) which is the foremost of
all military qualities.   Providence has gifted it with so many noble
qualities that this blessing has borne fruit.   He has committed to
the French nation the mission to preserve in all   extraordinary
attacks—the destinies of Truth on the earth.

It was France that under Clovis put its foot on Arianism and
crushed it :   it was France that by the hands of Charles Martel
drove for ever from our borders the danger of Mussulman invasion :
it   was   France   that   by   Charlemagne   delivered   Europe   and
Christianity from the formidable outburst of German barbarism : it
was France that by Godfrey de Bouillon, by Saint Louis, and by
means of the Crusades, gave to the Eastern Christians a security
which the East threatened.   This is the reason why the Popes of
the Middle Ages never feared to praise loudly France above all other
nations : this is why the old Pope Gregory IX.,—a contemporary
with our latest epic poets—had no scruples in exclaiming in magnificent language—thus—

" The Son of God to whose orders the whole world is subservient,
and whom the battalions of the Celestial army obey, has established
here below, as a sign of Divine puissance, a certain number of kingdoms, diverse in inhabitants and language.   And as in past days
the tribe of Judah received a special blessing from on high amongst
the sons of the patriarch Jacob, so the kingdom of France is above
all others endowed by the hand of God himself with special grace
and privileges."

Our poets have spoken of France in similar terms, and the commencement of the "*Couronnement Lovys*" is as worthy of notice as the Bull of Gregory the Ninth.

II.

The authors of our old poems are not less eloquent or decided when they concern themselves with the Fifth Commandment of the Code which refers to the valour of the knight, and it is scarcely necessary to enumerate the various virtues which the Code imposes upon all knights.

Amongst the old degenerate Gauls, amongst the Roman legionaries scientifically trained to victory, in the case of the young Frankish warrior who possessed the courage and instincts of the savage, and finally in the Christian race which already reckons so many millions of martyrs, there are undoubted traditions of courage. These four streams have formed the river of which we speak ; but it is necessary to state here as elsewhere, that the German and Christian elements have been the most powerful and the most fruitful. Chivalrous courage is only one spirit composed of these two strains of courage — it is made of these two "mettles." For the rest, the Code of Chivalry is more clear upon this than any of the other Commandments. Like Nehemiah, like that knight of the old land who wrote, " My peers have no fears, and never fly," our knights were most afraid of being considered cowards. This was their great fear. "*Miens vauroit estre mors, que couars apelés,*" was their motto which they continually kept repeating ; and added with a certain touch of terror, " *qu'un seul couart feroit un ost descouragier* "—a single coward was sufficient to discourage an army !

Again. When they plunged into the thick of the fight they would turn to their companions and exclaim in bold accents, " We will slay all, or all be slain ! " They were most desirous to meet their foes hand to hand, to feel him at the point of their swords. There have been some magnificent passages devoted to this subject which the poets of our time have happily popularized. " Cursed be the first who bent a bow. He was a coward and did not dare to come to close quarters." Javelins and arrows appeared to our knights the arms of villains, and this prejudice, which at first did honour to French valour, ended by being fatal to it. We remember the theatrical disdain which our knights entertained at Cressy for the Genoese bowmen, and the result. It was an excess of heroic virtue, and it is too true that the fourteenth century is, in too many instances, only an exaggerated copy of the twelfth, which, when all is said, remains the great century of the Middle Ages.

We said just now that there were in knightly courage two principal elements or factors, the Germanic and the Christian : they were not always sufficiently developed. Our knights too often loved fighting for its own sake, and not for the cause which they had espoused. The old barbaric leaven of the German forest was still working beneath the coat of mail. In their eyes the spectacle of gory sword or armour was a charming sight; a fine lance-thrust transported them to the seventh heaven of delight. "I enjoy such a thrust more than eating and drinking," exclaimed, very naturally, one of the ferocious heroes of " *Raoul de Cambrai.*" This naïve admiration is very apparent in our oldest epic poems, and in " *Roland* " in particular. In the midst of the terrible battle, when it was a question whether victory would declare for Islam or the Cross, when a handful of Christians were holding their own against thousands of Moslems, on that immense plain covered with the dying, our Frenchmen, more than half dead, still found time to criticise and admire good strokes of lance or sword. A fencing-master of the nineteenth century could not appreciate more calmly a pretty "pass."

It was art, but art of a brutal kind, which Christianity had some difficulty in realising. It was practised nevertheless, and the Crusades had from this point of view an influence which has perhaps been scarcely appreciated. Feudalism had not de-germanised the courage of our ancestors, and had not deprived it of any of its old roughness. The Crusades interjected into it the idea of God, and transformed it ; compare these two " Chansons " with one another, " *Raoul de Cambrai* " and " *Antioch.*" The barbarous German rages in the former, which is an echo of the tenth century; the Church triumphs in the latter, which is a narrative of the

Crusades, written in a measure after the dictation of the Crusaders themselves. Feudalism and the Crusades are the thesis and anti-thesis.

"Fight, God is with you." Such, in a few words, was the whole formula of Christian courage ; and the following old verse of the twelfth century, only in another form, expresses the famous saying of the most knightly of all knights : I mean Joan of Arc. "The men at arms will fight, and God will give the Victory."

There is in fact no more correct embodiment of the fifth article of our Decalogue than that.

To this law, all the heroes of our history and legend have been gloriously faithful ; and it seems that those two groups of knights— the real and the imaginary—rival each other in moral greatness and magnificent bravery. The personages pictured in " Aliscans," do not cede anything to those described in " Antioch ; " nor those of " Jerusalem " to those in " Roland." Legend is in this case, as in so many other cases, only the condensation and the quintessence of history.

Under the walls of Antioch—where were performed so many heroic deeds, grander even than those of the heroes of Greece and Rome—it was that this law was obeyed by that squire Gontier d'Aire, who entered one day, quite alone, into the beleaguered town, and so deserves to take foremost rank amongst knights. During a siege as memorable as that of Troy, this law was obeyed by the admirable Renaut Porquet, who, a prisoner of the Saracens, advised his Christian companions not to exchange him against a pagan. To this law, Foucart the orphan subscribed, when he would not permit his lord, the Count of Flanders, to mount the scaling-ladder before him—that perilous ladder which should have enabled the barons to ascend to the ramparts of Antioch—but who, after saying simply, " If I die, no one will lament me," offered himself as a victim, threw his *blason* behind his back, seized the ladder with both hands, offered a long prayer to God, hurried forward, and left only the second place to such heroes as Bohemond and Tancred.

Under the sacred walls of Jerusalem, where all the Christian West met, Thomas de Marne again obeyed this law. He caused himself to be thrown into the town through the air, by means of thirty lances of the knights. " So long as the world lasts, this exploit will be related," said the author of the "Chanson of Jerusalem." I am sure I hope so, and a thousand other exploits still, which I cannot relate here, which will redound to the eternal honour of the French and of the Christian race. A second "De Viris" might be composed for our children. The other is less beautiful.

This law was obeyed in the domain of legend, by all the heroes of a hundred fights whose names were throughout all the Middle Ages a loving lesson of highmindedness, honour, and courage. The Code of Chivalry which we are endeavouring to make clear, is not, like other codes, a dry and barren text, and our fathers as a commentary upon it recounted the examples of great knights. Instead of telling the young squires to be valiant—they rather said, Look at Ogier, and think of Roland. The mural paintings— somewhat gross perhaps—which covered the walls of chateaux and the open spaces of the enormous chimneys, the dull-toned tapestry, the brilliant mirrors, the quaint sculpture on the portals, all told of these models of chivalry, and the gaze of youth could not fail to dwell on them. They had Guillaume Fierebrace resisting unaided a hundred thousand Saracens in the plains of Aliscans. They had Ogier, withstanding the whole Empire in his dungeon at Castelfort: there was Vivien,—the child Vivien—panting and half dead, tying his entrails around his body and rushing again to meet death in the *mêlée :* they had the good knight Guron who in the "*Taking of Pampeluna*" successfully accomplished the most dangerous of all errands to the pagan King Marsilus and perished in a treacherous ambuscade, after an unequal and sublime struggle where his life would not have lasted a moment save for his high courage: there was Roland, the most glorious and popular of all these valiant warriors—Roland, who died, "extending his gauntlet to God," upon that rock of Roncesvalles, which literally dominates all the Middle Ages. There were, in fine, all our epic knights who vied with each other in repeating this grand sentence from one of our oldest poems—

"See, death approaches ! But, as becomes brave men, let us die fighting ! "

III.

From the Fifth to the Sixth Commandment is, we opine, a very easy transition, for the real employment of chivalrous courage, the only legitimate object and use of it in the estimation of our ancestors, was to fight against the Saracens. A murderous war, an endless duel. Some of our epic poems, it is true, are almost entirely animated by feudal rage; but these, no matter what people may say, are neither the most ancient, the most beautiful, nor the truest. To prefer " *Raoul de Cambrai* " to the " *Chanson de Roland* " is to give proofs of an intelligence which does not possess sufficiently either the " Christian " or the " French sense." Hatred for the Pagan animates most of our old poems; they exhale the air of the Crusades by which they were vivified.

No doubt we find many classic images of a more noble style in the letters of the Popes, wherein the crusaders are compared to " antique athletes," but our old poems express the same idea in more heroic and more popular words. Do we wish to sum up in one line the whole life of Charlemagne we immediately find it in eight words—" *Pas lui furent païen en maint leu encombrés* "— (The Pagan was in many places checked by him). Do you wish to have as brief a record of all the exploits of that historic liberator of our France, of that William whom we have too long forgotten? " It was he," they say, " who so severely punished both pagans and slaves." There you have said everything, and you cannot have a finer funeral oration.

Quotations are useless, and all our romances, to tell the truth, are only the recitals of this grand and formidable struggle. All that was not Christian became Saracen in our ancestors' eyes. Clovis himself was considered by them as a converted Mussulman, and it was at the head of our army of Crusaders that Charlemagne delivered Jerusalem. Each one of our epopœia concludes with the capture of an infidel town, and the three culminating points in our epic poetry are Aliscans, Roncesvalles, Jerusalem, two defeats and one victory, in which we were opposed by the Saracens. " They fought the Turks right willingly, and often baptised themselves in their blood." These two lines give us a very good idea of our knights, and resemble them more than all their other portraits.

This hatred of the Pagan was carried to the verge of madness, to spasmodic rage against them. "If we were in Paradise," said the rough soldiers of the twelfth century, "we would come down to fight the Saracens." The companions of Godfrey de Bouillon in the first flush of enthusiasm, which extinguished itself later, uttered a cry of rage which has not been surpassed in vigour—

"Were the walls of Jerusalem of steel," they said, "were they of steel, we would tear them with our teeth."

Many are scandalized by the exhibition of so much anger, but these people speak at their ease, and our fathers were better able than we to estimate the danger with which Islam threatened Christianity. We must not forget that the Mussulmans in the seventh century penetrated even to Poitiers, and that at Toulouse, in 793, they constituted themselves masters of all the south of France. In the ninth century they still infested our boundaries, and menaced our national independence. Two races, two religions, were there in presence of each other. It was necessary that Islam should retire, and the Crusade was only a process of driving back the invasion.

We also know that this scourge of Chivalry has delivered the world by protecting it against the ascendency of Mahomet. We have seen—we can see to what depths the Mussulman races can descend, and the rapidity with which they lose all moral sense, all honour of existence, all social vitality. Without chivalry, the West, vanquished by fatalism and sensuality, might to-day have been as decomposed and as rotten as the East!

Thanks to those of its commandments which appear the less *modern*, the Code of Chivalry has freed and preserved us. It would be perhaps only fair to preserve its memory in return.

CHAPTER IV.

THE CODE OF CHIVALRY.—THE LAST FOUR COMMANDMENTS.—
THE GROWTH AND DECADENCE OF THE CHIVALROUS IDEAL.

I.

THE strict performance of all feudal duties, and fidelity of the vassal to his lord, are the obligations of the Seventh Commandment of Chivalry. The vassal was bound to obey his lord in every particular, so long as the latter demanded of him nothing prejudicial, nothing contrary to the Faith, the Church, and the poor. "As soon as one holds fiefs or land of a baron, one is bound to come to his assistance on every occasion, provided that he does not attempt to destroy the churches, nor to harm poor people; for no one is bound to wage war against God."

Thus spoke the author of one of our old *chansons* (" *Girars de Viane* "), so at that time it appears people did not dare to war against holy things.

We have in a previous chapter recorded our protest against this doctrine, so strange and so widely disseminated, which confounds feudalism with chivalry. We have more strongly still protested against the creed of certain fanatics, who, instead of accepting feudalism as a necessity of history, designate it now as the most perfect of all forms of government. One of these enthusiasts said to us one day—

" Evil be to those who attack these two institutions—so evidently providential—feudalism and slavery."

One really cannot argue with such folly: it is sufficient to show one's contempt for it. But it is important that we should not go too far, and we may state that feudalism, so disastrous to the Church and to the Good, was really inevitable in the midst of the terrible troubles of the ninth century. No union was possible: the central power lost its head and abdicated; a thousand

ambitions surged on at the same time; Norman vessels entered
southern rivers; the last waves of Saracen invasion alarmed the
people of the southern maritime regions; the old German blood
raged again, and barbarism threatened to descend like a pall upon
the astonished world.

It was then, as we have said, that the weak entertained the very
natural idea of seeking the protection of the strong; and, rallying
round them, cried, "Defend us, defend us!"

Such was feudalism. There was nothing divine or perfect about
it: it was merely a phenomenon that took place from force of
circumstances, necessary and, in the good sense of the term, fatal;
inevitable.

It is also easy to understand that the great did not accord their
protection to the weak for nothing; and it was necessary that the
latter should put themselves in the hands of the former.

"We will serve you, we will be your adherents, we will follow
you to battle, we will be faithful to you—faithful to the death."
From this compact arose the incomparable strength of the feudal
bond. It was gratitude extended to the condition of social law.
What do I say? It was the gratitude which entered into all the
manners and customs of a whole race—of all the world. A brutal
and gross species of gratitude, I am ready to admit, but both
sincere and lively also. Without it and God it would have been
all over with us.

This devotion of the vassal to his lord was blind and insensate.
No matter what the baron's will may have been, the vassal always
responded by the words which have now become a formula:—As
you please, so let it be. Read and read again the barbarous
ultra-feudal poem, "*Raoul de Cambrai*," of which we have
already spoken. When this hero of this "Epic of Savages," when
Raoul proceeded to burn the convent of Origni, his vassal Bernier,
whose mother was an inmate of that very convent, consented to
follow him, even to the committal of this crime.

"My lord Raoul," said he, "is a greater traitor than Judas—
but he is my lord. I would not fail him for the world."

This is terrible, but there is more behind.

The crime was consummated. Origni was burned: the nuns, a
hundred poor women, perished in the flames, and Bernier's mother

was not spared. She lay there lifeless, with her psalter still burning on her bosom. Her son perceived her : what grief, what rage possessed him ! But Bernier is Raoul's vassal, and it is with a certain fear and respect that he seeks for his mother's murderer.

Raoul, who had never repented of anything he had done, treated Bernier as a slave, and struck him a terrible blow on the head. The blood flowed in streams over his face, already wet with tears,

Renaud de Montauban and his brother at the feet of Charlemagne.

but he, never rising from the position of a true vassal, calmly endured this supreme injury, and contented himself with asking for his weapons.

" *De ceste cort partirai sans congie,*" says the narrative. He did not strike the wretch, Raoul ; he did not render insult for insult, and blow for blow ; he went away—simply ; that was all. This was the type of vassal in the heroic age of feudalism ; and the terrible romance of " *Raoul de Cambrai* " is founded—and we must not forget this—on the historical facts of the tenth century. There is no need, I think, to go farther than that.

The bonds of feudalism were stronger than family ties : the lord was greater than a father, and a vassal was more than a son. Do we require another proof, really tragical and perhaps more horrible than that crime at Origni ?

A traitor of the name of Fromont one day murdered his lord and master, Girart de Blaines, and in his mad rage would have slain every member of the family of which he had slain the chief. There only remained, alas ! a child, a little lad of a few months old, and this only child of Girart had been confided to the care of a devoted vassal named Renier, whose wife was called Erembourc. The traitor ordered these good people to bring to him Girart's child, the little Jourdain whom he wished to kill. After lengthy and moving remonstrances, which we shall have opportunity to relate elsewhere, they refused, and ended by giving up their own child, which they palmed off as the son of their *seigneur,* to the assassin. Yes ! they sacrificed their very flesh and blood, and were suffering spectators of the agony of the child. They weep, they faint, they die ; but after all they are vassals, and those people believed that they were accomplishing a duty in saving the little son of their lord at such a price. It was hard !

The Code of Chivalry tempered this rudeness, but was also careful not to whittle it down too fine. The Church itself understood what would have become of these young and wild people if, in the excess of a false sensibility, they had undermined the fidelity of the vassal, if they had destroyed that barrier, if they had ameliorated the rudeness of those customs.

She was satisfied by giving to the duties of the sovereign lord the same relief as the vassal, and by throwing into their somewhat savage relations the spirit of toleration, and the spirit of sacrifice. "Dear son," said Odilon on his death-bed to his nephew Girart de Roussillon, whom he wished to reconcile with Charles : "Always practise caution and common-sense : love your lord, and be faithful to him."

This caution did not interfere with the devotion of the individual. William—that perpetual liberator of the kings of France—William was at church ; he was being married. They had reached that interesting part of the ceremony when the bridegroom places the ring upon the finger of the bride, when suddenly a messenger

RENIER AND HIS WIFE EREMBOURC SUBSTITUTED THEIR OWN CHILD FOR THEIR MASTER'S
INFANT.

[*p.* 64.

entered in a great hurry, and very much alarmed, bringing bad news of the emperor.

"My lord Louis in danger!" exclaimed William, and—quitting his place at the altar, the priest, and his pale-faced bride on whom he would not look, and whom he would never see again, leaving the happiness of which he would not think—he went away. His heart was broken, he was in deep grief; but he went. If Victor Hugo had versified this episode he would have made it a beautiful pendant to his *Aymerillot*.

There was the same heroism in the case of that Fouqueret whom the father of Aubri le Bourguignon had formerly brought up and made a knight of. Aubri was the mortal enemy of this vassal, whose nephews he had killed, and whose daughter he had intended to dishonour. But the Burgundian, as it happened, was defeated and forced to succumb. He was disarmed, dismounted, lost.

Yet immediately the loud voice of vassaldom made itself audible in the heart of Fouqueret: the memories of his infancy came back to him; he recalled the kind *seigneur* who had brought him up, and without hesitation he said to Aubri—

"Hold! take my horse and my sword: begone!" and he fled.

Didier did the same for Charlemagne in the midst of the great battle under the walls of Pampeluna, and many other vassals did likewise. It is true, nevertheless, that there were occasions in which this noble sentiment seemed to be extinguished in the hearts of our best knights. Yes, certain barons revolted brutally against their lords, and raised their hands against those who had nourished them.

But these were only moments of mental aberration and blindness. These revolts were not thorough, and sooner or later the rebels collapsed at the feet of their lords, bathed in tears and imploring mercy. The four sons of Aymon, the sons of Garin, Doon of Mayence and Gaidon, fell thus at the feet of Charlemagne; as the sons and grandsons of Aimeri of Narbonne fell later at the feet of the too easy-going and weak Louis. One day they saw (it is in "*Renaus de Montauban*") four thousand seven hundred knights proceed, with bowed heads, naked feet, and clothed only in their shirts, towards the tent of the redoubtable emperor against whom they had rebelled.

They scarcely perceived the king's majesty, when they fell upon their knees, and, weeping, swore never to be false again : that was the crime of crimes, which could only be compared to apostasy. Upon the walls of all the halls in all our castles of the twelfth and thirteenth centuries one might have written this threatening verse from one of our old *chansons*—

"QUI BOISE SON SEIGNEUR BIEN A DIEU RELENQUI."

If anyone committed such a crime he never could sufficiently repent. But this repentance was not sufficient for the unknown framers of the Code of Chivalry, and they showed themselves more severe. A penalty was instituted against vassals who had failed in their duty, and it was severely insisted on. That Bernier, in "*Raoul de Cambrai*," of whom we have already spoken, had many reasons for revenge against him who had burned his mother in the flames of Origni, and who had cruelly maltreated him, what matter! The bond of vassaldom was not broken, it could not be, and there was Bernier in tears, offering to expiate so great a crime as the spirit of revolt, by undertaking a pilgrimage beyond the seas !

Why did Renaud de Montauban leave his wife and children one day and make the pilgrimage to Jerusalem ? Why did he make his way towards Cologne, concealing his glory, his rank, and his name ? Why did he clothe himself in the humble garments of the least of his companion masons ? Why ? Because he had formerly rebelled against his lord, and the expiation seemed to him then a thousand times too lenient.

Such a law needs must have such a penalty.

II.

Another Commandment for the knightly ones, and one which the ancients were little acquainted with, is, " Beware of falsehood ; have a horror of lying." " Do not lie," is one of the conditions of chivalry which remains fixed and living amongst modern peoples. There is no necessity to quote a number of texts, and so we will only mention two, one of which is taken from one of our oldest *chansons* and the other from one of the most recent. These are, as it were, the two poles upon which revolved all the poetry of the middle ages.

"*Fins cuers ne puet mentir,*" says the author of "*Raoul de Cambrai,*" who wrote in the thirteenth century with the spirit and traditions of the tenth. We have the same injunction in the "*Entrée en Espagne,*" which is a work of the period of our epic decadence. When Roland undertook the fabled journey into Persia which is described in the second part of this curious poem, when he was called on to induct Samson, the son of the Pagan king, into a regular course of chivalry, he gave him a great deal of advice of a very valuable character, and notably the following counsel—

"Friend," said Roland to his pupil, "*Gart-toi de mentir. Car ce est une tache qui moult fait repentir !*"

We have seen in the foregoing pages that one of the most beautiful eulogies which has ever been addressed to noble France is this, "This is the most truthful of all nations :" that is to say, the most sincere. So writes the author of "*Berte ans grans piés,*" and it is as well to add that this Homeric epithet, a "sincere heart," is one of those bestowed on knights in the old *chanson* of "*Griatz de Rossillho,*" and in many others. If we wished also to go back to the true origin of the most justly praised of our modern sentiments, one would easily perceive that "respect for one's word" can be traced back to the epoch of chivalry. Respect for feudal engagements has carried in its train respect for all other engagements. Not to tell lies, and to keep to one's word, are, to this day, the two chief traits in the character of a gentleman.

It mattered little whether the word of honour had been passed under the form of an oath upon the open Testament or before the golden caskets which contained the relics of the saints, or whether the promise had been made simply by the knight extending his un-gloved hand, or whether the engagement was unaccompanied by any rite at all. The *parole* was in itself sufficient.

When Count William returned from that great disaster at Aliscans where Christianity was vanquished with him ; when he re-entered half dead and in tears into the beautiful palace of Orange, which had formerly embraced within its walls so much prosperity and such great glory ; when, out of breath, and without taking time to dress his wounds, the heroic Guiborne, his wife, turned him away to Paris, where he wished to obtain the assistance of the emperor against the Saracens, the poor countess, at the moment when she bade adieu to her husband, felt all her courage fail, and for a moment she became a very woman.

"Ah," she said, "you will see other women, yonder, more beautiful and younger than I. You will forget me."

Then William, to comfort her, swore to leave his hair and beard untrimmed until he came back to her again, and that he would never touch any other lips but hers in all his wanderings. He went away, and kept his word.

But what need is there of accumulating evidence? One word will suffice to indicate the estimation in which our fathers held *Sincerity*, the name of which is synonymous with Honour. Amongst all the titles with which the troubadours associated the name of God, the most in use was, "The God who never lies."

This formula is more significant than all our texts, and more eloquent than all our commentaries.

III.

The Code of Chivalry cannot be assimilated to the Decalogue in the Old Testament consecrated by the New Law, popularised by the Church, a truly divine and universal covenant for all centuries, and adapted to all nations. The rules for the use of knights are necessarily of a more restricted and of a more special character than the sacred Commandments. We will give a striking example. "Thou shalt not bear false witness," says the sacred text. "Thou shalt keep thy word," adds the commentator of the Middle Ages. The difference is easily perceived.

It is just the same as regards the precepts and evangelical counsel, and it is not worth while to pause and find them word for word in the decalogue of chivalry. It is certain (and here again we wish to take a decisive illustration) that chastity is more than once advised in our old poems to Christian soldiers. Elias of Saint-Gilles expressly enjoined this virtue on his son, and the author of the "*Ordene de Chevalerie*," of that almost mystic work, is as stern and rigorous on the subject as a preacher, and advises the knights to keep themselves pure. This is as it should be, and we have nothing but admiration for those who repulsed energetically any temptations, whether from Saracens or Christians.

So with charity, which is the essence of Christianity, and which must not be confounded with liberality, which is the essence of chivalry. This liberality embodies the Ninth Commandment of the legislation which we are attempting to set forth ; and, to tell the truth, charity holds but a small position in it.

Sometimes, nevertheless, these heavy mail-clad warriors, living amid the licence of camps, had really fine accesses of charity. The admirable Godfrey, the prototype of all knights, who exercised a notable influence upon the historical development of the chivalrous ideal, this leader of the first crusade was a true "brother of charity," and occupied himself continually in visiting the poor in his army.

Judas Maccabeus again, in the romance of "*Auberon*," is celebrated for being *as povres gens larges et visitens.* Huon de Bordeaux at Tormont in a manner acted as a deacon of the Primitive Church. *La povre gent servoit à lor mangier.* It is recorded of our heroes, that, in times of great danger they did not scruple to register vows, as sailors do in the midst of a great storm ; and one of these vows was to found a hospital, an alms-house, wherein *all* the poor could be accommodated. Such traits deserve a place in the history of Christian charity. And we may remark, in passing, that it is a shame that no one has ever written such a history.

All our barons were not so constituted as to understand this grand law of evangelic charity: their brutal nature put it aside, and the old selfishness resumed its sway in their savage natures. I cannot refrain from relating here the terrible lesson which was taught them, as told in one of our old poems, as follows :—

The Saracen king, Marsilus, was a prisoner of the great emperor. "Be converted, or die," they said to him, and they offered him the abominable choice between baptism or death ; an alternative which we have denounced more than once, and which disfigures all our old romances.

The pagan king did not hesitate for a moment ; he refused to be converted to the law of Christ. He had his reasons, and would not be baptized : he would rather die !

Then he said to Charlemagne, "Who are those fat personages, clothed in furs, who are seated at your table ? "

" The bishops and abbots," replied the emperor.

" And those poor thin individuals, clothed in black or grey habits ? "

" They are the mendicant friars who pray for us."

" And those beyond, seated on the ground, to whom the scraps of your banquet are sent ? "

" They are the poor people."

" Ah ! " exclaimed the king, "and so that is the way in which you treat your poor, irreverently, and to the dishonour of Him whose faith you profess ! Well, no : I shall certainly not be baptized—I prefer death."

Such is the legend, which has something alarming in it, and which makes one shudder like the scene of the poor in Molière's " Don Juan." Before it had passed into our songs, a great Catholic reformer made use of it to arouse the souls of his contemporaries and to bring home to them the evangelical view of it. We may quote it after the text of Pierre Damien.*

The virtue—the true chivalrous virtue—is liberality, and, to use the proper word, *largesse*. This beautiful term *"largesse"* is French as well as Christian, and it expresses a good deal in our language. Would you sum up the praise of a knight in "two words" ? They say of him that he is courteous and wise, and *larges pour donner*. There is also in " *Corneille* " a line which equals this dissyllable in beauty—

" A hennor fere doit chascuns estre larges."

One of the most striking examples of *largesse* is presented to us in this grand scene which an unknown poet has depicted at the commencement of the " *Chanson d'Aspremont*." Naimes, who had nobly undertaken to speak to Charlemagne, firmly said to him—

" Do not be stingy in your expenditure, even though not a

* This history of the poor is related (1) by Saint Peter Damien, who gives the honour to Wittikind ; (2) in the " *Chronicle of Turpin*," where it is attributed to Agolant ; (3) in the poem of " *Anseïs de Carthage ;*" (4) in the " *Anseïs de Charlemagne.*"

farthing may remain in your coffers. Give my property first, and distribute it chiefly amongst the poor knights, so that their wives may benefit by it. The old counsellor did not fail to point his moral, and exclaim—

> " Tant en donez as grans et as munus
> Que tuit s'en aillent de joie revestu."

And the poet adds—

> " Tiels i vint fix de povre vavasor
> Qui au partir resemblera comtor."

In fifty, in a hundred of our romances we find the same appeals, warm and impressive, to all poor knights. "Come, and you will be rich." They came, and were enriched.

"Let all poor knights approach," said Charles, on another occasion in this same romance of "*Aspremont;*" and there were distributed to them chargers and palfreys, furs and stuffs, sparrow-hawks, falcons, gold and silver. "Let all those who have neither land nor tenure, go seek Fouchier, my relative, and he will enrich the poorest amongst them."

Thus spoke Don Fouque, a messenger from Girart de Roussillon, at the time when the great struggle was proceeding between himself and the emperor.

But there may be in this last suggestion some little cunning and diplomacy, and we prefer to stop before the spectacle of the hero of the first crusade, before the noble Baudouin, who, ere he departed for the Holy Land, had listened piously to his mother's advice—

"Give freely!" and he did give so freely and to such an extent that he was one day obliged to go and request a loan from Tancred.

There is really nothing to be added to this trait, if it be not the beautiful verse of *Girart de Roussillon,* which does honour to the heart of a woman, but in which policy holds, perhaps, too great a place. The queen, says the poet, is very liberal and generous. "Give! aye, even to her towers and battlements!" It is a remarkable sentence, almost unparalleled in feudal times, "Her very towers and battlements."

As for the *largesse* which the heroes of our old poems are reputed to have bestowed upon singers and popular musicians, it is unnecessary to speak of it in this place, and it was not the true generosity. The minstrels of the twelfth and thirteenth centuries

were in reality thorough comedians. If they celebrated the legendary liberality of ancient knights, it was with the view to obtain
from living knights actual gifts. "The heroes of our *chansons* are
generous and liberal. The least that you can do is to be as liberal.
Give!" And they gave accordingly!

But such presents cannot rank either as works of charity, or as
true *largesse*, and the Code of Chivalry has nothing in common
with it. Let us pass on.

IV.

We must confess that the Tenth Commandment of chivalry has
not been clearly formulated by our poets, and that we owe it to the
Church as a matter of fact. "To combat all evil, to defend all
good," would not have come naturally to the minds of those
descendants of Germans who had not been affected by the water of
their baptism.

It would be quite possible to show, by a series of texts scientifically chosen and wisely graduated, that this philosophical and
definitive formula only introduced itself by slow degrees into the
current of our ancestors' ideas. They did not reach such an
astonishing height at a bound, and some of these apophthegms—like
certain poems, the "*Dies Iræ*" for example—had to submit to a
long incubation of four or five centuries.

In our old songs the maxim, "Combat all evil, defend all that is
good," presents itself principally, curiously enough, in a negative
form. When the author of "*Gaydon*" sets himself to put forth
the infernal Contra Code of Chivalry, he does not hesitate to put
this abominable advice in the mouth of one of his traitors—

"Le Mal hauciez, et le Bien abatez."
Elevate Evil and abase Good.

Nevertheless humanity could not be satisfied with these negative
counsels; it had need of clear decisions, and it is the Church which
has furnished them to mankind. The liturgy here rises on golden
wings, and we rise with it to the highest summits. When
William Durand collected, in the thirteenth century, the elements

of that pontifical to which his name is attached, he took care to choose for the " *Benedictio novi militis* " this magnificent prayer :—

" O God, Thou hast only permitted the use of the sword to curb the malice of the wicked and to defend the right. Grant, therefore, that Thy new knight may never use his sword to injure, unjustly, anyone, whoever he may be ; but that he may use it always in defence of all that is just and right ! "

" Omnia cum gladio suo justa et recta defendat."

There exists a text still more characteristic, still more beautiful, which belongs also to the same epoch in which William Durand lived. When a new knight was dubbed at Rome in the splendid basilica of St. Peter, which was the centre of the Christian World, a sword was very solemnly handed to the warrior, " So that he might energetically exercise justice, and that he might overturn the triumphant edifice of iniquity, ' *ut vim æquitatis exerceret, et molem iniquitatis destrueret.*' "

And again, farther on : " Remember, O knight, that you are to act as the defender of Order and as the avenger of Injustice. ' *Ulciscaris injusta, confirmes bene disposita.*' " And the conclusion addressed to him in a grave voice, was, " It is on this condition, living here below as a copy of Christ, that you will reign eternally above with your Divine Model."

That is the language they held at Rome, in the most august sanctuary in the world. Imagine, if you can, anything more elevated.

In any case, there it was ; and the grand formula was definitively found.

The poet of this century who had perhaps the most Catholic temperament, and who perhaps most misconceived his real vocation —Victor Hugo—has spoken of chivalry in terms scarcely less magnificent. In one of the most beautiful verses which the nineteenth century has ever produced, he defines the Christian knight such as the code of chivalry conceived him ; such as the Church wished him to be :—

" He listened always if one cried to him for help."

There are ten words which one may engrave upon one's memory.

There was even a time in the twelfth century when the Church
attempted to form a corps of knights, simply for the purpose of
maintaining peace in Christendom and to prevent the scandal of
private wars. These *gendarmes* of God were called *Paciarii*,
peacemakers; and perhaps a warrior had never a more beautiful
name bestowed on him. However, the institution did not succeed;
but we trust our readers will not esteem the value of institutions
and ideas only by the single success which they have achieved.
One success is not everything, and proud souls will not be
contented with it.

Such is the Code of Chivalry, and one should not be astonished
that anyone tried to oppose to it a Satanic Counter Code.

He who has been so well named the " Ape of Providence "
succeeded without very much trouble in apeing chivalry. Nothing
is more difficult to reach than the sublime—nothing is easier than
to parody it.

This Contra Code finds more than once, in our *chansons de geste,*
its brutal and perhaps exaggerated expression. It is to the race of
the Mayençais, to that race of traitors, that the honour of this
astounding legislation belongs.

" Thou shalt never be loyal to anyone; thou shalt never keep
thy word to thy lord and master; thou shalt betray and sell
honest men; thou shalt uphold evil and abase the good; thou
shalt ravish the poor and disinherit the orphan; despoil widows;
dishonour the Church; thou shalt lie without shame; and violate
thine oaths."

This terrible and horrible advice is accompanied in the poem of
" *Gaydon*" by a kind of infernal liturgy, in which is parodied the
sacrament of penitence and holy absolution.

There is the same brutality in " *Renaus de Montauban,*" and in
this instance it is Duke Aymon himself who gives the most
incredible and horrible advice to his son, but he only directs it
against the priests and the monks, whom he recommends should be
roasted.

" Their flesh is really exquisite," he said jokingly; "let some be
cooked and eaten."

The pagan tutor of the infidel Renouart was, at any rate, only
acting up to his principles when he said to his pupil :—

" Do not believe in anything. If you meet a good man, beat him. Do wrong, commit sin everywhere and anywhere."

We have already mentioned the fearful nihilism which is displayed in a celebrated page of " *Amis and Amiles*," thus :—

" Refuse all service towards Heaven ; make war upon all good people ; burn towns, villages, houses ; overturn the altars and the crucifixes. This is the true road of honour."

Thus spoke Hardre, who represents quite a line of renegades and liars. Herchembaud, in " *Doon de Maience*," holds the same language. With the joy of a condemned soul, he promised himself to burn all the churches, to destroy all the convents, to massacre all the monks, to throw down all the crucifixes, and to break in pieces all the images of the saints.

There is in this horror, the undoubted phenomenon of " possession," but the most terrible of all the texts is still, as we have seen, that of " *Gaydon*." It is the most complete and the most Satanic of all.

V.

The decadence of chivalry—and when one is speaking of human institutions, sooner or later this word must be used—perhaps set in sooner than historians can believe. We need not attach too much importance to the grumblings of certain poets, who complain of their time with an evidently exaggerated bitterness, and we do not care for our own part to take literally the testimony of the unknown author of " *La Vie de Saint Alexis*," who exclaims— about the middle of the eleventh century—that everything is degenerate and all is lost ! Thus—

" In olden times the world was good. Justice and love were springs of action in it. People then had faith, which has disappeared from amongst us. The world is entirely changed. The world has lost its healthy colour. It is pale—it has grown old. It is growing worse, and will soon cease altogether."

The poet exaggerates in a very singular manner the evil which he perceives around him, and one might aver that, far from bordering upon old age, chivalry was then almost in the very zenith of its glory. The twelfth century was its apogee, and it was not until the thirteenth that it manifested the first symptoms of decay.

" *Li maus est moult avant,*" exclaims the author of " *Godfrey de Bouillon,*" and he adds sadly, " *Tos li biens est finés.*"

He was more correct in speaking thus than was the author of " *Saint Alexis* " in his complainings, for the decadence of chivalry actually commenced in his time. And it is not unreasonable to enquire into the causes of its decay.

" The Romance of the Round Table," which in the opinion of prepossessed or thoughtless critics appears so profoundly chivalrous, may be considered one of the works which hastened the downfall of chivalry. We are aware that by this seeming paradox we shall probably scandalize some of our readers, who look upon these adventurous cavaliers as veritable knights. What does it matter ? *Avienne que puet.* The heroes of our *chansons de geste* are really the authorized representatives and types of the society of their time, and not those fine adventure-seeking individuals who have been so brilliantly sketched by the pencil of Crétien de Troyes.

It is true, however, that this charming and delicate spirit did not give, in his works, an accurate idea of his century and generation. We do not say that he embellished all he touched, but only that he enlivened it. Notwithstanding all that one could say about it, this School introduced the old Gaelic spirit into a poetry which had been till then chiefly Christian or German. Our epic poems are of German origin, and the " Table Round " is of Celtic, origin. Sensual and light, witty and delicate, descriptive and charming, these pleasing romances are never masculine, and become too often effeminate and effeminating. They sing always, or almost always, the same theme. By lovely pasturages clothed with beautiful flowers, the air full of birds, a young knight proceeds in search of the unknown, and through a series of adventures whose only fault is that they resemble one another somewhat too closely.

We find insolent defiances, magnificent duels, enchanted castles, tender love-scenes, mysterious talismans. The marvellous mingles with the supernatural, magicians with saints, fairies with angels. The whole is written in a style essentially French, and it must be confessed in clear, polished and chastened language—perfect !

But we must not forget, as we said just now, that this poetry, so greatly attractive, began as early as the twelfth century to be the mode universally; and let us not forget that it was at the same period that the *"Perceval de Gallois"* and *"Aliscans,"* *"Cleomadès"* and the *"Couronnement Looys"* were written. The two schools have coexisted for many centuries: both camps have enjoyed the favour of the public. But in such a struggle, it was all too easy to decide to which of them the victory would eventually incline. The ladies decided it, and no doubt the greater number of them wept over the perusal of *"Erec"* or *"Enid"* more than over that of the *"Covenant Vivien,"* or *"Raoul de Cambrai."*

When the grand century of the Middle Ages had closed, when the blatant thirteenth century commenced, the sentimental had already gained the advantage over our old classic *chansons;* and the new school, the romantic set of the "Table Round," triumphed! Unfortunately, they also triumphed in their manners; and they were the knights of the Round Table, who, with the Valois, seated themselves upon the throne of France.

In this way temerity replaced true courage; so good, polite, manners replaced heroic rudeness; so foolish generosity replaced the charitable austerity of the early chivalry. It was the love of the unforeseen even in the military art: the rage for adventure— even in politics. We know whither this strategy and these theatrical politics led us, and that Joan of Arc and Providence were required to drag us out of the consequences.

The other causes of the decadence of the spirit of chivalry are more difficult to determine. There is one of them which has not, perhaps, been sufficiently brought to light, and this is—will it be believed?—the excessive development of certain orders of chivalry!

This statement requires some explanation.

We must confess that we are enthusiastic, passionate, admirers of these grand military orders which were formed at the commencement of the twelfth century. There have never been their like in the world, and it was only given to Christianity to display to us such a spectacle. To give to one single soul the double ideal of the soldier and the monk, to impose upon him this double charge, to fix in one these two conditions and in one only these two duties, to cause to spring from the earth I cannot tell how many thousands of men who voluntarily accepted this burthen and who were not crushed by it—that is a problem which one might have been pardoned for thinking insoluble. We have not sufficiently considered it. We have not pictured to ourselves with sufficient vividness the Templars and the Hospitallers in the midst of one of those great battles in the Holy Land, in which the fate of the world was in the balance.

No: painters have not sufficiently pourtrayed them in the arid plains of Asia forming an incomparable squadron in the midst of the battle. One might talk for ever and yet not say too much about the charge of the Cuirassiers at Reichshoffen; but how many times did the Hospitaller knights and the Templars charge in similar fashion? Those soldier-monks, in truth, invented a new idea of courage. Unfortunately they were not always fighting, and peace troubled some of them. They became too rich, and their riches lowered them in the eyes of men and before Heaven. We do not intend to adopt all the calumnies which have been circulated concerning the Templars, but it is difficult not to admit that many of these accusations had some foundation. The Hospitallers, at any rate, have given no ground for such attacks. They, thank Heaven, remained undefiled, if not poor; and were an honour to that chivalry which others had compromised and emasculated.

But when all is said, that which best became chivalry, the spice which preserved it the most surely, was poverty!

Love of riches had not only attacked the chivalrous orders, but in a very short space of time all knights caught the infection. Sensuality and enjoyment had penetrated into their castles. "Scarcely had they received the knightly baldric before they commenced to break the Commandments and to pillage the poor. When it became necessary to go to war, their sumpter-horses were laden with wine and not with weapons: with leathern bottles instead of swords, with spits instead of lances. One might have fancied in truth that they were going out to dinner and not to fight. It is true their shields were beautifully gilt, but they were kept in a virgin and unused condition. Chivalrous combats were represented upon their bucklers and their saddles, certainly; but that was all!"

Now who is it who writes thus? It is not, as one might fancy, an author of the fifteenth century—it is a writer of the twelfth ; and the great satirist, somewhat excessive and unjust in his statements, the Christian Juvenal whom we have just quoted, was none other than Peter of Blois.

A hundred other witnesses might be cited in support of these indignant words. But if there is some exaggeration in them, we are compelled to confess that there is a considerable substratum of truth also.

These abuses—which wealth engendered, which more than one poet had already stigmatised—attracted, in the fourteenth century, the attention of an important individual, a person whose name occupies a worthy place in literature and history. Philip of Mezières, chancellor of Cyprus under Peter of Lusignan, was a true knight, who one day conceived the idea of reforming chivalry. Now the way he found most feasible in accomplishing his object, in arriving at such a difficult and complex reform, was to found a new Order of chivalry himself, to which he gave the high-sounding title of " The Chivalry of the Passion of Christ."

The decadence of chivalry is attested, alas ! by the very character of the reforms by which this well-meaning Utopian attempted to oppose it. The good knight complains of the great advances of sensuality, and permits and advises the marriage of all knights. He complains of the accursed riches which the Hospitallers themselves were putting to a bad use, and forbade them in his Institutions ; but nevertheless the luxurious habits of his time had an influence upon his mind, and he permitted his knights to wear the most extravagant costumes, and the dignitaries of his Order to adopt the most high-sounding titles. There was something mystical in all this conception, and something theatrical in all this agency. It is hardly necessary to add that the " Chivalry of the Passion " was only a beautiful dream originating in a generous mind. Notwithstanding the adherence of some brilliant personages, the Order never attained to more than a theoretical organization, and had only a fictitious foundation. The idea of the deliverance of the Holy Sepulchre from the Infidel was hardly the object of the fifteenth century chivalry ; for the struggle between France and England then was engaging the most courageous warriors and the most practised swords. Decay hurried on apace !

This was not the only cause of such a fatal falling away. The portals of chivalry had been opened to too many unworthy candidates. It had been made vulgar ! In consequence of having become so cheap the grand title of "knight" was degraded. Eustace Deschamps, in his fine straightforward way, states the scandal boldly and "lashes" it with his tongue. He says—

"Picture to yourself the fact that the degree of knighthood is about to be conferred now upon babies of eight and ten years old."

Well might this excellent man exclaim in another place—

"Disorders always go on gathering strength, and even incomparable knights like Du Guesclin and Bayard cannot arrest the fatal course of the institution towards ruin." Chivalry was destined to disappear.

It is very important that one should make oneself acquainted with the true character of such a downfall. France and England in the fourteenth and fifteenth centuries still boasted many high-bred knights. They exchanged the most superb defiances, the most audacious challenges, and proceeded from one country to another to run each other through the body proudly. The Beaumanoirs who drank their blood, abounded. It was a question who would engage himself in the most incredible pranks ; who would commit the most daring folly ! They tell us afterwards of the beautiful passages of arms, the grand feats performed, and the inimitable Froissart is the most charming of all these narrators, who make their readers as chivalrous as themselves.

But we must tell everything : amongst these knights in beautiful armour there was a band of adventurers who never observed, and who could not understand, certain commandments of the ancient chivalry. The laxity of luxury had everywhere replaced the rigorous enactments of the old manliness, and even warriors themselves loved their ease too much. The religious sentiment was not the dominant one in their minds, in which the idea of a crusade now never entered. They had not sufficient respect for the weakness of the Church nor for other failings. They no longer felt themselves the champions of the good and the enemies of evil. Their sense of justice had become warped, as had love for their great native land. One was of Armagnac, one was of Burgundy :

no one considered that he was a Frenchman ! They submitted to compromising alliances, they were compelled to extend their hands to those beneath them.

Again, what they termed " the license of camps " had grown very much worse ; and we know in what condition Joan of Arc found the army of the king. Blasphemy and ribaldry in every quarter. The noble girl swept away those pests, but the effect of her action was not long-lived. She was the person to re-establish chivalry, which in her found the purity of its now effaced type ; but she died too soon, and had not sufficient imitators.

There were, after her time, many chivalrous souls, and thank Heaven there are still some amongst us ; but the old institution is no longer with us. The events which we have had the misfortune to witness do not give us any ground to hope that chivalry, extinct and dead, will rise again to-morrow to light and life.

In St. Louis's time caricature and parody (they were low-class forces—but forces nevertheless) had already commenced the work of destruction. We are in possession of an abominable little poem of the thirteenth century, which is nothing but a scatological pamphlet directed against chivalry. This ignoble "*Audigier,*" the author of which is the basest of men, is not the only attack which one may dis-inter from amid the literature of that period. There has always been in French society an unworthy corner in which chivalry has continually been the object of ridicule and raillery in very bad taste. Some editors have done themselves the pleasure to publish and to analyse these coarse effusions, but it seems to us enough merely to direct the reader's attention to them. If one wishes to draw up a really complete list it would be necessary to include the *fabliaux*—the "*Renart*" and the "*Rose,*" which constitute the most anti-chivalrous—I had nearly written the most Voltairain— works that I am acquainted with. The thread is easy enough to follow from the twelfth century down to the author of "Don Quixote," which I do not confound with its infamous pre- decessors,—to Cervantes, whose work has been fatal, but whose mind was elevated.

However that may be, parody and the parodists were themselves a cause of decay. They weakened morals ; Gallic-like, they popularised little *bourgeois* sentiments, narrow-minded satirical

sentiments; they inoculated manly souls with contempt for such
great things as one performs disinterestedly. This disdain is a
sure element of decay, and we may regard it as an announcement of death. It killed us!

Against the knights who, here and there, showed themselves unworthy and degenerate, was put in practice the terrible apparatus of
degradation. Modern historians of chivalry have not failed to
describe in detail all the rites of this solemn punishment, and we
have presented to us a scene which is well calculated to excite the
imagination of the most matter-of-fact, and to make the most timid
heart swell.

The knight judicially condemned to submit to this shame was
first conducted to a scaffold, where they broke or trod under foot all
his weapons. He saw his shield, with device effaced, turned upside
down and trailed in the mud. Priests, after reciting the prayers
for the vigil of the dead, pronounced over his head the psalm,
" *Deus laudem meam,*" which contains terrible maledictions against
traitors. The Herald of Arms who carried out this sentence took
from the hands of the Pursuivant of Arms a basin full of dirty
water, and threw it all over the head of the recreant knight in
order to wash away the sacred character which had been conferred
upon him by the accolade. The guilty one, degraded in this way,
was subsequently thrown upon a hurdle, or upon a stretcher,
covered with a mortuary cloak, and finally carried to the church,
where they repeated the same prayers and the same ceremonies as
for the dead.

This was really terrible even if somewhat theatrical, and it is easy
to see that this complicated ritual contained only a very few ancient
elements. In the twelfth century the ceremonial of degradation
was infinitely more simple. The spurs were hacked off close to
the heels of the guilty knight. Nothing could be more summary
or more significant. Such a person was publicly denounced as
unworthy to ride on horseback, and consequently quite unworthy
to be a knight. The more ancient and chivalrous the less
theatrical is it. It is so in many other institutions in the
histories of all nations and especially in our own.

That such a penalty may have prevented a certain number of
treasons and forfeitures we willingly admit, but one cannot expect

it to preserve all the whole body of chivalry from that de-cadence from which no institution of human establishment can escape.

Notwithstanding inevitable weaknesses and accidents, the Deca-logue of Chivalry has none the less been regnant in some millions of souls which it has made pure and great. These Ten Command-ments have been the rules and the reins of youthful generations, who without them would have been wild and undisciplined. This legislation, in fact—which, to tell the truth, is only one of the chapters of the great Catholic Code—has raised the moral level of humanity.

Besides, chivalry is not yet quite dead. No doubt, the ritual of chivalry, the solemn reception, the order itself, and the ancient oaths, no longer exist. No doubt, amongst these grand command-ments there are many which are known only to the erudite, and which the world is unacquainted with. The Catholic Faith is no longer the essence of modern chivalry : the Church is no longer seated on the throne around which the old knights stand with their drawn swords : Islam is no longer the hereditary enemy : we have another which threatens us nearer home : widows and orphans have need rather of the tongues of advocates than of the iron weapons of the knights : there are no more duties towards liege-lords to be fulfilled : and we even do not want any kind of superior at all : *largesse* is now confounded with charity ; and the becoming hatred of evil-doing is no longer our chief, our best, passion !

But whatever we may do, there still remains to us, in the marrow, a certain leaven of chivalry which preserves us from death. The French nation, Heaven be thanked, still loves the soil of France, and (not to say more of our country) there are still in the world an immense number of fine souls—strong and upright souls —who hate all that is small and mean, who know and who practise all the delicate promptings of honour, and who prefer death to an unworthy action, or to a lie !

That is what we owe to chivalry, that is what it has bequeathed to us. On the day when these last vestiges of such a grand past are effaced from our souls—we shall cease to exist !

VI.

In the eyes of our ancestors in the twelfth and thirteenth centuries the Code of Chivalry was bound to have a more than earthly sanction. And it is of this that we would now speak.

The aim and object of every knight was—according to our old poems—"Rest in Heaven: " *conquerre lit en paradis.* Those rude warriors who had assembled together by so many different ways, submitted to all climatic conditions, slept night after night on the hard ground, and passed days without unlacing their hauberks or taking off their helmets : that was the simple idea which they had of eternal happiness, "Rest in a good bed !"

This is not very metaphysical, nor very elevated, but it is true. "He who dies will have his bed prepared with the Innocents," said the Bishop of Puy in his magnificent oration under the walls of Antioch, and it was his peroration.

"In the chief Paradise your places are already taken," exclaimed Turpin on the field of Roncesvalles, where some of the most noble blood in the world was shed.

Again, celestial reward was elsewhere presented in the form of a beautiful garden in which reposed the soldiers who had died in the service of the Lord ; and such is the sense attaching to the term "holy flowers" which so often crops up in the "*Chanson de Roland.*"

The better-known image of the crown presented itself equally to the minds of our forefathers. "Those who die here below will wear a crown of flowers on high," and there is a verse in the *Charroi de Nimes,* which in ten syllables sums up all the life of the Christian knight—

Tant fist en terre qu'es ciex est coronez.

If one has ever learnt how to die it is amongst the Christian races. The ancients too often in the hour of death preferred something theatrical or eccentric, and no one, on the contrary, dies more naturally than "The men of the Supernatural." That is, before all, true of the Christian soldier, who knows how to fall out easily, without disturbance. Roland himself did not die like a bully ; and his last gesture was the familiar action of a vassal who, in evidence of submission, extends his glove to his liege-lord.

"I can hear the angels singing overhead," exclaimed Vivien; and he adds with much simplicity—"If I could only see my uncle William once again; and receive the Body of my Lord!"

We could tell of many "incomparable deaths" besides, but it is necessary to give here a more general type, a more middle-class, a more commonplace one, so to speak. Listen then, and hear how the knight who all his life had been faithful in his observance of the Code of Chivalry, whose Commandments we have discussed, ended his life.

Renaud de Tor, the baron, has dismounted from his steed. He is smitten through the body by four darts, and when he perceives that he must die, what sadness, what anger possesses him!

For the last time he unsheaths his sword, and passes his arm through his shield. Everyone he meets dies! But his wounds bleed too abundantly. He can no longer support himself, and he falls to the ground. Then he addresses himself to Heaven— "Glorious Father, who wast and ever wilt be, take pity on my soul, for my body is lost." Then he turns in the direction of France, and bows to it five hundred times.

The poet then relates how the dying knight administered to himself the symbolic communion. "Then the soul fled, while the body lay extended on the earth. *Te Deum laudamus* sang the angels who carried him to Heaven." It was a common death, and the least knight died in that way. But what are we to say of the last words of Vivien, Roland, and Renaud?

Such an end is the enviable termination of chivalry, and it is by no means an unusual thing for the Church to hold up for our imitation the deaths of the most illustrious priests and the bravest knights. Each of our great epic cycles has for its centre a hero who became a saint. Formerly people spoke of *Saint* Roland, *Saint* Ogier, *Saint* Renaud, so it seems that these great knights have passed at once from our epic poems into our martyrology.

Such is the supreme consecration of the Decalogue of Chivalry: such is its eternal coronation.

CHAPTER V.

THE INFANCY OF THE FUTURE KNIGHT.

I.

THE old castle was never more animated nor more lively than on a certain evening when the birth of the son and heir was being awaited.

The master of the house, the expectant father, had no idea whatever concerning a daughter. A daughter indeed! What did he want with a daughter? The warrior wanted a boy who would himself be a warrior in his turn; who would learn to hunt the wild boar, to go hawking, to hold a fief, to defend his liege-lord, and some day to go beyond the seas to deliver the Holy Sepulchre and redeem the soul of his father.

And the father exclaimed joyfully, "It is a son!"

You know the fine verse of Victor Hugo, in his "*Revenant;*" "It is the cry of all our knights, and even of their wives."*

Do you see those gentlemen yonder running towards Fromont?

"God save you, sir, in the name of your son who was born the day before yesterday, and is so little. Tell me what name we shall bestow on him."

"He will be called Fromondin," said Fromont, "because he will succeed to the kingdom after me." Then he called all his barons and said to them, "Be glad and rejoice; he is born, the liege-lord of whom you will hold your lands; he is born who will give you the richest furs, the vair and the grey, splendid armour and priceless horses.

And the old Fromont added proudly, "In fifteen years my son will be a knight!"

This little quotation from "*Garin de Loherain,*" may serve as

---

* "*Par le foi que vous doi, uns danioseux est nez.*"

an illustration, and on every occasion there was the same joy and happiness displayed.

The cradle is prepared, and it is of graceful form, for even to the most commonplace objects our ancestors knew how to impart some artistic and pleasing appearance.

The newly-born child, the future knight, is first bathed before a beautiful fire, which has been lighted for him in a wide-mouthed

The Mother of Godfrey de Bouillon.

chimney; and this bath recalls to his father that other bath which the youthful noble must take by ritual, in some countries, on the day before he is dubbed knight. Then the child is well scrubbed dry in fine linen or "bouquerant." He is quickly clothed in a little fur-lined silken robe, and a little ermine pelisse, like his father's and mother's, and above all a charming little cloak.

When the beautiful Alais, "with the fair skin," gave birth to Raoul de Cambrai, she was in such a hurry to make him a Christian that she sent two barons off on horseback to the Bishop of Beauvais, her cousin, carrying the child with them. How delighted the bishop was to see the child, and did he not make haste to baptise him !

Rejoicing everywhere. Knights and sergeants, all are full of merriment. The Heir is born !

The hour of birth in the Middle Ages was regarded as the most blessed of all. *"L'ore fut benoite,"* and it was one of the anniversaries which was most joyously celebrated. On such a day kings held "open court," as they did at Easter and Whitsuntide. There was "Halleluia in the air."

But all this while the infant is in his cradle, and according to a strange legend, the origin of which is hidden in the darkness of ages, he is listening to music, the incomparable music which the stars give forth as they traverse the heavens. Yes, that which the most learned scientists cannot hear, the children hear distinctly, and are wrapped in contemplation—charmed. What a delightful fable it is which gives to innocence in its immaturity greater privileges than to science in its prime.

At any rate our ancestors were not hard to please, and willingly accepted the grimaces of the newly-born infant for the almost intelligent smile. All mothers are equally self-deceptive in our own day—and fathers, too, sometimes. The *incipe parve puer risu cognoscere matrem* is repeated in many of our romances. In *"Auberon,"* Brunhault "was hardly born ere he began to smile." That is a smile which scarcely lives, but which we all know quite well !

The child was covered with kisses and caresses : we need not say there was no lack of prayers.

But all birthdays were not so happy, and there are some recorded in our epic songs remarkable for their sorrowfulness. The finest, the best of our knights, Roland, was born in a forest near Imola, wherein his mother was on the verge of dying of hunger and misery. Yet this mother was Charlemagne's own sister, who had fled with the seneschal Milon, and had retreated as far as Italy before the wrath of the great emperor. Picture to yourself this forest full of robbers and wild beasts, fancy this child born in the open air, the poor knight already half mad; and the new-born babe who, the young rascal, would not let himself be put in swaddling clothes like any other child of the period.

The story of the Duchess Parise is still more touching, but we need not enter into any details here. For particulars we may refer our readers to "*Parise la Duchesse*," wherein the melancholy but interesting tale is told. The lady, daughter of Garnier of Nanteuil, a wife of Raymond de Saint-Gilles, was unjustly accused of having poisoned her husband's brother. She was, under the circumstances, exiled, though condemned to death. The remainder of the narrative may be sought in the old romances. The chivalry of the old baron Clarembaut is remarkable.

But whether the child came into the world in sorrow or in joy, the first idea of its mother was the baptismal rite. In those days there were none of the vain delays which now arise. Then the infant was hurried to the font—" Quick—quick to the font ! "

II.

A graceful poet of the period, writing of this quite Christian mode of hastening the baptism of the infant, has indited a strophe which is not according to our taste but is according to the spirit of the Middle Ages. " The guardian angel, full of zeal, must be, I think, inclined to take the child upon his wings, in order that he may be all the more quickly baptised."

In our older Western provinces, the parents themselves refused to embrace their children before they had been christened.

The Baptismal Day possessed, in the minds of our forefathers, an importance to which nothing can at the present time be fitly compared. When Parise recognized her son Huguet, who had been taken from her the very day he was born, it was to the baptismal ceremony that she referred when, panting for breath, she put to him those questions on which his life depended—" Who was your father ? Where were you born ? "

When, in the horrible battle of Aliscans, Guillaume and his nephew Vivien, who did not recognise each other, were on the point of coming to blows, Vivien, recalling the scene of his baptism, begged his unknown adversary to reveal his names and titles.

" I conjure you in the name of Christianity, by the Baptism and

by the Chrism which you have received, tell me your name—tell
me who you are ! "

The old baron, overcome by the memory of the past, replied—

"My name is Guillaume," and then the adversaries fell into
each other's arms and embraced with tears.

The essential rites of Baptism have not been materially modified
since the early days of the Church. They deserve to be better
known, for they abound in deep and original beauties of composition, such as our Litany so frequently presents. But we do
not sufficiently care for our origin to wish to know more of it.

Immediately persecution had ceased, Baptism by affusion was
combined with Baptism by immersion. But, without entering
into simple details here, we will content ourselves by observing
that, in all the course of the Middle Ages in the East, Baptism by
immersion never ceased to be practised. Thus it is said—

"Bas-reliefs, illuminated manuscripts, stained-glass windows,
are unanimous in putting before us catechumens baptised in this
way."

The testimony of our poetry is not less clear on this point, nor
less eloquent : there is never any question of any other baptism.

In two words, one dips the converted and the newly born into
the same basin. This basin or "*cuve*" was sometimes a kind of
oblong trough, but it was more often a kind of cylinder supported
by four pillars or columns. Those at Vermont and Montdidier
give us a very good idea of all the rest.* It is necessary to see
them to appreciate them, and to understand fully the old passages
of the poems. Nothing is clear without the illustration of it.

After this the infant was carried to the neighbouring church—
for every parish possessed one of these fonts. Nothing more joyous
and happy than these processions can be conceived.

The ladies, laughing, went before ; the knights, clothed in new
attire, followed after, two by two ; then came the child, beautifully
clad in cloth of gold or in saracenic silk, in the arms of a matron
or of a young girl. The baptismal rites then commenced. The

---

* The font at *Vermont* (Aisne) is a round, deep basin, set in square, carved stone-
work, and supported by four columns at the corners : the columns resting upon
carved boars' heads cut in a slab. The whole is massive, and well sculptured. (See
" *Histoire de Baptême.*")—TRANS.

child was carried up to the church door, where the procession halted. The priest put the question—

" What do you come to demand from the Church of the Lord ? "

He then blew upon the child's face three times, marked him on the forehead and the breast with the sign of the Cross, placed his hands upon him, put salt on his lips, and pronounced the solemn exorcism. The demon was then put to flight.

This is only the prologue of the drama. The real rite now begins.

" Open your ears," says the priest, touching the ears of the new-born babe. " Do you renounce the devil and all his works ? "

" Yes, yes," reply his sponsors.

Then the future defender of the faith, the future knight, is anointed between the shoulders with a certain unction to prepare him for the great struggle. Then the celebrant puts off the violet vestment, which signifies penitence, and clothes himself in the dress which signifies purity, joy, light, and blessedness.

" Do you believe in God, in his Son, and in the Church ? " he asks.

" Yes," reply the sponsors.

" Do you wish to be baptised ? "

" Yes."

Then he plunges the child three times into the font ; and at this point the Church addresses the most tender and pressing recommendations to its ministers. It says—

" Take you great care that in thus dipping the children you do them no harm."

After this nothing now remains to be done save to administer to the little Christian the complementary rites of Baptism : the anointing and so on. He is then reclothed in his white robe, in his hand is placed the taper which is the image of eternal glory and splendour. Then the blessing—" Now depart in peace : and may the Lord be with you "—is pronounced, and the ceremony comes to a conclusion.

But how few Christians in the present day are cognisant of the profound beauty of this ceremonial, and the incomparable benefits of these rites. They are a " dead letter."

Our forefathers of the eleventh and twelfth centuries possessed

this sense which is lacking in us. But, on the whole, everything
took place in their days as in our time, with but few exceptions.
The child was plunged quite naked into the baptismal font, as the
saying still is,—"As naked as when you were baptised," but we
can readily perceive that the hard usage of the olden times has
been softened and toned down : and in the *" Brun de la
Montaigne,"* which is a work of the decadence period, the author
even then speaks of clothing at the performance of the rite—"Very
soft garments"—in which the infant Brun is raised from the
sacramental water. They do not dare to wash off the holy oil
with which the child has been anointed on the forehead, and so a
kind of bonnet has been invented for the occasion, which in
Germany is called the chrisen-cap,—*Kres menhuot,* and in France
the *chrêmeau.*

The white robe of the ancient catechumens is still in use with us,
and there are families whose members are confirmed and attend
their first Communion in the same baptismal robe—enlarged and
altered.

The godfathers and godmothers of our future knight deserve
more attention. There are a goodly number of them sometimes,
and the " *Chanson de Roland* " speaks, in very high terms and very
decidedly, of those French women of high lineage who were given
him for godmothers by Queen Braminonde, when they conducted
the beautiful captive to the baptistry of Aix.

When the giant Fierabas received baptism "there was no lack
of sponsors," remarked the unknown troubadour who has dedicated
to him the strange poem which they sang at Landit.

It would appear that this became a luxury as well as another
custom, and in Germany they even went as far as a dozen sponsors
—male and female, godfathers and godmothers. The Church
ought to put a stop to such a practice, and oppose a fashion which
was too little in conformity with the spirit of such a custom. It
professes to give us at the first a new father and a new mother :
but a dozen are too many. However, reforms are not adopted
suddenly, and there are in discipline itself variations that may be
easily understood.

Christian society seemed to hesitate at a certain period of its
history between the principle of the Unity which seemed to be

so completely justified by reason; and the symbolism—the excessive symbolism—of the dogma of the Trinity. It seemed to oscillate between the Unity and the Trinity.

The greater number of the councils of the thirteenth and four-teenth centuries permitted two godfathers and one godmother for a boy, two godmothers and one godfather for a daughter. This number, three, became almost universal in the fifteenth century, and was the fashion up to the time of the Council of Trent. How were these three persons to hold the little child at the font at the same time?

Nothing was easier of course! One would hold him by the middle, and the other two by the feet. That was the idea! Never-theless, the thought, the old idea, of the Church was very clearly expressed at Metz in 888, again at Nîmes in 1284, at Bénévent in 1331, in the solemn statute of the Church of Bourges in 1368, " Let there be only one sponsor; " so in the statutes of Treguier in 1457, and in the decisive formula of the Council of Trent.

With its customary wisdom, this Œcumenical Council decided that the infant baptised should have but one sponsor thenceforth; or, at most, a man and a woman—*unum* or *unam!* This last arrangement is decidedly the best, for the child needs, in fact, the tenderness and care of a godmother as well as the manlier care of a godfather.

In a great number of our *chansons* unity triumphs. Raoul de Cambrai had only one sponsor, and he was the Bishop of Beauvais; the sole sponsor of Amis and Amiles, those two inseparables, was no less a personage than the Apostolic successor, the Pope Isoré. The celebrated Remir, son of Gontelme, took " out of the water " the child Jourdain de Blaives, son of Girart, and no one assisted him in that holy function. Remark the expressions, " Took him out of the water—took him out of the font." This is significant as well as full of imagery.

From a very ancient period sponsors were called in Latin, *levantes.* They were, in fact, the individuals who raised gently, in their almost paternal arms, the children from the font, and presented them to the priest so that he might anoint the infants on the head. The word " raise " (take out, " *Lever* ") has come to be synonymous with " baptise."

Notwithstanding some texts of German origin, it is quite certain that in France the sponsors were the people who most frequently bestowed the names upon those they "lifted up." Quotations from our songs bear witness to the fact that it was the province of the sponsor to choose the name of his godson, and that this name was generally his own. Garin le Loherain enjoyed one evening the hospitality of William de Monclin, and on that very night a baby-boy was born to the house of Monclin. So Garin had "to hold it in baptism," and the Lorrainer did not fail to give the infant the name of Garin.

But no doubt, in those days as well as in our own times, arrangements were made with sponsors, who occasionally waived their strict claims and rights. One thing, however, seems clear, viz., that godparents had then, as in our day, to offer valuable presents to their godchildren. In the case we have just mentioned, Garin bestowed one of the markets of the town of Metz, which could not be valued at less than a hundred livres per annum, upon his godchild.

Again, the Pope (Isoré) gave to Amis and Amiles "gold and silver and silk." He was one of those sponsors who "stretched a point" and promised to his godchildren a town, a county, or (but this seems almost too grand) all their feudal succession. The godmothers, more modest, contented themselves with the preparation of a *trousseau* more or less rich, scarlet cloaks, pelisses and stockings. These were the kind of presents made by the ladies.

Let us now resume our account of the ceremony.

By this time the procession has come out of the church, and it is evident that every individual composing it is very happy and joyous. At the castle the mother is counting the minutes, and is almost overcome with delight when she hears the sound of the footsteps of the approaching concourse, the clear tones of the women, the trampling of the horses, and the clatter of the riders' arms. Then the narrow winding staircase resounds with acclaim, and the ladies hurry into the châtelaine's room—but she has eyes and ears for no one but the child.

"Where is he? Let me see him!" she exclaims. "And when she saw him," says the chronicle, "her delight was so great that her heart jumped in its strong pulsations." Then came the important question, " What name have you given him ? Oh, how pretty ! Was the water not cold in the font ? "

After this, nothing but kissing and petting and chatter. " Heaven be praised ! " said the mother at last, and at length everyone retired.

The most pleasing account of a christening, of all those which we find in our old poems, is in *Macaire*. The young mother is no less a personage than the Queen of France : the child is no less an individual than the son of Charlemagne, the heir to the immense empire of his father. But on this occasion you must not expect anything of a cheerful nature—nor any ceremonial. It is on foreign soil, in the small house of a Hungarian tradesman that the unfortunate Blanchefleur—daughter of a king—wife of a king, and mother of a future king, brought into the world her first child —a child so impatiently looked for—and bathed him with her tears.

The empress had been accused of a terrible crime : the whole race of traitors, the whole house of Mayence had leagued themselves against her innocent self : the emperor believed the accusers and condemned the accused. Had he sentenced her to death, her execution would have entailed the decease of the heir to the throne, so she was quickly banished from France. Nevertheless the malignity of the traitors was not appeased ; for the good knight Aubri, who had been instructed to accompany the queen, was one day set upon unawares and treacherously slain !

The unfortunate lady was thus left alone and unattended in the midst of a forest, where she would certainly have perished of hunger and grief, had not a woodcutter, a *vilain*,—a man of no descent, but one who possessed the heart of a true knight—come to her assistance.

This man—one of the few plebeians whom our poets have immortalised—was named Varocher. He left all—his country, his house, his family—to serve as guide and protector to this lady, to the unfortunate queen. With her he crossed France, Provence, and Lombardy, Venice—the sea : and it was he too who kept guard at the door of her humble apartment, while Blanchefleur caressed and fondled her new-born babe !

Now nothing could be more extraordinary than the physiognomy

of this man, of this faithful guardian whom the queen attempted
to pass off as her husband.   He was tall, strong, square-
shouldered, large-limbed, with an immensely large head and dis-
hevelled hair.   He brandished an enormous knotty club, a kind of
rustic mace, which he never willingly laid aside, night or day.

In fact he was about as strange a man as it was possible to meet
with.   The poet of the thirteenth century has well described this
original figure, this sort of Quasimodo with a tender heart, and who
was only a "vilain" by birth.

Under the protection of this rough-looking champion, the queen
remained for eight days in her own apartments, as was customary
at that period; and then the question arose as to the baptism of
the child.   So the host of the lady—the owner of the cottage, the
good Primerain—came and carried the infant to a neighbouring
monastery.

Varocher was present, carrying his big stick, for he would not
leave his young *protégé*, and walked gravely in the rear of the little
procession.   The King of Hungary happened to pass by.

"Whose pretty child is this?" he inquired.

Primerain told him of the unknown lady in his lodgings, and,
while he was telling his tale, all the barons were laughing
loudly at Varocher, who was not in the least put out by their
merriment.

Someone then raised the child's cloak to obtain a better view of
him.

"Eh!   What is this?" exclaimed the king.   "He has a white
cross on the right shoulder.   By this sign Providence witnesses to
children of royal lineage—of princely race.   This infant must be
the son of a king, and," he added, "I intend to be present at his
christening."

When they had reached the church, the king summoned the
priest, and said to him—

"Baptise this child in a manner befitting the son of an
emperor."

The king dismounted from his steed, and a magnificent
procession was arranged.   They all entered the church, and the
abbé made ready the holy oil: then he turned to the king, and
said—

"What will you have him called? What name shall I give him?"

"Call him Louis, after me," said the king.

So the ceremony proceeded, and was completed before the eyes of Varocher, who was delighted, and more particularly pleased when a purse full of gold-pieces was presented to him.

The poet naïvely adds that the young mother was taken greater care of by her hosts when they found she had money to pay well for her entertainment. After a while she revealed her true history to the king, who then learned that he was the sponsor of a son of Charlemagne.

It is not necessary to relate any more of the story here. Our readers who wish to follow it will find it in *Macaire*, pp. 112—131. But we may, with reference to Varocher, mention a custom of a truly Christian character, thus:

Rich and aristocratic people frequently chose the sponsors of their children from the poor and lowly, " so as to remind themselves that the poor were really their brethren." This custom remained in vogue till a comparatively late period. Buffon, for instance, had for godfather a poor man of Montbard, and his godmother was a beggar-woman. The same principle had been followed in the cases of Montaigne and Montesquieu. Such godchildren did honour to the rags of their god-parents!

There was hardly ever a christening without a great feast, as in our day; but we have few details recorded of this banquet, which was of a more or less solemn character, and does not appear to have possessed any features to distinguish it from any other feast.

The infant, meanwhile, was sleeping in his cradle, and our poets have not had sufficient imagination to place the angels around the sleeping child. Alas, alas, man is ice as regards the truth, and as fire as regarding falsehood. The Romances of the Round Table possessed the unfortunate tendency to domesticate amongst us little fables, and to put aside the angels for the fairies.

We have elsewhere pointed out that a great number of our epic poems are pervaded by these dangerous and useless fictions. The same kind of stuff passes current for true tales of the fairies, and there it is found even to the terminology which Perrault has made so common. Such, for instance, is the curious romance of

Auberon, in which we are spectators, as it were, of the marriage—quite unexpected—of Julius Cæsar with the fairy Morgue. Two children, twins, are the offspring of this singular union : these are the dwarf, Auberon, and, who can credit it? Saint George!

It is related that, on the very day of their birth, three fairies descended close by the cradle in which the innocent children were sleeping, took them in their arms, caressed them, replaced them in the cradle, and, without waiting, bestowed their gifts and predictions upon them.

"Thou shalt be King of Monmur," said the first to Auberon. "Yes, but thou shalt never be more than three feet high," said the second, who preferred the other child, and who represents here our fairy Carabosse. "No doubt it must be so," added the third fairy, who could not set aside the fatal decree, but who attempted at least to mitigate its effects. "No doubt, but with the exception of the coming Saviour of the World, thou shalt be the most beautiful one in the whole earth."

So saying she kissed him gently on the lips, and placed him again in his mother's bed. The scene was not wanting in gracefulness, but nothing can compare with the grace of truth.

One of the most curious circumstances is, that the fairies of our romances are most frequently such good Christians. One of them tells Georges that he will be sanctified in Paradise; and another by the cradle of Garin de Montglane speaks in almost mystic language to the newly-born babe :—

"Thou hast been born in poverty, dear child, but was not Jesus born in a stable?"

These were fairies who must certainly have been baptised, and each of them could say with Auberon, "Our Lord calls me to Paradise on high, and my seat is prepared for me at his right hand." What a curious instance of truth and error have we here!

We do not wish to drop into the sentimentalism which people so justly condemn in Jean-Jacques; but we are compelled to chronicle the fact, and not without some regret, that the mothers of our knights did not nurse their children themselves, and that the custom of hiring strange nurses was very common. The author of the "Romance of the Seven Sages" does not dare to go so far as to criticise a fashion so little conformable to the laws of Nature, but he complains in round terms of the laxity displayed in the selection of a nurse. He says :—

"In former times when people were more sensible, and it was customary for the son of a king to be nursed by the wife of a duke, the duke's child by a countess, and the child of a vassal (*Vavasseur*) by a tradesman's wife, and so on."

"Can anyone be astonished after that," exclaims our satirist, "that the race of our time is degenerating, when one sees the child of a low-born woman nursing the son of an admiral!" And this moralist adds, with a touch of philosophy, "You always bear traces of the nature of her who nurses you."

In those days children were not satisfied with one nurse ; they had three or four if the infants were of noble birth. Quite a following! This was the vocation which one of the most pleasing heroines of the old romances selected—that Parise of whom we have already spoken when she was hunted from her castle and deprived of her child.

"I have lost the infant which Providence sent to me," she cried, "and I no longer care for the light of Heaven"—she no longer wished to live. So she offered her services to the Count of Cologne, and was well fitted for the position, as the chronicle puts it, in different terms. "Thus it came to pass," says the poet, "that we behold a noble lady becoming a nurse." He would have been almost as astonished to see her, in other times, nursing her own child !

Beside all these duchesses and *châtelaines* who so easily disembarrassed themselves of their prime duties, it gives us real pleasure to note one who was a true mother. Such an one was the mother of Godfrey de Bouillon, the Countess Ida. She would not permit the attendance of any stranger in such a capacity, for she held that any such bringing up would have been "unnatural." The expression is a happy one, but the astonishment which such a simple decision gave rise to only proves, too clearly, that the case was an exceptional one. Such a mother deserved to have a son who was the bravest of knights.

Then came the day of thanksgiving, which was quite a festal occasion. The knights attended in full dress, and one might almost have imagined it was a marriage ceremony, everyone was

delighted and happy. Congratulations were showered upon the
mother and child, and everyone paid court to the infant in his
nurse's arms. The minstrels sang their most charming ditties.
There was a splendid repast, and boisterous festivity reigned, from
which the lady, already fatigued by the ceremony, retired early—
as much display and exertion had wearied her.

III.

Until he was seven years old the infant knight was usually confided to the care of the women, and his nurses never left him. In
all the rudeness of the feudal age, the baron, sometimes of a rather
brutal disposition, had neither taste nor inclination for infantile
graces, and our old poets seem to think there was little appreciation
of them in his mind. Until the last century, till the commencement of our own, there still remained something of this ancient
severity of manner.

In the time of Philip Augustus, it may be remembered, the youthful
noble was not admitted before the age of seven years to the honour
of sitting down at his father's table; and, even as we write these
lines, there are some families in which children are only permitted
to come in after dinner. All this education was rough, and a
preacher of the thirteenth century summed up the spirit of the
time in a few words when he said, that the body of the children
ought to be "strictly treated"—*Dure nutriendi quoad corpus.*

To tell the truth, no advice can be more wise, and it ought not
to have been otherwise as regards the young men who were called
upon in after life to pursue the vocations of hunters and soldiers.
What would have become of them if they had been brought up in
the delicate and coddling manner of our youths—what would those
lads have become who were destined to fight the battle of life
during the whole term of their existence, and to take their recrea-
tion in the intervals of fighting in pursuing the wild boar for ten
hours at a stretch in the immense trackless forests of this country?
And so we must expect to find in the writing of the poets descriptions of the infancy of the children to which we are but little
accustomed.

But one of our epic poets, who wrote at the end of the twelfth century, upon the borders of the Langue d'Oc and the Langue d'Oil, the author of *Daurel et Beton*, nevertheless, lingers upon the portrait of a very young child. He says :—

"At three years old Betounet had a charming countenance, fair hair, eyes like those of a hawk after moulting time, the mouth fresh as a rose in summer, and skin as white as snow."

But there was a speedy limit to this gentleness, and we have done with the portrait. At four years old he carried off the embroidered gloves of the good king who had brought him up, and brought them playfully to the queen, who embraced him. At five he played draughts and at dice, spoke gracefully, and above all rode gracefully. Oh ! the horse was the great attraction for this tiny feudal child, and so the friendship between the animal and the lad was cemented at a very early age.

It is certain that the little men of that period were by no means indifferent to the games which are practised with such gusto by our own children. In the twelfth and thirteenth centuries they played at marbles, walked on stilts, played battledore and shuttlecock, ball, bowls, trap-ball, merry-go-rounds, and see-saw. The lads played all these and other games as they do to this day, and those who preferred the chances of hazard used to practise " odd and even." They amused themselves in building little houses as young Parisians do in the sand at Trouville or Villers. The joys of Guignol ! yes, even these were not unknown in those primitive days, and the lads of the period (that age is pitiless) willingly harnessed mice to the toy carriages in which their sisters' dolls were seated.

But these are mere details and count but little, no more than the enjoyment of the cold bath and the flower or strawberry gathering in the woods. There were only two phases of child-life. In the house there were backgammon, dice, and chess—the everlasting chess which children learned to play at a very early age, and which still held a place as it were in the life of the knight. Then in the open air, exercise on horseback—always on horseback. As soon as the little limbs could accommodate themselves to the animal, the child was hoisted up on one of the great spirited horses, which our forefathers so delighted in. The child was not slow in finding his seat, and listening gravely to the instructions which were given him ; striking his tiny heels against the yielding flanks of the animal he bestrode, and then galloping boldly away ! And this before he was seven years of age !

To substitute for the son of his liege lord his own flesh and blood, in place of some poor innocent traitorously done to death, was—according to the testimony of the poets of the middle ages—an act of heroism of which few of the vassals would care to undertake the responsibility. Supposing a mother capable of such a sacrifice, it would appear almost impossible and far-fetched. But that is precisely what the good vassal Remir and his wife Erembourc did when they substituted their own child for the son of Girart de Blaives, for the little Jourdain, for whom they sacrificed their own infant, as already related.

We only refer to this incident again — which an unknown *trouvere* had placed on record in "*Jourdain de Baivies*," so that we may reproduce the portrait—or rather the sketch—of a child of noble birth before the age of seven years. The poor mother set out to deliver up her own child to those who would kill him. The child smiled at them, "for he knew nothing of treachery," nor of traitors ; and his mother laments that she shall never see him playing at the quintain or other games, prisoners'-base and *ecu*, struggling with pages and lads of his own age—" I shall see them engaged in mimic warfare but not him, and my heart will bleed again ! "

We are too apt to attribute to modern times certain fictions, instructive and manly fictions, certain happy types which we suppose, not without some temerity and presumption, to have been unknown to our distant ancestors. Thus, for instance, we give credit to Daniel Defoe as having been the first of the Crusoes. There is not a book more human, or more absolutely vivid in its reality, than Robinson Crusoe. A man, one man by himself, struggling against Nature, against all the forces of Nature, and overcoming them by his own sheer industry and confidence in Providence, without any other assistance whatever ! An individual doing the work of Adam and primitive humanity over again, and performing it without Eve and without Abel : it is beautiful, it is grand ; and is, perhaps, the best to put before our children.

Well, the middle ages had also its Robinson Crusoe—who told his adventures to the children, to the youthful barons of ten years old. We must not be surprised to find that it is impressed with the feudal character, and only very distantly resembles the romance of Defoe. Each century has its own way of regarding things, and lending them their own colouring.

In the opening of this Robinson Crusoe tale of the thirteenth century, it was necessary to have the history of a traitor, just as a shipwreck is absolutely necessary in all the Robinsons—family or otherwise—of modern days.

Now, we find that the old Count Guy de Maience used to live in a castle on the bank of the Rhine, low down—near the mouth of the river, not very far from the " salt sea."

This gentleman was an indefatigable sportsman, and a mighty hunter ; in the whole course of his existence he had had only two desires—but they were grand passions—fighting, and the chase ! These were his hobbies. It came to pass one day while he was hunting the deer in the profound depths of the forest, he was very considerably astonished to see the animal suddenly take refuge within the little court-yard which enclosed a hermitage ; and to see the hermit fall at his feet, soliciting respite for the poor deer which claimed his protection.

"No, no ; no quarter," exclaimed the implacable hunter, launching the heavy spear he carried at the unfortunate animal. But, somehow or other, the ill-aimed dart missed the deer and pierced the hermit to the heart ! The angels descended to receive his soul, and he died !

Nothing could exceed the grief of the involuntary murderer, who exclaimed in his remorse—

" I make a vow ! I vow to take the place of the holy man whom I have just slain, and to remain in this hermitage all the days of my life ! "

Up to this time we have not encountered the traitor ; here he comes now ! Attention !

The traitor is the seneschal of the old count, who was thought by everyone to be dead. As a matter of fact, seneschals have not altogether a good time of it in our old poems. But this particular seneschal surpassed all other seneschals in treachery, and proposed to possess himself at one fell swoop of the widow and of the territory of his late liege lord.

But the lady resisted his proposals; so he beat her cruelly and would have slain her on the spot had not a beautiful little boy of seven years old, the eldest of Guy's three sons, named Doolin, interfered. This youthful partisan heroically came to the aid of his mother, and threw himself with all the energy of a young lion upon the miserable wretch who had dared to strike the widow of his late liege lord. Doolin is henceforth the hero of the poem: Doolin will turn out to be the Robinson Crusoe whom we are expecting.

Now, in order to rid himself of the three children, the most treacherous of seneschals made a dastardly attempt to drown them, but only succeeded in the case of the youngest, and the other two lads were launched into the open sea in a miserable little cockle-shell of a boat by themselves. They floated away; away out to sea, and were lost to view. Lost! No! . . .

Doolin never despaired. But his brother, alas! had not strength sufficient to endure the terrible trial. He was only five years of age, poor little fellow. So pretty too, and with such beautiful bright eyes, as keen as those of a falcon. Hunger assailed him; he could not endure it: he grew paler and paler, and at length his beautiful eyes closed and he rendered up his soul. Then Doolin was left all by himself.

A child of seven years of age afloat on the open sea in a small boat! Picture it! Just as his little brother had expired in Doolin's arms, his kisses on his lips, the sun set, and night came on! And what a night it was! Doolin could see nothing, and he was famishing. He fainted, and lay motionless in the boat for many hours; but at length the sun, which, says the poet, "Providence caused so beautifully to rise," reappeared in the sky, and Hope once more animated the breast of the now re-awakened Doolin.

There! There! Yonder is a black speck. What can it be? It is land! But alas it is seven leagues away, and yet he must reach it. Now the child is so terribly weak that he cannot even raise his hand to his head—*à peine peut ses bras vers sa teste lever!* Moreover, a storm was rising, and in a short time it burst in terrible fury over the ocean. The enormous waves tossed the tiny boat up and down like a shuttlecock; the wind howled and roared; the rain and hail fell in torrents, and thunder crashed over all.

In this fearful strait the child commended himself to the mercy of Heaven. But how hungry he was! He was constrained to catch a few hailstones in the palms of his hands, and to suck them, to allay his terrible thirst. There were fortunately some branches of trees now floating on the waves—he ate them—what do I say? —he *browsed* on the leaves. Mercifully the storm passed away, the sun shone out warmly again, and the breeze impelled the little boat towards the distant shore. The bark grounded on the beach, and not one moment too soon!

What land was this? What country was this on which the boat had grounded so fortunately, and on which the wind had cast our little navigator? It was covered with an immense forest, in which trees abounded with wild apples and nuts, upon which our little hero regaled himself and appeased his hunger thereby. But this forest was very extensive, very lonely, and very dark, and Doolin was tempted to regret his own bed. Then there were wolves besides!

"Bah," he said to himself; "if they come I will plunge my knife in their stomachs!"

Nevertheless he felt constrained to seek for a resting-place where he could sleep. An old and magnificent oak-tree suddenly came under his observation, hollowed out by time in most comfortable fashion. Here was a bed ready made! It was more, it was a hiding-place, and our Robinson soon concealed himself therein.

At the time these events occurred our poet would have us believe that lions and tigers frequented the country at the mouth of the Rhine. This is a fact in natural history which I confess I have not ascertained, nor can I altogether unreservedly endorse the science of the narrator, who also believes in a species of tiger— absolutely unknown to modern zoologists—a tiger with prickles, a porcupiny tiger. However this may be, it is stated that the lad witnessed from his hiding-place in the tree a terrific combat between a lion and a tiger of this porcupiny species.

That these two animals killed each other goes without saying, and then a leopard arose, but he did not dare attack the desolate child. Fancy a leopard in the neighbourhood of the Zuyder Zee! This is all that is necessary to complete the picture. But let us proceed.

The sun rose brightly, and the weather cleared up. The birds sang merrily; the wild boars and the deer rushed around him in the depths of the forest, and the wolves howled; but Providence, with a mercifully guiding hand, led the courageous child—who had never lost his presence of mind—through the greatest perils, armed only with his knife, and singing hymns.

This wood was the very one (as our readers doubtless have already guessed) in which Doolin's father was living in the hermitage. The time was approaching—as was to be expected—when the father and son would meet again and recognize each other—but not yet. This is double Robinson Crusoism, but it is not less instructive, nor less touching than is the original.

A sudden change of fortune, very happily introduced by the author of our romance, comes in to complicate, in a very curious manner, the situation of the old man and the child.

It seems that the father, the hermit, momentarily oblivious of the vow he had made, had thought of abandoning his solitary life, and returning again to his place and habit as a knight. He burned to regain his wife and his inheritance from the arch-traitor who had possessed himself of his property. This idea was only a vague one, and had no fixed tenure in his mind—had nothing precise in it at all; yet one cannot even in thought violate a solemn vow with impunity, and Providence punished the aged count. An angel descended from heaven, and deprived him of his eyesight. Thenceforth he was blind!

And now begins the most interesting part of our story. It seems to us that the episode is novel, original, and possesses sufficient power in itself to inspire a strong romancist, another Daniel Defoe. Here we have a child of seven or eight years of age destined to live in a desert place with a blind old man, his father, whom he loves, whom he nourishes, whom he guides in his walks—a conception which is not inferior to Crusoe. The poet of the thirteenth century was not of a calibre to develop such a happy inspiration, but his characteristics are very natural and very charming.

We follow him in the story for many years, day by day, interested in the life of this gallant youth, who makes clothes from the skins of wild beasts, who goes hunting every morning, and brings game home every evening to the blind man, who himself prepares all the meals of the family, salts his food with the sea-salt, and makes mats of the bark of the trees. But one can understand that such a childhood cannot last long, and Doolin's came to an end at last.

One day in the forest they heard the tramp of a horse and the clatter of the armour of his rider. This person was an envoy from the wicked seneschal, the traitor, from him who had incarcerated, and who wished to put to death, Doolin's mother.

The young man threw himself upon the wretch and killed him with a blow of a club. Then in a rapt condition of mind, he contemplated for the first time in his life—what he had never hitherto seen—a gilded shield, a glittering helmet, a coat made of little steel rings, and above all a sword—a steel sword! At the sight of this weapon all his true nature awoke, his heart bounded. How could he learn to bear those arms? He had never learnt to use them, he did not know how to wear them! . . .

But Nature taught him, and Providence directed him. In default of knowledge, he possessed instinct, and in a few minutes he was able to leap upon the back of the steed, helmet on head, sword in hand. Then he galloped to and fro in triumph. The blind man heard him, and cried—

"What is that? Who is there on horseback?"

He came forward as the rider halted, and feeling his way with his hands, came upon his son!

"Oh, Heaven," he prayed, "grant that I may see him, let me behold my son!"

Then a miracle was performed! The old count's vision was mercifully restored, and he gazed upon his son. Could he have looked upon a more beautiful sight!

Doolin, however, had no wish to remain in the forest. He had his patrimony to regain, his mother to avenge, and also to punish the traitor. He leaves his father in the hermitage, and so the story closes.

I am convinced that such a narrative as this must have interested

the youthful barons in former days as much as Defoe has amused
our generations of boys, and that it was of a nature to arouse
chivalrous and manly feelings in the mind of the young baron
whose portrait we are attempting to sketch. All these Robinson
Crusoe tales form men!

IV.

At seven years of age the education of the noble child commenced. We intend to let our readers be present at the teaching.

The religious instruction was so far good that it did not then
constitute a special course. The fatal separatism which consists
in isolating the faith from all other knowledge did not exist, and
nothing was more healthily and wisely Christian than the means
by which the mind of the future knight was developed. The priests
were intimately acquainted with the life of the château; they were
present on all occasions of mourning or of festivity. Their failings,
which people saw very clearly, did not deprive them of the respect
they had won. It seems as if people sometimes felt the point of
the words of the old knights; "Honour all clerics, and speak to
them politely," they would say to their sons, "but leave them as
little as possible of your wealth."

This, however, is nothing but an innocent epigram, and has no
poison in it. In the paternal counsels piety bursts out—"Hear
mass every day, and make no noise in the convent."

There may well have been at the bottom of the hearts of some
old veterans an unconscious contempt for these men of peace who
were prevented from fighting: something akin to the disdain entertained by the soldiers of Napoleon for *pékins*. Let us go further;
there existed outside a small lay school, and Hervis of Metz exclaimed one day with all the fury of the sectarian—"They ought
to become soldiers, all these fat monks; all these canons, priests,
and abbés. Ah, if the king would only give them to me!"

We must take this tendency into consideration, no doubt, but
that is not the true character of the religious education of the
twelfth century. The idea, the spirit of the Crusades dominates
and penetrates everywhere and everything. In the castles the

children and young people are told with enthusiasm of the grand expedition of Peter the Hermit, fighting so bravely with an axe ; and the recital which appeals so directly and forcibly to the youthful auditory is the episode of the famous nineteenth battalion —of that battalion of priests which was perceived beneath the walls of Jerusalem at the great attack.

" They were all clothed in white, with a red cross on the breast, unarmed, each one carrying a consecrated wafer, all intoning the litany and blessing the army with one voice." Ah ! such action as this caused one to forget all the failings of the clergy, and this was also the catechism of the child of the Feudal age. It had its value.

At a very early stage of life children were taught prayer, and they prayed. When the poor little Doolin was lost in the forest, he concealed himself in an oak tree, made the sign of the cross very calmly, and said his orisons which they had taught him. And who had taught them to him ? It is scarcely necessary to say, his mother. But all around him were in the habit of praying.

Moral instruction came also from the lips of all those who surrounded the youthful baron, and he assimilated them, with the injunctions as to politeness, deportment, and manners. A single word embodies all this elevated teaching—a word which is one of the most beautiful in our language, which means the same as chivalry and honour—we refer to COURTESY !

It is then a lesson in courtesy which the professor is about to give us, and this lesson is inculcated on the youthful baron by the united voices of his father and his mother. One may readily imagine he hears the two semi-choruses of the Greek Tragedy.

"It is with God, my child, that we must begin," the mother would say. "In the most momentous hours of your life, God will never desert you if you put your trust in him. Recall the beautiful story of Aiol. His father, Elie, was banished from France, disinherited, absolutely in poverty, and an invalid for forty years. He lived in a wretched kind of cabin with his wife Avisse, and his horse Marchegai. The roof was so low that the knight's lance could not stand upright within it, and was placed outside (how sad !) exposed to rain and wind.

" The day at length arrived when Elie had to send his son into

France to reconquer his 'marches,' and he could only give him a bent lance, an old shield, rusty armour, and four pence—yes, only four pence. But he addressed to him these noble words, which you should always bear in mind :—'*Fiex quant iceus fauront, Dieus est es cieus.*' And the child on his part would reply, '*Si vos n'ave's avoir, Dieus a assés.*'" *

"It would not be sufficient for you," the father would say, "to have confidence in God, if you have not justice on your side ; but be assured, my son, that if you fight for God and for the right, you will conquer ! "

"Above all things," continued the mother, "be humble. Had you a hundred horses in your stables, and all the wealth of the world ; were you the Constable of France, nothing would go well with you if pride effected a lodgment in your soul. The proud man loses in a day what it has caused him seven years to gain."

"Be liberal, give largely ; then give again, and still give. The more you give away, my son, the richer you will be. Whoever is avaricious is not a gentleman, and it is really sad to see princes living in such a dishonourable vice. They sully the title of royalty !

"Remember it is not enough to relieve the poor, the widow and the orphan ; you must go further and embrace in all its widest scope the word *largesse.* The *vilains* in their proverb say that it is one's true interest to be liberal : *Ne fu pas fols cil qui dona premiers.* But it is not a question of interest which ought to guide you, and you are not a *vilain.* In the poem which a troubadour was singing to us yesterday, there was a verse which I retained in my memory to be my motto :—

'*En vos tresors mar remanra dernier.*'

To portionless knights, to disinherited good men and true, distribute your wealth, rich furs, the vair and the grey—all ! Do not consider ; do not make promises—give ! "

"As your father has spoken of knights, I will add that there is another tribute you should pay them, and that is respect ! When-

---

* These words were repeated almost exactly by the young Ameri when he proposed to the emperor to capture Narbonne—"You are as poor as proud," said Charlemagne. "Poor ! " he replied. "Is not God in Heaven above all ?"

ever you see a good and true man, rise up in his presence and put yourself at once at his service. When you are on the road, salute everyone. In your words as in all your actions be always courteous, for civility costs little. Above all things do not jest and banter with the poor, and be humble in your dealings both with small and great. When you are a man's guest show yourself of a smiling countenance and joyful mien. Cultivate the art of not hearing and seeing everything, and persuade yourself that they mean to behave kindly towards you.

"I need scarcely exhort you, my son, to avoid with horror that particular vice they call drunkenness. Eat well, but do not drink too much wine—'on the lees.' As for play, it is, alas, the source of many disputes; and that famous chess, of which they boasted so much, has cost the lives of many knights, as you are aware. It was because of a check 'that' Galien slew the traitor Tibert; it was on account of a game of chess that the youthful Landri, in '*Doon de la Roche*,' smote the traitor Tomile.

"But traitors were not the only people to suffer from this terrible game. The charming Bandouinet, the nephew of Ogier the Dane, succumbed beneath the blows of the son of Charlemagne, who was armed with a chess-board; and in the same manner died the nephew of the great emperor, the poor Bertolais, smitten down by Renaud de Montauban. Those who did not lose their lives in this accursed game often lost their money at it, and even their horses. Beware of chess!

"But, my son, you must beware of some people more than the game of chess—and they are the *vilains*. You must never have any intercourse with them, but be particularly cautious not to make them your counsellors and friends. Never confide to them a secret, nor give them any function, nor permit them to approach you. Ah, we are spectators now of sad sights which disgust me greatly. And never think of conferring on a villein the holy order of chivalry. I tell you, the Sacrament was not intended for him. I tell you that it would be a scandal, and, what is more, a danger! Such people, naturally, have not nobleness of heart; they are not noble, save on the surface, and they are capable of any felony.

"Girat of Roussillon was sufficiently attached to the son of a villein to make him his seneschal and his counsellor, and even bestowed on him a rich farm and good land. He was well punished for it, for it was this wretch, the same Richier, who delivered Roussillon to his most deadly enemies. No, no, a villein,—whatever you may make him—will remain a villein still, and his brain is so dense that no good will ever enter into it. In brief, a gentleman should only live with gentlemen who are his peers, and it is only in such intercourse that one finds good.

"A true baron should not compromise himself, he ought not to associate with a man who is not a baron like himself; and I cannot admit—yes, I will even go so far as that—I cannot admit that a valet should seat himself at table with his master. A little pride is not unbecoming a knight, and that is a lesson, my son, which you will do well to meditate upon.

"There is, nevertheless, something which you may learn from the villeins. These are the proverbs which they use incessantly, and which our poets quote so fully to our bachelors (knights). They contain a course of knowledge which the old men themselves may turn to profitable account. You are very young still, my son, but already very anxious to have adventures and to quit the maternal nest. Well, then, remember this proverb—

'The bird that wishes to fly before it can sustain itself falls to the ground.'

"Young people talk too much. Remember that a

'Wise silence is better than foolish talking.'

"Young people love danger. Tell yourself that some prudence is right and necessary ; and that

'He who would warm himself burns himself sometimes.'

"Beware of traitors and of those dangerous companions whom your father has just indicated to your attention and to your contempt. Do not blindly rush into the lion's mouth, or—to quote our villeins again—

'Do not imitate the lamb that plays with the wolf.'

"Beware even of your neighbours themselves, as the proverb says—

'He who has a bad neighbour often has a bad morning ;'

and persuade yourself that there are traitors everywhere. From treason no one can guard himself. Do not permit yourself to accept fine promises from the first comer. It is better to have one thing in hand of your own than four in the bush : and do not attach too much importance to the recognition of those who call themselves your best friends, for—

'Once a man is dead and buried he is forgotten.'

"If ever you become poor, remember that all the flatterers will very quickly turn their backs upon you, and it is well known that

'The poor man is in bad odour ; '

and poverty is the more detestable as it changes the heart of man and makes him do very much mischief (*lui fait faire maint méchef*).

"After Providence, depend on no one but yourself, and do not forget that 'who stag hunts, stag finds.' But be sure remember that you come of a good stock, and as the villeins say in one of their picturesque proverbs—

'The son of a cat ought to catch mice.'

"Imitate your father in all things, and you will do well."

"Your mother, my child, has correctly quoted the familiar sayings which are in vogue amongst young people. But it is with the prouder words which have sprung forth from the hearts of our poets, and which will one day attain to the dignity of proverbs, that I would have you to do. These are more worthy of you and constitute the code of honour.

" 'Death rather than dishonour,' was the cry which Roland uttered in the valley of Roncesvalles before the great battle with the infidel ; it is the cry of every Christian baron, and will be yours too, my son, on every solemn occasion of your life. They told you the other day that ' the heart of a man is worth all the gold in the country,' and that '*fins cuers ne peut mentir.*' Weigh all these in your memory, and so act upon them that people may say of you as they said of Ogier—

'*Molt fu preudom ; si ot le cuer entier.*'

It is the most beautiful funeral oration that any true knight could desire."

"Since they have held up Ogier to you as a model, remember, my son, that the knight has models in Heaven, and so lift your eyes on high. The Prince of the Celestial Chivalry is Saint Michael: he is the conqueror in the great and invisible battle in which were vanquished those vassals of God who one day revolted against the Sovereign Lord. I hope, my son, that you and I will soon go together, and perform the pilgrimage of 'Saint Michel de Peril de la Mer,' for the archangel is the great patron, not only of chivalry, but of the whole of France.

"In imitation of such a champion the very angels and saints have not disdained to be made knights, and to fight in mortal forms amid the ranks of the Christian army. At the commencement of the celebrated battle of Aspremont, in which Roland revealed himself and gained the sword Durendal, three mysterious knights were suddenly perceived descending in light from the mountain, seated upon great white horses : these knights were Saint George, Saint Domininus and Saint Maurice, who had quitted the 'flowers of Paradise' with the express object of couching a lance and striking a blow for our knights below.

"But why go back so far? You are aware, my son, of the incomparable expedition which ended in the capture of the Holy City of Jerusalem. There were saints and angels everywhere. It was as if a flight of falcons were hovering over our army, and had then cast themselves in terrible attack upon the infidels. On one day there were thirty thousand amongst us *plus blaus que flors de pres*. There, there, my son, are your models, and I often permit myself to hope that you will become another Saint George—another Saint Maurice. Let me retain this hope."

"Your mother has high aspirations, and she is welcome to them. I am more moderate, and propose to you only human models. Still, do not let me go too far in the impetuosity of my wishes. Certainly, it would not be displeasing to me to see you resemble Roland, who knew how to meet death in a manner which no mere mortal man ever did (save One) ; to that Roland who expired on the mountain, where he could overlook Spain and the infidels, holding his own against one hundred thousand men, preserving his sword, having time to repeat his *meâ culpâ*, and gaining the victory just before his death. I prefer to him, perhaps, Oliver, who is less sublime and more practical; but that is an opinion which I would not wish to defend too far.

"I also delight in the rough Guillaume—' *au fier bras* '—whose sword many times freed the Christian race, and who died a monk at Gellone : or the youthful Vivien, who fell in the field of battle at Aliscans when the angels came down to carry his soul to Heaven. Or again, Renaud de Montauban, who to expiate his sins consented to conceal his glorious name and to become a bricklayer's labourer at Cologne.

"For some time we have heard of the Nine. Nine heroic examples or models, which should represent to our eyes all that has ever been the most valiant and generous in the enterprises of the greatest captains. Joshua was for a long time the arm and the sword of Moses : David distinguished himself both as a soldier and as a knight, as well as a penitent and a prophet. It was Judas Maccabeus who delivered his countrymen.

"These form the first group of the nine heroes, the first and not the least grand.

"Hector, Alexander and Cæsar compose the second, which sums up Troy, Greece and Rome. But I would prefer to direct your attention to the third group, in which shines out the glory of Arthur of Britain, Charlemagne of France, and Godfrey of Bouillon.

"I do not wish to hide from you the opinion that I prefer Godfrey of Bouillon to any of the other eight heroes, and that he is the hero upon whom I should wish to model myself and you after me. I consider that he resembles Roland as much as Oliver, with, I cannot tell how much, more piety and sanctity. He was as gentle as he was brave, and this man, of whom all the Crusaders could say as they saw him pass by—' There is duke Godfrey, who has the heart of a lion '—that warrior was as gentle as a lamb.

"I am of opinion that no one like him knew the great mystery of the Crusade, and he ceased not for one moment throughout that war of unparalleled duration to distinguish himself by a singular moderation, which, however, never permitted anyone to question his courage. His companions could perceive that he was always thinking of Christ even in the very thick of the battle, and the idea of the Cross was ever present in his calm and tranquil mind. Two sayings of his, two sayings only, paint the character of the man. He pronounced the first at the Gate of David during the final assault on Jerusalem. He said, 'Do not fear death—seek it!' It was to his brothers—remark, to his brothers—that he addressed this grand exhortation. You know the other utterance, which will be repeated to the end of time by all true knights.

"'God forbid,' said the newly-made King of Jerusalem, 'God forbid that I should wear a crown of gold where He wore a crown of thorns.'

"He remained during the rest of his life grave and pensive, thinking always of his Master.

"No one ever saw such a crusader as he. But perhaps I am putting before you too elevated an example, and I think it would be better to propose to you a more accessible model.

"In fact I would not desire a better model than the cousin of Girart de Roussillon, who was called Fouque, and whose exploits the troubadour sang to us the other day, thus—

"'Fonque was heroic, courteous, frank, good, and a facile speaker. He was a most skilful hunter in the forest, the wood or the marsh; he knew chess, backgammon and dice. His house was never closed to anyone. He gave as he was asked. Good or bad, everyone had a share in it, and he was never slow to bestow largesse. He was supremely pious, for, although he was of the world, he never was in a court where was proposed or accomplished a single act of injustice, without being profoundly moved if he could not prevent the execution of it. He detested war, and loved peace: when he had his helmet laced, his shield around his neck, his sword by his side, then he was proud, furious, impulsive, superb, merciless, pitiless; and when pressed by a crowd of armed men, then he showed himself the firmest and most brave. They could not make him budge an inch, and there was not one man on earth who would cope with him. He always loved brave knights, and honoured the poor as well as the rich. Everyone, powerful or weak, found in him their support.' Decidedly, my son, he is your model."

"Yes!" repeated his mother. "There is your model. Now, my dear child, go and rest, after this long lesson. If you only retain a sentence of it, let it be this, in which all your father's teaching and mine is summed up :—

'Do your duty come what may.'

" The rest matters little. Kiss me, my child."

V.

Readers may perhaps be surprised that, while on the subject of the religious education of our youthful baron, we have not yet spoken of that festival of Christian infancy which, in the eyes of our sceptical generation, has retained all its touching majesty, and marks so happily the entrance of the child into the busier days of a later youth. The rite of Confirmation does not appear in those somewhat rough times to have been celebrated with the same tender solemnity, or with the same display as in these our days.

Our *"Chansons de geste"* somehow are silent concerning this festival, which is calculated to bring tears to the eyes of the most hardened : one can find only a single reference which leads us directly to this grand ceremony. It is true, that this episode is incomparable, and ought to be placed beside—quite on a level with —the death of Roland.

This occasion was the first communion of Vivien, on the evening of the battle of Aliscans.

We must picture to ourselves, here, an extensive field of battle, upon which two nations—what do I say? two races—are rushing one against the other furiously, and occupied for two hours in endeavouring to exterminate each other. The French, the Christians—these two names were gloriously synonymous—the "men of God " are beaten, and Islam is conqueror !

Almost interminable piles of knights and dead horses indicate the places in which have taken place the thousands of duels of which a battle in those days consisted. All the French, with the exception of fifteen, have bitten the dust, and the infidels still number one hundred thousand !

Everywhere around arise the cries of the dying and the wounded, the whinnying of riderless horses, and the joyous cries of the

victors.   And yonder, not far off, in a beautiful green valley
beside a spring—in a beautiful spot in which the cries of the
combat are but faintly heard—a very young man, almost a youth,
is lying stiff, perfectly white, his hands crossed.   One would have
pronounced him dead, if his clasped hands did not now and then
beat his chest, and if his eyes had not occasionally been turned
upwards to the heavens, and if one had not heard him murmur the
word " God."

This youth is the nephew of William of Orange—it is Vivien
who is dying!

William himself is yonder in the midst of the fourteen survivors
of the Christian army, whom he overtops in his great height.   He
is there seated upon his horse *"Baucent"* and is thinking of his
nephew whom he loves as a son.

" Where is he ?   Where is Vivien ? " he cries.

Then he adventures across the battle-field in search of him
living or dead.   " Where is he ?   Where is Vivien ? "

Providence has pity upon William, and conducts him to the
corner of the secluded valley in which Vivien is dying; and there
is the Count of Orange, in the presence of the young man with the
blanched face, who scarcely moves and hardly breathes.

Suddenly an idea occurs to this grim warrior, who is himself
covered with blood, for he has fought since morning like a furious
lion :

" He will die without having partaken of his first communion."
Then he exclaims, " O why did I not arrive sooner ? "   The good
William actually has the sacred elements in his possession, and he
regrets that he cannot place the wafer piously upon his nephew's
lips.   But alas those lips are cold and dead !

Suddenly the young man stirs : it is an almost imperceptible
movement. Life, as the old poet says, returned to him for an
instant, and "leaped into his breast."   William, then, possessed
by one idea, speaks to him very gently—

" Do not you wish to eat the consecrated bread ? " he says.

" I have never tasted it," replied the dying man, " but as you
re there I feel as if God had sent it to me."

Then in that little grass-grown valley, beneath the great tree
near the spring, an indescribable scene took place.   William

"A VERY YOUNG MAN IS LYING STIFF, PERFECTLY WHITE, HIS HANDS CROSSED."

became grave as he assumed the priestly office, and said to his nephew—

"You must confess to me, because I am your nearest relative, and because there is no priest here."

"I am quite willing," replied the youthful Vivien in a weak voice, "but you will have to support my head against your chest. I hunger, yes, I hunger for that bread. Hasten, for I die, I die!"

Then he makes his confession, but can remember only one fault.

"I made a vow that I would never retreat one step before the Infidel, and to-day I have failed to keep my oath!"

The supreme moment has arrived. William takes the wafer and places it between the parted lips of Vivien. There are thousands of angels present to witness the sight and to bear that soul to Heaven. Vivien's countenance lights up once again, but Death descends from his head to his heart. He falls back with a sigh; he is dead! Gone from this world to Paradise, to never-ending happiness, to complete the day of his first communion.

VI.

Such was the instruction which the youthful baron of the Twelfth Century received every day, and on which he modelled himself; such was the religious and moral education of the future knight. But he was still ignorant of the first elements of human scientific knowledge, and here we find ourselves in the presence of a grave problem.

Did the youthful noble of the Twelfth Century know how to read and write? Was not his ignorance, on the contrary, something astounding, and did he not even go so far as to derive some glory from it?

The almost general opinion is in favour of this state of ignorance, and it is unquestionable that a certain number of knights did not know their letters. There was once actually a Grand Chamberlain of France, who, in the reign of Saint Louis, was obliged to confess as much. This is related of Jean de Nanteuil, who subscribed to the will of Jeanne, Countess of Toulouse and Poitiers:—"Ego

Petrus canonicus de Roscha, de mandata domini Johannis de
Nantolio qui rogatus huic interfuit testamento et sigillum suum
apposuit, testamento huic subscripsi pro eo, *cum ipse non haberet
noticiam litterarum."*

But I may be permitted to remark that the majority of the heroes
of our old poems did not in this respect resemble the unfortunate
Jean de Nanteuil.   If I open that terrible epic of the Lorrains, in
which one finds recorded a very rude and barbarous social state, I
perceive that Hervis and Garin knew how to read in Romansche and
in Latin, to write and to engross.

We find the same knowledge claimed for the son of Parise, la
Duchesse ; for the three children of Gui de Mayence ; for the
young Aiol ; for the sons of Count Witasse de Boulogne ; and (it is
unnecessary to say so) for the son of Pepin, for the great Charles.
We could easily multiply instances and make quotations which
would prove to demonstration the accuracy of our conclusions, and
place the question beyond a doubt.

I do not refer to the proofs which many learned men have
extracted from our romances of adventure, or from our didactic
poems of the Thirteenth Century ; but I would just bring to the
knowledge of the reader, and put before him, the charming picture
which the author of *Dolopathos* has limned.

" There, seated on the ground before their master, were the
children of many a haughty baron, attentive to their instructor's
words.   And every pupil had his book in his hand !   So he taught
them ! "

Now I am not altogether sorry to be able to make you spectators
of a writing lesson, with or without blows with a ferule, as the case
may be.   The children first learn to write on wax tablets with a
stylus, and care is taken to prevent them from spoiling the good
parchment, which is expensive.   When they have made a sufficient
number of " pothooks and hangers," which are in turn effaced from
the wax ; when they have arrived at a certain pitch of perfection as
scribes ;—they are then—but only then—entrusted with some
sheets of parchment, which is scarcely of the first quality.   It is
necessary to be economical.

Regarding the ignorance of our barons, it behoves us to be cir-
cumspect in our statements, so as not to fall into any excess of

criticism. People will never make us believe that, in an age when every little village boasted its school (a fact which is indisputable, and which has been proved in certain provinces), the feudal youths were destined to be less instructed than their inferiors. On the contrary, it is certain that the nobly-born youth often had a private tutor in the paternal castle who was always with him. Such an one was the tutor of Doolin de Mayence; such, likewise, was the pedagogue mentioned by the author of the *Romance of the Seven Sages,* "who had to attend his pupil everywhere; who accompanied him to school, who (interesting detail, this) prevented him from eating too much; who taught him polite language and good manners; and who did not even quit him when he dressed, and when he retired to bed.

Again, it often happened that in good families and in well-managed households, the worthy task of education was ingeniously divided between the father, the mother, and the tutor. In this manner did Aiol learn from his father military prowess, and particularly the art of riding; for to these grandsons of Germans one certainly could not apply the words of Tacitus, addressed to their ancestors of the farther Rhine: *In pedite robur;* and we have already seen that the baron was almost one with his horse. Aiol's mother instructed him in the courses of the stars; and taught him the reason for the waxing and waning of the moon. This branch of instruction, I admit, was unusual on a mother's part; but such knowledge was very necessary to those who later in life would be compelled to pass many days and nights in the open air, like the shepherds, who were also somewhat of astronomers.

Finally a hermit instructed the youth in "the art of reading and copying Latin and Romansch." That was an education which, notwithstanding all objections, would appear to have been pretty complete. Some barons of the Nineteenth Century are, perhaps, less enlightened than the sons of Elie de Saint Gilles.

We see these knights, whom it pleases some people to regard as "paragons" of ignorance, in their tents in the interval between two battles reading to each other, and seriously discussing military matters, literature, and law. Philippe de Navarre has bequeathed to us, in this regard, a little picture which is worth studying, and might have inspired Meissonier. There are in it no dullards ignorant of their letters, but men of talent who have received some fundamental instruction, and who have improved upon it. It is true that they are neither gluttons nor pedants; and it is equally beyond question that they are less instructed than our officers of the present day. But, when all is said, they are still of the same race.

I am quite aware what the enemies of the Middle Ages will say, and what quotations they will bring forward to oppose me. It is too true, in fact, that a certain number of our ancient poets are of the same mind, for we read—

"A ruler, a king, receives a letter: he breaks the seal himself, but hands it to some one else to read."

Let us add, by the way, that it was quite usual for the chaplain to open and read publicly the notes addressed to his lord and master. Well, at any rate, I opine that this argument is not irrefutable, and that rulers and kings sometimes did cause their letters to be read for them because they were written in Latin. But I do not, however, wish to give a too rigorous character to my conclusions; so I will content myself with stating that if a certain number of young men then remained in their pristine ignorance, the greater number of youths in our best provinces were sufficiently well educated to be able to read a romance, to write a letter, and even (but this was rare) to understand more than one language.

This last sentence may, perhaps, cause some astonishment; but our old poems favour such an hypothesis, although one which we must not push too far.

The Duc de Nevers, in *Gaufrey*, boasts of knowing "French, German, Lombardic, Spanish, Poitevin, and Norman." Baudouin, in the *Saisnes*, passes himself off as a Persian because he knows a little "Tiois!" Mirabel, in *Aiol*, is still more learned; for this surprising lady speaks no less than fourteen "Latins," amongst which figure Greek, Armenian, Saracenic, and Burgundian.

Furthermore, there were professors of languages, who, like the interpreters, bore the name of *Latimiers*. The celebrated text of Arunetto Latini, and many others of the same order, have often been quoted, which have inspired a poet of our own day to write this fine, bold verse :—

"Every man has two countries—his own, and then France."

We recall also this verse of *Berte*, which possesses a high historical value, and which one can never quote too often :—

"It was then the custom in all the 'Tiois' country, in all Germany, for all the nobility, the counts, and the marquises, to have Frenchmen in their train to teach their sons and their daughters the French language."

O beautiful language, which was then spoken all along the Mediterranean border, and which was the almost universal tongue!

Of all other sciences the young baron was taught only the rudiments. In his conversation with the clergy he gleaned here and there some information, but it must be confessed that it was but a taste. Many errors (worse than ignorance), and many prejudices were absorbed. All this tended to form the singular love for the "Encyclopædia," which is the noble character of all the period of the Middle Ages. The mixture was strange, I admit; but it is perfectly certain that it was *real*.

VII.

The young baron scarcely knew by hearsay the admirable classification of the Sciences which the Twelfth Century had formulated with so much lucidity, and to which the encyclopædic genius of the Middle Ages had added a new element with the gifts of antiquity. The youth had heard, vaguely referred to by the domestic chaplain, of the Seven Arts, with which he desired no more intimate acquaintance : of the *Quadrivium*, which embraced arithmetic, music, geometry, and astronomy; of the *Trivium*, which included grammar, dialectics, and rhetoric. But he had no idea that the boasted *Quadrivium* and *Trivium* were far from representing all the science of his time, and only were part of a very much greater whole, and a much more imposing array of subjects.

He was quite ignorant, for instance, that the term Philosophy

then indicated the totality of human knowledge ; that Philosophy
was divided into theory, practice, logic, and mechanics; that Theory
was sub-divided into theology, physics, and mathematics ; and that
it was this third sub-division which constituted the *Quadrivium.*

He was equally unaware that Practice included morals, economy,
and politics ; that Logic was equivalent to the Trivium ; and that
one was bound to include in Mechanics the principal industries of
the period—which were the making of cloth and armour—by the
side of navigation, agriculture, medicine, the theatre, and (oh,
happiness !) the chase.   This last fact—must I confess it ?—had
most weight with the feudal youth—it was the only part he
understood.

The chase was part of the great sum of human knowledge ; the
chase was becoming a science.   " There it is," he exclaimed ;
" what a fortunate discovery—and how true it is ! "

That the future knight ignored this Encyclopædia, destined for
the clergy, I can understand, and can excuse him for so doing;
but it is unfortunate that he did not content himself with this
ignorance, natural as it was, and avoid forging twenty false notions.
First of all, as a matter of course, he confounded Astronomy with
Astrology.   If you want to know the future—do you wish to know
in advance who will be the victor in a duel ?—learn Astronomy.

Nothing is more simple ; but our *ignoramus* goes farther, and
plunges into " Necromancy "—that is to say, into Magic, in the
degraded list of the Seven Liberal Arts.   " It is by means of this
incomparable Art (!) that one may discover all thefts ; understand
the language of all animals ; that one may journey through twenty
countries in a single day; that one may escape from all prisons ;
and in an instant level with the ground the most celebrated
fortresses and the most impregnable castles."   But it is the Art of
the Evil One, and so it must be avoided.

However, these superstitions are few, and without any real
weight.

It happens, perhaps, one day that our youthful baron is
engaged turning over the leaves of a beautiful large volume entitled
The Mirror of the World.   One of the plates in it remains impressed upon his memory, and a much longer time than all the
others : it is a picture in which the whole plan of the universe

is set forth. The idea has its origin in a false interpretation of Scriptural texts; but it is not lacking in force or beauty, and the youthful reader has been greatly struck with it. Let us glance at it.

See, there are seven concentric circles, enlarging into the infinite. The centre is the world, and in the centre of our earth is fire. The earth is surrounded and enveloped in air; the air by ether; the ether by the firmament; the firmament by the aqueous heavens; the aqueous heavens by the immaterial Heaven; that, which is the abode of the blessed, is surrounded by the Heaven of Heavens—in which resides eternally the Creator, Who thus embraces the entire universe, and all created beings in a living, eternal, infinite circumference. It is a grand conception.

VIII.

It is no doubt a good deal to know the general conformation of the Universe, but one feels happy when one returns to Earth and stays there. Our youthful baron is not of age to remain very long amid the grand syntheses of science, and all those circles are apt to tire him. He prefers to study one of those immense maps—one of those strange Mappe-mondes which give us such an exact and picturesque idea of the geography of the Twelfth and Thirteenth centuries.

Our student cannot take his eyes off it, and he makes his tutor show him the way by which the Crusaders journeyed. He will not see, he does not want to see, anything else. Then, in thought, he follows the Christian army, he halts with it at Constantinople, he crosses Asia Minor, arrives at Antioch, and exclaims "Jerusalem, Jerusalem!"

Although they had some vague notions of the rotundity of the globe, the simple-minded geographers of the Feudal epoch, have only left us flat maps: but how interesting these are! In them our planet is represented in a round or oval form, and in the latter case its greatest extent is from north to south. It is completely surrounded by the "Ocean Sea" as by an immense ribbon. In this sea, which recalls to us the ancients' "Ocean River," our primitive draughtsmen have delineated fish which are as large as the islands ; vessels which, according to the law of proportion, are several leagues in length, and islands drawn in all shapes.

These islands our forefathers made a fourth part of the globe. There are Great Britain, Ireland, the Fortunate Isles, and many others besides, which are in some cases fabulous. And everywhere, fish in shoals ! As for the great oval or circle, it is cut into several continents by the Mediterranean and other branches of the Ocean. All the upper portion of the map is occupied by Asia ; Europe and Africa share the lower portion ; the former to the right, the latter to the left. It is symmetrical.

Then, leaving the side of the Islands—read what says an old poet :—

> " Il sont trois terres que je sai bien nomer
> L'une a nom Aise et Erope sa per ;
> La tierce Aufrique plus n'en poons trover—
> Ices trois teres so partirent par mer
> Qui totes terres fait partir et sevrer."

Thus wrote one of our old poets,[*] of whose work our young pupil has retained some rudimentary knowledge.

At the top of the map there is a square indicated, which represents the terrestrial Paradise. An enormous Adam and an immense Eve are standing upright near a Serpent which is coiled around the fatal tree. There is the point of departure indicated for those who wish to travel . . . on a map. " I will start from Paradise," says the youth, " and hope to return thither some day." He makes believe to go to the end of the world, but where are those ends of the world to which our poets gave such curious names, designations now so obscure ?

Where is now the famous "Arbre qui fent ?"[†]   Where are the " Bornes d'Artus ?"[‡]   Where is the " Mer betée ? "[§]   The lad does not know, and he very much wants to know.

---

[*] Aspremont ; Guessard edition, p. 4, v. 10–15.

[†] The " Arbre qui fent " has been stated to be the Arbre sec (or dried tree) so celebrated in the Middle Ages, and which figures on the maps of the 12th Century. It is placed to the south of the Indus, near the Paradise from which the Angel drove Adam. Marco Polo puts it at the " end of Persia towards Tremontania, in the Kingdom of Tonocane." He describes it as like a plane-tree standing alone on an extensive plain.

[‡] The Bornes d'Artus are synonymous with the Pillars of Hercules (*Romania*, xi.).

[§] A sea mentioned by Plato as absorbed or engulfed in the ocean (Gautier de Metz).

The terrestrial Paradise still exists, and the Tree of Life still puts forth its divine branches; but nobody can enter into it, because of a wall of fire, which ascends even up to Heaven to preserve it from the observation of mankind. All around there are only sandy deserts extending as far as the Caspian Sea, endless sandy wastes, on which the foot of men would not dare to enter. To the north lies Asia Minor up to the borders of the Black Sea. To the south extends China, and more particularly India—"India the lost," * which shelters no less than forty-four different religions. If we cross the Ganges we find ourselves in Parthia.

At the southern extremity of our map, the Persian Gulf opens with the celebrated island of Taprobane, where the verdure is immortal, and which enjoys the privilege of having two summers, and alas! two winters also. Arabia is not far off, dominated by the enormous mass of Sinai.

To the north is Aracusia, Mespotamia, and Nineveh; then, inclining to the west, the river Orontes, the first shores of the Mediterranean, Phœnicia, Mount Libanus, and finally Judea, with the city of Jerusalem, upon which our young baron had fixed his eyes.

"It was thither," he says, "that Peter the Hermit led all the Christian Knights, and all the cowardly ones only remained behind at home. There my grandfather rushed to the assault; there he slew twenty Turks; there he died!"

The youth is so moved by these grand and holy memories, that he does not take the trouble to listen to the singular lessons which his tutor is attempting to teach him regarding the countries and the inhabitants of Asia; thus:—

"It was Queen Asia who bestowed her name upon this portion of the world, and how many kingdoms thus owe their names to one of their rulers: Persia to Persus, Bithynia to Bithynus, and many others besides. At the foot of the Caspian hills lived the race of Gog and Magog, who fed on human flesh. In India pepper is naturally white, but becomes black under the influence of fires which are lighted underneath to scare away serpents.

"In Albania the men are born with white hair. The mares of

* "Il vous vausist miex estre en Ynde la perdue." *Aye d'Avignon.*

Cappadocia are fecundated by the wind. Ephesus was founded by the Amazons," and so forth. But all the while the pupil remains inattentive and murmurs between his teeth, "Jerusalem, Jerusalem!" He is only aroused from his reverie by the pronunciation of the word "Mecca."

"That is the key of the Pagan's Empire," they tell him.

"Well," he replies, "we will get there as well as to their Babylon. Ah, when shall I be a knight!"

"When you are a knight," replies the clerical tutor, "you will have to fight with people who bear little resemblance to our countrymen, and who are of terrible aspect."

Thereupon he proceeds to speak to him concerning the "Canelians," who are the Canaanites, and of the Achoparts who come from Africa, where one can see the descendants of the ancient Ethiopians. The troubadours have already told him of twenty tribes still more wonderful. He has, in *Roland*, become acquainted with the country of the pagan Churnuble, where the sun never shines, where the corn will not grow, where all the stones are black, where there is no rain nor dew, and which is justly designated as the dwelling-place of demons.

Again, in the same poem, he has met with the men of Occiant-in-the-Desert, whose skins are harder than iron, and who go into battle without armour. In the country of Arcaisia, the Sagittaries and Neros live with Lucifer, another district where corn will not grow. The Canelians, whom we mentioned just now, the Gauffres and the Bougres eat dead bodies in a state of decomposition, and, what is still more horrible, their chins and teeth are united with their chests!

The tribe Bocident is better off, although the people live on spices, and do not know wheat; but they bathe in the river of youth, and get on very well. The men of Bucion have horns like sheep. Those of Buridania bay like mastiffs; the Espes have lion's claws on their feet and hands, and when they roar the earth quakes for three leagues round. As for countries without sun or moon, we need not take any notice of them, they are too common and trivial for consideration.

All these marvels do not scandalise the youth one bit. He believes them freely; and one must say in his defence that the clergy themselves accorded perfect faith to many other geographical fables. The " teratology," or " science of monsters," plays, alas ! only a too important part in the Encyclopædia of the Middle Ages, and the true country of monsters is Asia.

Our pupil does not know much about it. More correct, however, as regards Europe and Africa, he gives them almost their normal situations ; however we need not exaggerate this "almost." But he still lends himself to incredible mistakes and regrettable errors. He fancies that, south of Africa, the ocean boils like hot water ; he pictures Spain, Italy, and Greece, like three great, nearly square, tongues protruding into the Mediterranean, which is parallel to the Red Sea. Just opposite Italy is Egypt. Spain has no depth southwards ; beyond the Ebro he knows nothing, and our poets, equally ignorant, crammed into the limited northern zone of Spain all the celebrated towns of which they had heard—as Cordova, Toledo, and Seville.

Three cities, moreover, appear to the youth the wonders of the world—Paris, Constantinople, and Rome ; and descriptions of them abound in all our songs. Rome is the grandest, and all solemn oaths are sworn " by the apostle who perished on the Pré Noiron." *

But Constantinople is more magnificent, more cheerful, more beautiful, and the surroundings are charming.

" There. are beautiful walks planted with pines and laurels ; there the roses are always in bloom ; twenty thousand knights are seated there, clothed in white silk, and bearing falcons on their wrists ; three thousand virgins are there arrayed in robes embroidered with gold, and illuminating the country with their beauty."

But all this is nothing in comparison to the city itself, and one of your most ancient poets has described Constantinople—

" Such as the popular imagination, inflamed by the reports of travellers, may conceive. In the palace, all the furniture is of gold ; the walls are covered with paintings representing all the beasts of the earth, all the birds of the heaven ; and accounts, which now appear fantastic, almost understate the magnificence

---

* The Pré Noiron was the Garden of Nero where Christian Martyrs were burned.

which is really presented to the eyes of the astonished Franks in the Imperial palace of Byzantium." *

These are the luminous points of Europe, but nothing in the eyes of the Feudal baron is worth the two places valued by us— Jerusalem, where the tomb of the Saviour is, and the Castle in which his wife and children live. Many knights know no more geography than this, and this knowledge is perhaps as good as the other which I have detailed.

IX.

One day when our young aspirant of Chivalry was going into the town adjacent to his father's castle, he had the pleasure to witness a grand *fête*. His delight knew no bounds. The king was making a solemn entry into the town. All the streets were garlanded with flowers; all the houses were draped with painted canvas. The aspect of the town was joyous and imposing.

Three wide thoroughfares led to the Cathedral, and I do not know what originally minded artist had conceived the ingenious idea of painting the roofs of the houses in the first street with representations of events in sacred history; on those of the second street, all the annals of Pagan nations; on those of the third, all the history of France.

Nevertheless, from these pictures our pupil learnt his history.

From the sacred historical representations he learned nearly as much as a little peasant lad of our own days can learn from the Introduction to his Catechism. He passed rapidly before the first painting, in which the unsophisticated brush of the artist had represented the creation of the world by the Creator, Who was and is for all time; Who sees everything from his throne on high; Who makes the birds fly, causes the grass to grow, the flowers to flourish; and who with his own hands fashioned and formed man and woman.†

Paradise detained the youthful spectator longer, and he was

---

* Gaston, Paris ; *Pilgrimage to Jerusalem.*
† Ogier : "Renans de Montauban."

particularly struck by the first of the dramas of which our Earth was the theatre. He examined with much curiosity that Adam and Eve by whom the world was peopled (*dont li mont est peuplés* —Fierabras), and with grief saw them both succumb to the deceitful machinations of Satan (*l'engien du Satenas felon*). In vain did his tutor point out that Satan did not enjoy one single hour of Heaven, whereas Adam was happy there for seven hours ;* this legend did not console the youth.

It mattered little to him that the first man had thirty sons and thirty daughters, and that " he had been buried at Calvary " (*Honoré d'Auteur*); what really struck and affected him deeply, was the fact that, since that unhappy day, all the descendants of Adam are doomed to pain and suffering (*en painne et en frichon*). There was the fact that Cain killed Abel in the desert of Abilant. There was the Deluge, which engulfed humanity while the Ark floated on the waters !

It is not without some surprise that our scholar learned that " All free men are descended from Shem, the serfs from Ham, and the knights from Japhet." So he could at anyrate congratulate himself upon a good genealogy. The picture of the Tower of Babel did not appeal sufficiently to his feelings, but rather amused him too much ; and there did not appear to him anything remarkable in the fact of the terrified men suddenly breaking into speech in ninety and nine different languages, and no longer understanding each other in the least—when one asked for a stone the other understood him to want cement (*Qui dermandoit le pierre chins entendoit chiment*).†

On the other hand the pupil could not regard without real grief, " the baron Abraham about to sacrifice his son, whom the Angel of the Lord took in his arms and carried up to Heaven amongst the Innocents."‡ Beyond these he was only pleased with great battles and great miracles. He followed with interest Joshua, the Judges, and the Kings, when they valiantly pursued and put to flight all the horrible Canaanitish people by whom they were surrounded. " Why was I not there ? " he cried, quivering with excitement.

---

* Honoré d'Auteur : "De Imagine Mundi."
† Bastars de Buillon.
‡ Amis et Amiles.

But there were three miracles which included for him the whole history of the Old Testament; these three miracles, which in the Middle Ages enjoyed so great popularity—an incomparable popularity, which extends back even to the epoch of the Catacombs—were—

(1.) Daniel in the Lions' Den.
(2.) Jonah in the Whale's belly.
(3.) The Three Children in the Fiery Furnace.

Thence, in one bound, our young pupil hurried to the time of the Saviour, casting a longing look, as he passed, at Judas Maccabeus, who had so many claims to enter into the *corps d'élite* which was called—or was to be called—the Nine Champions ("Les neuf preux"). But we find the student contemplating the Star of Bethlehem and the Holy Child born of a pure Virgin. He was acquainted with the life of the Saviour better than with the incidents in the life of his own father; but in it there were also certain occurrences which had more attraction for him and which he liked better than others, and which dwelt more vividly in his memory.

Merely mentioning in this connection the Marriage Feast at Cana, which always pleased him (and in which he transformed the host of the Evangelist, the *Architriclinus* into Saint Architriclinus), the chief incidents which appealed to him were the Raising of Lazarus; the repentance of Mary Magdalene, who washed His feet with her tears and wiped them with her hair; and the miraculous conversion of that Longin who was blind. He could read and relate the incidents of the Passion, weeping copiously over them; the terrible Crucifixion inflicted by Marcus and Jonatas,* the crown of thorns, and the interment in the tomb (which the hatred race of Saracens had so long held in possession, to the shame of the Christian Race); the "descent into hell," the resurrection the third day and the ascent into the Heavens, where are no iniquitous judges, nor wicked barons; no cowards nor traitors.

Such is the Scripture History studied by the young Feudal Baron. He knows neither much less nor much more; and, to tell

* These two names were chosen to represent the two nations that were responsible or our Saviour's death: Marcus referring to the Romans, and Jonatas to the Jews.

the truth, mingles with it many ridiculous legends borrowed from apocryphal gospels, and I know not what puerile and silly super-stitions. But, when all has been said, we have shown the exact extent of his knowledge; for we have been careful to search principally the volumes of the " Chansons de geste," the old poetry, which lay upon his father's table, which was popular, and which formed an Encyclopædia within his reach.

The painted and stained-glass windows, work of the clergy, had a more erudite tone about them, and were not always clear to the youthful noble. The tapestries and the pictures held a middle place between the epic poems and the stained windows; and it is upon them that we would fix the attention of our readers.

X.

Of profane history our youthful baron is almost entirely ignorant, and he has some difficulty in understanding the pictures which decorate the squares and streets of his native town. Three episodes, three names, sum up in his mind the whole history of humanity before the Christian Era, outside the true peoples of Scripture—Troy, Alexander, Cæsar.

The rest is night; the rest is nothing.

The history of Troy seems to him scarcely more than a chivalrous episode, and he pictures the Greeks and Trojans simply as knights, like knights of his own time, helmeted, arrayed in armour, lance in hand. No idea of local colour has ever entered his head, and the fair Helen, in his imagination, resembles a young *châtelaine* of a neighbouring castle. The same long, fair tresses, the same high colour, the same coquettish manner and appearance, of which the youth, fortunately for himself, does not take any particular notice.

To speak frankly, he prefers Hector to Achilles, and, for my part, I congratulate him on his choice; that taste for the vanquished is a Christian trait, and I should not be surprised one day to see him admit Hector, instead of his conqueror, amongst the " Nine Champions." The sympathy which our future knight professes for the Trojans is so much the more surprising, inasmuch as he quite seriously considers France as a sort of colony of " Troy the Great," and that strange legend is in circulation in his neighbourhood.

But the glamour of old Homeric fictions, although distorted by twenty unintelligent copyists, is sufficient to captivate him for a long while. Achilles, the Warrior; the beautiful Helen, "*qui tant fist à prisier*," whom Paris "*embla à Menelaus*," and whom "*Menelaus conquist puis a l'acier*," "*Quant chil de Troie furent terit essillie*;" old Priam with "*la barbe chenue*;" and the ten years' siege, during which 870,000 Greeks and 680,000 Trojans were slain,—all these descriptions carry the imagination of our young pupil into dreamland and to the ideal.

On the day upon which the warriors showed to young Alexander the pictures in his tent which represented the taking of Troy: "It is thus," said the son of Philip, "that I will treat the kingdom of Persia." Our youthful warrior is less ambitious, and when the same history of the fall of Ilion is presented to him, he contents himself with saying to himself, "I would rather resemble Hector."

More popular still is the history of Alexander, which only reached the readers of the Twelfth Century with all the legendary embellishment of the Pseudo-Callisthenes, overlaid with ridiculous fictions and ornament in very bad taste. This history of Alexander would almost appear to have been a veritable magnet to which were successively attracted by the simple force of circumstances, all the myths, superstitions, and fables of antiquity. Not Cæsar himself—no, not even Cæsar—has been a magnet so powerful! and he has not given such a stimulus to the oriental imagination.

Even had this marvellous history not been represented on popular tapestries and in the street decorations we have mentioned, our youth would certainly have become acquainted with it from other sources. However, he had learnt it; he knew by heart this marvellous legend, and could repeat it throughout. He knew all about the youthful days of Alexander, and how he conquered Bucifal:—

> " Monet fu liés Alixandres quant il vit le ceval
> Qui vers lui s'umelie et ne li fit nul mal."

Our Feudal Youth often compared the education which Aristotle of Athens gave the young prince with that which he himself received in France. He saw the son of Philip triumph over a Grecian prince, whom he called Nicholas; saw him create twelve peers, all like Charlemagne; saw him invest Athens; accept proudly the defiance of King Darius; initiate the great war by the famous advance through the defiles of Cilicia to Issus; saw him lay siege to Tyre; defeat the Persians in the great battle of Pylos; punish mercifully the miserable wretches who "*Daire lor signor lige ont mort en traison;*" saw him descend to the bottom of the sea in "*un moult riche tonnel qui fu de voirre blanc;*" sail to India under the guidance of king Porus, who had been his mortal enemy, and reach with him the famous pillars of Hercules; saw how he escaped from the Sirens, and from twenty other enchantments not less dangerous, and not less astonishing; how he took the miraculous bath which all knights take at the fountain which springs from the River of Paradise; saw him stop before the prophetic trees, interrogate them concerning his destiny, and learn from them that he would die in one year and one month; saw him resume the war, and march, after many successive victories, to Babylon; saw him bring into subjection the country of the Amazons, where there were only women, and whose Queen, Amabel, came to do homage at the head of a thousand virgins—"*laissant dehors la crine qui peut bloie.*" Our pupil beheld all this, and then saw the hero die, poisoned by the felon Antipater, lamented by the entire world, and having but one regret, that he had not time to conquer France—the head of the world—and Paris, which it had created its capital.

So lived, so died, Alexander; and it was in this form that our pupil loved to relate the marvellous history, which, for him, was more amusing, more varied, and much more sparkling and interesting than any fairy tales.

We must state, or rather repeat, that Cæsar, more modern, and throughout less legendary than the son of Philip, did not stand out so clearly in the Middle Ages as did Alexander. He did not appear to our ancestors with the same halo, with the same star in his forehead. They were reduced, to do him honour, to translate the *Pharsales* into verse, and these verses were very mediocre.

Our young baron himself was really too intelligent to accept as correct the bungling statements of the wicked author of *Auberon*, who stupidly makes Julius Cæsar the happy son of Brunehant, the happy husband of the Fairy Morgue, the happy father of the illustrious dwarf, who was the friend of Huon of Bordeaux. Although represented on the tapestries, these fables irritated him, and two ideas perturbed his mind—that Cæsar had been one day master of the world, and that his murderers—a strange thing—had been the ancestors of Ganelon. How could he reconcile these ideas with each other ? He knew nothing of the facts himself, and we must here respect the candour of his ignorance.

France ! Here is France, and the heart of our future knight beats more quickly in spite of himself, when he finds himself before the popular pictures which are devoted to the history of his country. Greece and Rome have disappeared. France, that he loves, remains. Do not question this love, profound and sincere ; do not demand the form which it had assumed in 1789—that would be neither scientific nor reasonable. He loved a France which was composed of fifty of our Departments, which had thirty others— those in the south—as tributaries. The limits were rather vague, but the affection was precise enough. With it he held a thousand curious errors, which have met with a strange fortune in the world. Where could have arisen the idea that our race was descended from the Trojans ? And to whom do we owe the first conception of such a strange idea ? From Fredegaire, past the author of *Gesta regium*, past Paul Diacre, Aimoin, Sigebert de Gembloux, and Vincent de Beauvais, it was accepted by the clergy, and has scarcely made way amongst the ignorant, nobles or others.

Besides, the legend is of the most childish description, and takes liberties with history which cause one to smile. The good Philip Mouskes, following twenty other writers, tells the tale with an artlessness which loses none of its effect. He says :—

"When the Trojans had been obliged to fly from their burning city some of the fugitives took refuge in Pannonia, which is now-a-days known as Hungary, where they built a city which they called Sicamber."

So much for Sicamber ; but it is also a very curious circumstance that we are suddenly transported to the epoch of Valentinian the First. This emperor, threatened by the Alains, threw himself into the arms of the Trojans, and forgave them their tribute for a period of ten years.

The Sicambrians came to his assistance, but there was no necessity after these ten years to claim any tribute whatever from them. They determined to be independent, and in this laudable endeavour conquered the whole of Gaul. Upon that died Antenor—who, we should have thought, had died long before—and it is a fortunate circumstance that we are enabled to find a son of Priam, Marcomirus, who was the first King of " Gaille." His son was Pharamond, and the rest is plain enough. What history! And how beautiful is truth!

These Trojan " origines " were not very popular, and the youthful baron only became acquainted with them through the statements of his clerical tutors or through some *jongleur* more learned than his fellows. The great incursions of the Barbarians, left on his mind a deeper impression; he knew that there had been a very solemn hour in our history—one terrible hour when the Vandres nearly nipped France in the bud. Now the Vandres, in his estimation, were not only the Vandals of the year 406, but also all the German and Finnish tribes. He did not distinguish them very clearly from the Saracens, and attributed the honour of their defeat to a Charles Martel, whom he was inclined to mix up with Charlemagne: and so on.

Of the illustrious Clovis, to whom we are indebted for the first real attempt to solidify our national unity—of that grand soldier and politician he scarcely knew the name.

" He was," he used to say, " a Saracen, who for twenty-six years persecuted the Christians, hanging or quartering them. But God loved him so much that he caused him to be baptised at Saint Denis, and since then, he has been more than ever valiant and celebrated in poetry."

Such was the whole history of the first King of France who became a Christian.

From Clovis our scholar makes one leap down to Charlemagne, and for him the whole history of France is centred in the " monarch with the florid beard." The son of Pepin is followed in imagination from his cradle to his grave, with an attention begotten of admiration and affection. He contemplates, with an almost educated

enthusiasm, the series of paintings which the popular artists had
devoted to him.

A medallion first showed him the youthful Charles in pagan
Spain, where he had taken refuge under the name of Mainet, in
order to escape the traitors who had usurped his father's throne.
The future emperor soon ascertains from what stock he has sprung,
and offers to a beautiful Saracen maiden, the lovely Galien, the
charming first-fruits of his coming glory.

A second picture represents him in Rome, into which he has
triumphantly reconducted the Pope with the powerful aid of the
Dane Ogier; a third painting introduces us to the battle-field of
Aspremont in Southern Italy, from which Charlemagne drove and
dispersed the invading Arabs, and where he was witness of the first
exploits of his nephew Roland. The three following scenes represent the grand struggles of the King of France against his revolted
vassals—against Girard de Viane whom our painter has unfortunately confused with Girard de Roussillon, against Ogier the Dane,
and against the four sons of Aymon.

Then again we perceive the great emperor in Jerusalem, where he
is represented kissing the Holy Sepulchre and bathing it with his
tears; and at Constantinople, whence he carries home the relics of
the Passion. Afterwards the whole of the incidents of the war in
Spain are unfolded to the eyes of our typical pupil, as to our own,
in a series of original illustrations strongly accentuated, which
terminate with the gigantic figure of Roland, dying hard by the
corpses of eleven other peers on a hill from which Spain can be
seen.

There remains for us now only to view in our mind's eyes, or
with our bodily vision, the horrible, the interminable war of
Charles against the Saxons and their King Guitechin: but the
closing years of such a splendid life have not, alas! the victorious
character of the former decades. Charles, ere he died, sadly placed
the golden crown on the head of a weak and unstable successor,
who was surrounded by traitors and succumbed to their machinations.

Nevertheless Providence did not permit such crime to triumph,
and sent to Louis the illustrious liberator of Christianity and
France called William, "au fier bras," or William of Orange: a

hero comparable to Charles himself, who, after having punished the traitors and raised up the throne of the new emperor, was beaten by the Pagan hordes at Aliscans, and finally triumphed over the accursed race in a subsequent engagement fought on the same field, the memory of which has filled the Middle Ages with its glories.

After Aliscans, our future knight knows nothing of our history. He loses himself amongst all our Charleses and Louises, and arrives without transition at the council at which the Frst Crusade was preached by the "Apostle of Rome." The leap is prodigious, but the youth has no doubt it is all right.

There! we are now acquainted with all his knowledge. It must, however, be stated in conclusion that this is the maximum of the instruction given or absorbed, and all the youthful nobles were not so conversant with all the subjects of which we have attributed a knowledge to our typical pupil.

We do not wish to exaggerate in anything.

XI.

The education and training of the body were, in fact, held most in esteem by these military-minded and rude generations, and it would be wrong to exaggerate the importance of these practices.

From the age of seven to fifteen, the youth was particularly instructed in fencing and hunting, and we need here only refer to horsemanship, of which even before that age the child had mastered the rudiments. About this time he began to live familiarly, I had almost written fraternally, with his horse, and did nothing without his companionship.

Fencing, however, cost the youthful aspirant more trouble, and was sometimes quite a business. If good fencing-masters could not be procured in the country, the youth was sent away to the residence of some more accomplished knight.

"Remember," his friends would say, "that some day you will be too happy to possess such science and skill, and your enemies, (for you will have enemies,) will know something about it."

There were as many kinds of fencing as there were arms : fencing with the sword, lance-practice, and single stick. It was to this last-mentioned exercise that Aubrey the Burgundian was one day challenged, and which he accepted with very great repugnance. Fencing was generally the chief amusement, the favourite pastime of young people : while the elders played gravely at backgammon or chess, more probably the bachelors after dinner would amuse themselves in fencing or in leaping in the field. Do we not remember the delightful description given by the author of *Roland ?*

" Under a pine-tree near a briar is a massive gold chair. In it is seated the king who holds sweet France. His form is handsome as his features. Fifteen thousand knights of fair France are seated around him on the greensward. The oldest are playing chess, the youths are fencing."

It is not difficult to reproduce this scene which took place in a meadow one lovely day before the entire court, ere the arrival of the infidel messengers. But it must be added that the sight was not always so pleasing, and nothing could be more dangerous than these encounters at times, nothing more fatal than these factitious duels in their results. The young men were hot-blooded and very quickly quarrelled : these quarrels led to jealousies and blows. After amusing themselves they killed each other !

One of the principal peripetia of the wild romance of *Raoul de Cambrai*, is just the death of the two sons of Hernaut de Douai, who were killed on Easter Sunday after a fencing-bout. What evil resulted from this murder, against which the poet does not sufficiently inveigh ! What blood was shed ! What crimes committed !

The chase presented less danger with greater attractions. He cannot know the society of the middle ages who is not acquainted with the passionate pleasure which our ancestors had for the chase. After war it was their passion, their life. Those castles of the Twelfth Century, notwithstanding the pleasing aspect which ingenious painters have bestowed on them, those great heavy *châteaux* were gloomy dwelling-places, and their inhabitants, whenever they could, sought the open air. Covered with forests which the lieges were in no hurry to clear, and in which great wild boars and magnificent stags roamed freely,—France was specially suited to the sporting tastes of our barons: but as a result of this, the chase became a veritable science, very complicated, and a very serious business for which a long apprenticeship was absolutely necessary. It was a business which the youthful noble learnt between his seventh and fourteenth years, and we will glance at the working of it.

The youths, as we have just said, commenced to learn the elements of the chase at the age of seven, and for their instruction bows and arrows of a size and strength suitable to such young hunters were made. There were instructors, professors of the chase. The course of study naturally divided itself into two parts, Venery on the one part and Falconry on the other. The latter formed quite a science of itself, very extensive in its ramifications, very abstruse: and the four principal lessons in which may be said to have borne these significant titles—

(1.) How to fly the birds.
(2.) How to feed the birds.
(3.) How to call the birds.
(4.) How to hold the birds.

It will therefore be understood that a considerable time would elapse before the pupil would be able to really profit by the lessons of his master, and ere he could exclaim proudly with the youthful Huon de Bordeaux—

"I know how to *mew* the hawks, I can hunt the wild boar and stag: I know how to wind the horn when I have slain the animal, I know how to give the quarry to the hounds."

That is what one may term a good education, and we may say so in all seriousness. For we must not judge the manners of the Twelfth Century by our own, and there is no worse historian than he who compares and refers everything to the circumstances of the epoch in which he is living.

Let us rather transport ourselves in imagination into one of those old forests which existed in the neighbourhood of the *châteaux:* in such woods as this our young noble passed two-thirds of his life, like a rough well-made fellow who breathes the fresh air simply and solely like a countryman, but is not idyllic. What he sees, what he seeks in the depths of the forests are not the streams or the flowers, but the track of the wild boar or the stag in the damp ground or in the light grass. He is a realist, but a true one. These will be the occupations and passions of his whole life, with the addition of war for which the chase is merely an apprenticeship. What was Ganelon's reproach to Roland, to the greatest of our legendary knights? It was for passing a whole day in the pursuit of a hare or a brace of plover! And when one of our ancient poets wished to eulogise the greatest of our historic knights—Godfrey de Bouillon, of whom no one can speak without feeling his heart beat the faster, "He would fight the infidel rather than possess pure gold and silver money, rather than amuse himself hunting or in flying the hawks." What, rather than fly the falcons? This is saying a great deal in a few words!

So, as we have stated, the youthful baron was accustomed to live in the woods, in the midst of the forest occupied by the game he was learning to know and to hunt. On his return to the castle he would proceed to visit his harriers, or the hawks in his father's mews, "*Faucons sur perche avez, et vair et gris.*" Those who had such as these were counted rich. To possess "birds of chase" and furs was to be considered a millionnaire many times over. If one wished to make a handsome present—notably to a lady—one sent a falcon. Nothing could be more polite. Children had their own dogs and falcons, and attached a high value to them. Many charming episodes in our *Chansons* set forth in brilliant colours this "savage passion" of the youthful "noble," that love for the hound or for the hawk, stronger than any other love: for the young ladies were only relegated to the second rank: *longo proximo intervallo!*

Vivien was the son of Garni d'Anseüne: the grandson of Amieri de Narbonne, and the nephew of the great William of Orange. But the poor Vivien, alas! was as a child handed over and delivered to the Saracens in order to preserve his father's life, and the King Gormond, a Danish pirate, one day took possession of him, and sold him for a hundred marks to the wife of a merchant named Godfrey. This woman passed him off as her son, and attempted to give him a good education to fit him for a tradesman and a merchant.

But the old blood was in his veins—the old blood was there—

the vocation was there, and the son, the grandson, the nephew of chivalrous heroes, Vivien, had only the tastes and appetites of the knight. The merchant said to him—

"I am about to teach you how to buy and sell!"

"No," replied the youth, who was eight years old. "I do not want anything but a horse, two hounds, and a hawk!"

He was so very anxious to possess them, and so determined, that on one occasion, when intrusted by the merchant with some negotiation in business, one fine morning he exchanged one hundred bales of merchandise for the much desired hounds and hawk. We need scarcely ask whether he was not beaten, but the blows could effect nothing, and with a simplicity worthy of a better cause, the child said to his patron who had beaten him—

"I assure you, my father, that these harriers are excellent animals!" That was the feudal youth all over!

The youthful Hervis of Metz bore a striking resemblance to Vivien, and they vainly endeavoured to make him a merchant. His blood revolted at it, his nobility revealed itself to him. His employers conceived the unfortunate idea of sending Hervis to the fair of Provins, and there he purchased for three thousand marks (paid on the nail, if you please), a charger, a falcon, and a harrier. They were expensive. Ah, how the barons of the twelfth and thirteenth centuries laughed as they listened to these recitals of incidents which were so entirely in conformity with their most cherished habits and tastes!

This was the comic side of the question; but the love of the youths for the chase and for the animals they used to hunt, gave rise to narratives otherwise dramatic. The great duel between Oliver and Roland, that never-to-be-forgotten encounter under the walls of Vienna, which has had the honour to tempt the pen of Victor Hugo to a description—do you know what the cause of that celebrated duel was? A hawk! It happened as follows:—

One morning Roland came forth from the French camp, falcon on wrist, and perceived a mallard flying over Vienna. The young knight unhooded, and let fly his hawk, killed two mallards and two ducks, but by chance he lost his hawk in an orchard. Oliver hurried thither and called the bird to him, which, being well trained, came down and perched upon his left arm.

Roland had seen the whole affair and got into a terrible rage.

" Who are you ? " he shouted to Oliver.

" I am called Oliver de Gennes," he replied, " and I am the son of Count Renier. My uncle is Girard the Proud, whom Charles banished from Vienna by great treachery and treason. And whom do you call yourself ? "

" My friend," replied the other, " they call me Roland, and I am the nephew of Charles, the mighty Emperor. I will cause your uncle Girard to be hanged. Meanwhile I will trouble you for my hawk."

The young men then proceeded to vilify and to threaten each other. The scene was of the most primitive order, and one must be very blind not to perceive the plain analogies between this poetry and Homer's.

All youths of the period of which we are speaking were fond of the chase, but there were many of them who preferred falconry and others venery. The former " went in " for birds ; the latter for hounds. These different pursuits gave rise to interminable discussions in those peaceful intervals of leisure which the barons sometimes enjoyed in their castles, where life was not without monotony and where *ennui* was not always absent. Thus—

" Can anyone," a lover of falconry would say—" Can anyone imagine anything more beautiful than a properly dressed falcon ? It is even a delightful pleasure to take it from its nest when young. It is true that such an undertaking is not without danger, and that one must climb the trees to catch the young hawks, in pursuit of which many a brave man has broken his neck. But how delightful it is when the birds are captured and when we begin to educate them in their *demure*, when we sew the pupils, when we trim and point the claws, when we attach the jesses and the bells to their feet. And how delightful is the noise of their *campanelle*. I prefer the jingle of their bells to the most beautiful songs of the troubadours.

" But I must say I would rather have the hawks in their wild state, and their ' setting up ' is the most picturesque and most lively. One can imagine nothing more droll than the sack, the *maileolet* in which the bird is enclosed in order to ' doctor its eyes ' or to trim its claws. And what sight more pleasing than to see it sit on its perch or on a *sedile* on which the hawks hold themselves so upright and motionless.

" Still the joy which exceeds in joyfulness all mundane delights, is when on some fine September morning under a blue sky, and in the fresh air, the cavalcade quits the *château,* the ladies riding alongside their knights, the huntsmen and their wives carrying on their leather gloves the beautiful hawks, *monteniers* of four *mues ;* and all this little army of horsemen and horsewomen hurrying gaily forward in pursuit of the crane, the heron, the mallard, and the lapwing.

" The pages and the youths are not in the first flight. They let fly and cast off their hawks at the first game they can perceive : the bird darts off, makes her point, darts down upon her quarry, plunges her talons in its flesh, and couches on her prey until the arrival of the hunter, who takes the bird up and replaces her on his wrist.

" Such enjoyment as this is far superior to all your great hounds and their endless baying and barking, and your ignorant huntsmen with absurd and ill-justified pretentions. Venery is but a habit : Falconry is an art."

These are the arguments of the falconer, and before inditing the reply of the huntsman, we will give our young readers some few particulars concerning the training of the hawks for the chase. Considerable skill and science were necessary in this training of the birds—now almost a lost art. We will now proceed to give our readers an idea of an elementary course of the falconry of the twelfth and thirteenth centuries. There is an excellent and celebrated treatise, *De arte Venandi* of the Emperor Frederic the Second, in which the details are very clearly given, and to which we are partly indebted for our explanation, only putting the information in a more simple style.

I.—THE VARIOUS SPECIES OF BIRDS FOR HAWKING.

These are the *Gerfalcon,* the *Sacre,* the *Pilgrim* (*pélerin*) or *passager,* the *Gentil* and the *Lanier.*

(a) The *Gerfalcon* is of all the superior and of the best flight ; it also is the best proportioned. Its plumage is grey or white, but the white variety is the most valuable and sought after.

(*b*) The *Sacre* has a rounded head, the beak shorter, the neck more delicate, the feathers longer, the claws shorter than the *Gerfalcon.*

(*c*) The *Pélerin* or *passager* ought to have the *cere* (or skin of the beak) and the feet, of a greenish hue.

(*d*) The *Gentil* falcon is only a variety of the *Pélerin ;* it has a smaller head : the feet are also smaller, and the colouring less brilliant.

(*e*) The *Lanier* is inferior to the *Gentil,* and has a more slender neck, the body long and fleshy, the feet blue, short and thick.

Every species of hawk emigrates every year in order to pursue the migratory birds upon which it preys. The *Pélerins* are taken in October, and the *Gentil* falcons in the months of June and September.

A falcon taken from its nest in the wild state is called a *ramage* falcon : those taken from the nest very young, are termed *niais* hawks. The merlins, goshawks, sparrow hawks and gerfalcons are termed wrist-birds (*oiseaux de poing*).

We now pass on to the—

II.—NIAIS FALCON, AND ITS EDUCATION.

It is by no means an easy task to capture the young falcons in the nest, which is situated at the top of a high tree, or on the summit of a rock. As soon as the young birds have been captured it is necessary to protect them with the greatest care from cold, rain and hail. For this purpose the master of the hawks, places them in a *demure* which ought to be elevated in the air, and in these "cotes," furnished with a pan in which the young falcons can have their bath. It is not necessary that the *demure* should be placed very near a wood, which might prove too attractive to the young falcons.

III.—CONCERNING THE MUE.   (THE CAGE.)

The young hawks, when taken from the nest and carried away from the parent-birds, undergo the confinement of the *mue* with great difficulty. The birds are cleaned and purified and placed in the *mue* about the middle of April—say St. George's Day,—and the *mue* is of two kinds, " on the stone," or at " liberty," " *sur la pierre, soit en liberté.*" The *mue sur la pierre* is carried out in a room far removed from all disturbance, and in this apartment the falconer sleeps ; he takes the bird out, and is very careful with it.

The *mue en liberté*, is managed without the assistance of the falconer, and is a much less costly plan. There are no really good falcons except those which have passed through the ordeal of the *mue*, the falcons and the gos-hawks, *muiers.* The best are those " *de quartre mues.*"

IV.—CONCERNING THE FEEDING OF HAWKS.

When a falcon is taken from the nest, it is necessary to avoid choosing specimens of those birds which live on fish. In feeding the falcons, in default of the flesh of birds, that of quadrupeds is used, preference being always given to wild over domesticated animals. The flesh, which should be a portion of a not too young, nor yet an old bird, or other animal, should be given to the hawks bare, and stripped of all the nerves and tendons still warm, or artificially warmed. It should be cut up upon a wooden table.

If flesh cannot be procured, fresh or re-made cheese should be substituted for it—stale cheese never ; or, failing cheese, hens' eggs beaten up and cooked in milk.

V.—THE TAMING OF THE HAWK.

To tame a bird of prey is to train him, and there are two methods of doing this, according to whether the bird is a *niais* or a *ramage* falcon. If the former, it is deprived of its liberty as soon as it is old enough to fly. In its *demure* only one opening is left unclosed; this is a small door called the *treillette* or *jaiole*, and it is only after four days that, at night time, the falconer proceeds to the operations of the *cilieüre* and the *rebouchage* which we refer to again farther on.

If the falcon is a wild bird it is enclosed in a *maillolet*, that is to say a kind of small sack of linen, which fits very tightly, and from which only the head and the extremity of the tail of the bird protrude. It is in this *maillolet* or shroud, that the *ramage* undergoes all the operations of the *cilieüre* and the *rebouchage*, while the *nïais* submits to them in the *demure*.

The first important operation of the taming business is really the *cilieüre*, which consists in sewing the eye-balls of the falcon to *seel* it. Then comes the *rebouchage*, which consists in clipping the bird's claws. After that the *jesses* are put on. That is to say, straps, which ought to be placed sufficiently loose around the feet, to do no harm to the bird. At the other extremity of a *jess*, which is very thin, are two meshes of a hauberk, or two rings fastened together, called *tournet* which unite the *jess* to the tether.

This tether ties the falcon to his perch. Outside these fetters is fixed on the foot of the falcon, a little above the *jess* a little silver bell, called a *note* or *campanelle* which serves to recall the bird when it strays away. To rest the falcon it is placed on the high perch or on the *sedile*. The high perch is elevated above the ground, about on a level with the eyes of a man of ordinary height. The *sedile* is a cone of wood supported by an iron stem, which is fastened into the ground. To the iron rod is fixed a wooden or iron ring which holds the tether.

The falconer *unseels* the hawk by degrees and with the very greatest precautions, so as to accustom his charge by degrees to the light. The falconer accustoms himself to carry the bird on foot or on horseback. The upper portion of the arm (in some countries only the right arm is permitted to be used for this purpose) should be held down parallel with the body, with which, however, it should not be in contact; the forearm is held at a right angle.

Care must be taken not to hold the hawk too near the face, as the bird will be alarmed, and it ought to be held with its chest to the wind. No falconer is any use if he become intoxicated frequently, as his hand will shake, and he will not carry the falcons properly. The hawks are taken out in the morning, in preference when a light rain is falling, and, with a view to excite them, they are given what are termed the *tiroirs*—one consisting of some morsels of fresh meat, the other of a bone or muscle covered with feathers.

After this the hawk is trained to obey the voice of the falconer, his whistle, and even his gestures. To accustom it to throw itself upon its prey, living, the *lure* is employed. This lure consists of the image of a bird made in red cloth, fitted with the wings of a partridge or the skin of a hare.

This lure is attached to a lasso of a greater or less length, which the falconer twirls around him with considerable rapidity. The training or taming of which we have been speaking, is carried on without *chapel* (*sans chapel*), but there is another method which the Emperor Frederic boasts of having imported from the East, and of which he perfected the mechanism. This is the *adebo-nairissement avec chapel* (hood).

The *chapel* of the falcon is of supple leather, and takes the form of the bird's head, which it closely envelopes as far as the neck, only leaving the beak and nostrils free. The bird is not inducted into the *chapel* until the other operations and attachments have been performed—the trimming of the claws, &c. The *chapel* ought to be put on in a dark room with very great precautions The strap of the *chapel* passes between the wing and the tail, and is held by the falconer between his third and fourth fingers.

These are the general principles of the art of falconry. The rest of the management will depend upon the dexterity and tact of the individual falconer, and the manner in which he trains the birds to strike their quarry and to return to him. The study is by no means an easy one, but it will repay the time and patience expended on it if hawking should ever be revived.

We will now resume our defence of hunting as set forth by its votary, who has taken our youthful baron as umpire between the two enthusiasts for venery and falconry.

"One may easily perceive," replies the lover of the chase, "that you have not been accustomed to associate with intelligent animals like my hounds and harriers. The education of one good blood-hound, I can tell you, requires as much care as do all your falcons, and at least the beast is fond of you, and reciprocates your caresses. Do you tell me of your going out hunting, indeed? The really animated and delightful scene is on a hunting morning when we go forth to chase the stag or the wild boar. There is the pack baying round you with the beaters, and the attendants with the relays. The favourite hound is encouraged by name, 'Eh, Brochart, hie away, lad.' Then the hounds are uncoupled and set upon the

scent of the game. On, on! Then the hunt plunges into the
wood, and reposes there in the middle of the day in the leafy
glades beneath the overhanging trees.

"Then after a while the baying of the hounds again arises, they
are again on the scent, they bark, they bay, they have reached the
boar, they attack him! The enormous beast defends himself
stoutly and fiercely: he places himself against a tree and rolls over
and disembowels ten of the boar-hounds. Blood flows, not only
that of the dogs: the boar's blood ensanguines the sward, and the
noble blood of the huntsman mingles with it. The hounds
redouble their cries and their efforts to avenge their master. The
animal is at length overcome; pierced with twenty spears he is
nailed to the ground; dead!

"There! That is much more exciting than your petty pursuits
of lapwings and partridges, your herons and your cranes. This
chase resembles war much more than your hawking, and is much
more enjoyable! And, for my part, I only hope that after my
death people will say of me as they said of that great hunter,
Begon de Belin—'*Gentis hons fu, moult l'amoient si chien.*'"

Such were the opinions of the falconer and the huntsman; such
were the controversies which our future knight heard every day,
and in which he was compelled to take an active part. Sometimes
they even put him in the *demure,* so as to compel him to decide
once for all whether he preferred Venery or Falconry. When his
mother was present the youth preferred Falconry, because his
mother did not disdain to hunt with the hawks, and he was pleased
with it. But at the bottom of his heart he was still of the same
opinion as his father, and preferred hunting with the hounds.

Almost every morning he calls *Brochart,* and sets off to hunt.
On wet days he plays chess, and works hard at the game so as to
become a proficient. By these means he completes his education.

Chess, moreover, is a serious game; and frivolous people prefer
dice. But our youth is not frivolous, and often asks his father
"When shall I be out of leading strings?"

Alas, these periods of youth are just the same as all others, and
finish too soon!

CHAPTER VI.

THE YOUTH OF THE BARON.

I.

ALL that could be learnt in the paternal castle the youth has learnt. He is now, we will suppose, twelve years old. Already, he is envious of those who go to seek honour in foreign lands (*qui vont querre honor en estrange contrée*). He feels himself cooped up at home, and becomes very restless and weary. This is the time for him to throw himself into the full tide of the feudal world-current, far from his own people, in the houses of strangers —the time for him to learn manliness and the rough side of life.

But before becoming knights themselves the youthful nobles were attached to other knights. The lads quitted the paternal mansion or castle, and went far afield, often for many, many years to follow a course of Chivalry at the *château* of a master more severe and more illustrious than their own parents. This new teacher of the future knight was very often some powerful baron ; it might be the " seigneur suzerain," it was sometimes the king himself.

Monarchs did not consider this education as a charge, but as a privilege to which they attached great value. There are certain of our romances which are exclusively anti-feudal, and which attribute to the emperor alone the power of conferring the honours of Chivalry : these are historic texts in which one may read how the prince claimed as a right this education of the youthful nobles in his palace.

It is at any rate certain that royal personages by these means affirmed their supremacy over all other seigneurs, created devoted partisans, and formed the nucleus of an excellent army. We need scarcely add that these youths embellished and animated the courts at which they resided, "*De leur beauté le palais resplendit.*"*

This custom was not confined to France. Schultz quotes German texts in support of the same conclusion: Sainte-Palaye says the same, and also as regards France in particular. The same custom obtained in Spain, "In regali curia nutrirenter."

As for the great barons they made a point in this as in other affairs, of imitating, and following the lead of, the king; and attracted to themselves the sons of the knights—their retainers. So each one had around him a school of Chivalry.

This education of the future knights was called nursing them (*nourrir*). "There goes one of my 'nurselings' (*un de mes nourris*)!" the baron would say, as he pointed out one of the youths who was domiciled in his *château*. This was the technical term. It was very significant.†

The more celebrated a baron was, the greater number of " nurselings " he had under his charge. When the author of " Raoul de Cambrai " wished to pass a eulogism upon his hero, he remarked that from Cambrai as far as Ponthieu there was not a baron who had not confided to his charge his son or his *nourri*, his cousin or his nephew.‡ It is true that sometimes the vassals hesitated to send away their children from them, and in " Jourdain de Blaives " the traitor Fromont is obliged to display very great firmness when he desires Renier to leave him the youthful Jourdain in order that he may prepare him in his course of Chivalry.

But the emperor on such occasions did not hesitate to give the most peremptory orders concerning the youths. Thus when Charles sent a mandate one day to Aimeri de Narbonne to cause to be sent to him his four elder sons at once, without delay, he said—

"They shall serve me six years. Then I will make them knights, and I will bestow upon them good fiefs."

No one thought of disputing the command; the young men were immediately despatched to the Court.

---

* "Nunius vero pater ejus fere ab omnibus castellæ militibus domicellus filios petit nutriendos."—*Rodrigo de Toledo.*

† The lads were in fact " nourished " at the residences of the kings or the barons who educated them.

‡ "Or n'a baron de ci que en Ponti—Ne li envoit son fil ou son nourri ; Ou son neveu on son germain cousin."—*Raoul de Cambrai*, b. 1, p. 21.

There is no doubt that the education and the "nourriture" of so many young people plunged the barons and the king into very great expenditure ; but they indemnified themselves by demanding from these youths real service near their persons. At a very early age they appointed them " squires," and we shall see later on that such an appointment was very far from being a sinecure. Then the *patrons* always considered it a fortunate thing to possess a

An episode in the youth of Roland.

numerous following, and paid for it. Now, this assemblage of youths was the exercising of a kind of patronage. It was the military and feudal patronage.

The period which we are endeavouring to present to our readers in many points of view was really very primitive and unsophisticated. Between the nurselings and those who brought them up there was very soon a distinct line drawn, and nothing was permitted to break through it. The youthful noble owed to his instructor a deep and unswerving devotion, and his respect for him invested it with a filial character. The master was really a second father. When Roland in the *Entrée de Spagne* received from his uncle the most sanguinary insult to which any knight could submit, when the emperor struck him a blow with his gauntlet in the face : the knight, insulted, bounded up under the affront, blushed and trembled with rage ; he rushed upon the king and was about to strike him : but suddenly he checked himself, his arm fell powerless to his side.

Now what was the cause of this sudden checking of his passion ; simply because he remembered that Charles had brought him up when a young lad !

Later on, at Roncesvalles, when the same Roland was on the point of rendering up his soul to the angels who were waiting to receive it, one of his latest thoughts—perhaps the most touching of all—was still for the instructor of his youth.

> " He lies there beneath the pine tree, brave Count Roland,
>   He recalls to his memory many things—
>   He remembers all the nations he has conquered,
>   He dwells upon fair France and the men of his race,
>   And upon Charlemagne, his lord, who had brought him up."

But there is again another poem in which the "nourriture" system occupies even a more important place, and this is *Raoul de Cambrai*, that "Song of Cannibalism," that epopœia in which blood flows in great streams, "bank full."

In this poem there are two personages of the first rank, who attract and retain the reader's observation. These are, on the one side, the gross and cruel Raoul, who, as we have already seen, set fire to the convent of Origni, and committed twenty other crimes as heinous ; on the other side, we have the good vassal Bernier who had in former days been raised to the rank of knight by Raoul.

Now amongst the nuns of Origni, Raoul had burned Bernier's mother. He had done more ; he had insulted his vassal twenty times, and finished by striking him a violent blow on the head. You may be astonished to read that Bernier made no reply to these insults by other insults, to these blows by other blows, and contented himself by quietly quitting the service of such a brutal master !

Why? you may ask, why did he display such mansuetude ? Because he had been "nourished" by him. This is the sentiment which animates the whole poem, and the expression of it may be termed even redundant. It is true that at the termination of the *Chanson*, the "nurseling," the former *nourri*, slays his liege lord in single combat, but only in self-defence *en larmoient sur son elme*.

Then how bitterly he repented! "I was mad to kill him! He nourished me and made me a knight!" Full of remorse, which continued to increase and not to diminish as time went on, Bernier determined to make honourable amends by undertaking a difficult and distant pilgrimage; he died by the dagger of the assassin, without having been able to forgive himself for having been compelled to kill Raoul, "who had nourished him."

In this episode one feels that many centuries of our history live and move. Is it not so? Many kindred circumstances and incidents might be quoted. But the above will suffice to illustrate the depth of the feudal respect and regard with which those who had been brought up by knights and barons regarded their former *patrons* and masters in Chivalry.

II.

Whether brought up in the court of some prince, or in the castle of some lord, or whether the youthful noble received his education in Chivalry at the paternal mansion, he was known by various names, in the various grades to which he attained, and it is necessary that we should acquaint our readers with the significance of these. He was first known as a page or *damoiseau*. But it is expedient, to clear the ground, that we should inquire whether the term "Bachelor" has the same signification, and if it, like the preceding terms, means an "aspirant for Chivalry."

It is certain that originally this word was somewhat ambiguous, as it is referred to a small rural proprietor, and later on, in the age of feudalism, meant the possessor or owner of a very small domicile or holding. The *baccalarius* was a poor but a free and ennobled individual. Briefly, he was a country gentleman, but one possessing only a *prædium*, and who in response to the *ban* enrolled himself alone, without any vassals, in the army of the king, or in the *ost* the contingent) of some lord.

The term, during the period of the Middle Ages, retained its primitive signification and implied, as often as not, a somewhat inferior condition, and in any case one verging upon poverty. This is its original meaning, one very happily embodied in the following quotation from the *Couronnement Looys*—

> " Bacheler estes, de tere avez mestier."

and from it the second meaning is naturally derived.*

[In Spain, we may add, the term *baccalarius* sometimes signified a person of low character and referred to the rustic who was by no means noble. Everywhere and always the *bachelors* are represented as inferior to the counts, viscounts, barons, and even to the *châtelains* or owners of castles. They are in particular opposed to the *milites vexilla ferentes* of Mathew Paris, to the *gaudentes insignibus vexilli* of Rigord ; to the bannerets in fact who possessed *plura et majora prædia;* and to whom they are plainly inferior. In an account dated 1340 A.D. we find the sum of thirty sous paid to a banneret, while only fifteen sous—or just half the sum—was paid to a "chevalier-bachelier." Bachelors were considered as a second-rate, and even as a third-rate kind of knights—*Milites secundi et tertii ordinis*, like the *minores milites* or *milites mediæ nobilitatis.* By some system of ridiculous derivation it has been stated that " bachelor " means bas-chevalier.]

By an extension of the sense, easy enough to understand, the same word was one day employed to indicate the youthful noble, who being unmarried,† and (his parents being still alive) possessing no *fief*, was compelled to surrender himself without a vassal to the *ost* of the feudal baron or of the reigning monarch.

We must note here that it was not the idea of *poverty* so much as *youth* that was in question, and that is how the term *bachelor* came to be synonymous with youthfulness. When in after years the notion of " chevalier-banneret " (knight-banneret) became more clearly defined, and in a manner more official, the bachelor was placed in contradistinction to the banneret; this opposition is

---

* The Baccalaria was a kind of rural dignity—*prædii rustici* species. There were Bacheleries of five or six manses. The proprietors, or possessors, of the baccalariæ were called Baccalarii.

† They were called *varlets d marier.*

clearly shown in the writings of the fourteenth and fifteenth centuries — Messire Fouque, chevalier-banneret — Messire Jehan Luce, chevalier-bachelier, &c., &c. The squires came naturally in the third place.

The knight-banneret was a knight who had already acquired his fiefs by inheritance or by marriage, and who proudly went forth to join the army of the king or of the baron with a number of vassals or retainers serving under his banner.* But still the idea of youth is implied, and a very excellent definition is given in *Foulques de Candie,*

" Joenes hom estes et encor bacheler ; "

and elsewhere—

" Bachelers fut et de joene jovent."†

This delightful youthfulness was, moreover, the military element upon which princes counted most in really difficult and trying circumstances. Did the pagan hordes threaten Christianity, did they menace Rome or France, it was to the bachelors that the appeal for assistance was addressed! Having neither wives nor children the bachelors feared death least, and were not so dearly attached to existence (*Qi n'orent ni femme ni enfants*). They formed a separate *corps d'armée*. They composed the " young guard."

In the great battle of Aspremont, Ogier comported himself splendidly at the head of a body of two thousand bachelors, and in that decisive battle against the Emir, in which Charlemagne avenged the disaster of Roncesvalles, and the death of his nephew Roland, the first line—the first corps d'armée—was composed of fifteen thousand bachelors of France—" *de nos meilheurs vaillanz.*" In the midst of these picked troops, and to encourage them to noble deeds, Rabel and Guinemant were conspicuous, the one with the sword, the other with the horn of Roland. Such relics could not have been confided to a braver and more devoted guard of honour.

[The second corps d'armée was also composed of fifteen thousand bachelors of the same race, and in the tenth *echelle* (or line) came the old knights, the barons of France. The distinction is very marked.]

---

* A bachelor could " by age " become a banneret.

† Bachelor in other old poems is used as synonymous with youth. See *Raoul de Cambrai*, &c.

In the wars of the feudal period it was still to the bachelors that the appeal was always addressed. When the Emperor bestowed upon Gibouin the fief of Cambrai, Gueri le Sor set forth against him and hurled at him a brutal defiance—calling upon him as a "recreant bachelor." When there was any adventure to be undertaken, any rash enterprise to be entered upon, some more than ordinary risk to be run, the bachelors, the youths, were called for. They had nothing to lose and everything to gain—Forward!

So we need only now inquire whether or not the bachelor was a knight? And in this question consists the most important problem which we propose to ourselves to solve.

Notwithstanding the authority of illustrious and learned men who have defined the bachelor as "a young gentleman who aspired to be a knight," and who held a position between the knight and the squire, I am of opinion that, with reference to our poems of Chivalry of the eleventh, twelfth, and thirteenth centuries, the bachelor must be regarded as a knight. A knight without fortune, without fief, a very youthful knight it is true, but still a knight.

Indeed the question need not have been put, and need not be discussed. It is settled by a hundred texts from our ancient poetry which leave it in no manner of doubt. When William Fièrebrace returned from hunting he was accompanied by forty bachelors "who were all newly-dubbed knights" (*chevaliers de novel adobé*). So says the author of *The Charroi de Nimes*, and the author of *Parise* is not less clear when he brings upon the scene a bachelor named Beuvon who had been recently created a knight.

In the poem *Renaus de Montauban* the same individuals are mentioned within the limits of a few verses as knights and bachelors, and from the context one can perceive very clearly that the two words have exactly the same signification and value. Aiol is described as having been for a long while a knight when he is spoken of as a bachelor. The bachelors in the *Chanson de Roland* fight with lance and sword, that is to say, with the same weapons as the old knights fought, and were nowhere placed in the second rank. It is thus in every instance, and the few texts which we could quote in favour of the opposite opinion only serve to bear testimony in favour of the youthfulness of the bachelors.

But, instead of multiplying such proofs, I prefer to relate a touching episode which I have borrowed from one of our most truly primitive poems, one of those which should have prevented Cervantes from writing his Don Quixote as he has written it.

The circumstances referred to are these. It was once more William who was in question, and on his return from the hunting party to which we have already referred. He came back surrounded by the sons of princes and counts *chasez:* the hounds bayed behind him, the falcons were seated upon the wrists of the satisfied huntsmen, and they thus made their noisy entry into Paris by the *Petit Pont.*

But William's nephew stopped him and put an end to all this enjoyment.

" You arrive very opportunely, good uncle," said he, " for the emperor has just made distributions among his barons of fiefs, towns and castles."

" And what has he given me ? " inquired William.

" Nothing," was the reply. " He has forgotten you, fair uncle, and me with you ! "

A flush of rage mounted to the features of William. He trembled with anger, and his glance was terrible to see.

" I will go," he said, " and have some conversation with your emperor ! "

He mounted the steps which led to the presence-chamber, and the loud echo of his footsteps was heard in the palace, as formidable as those of the Commandatore in Don Juan.

" 'Tis I," he exclaimed, " 'tis I ; " and he made as if to insult the poor emperor, who was trembling like a leaf.

We shall have an opportunity to depict elsewhere this historical event, but, nevertheless, it is necessary to note here the words of William, the utterance of that knight who had already rendered himself celebrated by so many exploits, and who was no longer a young man.

The son of Charlemagne said to him hesitatingly that, one day in after times, on the occasion of certain deaths which were supposed to be imminent, he would be presented with some extensive fief.

" Great Heaven ! " replied the Count, " what a long period of waiting we poor portionless bachelors are obliged to submit to. I have not even the means to feed my horse ! "

And a little later he repeated the same idea in different words—

"Great Heavens! What a time they keep waiting a ˙   ˙lor who is of my years!"

There is certainly in this speech an ironical meaning not difficult to seize: but the sense of the word bachelor ought to be no longer in doubt at all. The speech of William is worthy of a treatise to itself: it quite confirms our system.

Briefly, it is not correct to regard the bachelor as merely an aspirant for Chivalry like a page or a youth (*enfant*). The ground is now cleared.

III.

The term youth (*enfant*) always and invariably denoted the young man who had not as yet been inducted to the Order of Chivalry. The *enfances* of a hero, refers to the space of time— more or less long—which preceded his elevation to the knightly dignity, and the poems which are entitled *Les Enfances Ogier, Les Enfances Garni, Les Enfances Vivien* are devoted to singing the praises of youths who had not yet become knights; from the time of their birth until the day on which they receive the *accolade*, and the sword.

It would be easy to prove to demonstration the exactness of this interpretation. In the beautiful and antique *chanson* attributed to Raimbert de Paris, Ogier is called *enfant* up to the very moment of his being dubbed knight. In *Girars de Viane* and in all other romances we find the same exactness and the same justice in terms.

The period at which the *infancy* of a knight terminated is some-times represented by our poets as that at which he becomes a "new man," so to speak. In this light Aubri, the Burgundian, appears to us; in all his period of *infancy* he was a brutal, cynical, cruel personage, loving strife and bloodshed, and delighting in administering punishment unjustly.

But scarcely has he become a knight, when lo! he is trans-figured! and the poet is careful to tell us that:—

> " Sa legerie est tout remainsue
> Qui il avoit en s'enfance tenue ; "

that, in fact, he has corrected himself in manners and morals. It is hardly necessary to add that these conversions were not of long duration.

The authors of our old poems have not been the only persons who have adopted this meaning of the term—the Law has consecrated it. In the celebrated *Observances du royaume d'Aragon* there is a chapter entitled " Of the condition of the infant." He receives the name of *enfançon*, and his condition, regulated by the law, is l'enfançonnat (infancy). It was established as a principle that every knight could make an "infant" a knight, and the Feudal hierarchy was, in Aragon, composed of three degrees ; at the top of the ladder the *Richombres*, at the bottom the *Enfançons*, in the middle the *Knights*. Nothing can be clearer than this, and we see once more that our poets display as much precision as lawyers.

Damoiseau has the same significance as *Enfant,* but with some shades of difference which we must notice. The word *domnicellus* is only the diminutive of *dominus,* and the damoiseau was always the son of a more or less powerful baron.

In some countries the title was reserved exclusively for the sons of sovereign lords—kings ;—the term signifying "little lord " or *seigneuret.* In Béarn the aristocracy was divided into three principal groups, the *Barons,* the *Cavers* and the *Domengers.* The two latter deserve notice. They were knights.

But, as we shall see further on, one was not created a knight without being put to very considerable expense. In France and elsewhere all damoiseaux could not afford such sums as were deemed necessary, and they remained damoiseaux for a long while —or perhaps all their lives.

A synonym for damoiseau is *Valet.* The term valet means "little vassal " just as *damoiseau* means "little lord." It was applied to the youthful noble who had not yet been admitted into the Order of Chivalry, and who was being prepared to enter it. It is certain, however, that the word *valet* has never been like *damoiseau* reserved for the sons of kings, and its destiny has always been somewhat less elevated, but in any case during the twelfth and thirteenth centuries it never was used in an inferior or despicable sense.

" When well-born knights considered themselves honoured in

being called *vassals*, gentlemen who had not yet taken rank in Chivalry did not blush to be called, or to call themselves *vassalets!*" In truth, it was not until a very much later period that the term was derogatory or humiliating, and we may assign the fourteenth century as the period in which the decadence of the term first set in.

The word " page " has been more fortunate, and has achieved a contrary destiny. It was first used to designate a man of a low position, and almost a " cook's assistant,"* but subsequently attained the signification of a beautiful and almost etherial being of whom the librettists of our operas have made such wondrous use. The avowal is painful, and I am really sorry to displace this personage who plays such a prominent part in our lyric dramas ; but it must be confessed that before the time of the Valois one never thought of inflicting the name of page upon a damoiseau, upon an *enfant*, or upon a valet. In proportion as the valet descended, the page rose ! He has had his revenge !

On this question we may quote Fanchet. " The word *page*, till the time of Charles VI. and Charles VII. seems never to have been bestowed on any but low-class persons such as ' *garçons de pied* '— (messenger lads)."

Up to the present we have only had to do with the terms (*enfant, damoiseau*, or *valet*) which indicate the youthful noble as a platonic candidate for Chivalry. In the twelfth and thirteenth centuries, one word—a single word—"*Ecuyer*" (Squire) implied certain functions.

The Squire was the " enfant," the valet, the damoiseau, called upon to perform certain duties personal to the lord who appointed him. The duties had something of a domestic character. (We read of this little change of position first in *Guillaume Guiart*.)

The Squire is the *enfant*, the vassal, the damoiseau, employed (*occupé*).

We must now speak of these occupations, which were many, varied, and tiresome. So let us glance at the Squire for a moment.

* These were pages of the kitchens and pages of the stables (grooms' assistants), see *Ducange*, " Pagius."

IV.

The meaning of the word is not exactly happy or clear, and at any rate there was some doubt about it in the eleventh century. In the *Chanson de Roland* the squires cut a sorry figure beside the " garçons " of the army, and it would appear that the squires were regarded as the villeins or serfs who were charged with the lowest duties. When Charlemagne in tears made his first painful excursion over the battle-field of Roncesvalles on which reposed the dead bodies of so many heroes, he gave the most strict orders to Gebouin and to Otho, to Thibaut of Reims, and to Count Milon, to protect them.

" You shall guard this field, these valleys, and these mountains. Let the dead remain as they have fallen. But be careful that the lions and other wild animals do not molest them, any more than the squires and the lads (garçons) ! " He likened the squires to the wild beasts of prey, and to the scum of the army !

Decidedly, they were then people of very little account.

Certain quotations from writings of the period—the end of the eleventh and the beginning of the twelfth centuries, principally Norman and English records—assist us to trace the transformation of the original meaning, and appear to bring us into the society of young noblemen, who, under the formerly despised title, are attached to the persons of the knights. But there are still many points to be cleared up.

It was about the meeting-time of the eleventh and twelfth centuries, that, by degrees, was regulated the position of the young noble, charged, during his apprenticeship to Chivalry, with certain functions in the households of kings and barons. It was about that time that the noble squire, *armiger, scutifer, scutarius,* saw his duties defined and regulated.

As soon as the damoiseau arrived at the castle or mansion where he was to be brought up, he was made a squire. There was no delay in the transaction.

" Leave me your son," says (*in Jourdain de Blaives*) the traitor Fromont to the good Renier. " Leave me your son. I will arm him and clothe him until he can sit securely on his horse, and carry lance and sword."

Without an instant's hesitation, the lad was transformed into a squire, and nothing could be wiser than this immediate induction into the duties of his position. How long did this apprenticeship last? This is not an easy question to answer precisely by the light of extracts and texts. Five or seven years, rarely more, and often less.

As the squire was generally dubbed a knight between the fifteenth and one-and-twentieth years of his age, it is easy enough to arrive at the age of the squires, bearing in mind, that physical weakness scarcely ever permitted the lads to undertake the duties of squires before they were twelve years old. This extreme youthfulness was well fixed, so that the valets or lads should not find their conditions of servitude too rigorous. It would seem that it was desirable to accentuate their inferiority *vis à vis* with the knights in everything.

Thus, in public acts, their names did not appear till after the superscriptions of the militia.

They had no right to touch a sword. A sword is a holy weapon, and in the pommel are the bones of the saints; the sword is a reliquary!

Then the lance again, in the first severity of the military code, was interdicted to the squire, who was obliged to console himself by fighting with a javelin or a pole.

Even the helmet and the hauberk were forbidden to these youths, and it was with bare heads and without coats of mail that they encountered the enemy. But these hardships were subsequently modified, until the spurs only remained to accentuate the difference between the knight and the aspirant for knighthood.

It is scarcely necessary to add the poet's verses—

> " Que ne se doit un escuier
> Armer encontre un chevalier."

These lines from *Flore et Blancheflor*, are of a conciseness and clearness that leave nothing to be desired. In other words, the squire had no right as against the knight in the *duello*, nor in gage of battle. He was not his equal—his peer.

The reader will at once comprehend how such a state of inferiority might often have depressed our youthful nobles, and in those

days there was a saying in circulation, "Squires are envious."
But they were able to console themselves in repeating another
proverb, "The good squire makes a good knight. So wait and
hope."

At a period in which all children were but imperfectly educated,
one must not expect that our young squires were versed in all the
delicacies and sweets of life. They were not spoiled, and there is
a verse in "*Garin*" which describes them exactly, and which
might then have passed for an axiom. "*Li escuier se painent de
servir.*"

Poor lads! They certainly did not eat their white bread first,
and that is true literally: for they had to contrast the white bread
of the *château* and the convent, with the squire's bread, *panis
armigerorum*, in which the rye and barley occupied the most space.
But at their time of life, one hardly takes notice of the whiteness of
the bread, but cheerfully eats it with avidity as it is.

The most pleasant time for the squires was not the period passed
wearily and slowly in the castles, but on the morn of battle; and
their first duties, those from which they derived their title, consisted in carrying their master's shield, and also in arming and dis-
arming him. We may picture these fine young men before the
battle, trotting in front of their lords, seated on their enormous
roncins, and wearing round their necks, suspended by the *gingas* of
Eastern stuff, those long large shields of twelfth century pattern which
covered a man on horseback entirely. But they were not entrusted
with the shield alone; they carried all the arms of the knight, and had
to keep them in good condition; bright, polished and free from rust.

A battle in the eleventh or twelfth centuries was generally
nothing more than a series of duels. There was no strategy in those
days. The opposing armies arrayed themselves in lines—something like the array at Solferino, only of greater depth. Behind
each knight was his squire, and this arrangement caused an
erudite gentleman of the last century to remark that the squires
formed a second line of battle ("Sainte Palaye," Memoirs).
Nevertheless, I am of opinion that this regularity of formation
scarcely existed, save in theory, and that there was more disorder
than arrangement.

But it is an established fact, that while the *mêlée* was at its height, the squires held the horses of the barons, the *destrier* of the knight in their *destre* (right hand).   For instance, we read :

> " Messire Gauvains fut armez
> Et si fist à deux escuriers
> Mener en destre deus destriers."

The word *destrier* answers to a type of bad Latin *dextrarius*—*dextra*, right hand.   The vassals leaped forward on a *ronchin* and held the *destrier en destre*.   At jousts and tourneys the same custom obtained, and to the squires were consigned the horses of the knight's slain foes, horses being then a source of income, and valuable property.

In battle the squires led the chargers to their masters as soon as the foe came in sight.   Then the engagement began.   Each knight selected his adversary and charged him with his lance.   If the lance was broken the fight was continued with the sword.   The good squire did not fight at all, and was the anxious witness of many combats.   With his eyes fixed upon his master he followed anxiously the varying fortunes of the duel, handing to his liege-lord fresh weapons which he had in reserve ; he was also charged with the duty of guarding prisoners.

Of course, this attitude of armed inactivity could not last long ; before the day was over the squires themselves sometimes had engagements on their own account.   Under such circumstances, and on these occasions, which were frequently repeated, they manifested knightly attributes, and such an one who went as a *damoiseau* to the field of battle, quitted it a knight, sword in hand, and proud in bearing.

But they could not be always fighting, and the *château* was sought in peace ; and in such periods of rest, the duties of the squire were very modest and unassuming.   Perhaps some reader may remember the beautiful verse of Victor Hugo in his first " Legend of the Centuries," in which the Cid is the hero, and which are entitled " *Bivar*."   An Arab Sheik came to visit the Cid Campeador, and found him prosaically employed in grooming his horse, rubbing him down, and washing him, and " doing what was the squire's duty to do."   The great poet has here touched the true note, and this was exactly the squire's duty.   It could not have been better described.

Immediately he had risen in the morning the squire's duty called him to the stables, where he was destined to pass several hours every day, curry-comb and brush in hand : first attending to his master's horses and then to his own. The squire was obliged to be very particular as regards the shoeing. It was always his duty to break in the young horses, and he had to get accustomed to this rough and dangerous exercise. Then he had to watch for his master's waking, for upon the squire devolved the responsibility of getting him up and dressing him. If a stranger or a guest arrived at the castle it was the squire's duty to attend him, to relieve him of his arms, to look after his horse, and conduct the new arrival to his chamber, to undress him, to dress him, and to entertain him.

The horn is sounded ! It is the dinner hour, the horn winds a " water " call, and the guests wash their hands before seating themselves at the table. But who has supplied the water ? who has set out the table, who stands there behind the chair of each dame or baron, silent, attentive, assiduous ? who hands the bread, who carves the viands, who pours out the wine ? The squires ; always the squires, and they congratulate themselves upon being as quick and clever at all these occupations as the most expert of the attendants. If their lord and master leave his home to travel, they guard his coffers, which are full of money and jewels. If he proceed to a tourney, they are delighted to accompany him, and to perform for him the same offices as in war, calling out his name, collecting the horses which he has won, and looking after the " spare armour." At hunting-parties we find the same zeal, and the same delight in these duties.

The knight is always the " double " of his squire ; they are, so to speak, inseparable. On the return from the chase, the tourney, or the battle field, the *damoiseaux*, the *meschins*, the squires also receive the baron at the castle gate, and bring him wine.

" The Count Raoul has asked for wine. Fourteen varlets run to fetch it, all arrayed in ermine ; amongst them is a page, born at Saint Quintin, son of Hubert Count Palatine. He has seized a cup of fine gold, full of ferments and wine, and he kneels before the Palatine Raoul." The Count, who is in an angry mood, seizes the cup from the hand of the squire, and utters a cry of hatred directed against his mortal enemies.

"Listen to me, ye hardy French knights. By this pure wine which you see here, by the sword which is by my side, and by the holy saints, evil, evil, befall the sons of Hubert." *

Such violence as this fortunately did not often sadden and disturb the halls of our castles, and the *damoiseaux* had not often to be witnesses of such scenes.

Well, it is nightfall again, but the day of our squires has by no means ended. They have still to disrobe their master, whose bed they had to make after he had got up that morning; at any rate, their duties are then over? No, for a last glance has to be directed over the stables, and "rounds" have to be made during the night over all parts of the castle. After such a day's work as this they deserve to sleep!

V.

All *damoiseaux* did not perform the duties of squires, and many certainly did not perform them thoroughly. Nothing in the Middle Ages was very rigorous, and there were numerous exceptions which are mentioned. One fact is certain, the "infants" were in the hands of their master, and he was free to employ them near his person as he pleased. Thus it came to pass that the varlets had sometimes to carry messages for the Barons. This fact deserves some little notice.

Occasionally a *damoiseau* was directed to write the letter himself, the *bref*, which he had to carry, but the writing of the epistle was usually the act of the clerics. No letter was ever despatched without being sealed; but while the finishing touch is being put to the toilet (so to speak) of the message, we must not forget the messenger.

Those hissings and noises which we hear from the direction of the steps are the sounds of preparation of the horse, the animal

"Qui est legier pour courre et legier pour aler."

The directions are particular. Above all things they say to the

* Raoul de Cambrai.

messenger, "Arm yourself, and arm yourself well, for a courier ought never to be without means of defence."

Then he sets off: where does he carry the letters with which he is charged? There in that little box or small barrel hung by a strap around his neck, he also carries with him the necessary provisions, bread, cheese, wine; but he has no sleeping-place, save under the canopy of Heaven, unless he can find a bed in the house of some friend.

Would you behold him on his passage? He sings a merry song, and has not forgotten to carry with him his hawk, wherewith to enliven the journey. But, notwithstanding, the way seems long, and he hastens to reach his destination. As soon as he is in the presence of the individual to whom he has been sent, he addresses the person gracefully, and bows respectfully, often giving him a verbal *résumé* of the letter. His address is polite and pious, somewhat after the following fashion :—

"May the God who has created the world and the sea, and placed the fishes in it—may that great God give you strength against your enemies. Here is the letter I have brought you." Then he hands the letter to the individual to whom it is addressed; he breaks the seal and reads it. We know the rest: there is no need to add more, and we may add for the benefit of sympathetic souls, that the messenger is well paid for his trouble. He was even paid twice over; by the sender and by the recipient of the letter. Clothing, horses or money; there were few fine things which were *not* offered to him—and he accepted them.

But neither fatigue nor presents could prevent our squire from thinking of the day on which he would become a knight. His great consolation was that the grade of squire was the last degree to pass before he arrived at that of knight so greatly desired! He kept this fact continually in mind, and counted the days until his aim should be attained.

Let us count them with him, and profit by this delay, to give a physical and moral portrait of the youthful candidate for Chivalry.

VI.

With some rare exceptions the beauty of our *damoiseaux* was of the blonde order. All our heroes were fair men.

The ideal of mothers, which was that of all wives, was a fine boy, quick and active, with regular features. This accomplished young man ought to have golden hair, and even hair of " more than golden hue," as some poets insist. This beautiful hair ought to be curly, and curled with the curling-tongs, too; no other style could be permitted. But to the eyes the greatest importance was attached, and there were no eyes beautiful but those of *vair* colour (an heraldic term), " the eyes of a falcon." Even if large, or even somewhat " goggle " eyes with a proud look in them, they did not displease. The carnation is white and red, a " carnation of blonde," and our poets who praised the golden hair praised, above all attributes, a " skin whiter than silver or crystal." A nose straight and thin, a laughing mouth, and I don't know what species of down to represent a beard. These points constituted the personal features of the youth and fresh face.

As regards the body, the principal *desiderata* with our poets, and the great physical qualities which they were never tired of praising, were wide chests and shoulders, with otherwise a slender form and figure. The chest heart-shaped was almost a *sine quâ non*, and this, in the ideas of our grandfathers, was the supreme and perfect beauty. Thus,—

Par espaules fus lés, graisles par la ceinture—

that is, " broad shoulders and slender waist," is a verse which occurs with variations many hundred times in the old " *Chansons de geste.*"

The remaining attributes of the squire or *damoiseau* are of little interest, but it was desirable he should possess—and in those days people were fond of the young valet with—nervous arms and large fists, white hands, and well-trimmed nails; nor did they disdain well-turned limbs, " long enough to mount a horse," nor, particularly, well-shaped and arched feet, " *pieds bien voltis.*" In two words, they desired in a young man the happy combination of elegance and strength. It would appear that, after all, our grandmothers had not such bad taste.

Strength, it must be admitted, was held in greater esteem than good looks, and this preference is not astonishing when we consider the rude manners and uncultivated tastes of the period. The effeminate type of page was the outcome of an epoch of decadence, and would have had no charm for the burly barons of the twelfth century.

How was Charlemagne, that august ruler of the Christian race, that Agamemnon of the French epic poetry, represented? As a giant seven or eight feet high, who could easily bend three or four horseshoes, and who could lift, without much difficulty, in his hands a fully-armed knight! These are the kind of feats which are now performed by the Hercules of the village fair; but our forefathers did not laugh at them, they admired them! They did not stop to consider that force was brutal,—it was *force*, and they bowed down before it.

However, these strong men have rarely much intelligence, these Hercules are generally devoid of mind,—their powerful brutality usually is sufficient for their vulgar admirers. There never has existed a being more gross, more stupid, and more brutal than the illustrious Renoart, that friend of William of Orange. Not one single ray of intelligence illuminated his gross visage, and he never did anything which was not either silly or cruel. But he was a giant, a giant of extraordinary strength, who flourished an immense mace, a *tinel* with which he, like a butcher in a slaughter-house, ceased not to beat out the brains of Arabs or Frenchmen. One day he, with one stroke of this plaything, smashed the skull of a monk of Brioude who would not exchange garments with him.

Our forefathers considered this very amusing, and laughed at it till tears rolled down their cheeks. Such a primitive-minded people, such an infant nation, were really in need of enormous material force to fight against their enemies, and it was not desirable to have too bad an opinion of those habits which very properly shock our delicacy. We now prefer more refined specimens; our forefathers liked them before all things robust and strong—" iron-breakers."

For instance, they were hugely delighted, and greatly amused, always, by a recital of the exploits of the infancy of Roland, such as are related by a bard but too little known. That most illustrious of our knights (Roland) was of enormous size even when he was born. Never before and never since had or has such a big strong child been seen. His arms and legs were those of a giant! His anger as a child was already terrible! The swaddling-clothes were regarded by him as a restraint and an injury. He would not permit himself to be swathed, and thumped his mother furiously, struggling in her arms, which were too feeble to restrain him. Our forefathers uttered exclamations of admiration and astonishment at this, but it is not necessary to regard them as more gross than they actually were, and they only admired material force. Those old Christians had a very elevated notion of the human soul, and had an idea that if it would be really great it ought to endure here below much grief as the true complement of its existence in the world.

Young Roland, before attaining to celebrity, travelled over this good and necessary path of misery and adversity. His father Milon and his mother Bertha had been banned by the great emperor; they had to fly from the anger of the son of Pepin. So they went away half-clothed, and without food, across country, and through towns in Italy. Bertha, who was the sister of the King of France, pressed young Roland to her bosom: Milon turned woodcutter, so as to be able to support the nephew of Charles. Nothing could be more painful and distressing than such a beginning, and no one could have foreseen how Charles eventually was destined to find his sister's son, and how he would be reconciled with Roland's mother.

An expedition undertaken by the French to the Holy City, which it was necessary to snatch from the Saracens, a military promenade by the emperor into Italy was the means whereby everything was arranged. It happened that Charlemagne was, with his whole army, proceeding to the town of Sutri, the very place in which Roland and his unhappy parents were living. There was a great disturbance in the little town, which was not accustomed to such excitements, a great noise and tumult of armed men. The emperor, installed in his palace, was very generous and openhanded, giving liberally to all who asked his assistance.

However, there came a visitor whom no one expected. This was a youth, fair, "with the eyes of a lion, the sea-dragon, or the falcon." His beauty was something quite out of the common, and "launched rays around him." He was as bold as good-looking, and at the head of thirty young fellows of his own age penetrated

into the palace as into a conquered city. What he sought under
the gaze of all was not the golden throne on which the emperor was
seated, nor the tapestries on which were embroidered the exploits
of the old knights, nor the Oriental stuffs which were extended
between the pillars, nor the flowers which thickly overspread the
ground. No, no ; he sought something very material indeed,—
the tables ! On them was displayed an exquisite repast ; he began
to eat ! Nothing interests and amuses people who have no appetite
more than to assist other people to satisfy their appetite. You
may remember the beautiful verses of Victor Hugo—

> " Nous mangions notre pain de si bon appetit
>   Que les femmes riaient quand nous passions près d'elles."

Charlemagne and his courtiers behaved as these ladies did : they
laughed heartily as they watched the quickness of the fair child
with the blue eyes. They were more astonished to see him carry
away a portion of the banquet which he had kept in reserve.

"This is for my father and mother," he said, gravely ; and he
forthwith carried the viands from the royal table to his parents ;
his mother being the daughter of one king and the sister of
another. The inevitable discovery was made. This wonderful
child of Sutri was Roland ; and Charlemagne, overcome by his
gracefulness, ended "by extending his arms to his sister." Gracefulness alone would not have sufficed to obtain such a victory :
material, brutal force had been the useful means. The King of
France, moreover, did not make peaceful overtures to Roland's
mother : he attempted to stab her. But Roland seized him so
violently by the hand that the blood gushed from beneath his nails.
This argument admitted of no reply. But Charles, delighted at
being vanquished by a mere lad, so charming *and so strong,*
exclaimed, as he gazed enthusiastically upon the youth—

" He will be the falcon of Christianity ! "

Then all ended happily : reconciliation came with tears and in a
Hallelujah of Concord. Roland, however, who was less impressed
than anyone present, looked on, tapping the table and demanding
(O ! Nature) some more to eat !

However original this episode may be, it must be confessed that
in it grace was too much sacrificed to force, and elegance to gross-

ness. There is in it not exactly the "infant" type of our romances; but there is in it none the less the infant complete. For my own part I prefer the Roland of *Renans de Montauban*, and the delightful coolness with which he entered the court of Charlemagne. On a certain day a great noise was heard in the precincts of the palace; quite a "bombardment" of youthful feet. A valet was seen to descend the staircase, followed by thirty *damoiseaux* "*de gente faucon.*" Not one of them boasted a beard; but what a refined appearance, and what good clothes they wore! Their young chief wore an ermine cloak upon his shoulders, he wore heuses— African boots—and (although he was not yet a knight) golden spurs.

He was well made, upright, and had the head and features of a true baron. We can only compare his gaze to that of a leopard or a lion. With determined steps he ascended the staircase of the palace and came into the presence of the emperor.

"In the name of Him who was crucified, I salute you," he said to Charles.

And the king replied immediately—

"In the name of Him who ransomed us, I salute you. Who are you, and whence do you come? What is your name?"

"Sire," replied the valet, "they call me Roland, and I am the son of your sister with the fair face."

Charles listened to him, raised his head, took the "infant" by the sleeve of his fur cloak, and, kissing him four times on the mouth and chin, replied:

"Fair nephew, we will make a knight of you!"

*   *   *   *   *   *   *

We will now quit these scenes, which are both primitive and charming, and come to the moral aspect of the *damoiseau*, whose outward appearance we are now acquainted with, and whose moral aspect remains to be considered.

The first quality which was desirable, and was exacted from a candidate for Chivalry, was "to have the vocation." This term is rather ambiguous in a study of Middle Age literature; but we must excuse it and take it as it stands. When the valet was brought up in the paternal castle or in the palace of another baron, such a "vocation" was only natural. Everything contributed to entertain and to excite the youth. There were the interminable chaunts of the troubadours after the long dinners, and the reading of the roughly illuminated old romances. There were the historical events embroidered upon the tapestries in the castles, or painted on the large chimneys. The nobleman devoted to the chase and war kept our *damoiseau* continually in practice. In fact, he lived amid surroundings which only admitted of his becoming a Churchman or a knight, and we find him most frequently preferring the helmet to the tonsure.

But there were "vocations" which had a less favourable conjunction. Some "infant," nobly born of unknown parents, was thrown by circumstances into the family of some common persons who regarded him as common as themselves and brought him up as a tradesman. A Montmorency educated by a grocer! Ah, it was beautiful to see the development of the chivalrous vocation in the youth. The young noble from his earliest days detests business, money, petty calculations and economies, and all the tricks of the trade. The meanness of it annoys him, he reddens with shame, his heart beats, and he proclaims himself a knight.

Our poets were fond of bringing forward this phase of the character which developed itself in "trade" surroundings. I can imagine that the stout barons laughed heartily when the troubadours thus sneered at the merchants in their presence. The nobles always were pleased to laugh at the tradesman and at commerce, and our bards were sure to succeed in the castle when they "made fun" of the shop.

On the other hand, I am persuaded that stones would have been thrown at the ill-advised singer who would have sung in the open street, the *Enfances Vivien* or *Hervis de Metz!* and before an audience of tradespeople.

You shall judge for yourselves.

Vivien was the son of that Garin d'Anseüne who on the field of Roncesvalles and not far from the inanimate body of Roland had been made prisoner by the infidels. Vivien was the nephew of Guillaume *au fier bras*—Vivien is the Roland of the poem of Aimeri de Narbonne.

When scarcely seven years old he fell into the hands of Norman pirates, who hastened to put to sea. He was a lovely child, "who had fair hair, curly too, and eyes like a falcon, his skin as white as a flower in summer." There he is, poor little fellow, in the midst of the horses and mules. A female merchant happens to perceive him and buys him. This lady had always wished to have children of her own. "It is seven years since my husband went away. I will say he is our son and he will believe me."

As a matter of fact this is exactly what happened, and the good merchant Godefroy is very willing to believe what his wife tells him. Even he displays for his son the most tender and touching affection. It is a good thing to have a son; it is right and it is wise to plan out a future for this long-expected heir. "He shall be a merchant," said the worthy man, and he at once began to instruct him in the business.

"I am about to teach you how to buy cloth, corn, pepper, and cummin, and above all how to sell them," said he.

At these words Vivien blushed and all the blood of the race of Aimeri boiled within his breast. A merchant! He! He the grandson—the son and the nephew of so many heroes. He who would have been born a knight, if any one could be born a knight.

Thenceforth began a struggle between the merchant and this singular apprentice, an incessant struggle, the issue of which it is not difficult to perceive. It was the ancient, the immortal dispute 'twixt sword and counter, between the villein and the nobleman, between the real and the ideal.

"I will teach you weights and measures."

"No, no," replied the lad, "I would rather fight."

"I will instruct you in money-changing."

"Oh, what a delight to exchange some good lance-thrusts!"

"I will shew you the best fairs and best markets."

"Oh, were I only in the saddle, had I but a good horse, hounds, and falcons."

"I will purchase some good cloth for your clothes, and strong boots which will last you a long time."

"The infidels, the infidels! where are they? There! Kill them! Take their silver, it is there!"

Such is the dialogue which was heard day by day in the house of honest Godefroy. Those possessed of quick ears may still hear something to the same effect in these days, for the human soul changeth not.

But the time arrived for Vivien to replace words by deeds. To him was confided one day the sum of one hundred francs to make his first purchases : he was launched into business. What imprudence ! The gold burned the fingers of the future knight.

" Will you sell me that good steed for one hundred francs ? " said he to a squire who passed him on the road.

The squire relinquished to him his steed on the spot and pocketed the hundred francs, but our hero found that the good horse was, alas ! only a wretched hack, and our youthful merchant had been impudently robbed. Then succeeded the reproaches, the anger, the fury of Godefroy, who heaped reproaches on Vivien's head. But our hero was very calm and pleasant notwithstanding his discomfiture, and gravely asked for the news of the war at Constantinople !

It was evident that these two minds were destined never to understand one another. One never thought of anything but of the picking up of little profits, and of leading his petty circumscribed tradesman's life in peace and quietness. The other dreamt of nothing but horses, the chase, and the battle.

" Do you know," said the lad one day to his master, " what I would do with all your money if I possessed it ? I would build a big castle with a hall in which we could sit all day and play chess or draughts."

The unfortunate merchant could by no means understand this singular idea, and shook his head with a discouraging smile. Nevertheless he still tried—he committed the fault of making a last attempt, and sent his son to a fair at Tresai.

This time a regular disaster supervened. Vivien, who had nothing of the merchant in him, sold three hundred *vairs* for sixty francs (and now-a-days we must reflect a little to properly estimate the enormity of the crime), and got rid of his merchandise in order to purchase hawks and hounds.

" Wretch ! " exclaimed Godefroy, " you have squandered my fortune—it is all lost ! "

" You will have some trouble, father, to find better dogs than these for quail."

He was quite happy under the circumstance, and vainly endeavoured to cheer up the inconsolable Godefroy. The question was decided. He must make Vivien a knight, and what a knight he became !

The inclination or "vocation" of the youthful Hervis de Metz was exactly similar to that of Vivien, and one might almost be excused for believing that the action of the one was copied by the other. However, there are in the adventures of Hervis certain incidents which may be considered original so far as he was concerned. This chief of the terrible *geste* of the Lorrains had a semi-vulgar origin. His mother was nobly born, but his father was only a tradesman. Provost of Metz in the place of the absent duke he was, but only a tradesman for all that.

There is a pretty saying of a Father of the Church which applies very happily to our young *damoiseau* of Metz. *Filii matrizant;* 'tis their mothers whom the sons resemble. But this resemblance did not prevent the youthful Hervis from committing a hundred follies, but they at least were not stamped by vulgarity. His parents entrusted him with four thousand marks to attend the fair of Provins, and his only idea was to play the grandee with the money so laboriously amassed by his father.

In his course of enjoyment the young man expended one thousand marks in entertaining the tradesmen of Provins, who were perfectly astonished and delighted with such banquets. The first day he invited eighty of them to dinner, the second day he entertained one hundred and sixty, the third day two hundred and forty, the fourth day three hundred and eighty, and what dinners they were ! Game of every description, cranes, mallards, *jantes,* partridges, &c. As he rose from table each guest was presented with an immense taper, a *tortil* of wax. No one is more liberal than your true baron.

The following year the entertainments were repeated at the fair of Lagny, but he did not this time bring back a horse, a falcon and three hounds as he had done from Provins. No. On this latter occasion he returned triumphantly to Metz (will it be credited ?) accompanied by a beautiful young girl, who had fallen into the hands of some squires and scoundrels, from whom our hero had purchased her, money down, for the sum of fifteen thousand marks.

"Ah," exclaims an old poet, "what a splendid bargain he made when he purchased the beautiful Beatrix in this fashion. This lady was in after years the mother of Garin le Loherain and of the Duke of Bégue of the castle of Belin."

Beatrix was indeed worthy to be the bride of Hervis: she wore on her forehead the double crown of purity and regal nobility. Daughter of the King of Tyre she was a true Christian, and notwithstanding her adventures had been able to declare proudly to Hervis—her fitness to be his wife; for he never should lower himself in taking her to wife, she declared, if she were not pure.

" De vostre pris n'abaisserez por mi."

All things considered, we may perceive that the " infant " had no reason to complain of the temerity with which he had pursued the irresistible demands of his " vocation."

Another " vocation " not less imperious, and which manifested itself under very strange circumstances, is that of Betonnet, son of Beuves d'Hanstonne. To save the son of his liege lord, whom a traitor was about to put to death, a poor fellow, a *jongleur*, carried heroism to such an extreme as to substitute his son for the son of his master; and had the unutterable grief to see the child killed before his eyes! The same act of self-sacrifice was performed by the good knight Renier, in order to save the youthful Jourdain de Blaives, and this incomparable devotion is, as has been said, " one of the common bonds of Feudal literature."

A literature which has such bonds is perhaps not unworthy of the esteem of good judges. However that may be, the *jongleur* called himself Daurel, and the child whom he had saved at the price of his own flesh and blood was named Beton. Daurel took care of the child, and was as a mother to him; he kept watch to see whether this son of a baron, brought up as the son of a singer, would not some day give tokens of chivalrous tastes.

These signs the good Daurel, as a *jongleur* distrusts, and as a vassal hopes for. The situation is really dramatic and interesting. The little Beton, however, did not keep his protector waiting long for the symptoms which he both feared and desired. As soon as he had attained the age of seven, he cared for nothing but horses and arms, but it was desirable to put him to some decisive proof, and that proof was typical. It was as follows:—

One day they presented him with a hundred marks of silver— " If he takes them he is the son of a singer," they said.

Need we relate that Betonnet refused them with superb disdain,

and with the gesture of Hippocrates rejecting the presents of Arta-
xerxes ?   At nine years of age he went off to the chase by himself,
followed by dogs, and with his falcon on his wrist.   At eleven he
was a past master in fencing, and gave many proofs of it.

Nevertheless all these accomplishments did not satisfy the
jongleur, and the vocation of the son of Beuves still seemed to him
uncertain.   He pressed his argument home.

"Fair son," said he, "take thy weapons, and thy courser and
let us fight—let us fight together."

The youth resisted the invitation : he did not wish to contend
against him whom he believed to be his father.

The other insisted and commanded.   The fight began and was
not of long duration.   The happy Daurel was unhorsed by the
youthful baron, who ran weeping to pick him up, and to take him
by the hand.   The good *jongleur* could contain himself no longer ;
delighted at his defeat he revealed to the son of Beuves his origin
and the secret of his birth.   Over what obstacles will not a vocation
—a true vocation—triumph ?

We will now turn to find ourselves in the presence of a
damoiseau who is placed amid the ordinary surroundings of Feudal
life, who we know is noble, and only waiting the time when he shall
become a knight.   But even he is not spared some tests, and it is
in fact very necessary to know if he has a heart and soul truly
chivalrous.

That these proofs or tests were brutal, no one who knows the
savage races of those iron centuries will be astonished to hear.

Our type will be Aimeri de Narbonne, the same of whom Victor
Hugo has sung.

It is the birthday of the "baron," St. John the Baptist, the 24th
June.   Duke Girard is in his castle in Vienna, and feeling rather
wearied, no doubt ; for there is no hunting, nor tournament, nor
battle to amuse him.   He places at one of the windows a very
"rich falcon" and permits it to gaze through the glass far and
wide over the plain.

Staring at the passers-by is a never-failing occupation for those
who have nothing to do, and it is not without its charms.   Suddenly, between two hillocks in the midst of a deep valley, Girard
perceived a troop of young people, well arrayed, who came prancing

along on Spanish mules, and ere long debouched beneath the walls of the château near the steps.

They were all well mounted; their saddles were embroidered, and their reins studded with golden buttons. Their chief was as young as any of them, and as good looking. He leaped from his mule, and lightly ascended the stair-way to the hall, carrying on his wrist a falcon whiter than the poplar or the willow leaf.

At his very appearance Girard was thrilled; his blood ran cold, and he muttered as his countenance changed, "How greatly he resembles our family!"

The Duke of Vienna, once possessed of this doubt, was anxious to see what the new-comer was made of, and he proposed to put him to the proof.

"Do not take any notice of him," said he to his attendants, "do not announce him, nor speak to him."

At this strange silence and chilling reception, Aimeri began to get angry, and his temper rose.

"Is it thus that you receive your guests?" he cried. "Know then that there are inns in the town, and that I have still fifteen golden livres;" and he added—

"You have all the appearance of *gloutons losengiers*, and I will be avenged upon you."

Thereupon Girard burst out laughing, and when he had recovered his gravity, he said to his nephew—

"Are you not a *jongleur*? Keep to your business."

Then, turning to the steward of the castle, he continued—

"There is a lad who does not even know how to carry a falcon. Take his bird from him, and put it on the perch."

This speech made Aimeri more angry than ever. He only perceived that he was being treated very "cavalierly," and that his talent as a falconer was being called in question."

"Most certainly," said he to Girard, "I must return to my father, for my uncle is not here."

"If you are a *jongleur*," replied the other, who wished to carry the test as far as possible, "this is just the time to sing us a little song. See, yonder is my ermine cloak. That shall be your recompense. Go on."

This time the young fellow could not contain himself; he took his hawk, and, using it as a weapon, struck Girard a blow full in the face. Blood flowed from the poor count's visage, and in pretended anger he cried to his attendants, " Seize him, seize him. Hang him."

Sixteen squires and vassals threw themselves upon him, and seemed quite ready to give him a bad time of it. Pale and trembling Aimeri kept them aloof with his haughty gaze, and said—

"I am the son of Don Hernant the baron. I am the nephew of Girard. Back! Stand back!"

Girard heard him, ran to him, and clasped him in his arms, kissing him at the same time on the mouth and chin.

"Ah," he exclaimed, " you are indeed one of the family, and you have the heart of a baron!"

The proof had been established. The test was completed by those tears and kisses.*

Other proofs were those which events themselves imposed upon barons and kings. The Feudal system gave openings only too readily to wars and private hatreds, to competition for lands and rights, and the Feudal " minor " was only too often exposed to real and grave dangers. It was sometimes found necessary to put him in safety under the protection of some powerful personage, and it was necessary for him to wait until the aggrieved one became a knight to regain his rights. It was a long and weary waiting.

Besides, all the *damoiseaux* had in this an example which they did not fail to reflect upon ; incomparable knight, the records of whose youthful days were chanted in all the castles of Christian Europe, who could complain of having to endure a rough and rude existence in his youth, when that of Charlemagne himself—that of Charles " whose grandeur has penetrated his name"—had been neglected, solitary, painful ?

Ah, they consoled themselves easily under all their troubles when they remembered the formidable obstacles which the great soul of the son of Pepin had overcome. Scarcely had his father died ere he became acquainted with grief. His father had been poisoned by two bastards who were equally desirous to get rid of the legitimate son, and there was little Charles in the power of those

* See *Giars de Viane*, pp. 43, 46.

two traitors, whose names history has preserved to us—Hendri and Rainfroi. Unfortunately the child was not tall enough to fight with his brothers, and he had no other defence save his pride.

On one occasion his friends snatched him from the wretches who wished to do away with him, and found him a safe asylum with his own sister in the duchy of Angers. But the traitors, by duplicity and *ruse* managed to lay their hands again upon their victim, and proposed to make an end very quickly of the little king, the young lion, who so decidedly interfered with their ambitious views. It was easy enough to kill him outright, or to poison him was easy enough, but by so doing they perceived that their vengeance would be incomplete, for they wished to humiliate the true heir to the crown of France before their bastardy.

"You shall go with us," they said, "and wait on us at table."

Then all Charles's blood mounted to his face: he seized a roast peacock and threw it with all his force at Rainfroi's head. Then seizing a spit he brandished it as bravely as he subsequently wielded his sword. He thrust it at the bastard, who raged furiously, and attempted to cut his assailant's throat on the spot. The whole palace was in an uproar, the repast was interrupted; cries of rage were mingled with shouts of victory and the clash of arms.

The youthful Charles, still very proud of his first exploit, but too weak to resist long, was literally carried away by the partisans of the legitimate sovereign, who departed at a gallop and placed him in a fortress at some distance from Reims. But Reims was in the vicinity of the bastards, and they were very powerful. So, in dire necessity, the youth was hurried away to a safer place of refuge.

It is a hard thing to say, but Christianity could not offer this refuge to him who was destined to wear the principal and the most beautiful of all Christian crowns; and it was amongst the Infidels that the youth of their future implacable enemy was destined to be passed.

They crossed the Pyrenees in haste, and arrived at Toledo, at the palace of the Saracen King Galafre. It was in such a place that Charles was obliged to hide as a criminal; where, alas, he was constrained to dissemble as regarded his birth and to conceal his name. He was no longer Charles but "Mainet." A few devoted friends watched over him in secret, and their principal trouble consisted in preventing this son of a lion from revealing himself as a lion prematurely.

This royal "infant" was eating his heart out! he thought of nothing but battles, and irritated his followers by his restlessness—angry as he was at being restrained by them. They were reserving him for the throne of France, they made him understand that and told him so repeatedly, but he was then too young to care for politics, and could not comprehend why they counselled prudence so continually.

It happened that the Pagan king who had received him so kindly, the good Galafre, was himself at war with his neighbours, and the son of Pepin desired nothing better than to show off his skill with the lance, and prove his knowledge of arms at the expense of his host's enemies.

At length the day arrived—and it had been long waited for—when "Mainet" like a young wild animal made his escape notwithstanding the vigilance of his keepers, and came into the midst of a battle in which his youthful courage had full scope. He fought, he overthrew, he slew his enemies. But it was the Emir Bruyant whom he wished to attack, for he was the mortal enemy of Galafre. "Mainet" found him, rushed upon him and attacked him. The great duel then began but did not last long; and when the dust cleared off the spectators perceived a corpse, beheaded, horrible, and standing by it a *damoiseau* like to David, holding the bleeding head of his adversary.

This *damoiseau* was "Mainet" and the head was that of Bruyant the Emir.

However, the "*enfances*" and exploits of the son of Pepin were by no means ended; but the smiles of a young damsel soon came to console the conquerer for this his first exploit, and for many others of which the recital would be too long. The lady who thus appeared to console our hero was the amiable daughter of Galafre: we behold the smiling face and charming figure of Galienne who was so soon to become the wife of "Mainet," or to speak correctly, of Charlemagne.

One of the most severe tests to which one could put the young *damoiseaux* was to deprive them of their fortune, and say to them,

"We will give you nothing. Depart and seek your fortune else-where."

We know the advantages, the really enormous advantages, which the Feudal system assured to the eldest son, and it is not astonishing that the cadets desirous of a better lot, had sometimes a thirst—a noble thirst—for adventure, when they did not enter the Church, (of which they often made very mediocre ministers). They devoted themselves to rash enterprises in distant lands. The heroic poems which they had heard sung every day in their father's château were still calculated to develope such ideas in their youthful heads.

They saw only *damoiseaux* despoiled of their inheritance, going forth to conquer kingdoms at the point of the lance. The spec-tators of this prowess, always so interesting to the disinherited ones, were poor people whose merit alone led them to fortune.

"When I first came to Paris I wore *sabots*," is not a saying of yesterday, and Aimeri de Narbonne repeated it, as it stands, to his children whom he disinherited; "when I went to Vienna I had nothing," he added.

In all courts, and about the person of princes, there were a great number of "younger sons," portionless lads—valets who looked to every point of the compass in search of distinction and glory . . . and the rest.

> " Jouvencel somes, acroisons nostre pris
> Et querons los en estrange païs."

No doubt they were acquainted with all the dangers of the adventures they sought, but they repeated to themselves the fine chivalrous proverb,

> " Car ne puet estre ce est chose passée
> Honnours par armes sans perill conquestée."

And in strength of this, they departed.

Another ideal which our youthful nobles presented to themselves and which our poets also offered voluntarily for their acceptance was a grand marriage which would give them fortune as well as glory. I know nothing from this point of view more improbable and more delightful than the *Department des Enfances Aimeri.* Ah ! there is a poem which was sufficient to delight the *damoi-seaux* and to make them dream for many a long day. Listen—

Aimeri is poor, and he only possesses Narbonne, which he wishes to leave, not to his eldest son (mark you), but to the youngest of his seven sons. There was nothing absolutely contrary to Feudal custom in this, as he could make his will as he pleased; but one thing is certain, that the decision of "the old man of Narbonne" was not of a nature calculated to please the other six young gentlemen who saw themselves put aside, and forced to hold their tongues, for they knew their father was headstrong and even brutal.

But they were speedily consoled, and you will now be able to see how a Feudal baron used to establish his sons in life. Aimeri sent one day for his eldest son, whose name was Bernard, and said to him in terrible accents—

"You make a great mistake in your fancy that you will ever get anything from Narbonne! By the faith which I owe to St. Peter in Rome, you shall not have the value even of an apple!"

The lad gazed at his father in astonishment, and the latter continued:

"Take a hundred knights with you and go straight to Brubant. There is a duke there—a very proud individual—who has the most beautiful daughter in the world. Go and demand her hand in marriage! Begone!"

Without appearing in the least taken aback, Bernard simply replied: "Since you wish it, father, I also wish it."

Then turning to his knights, he cried: "To horse!" and in a few minutes they were in the saddle. The wife of Aimeri, Bernard's mother, took only time to embrace her son, and to make him a present of three purses filled with gold and silver. A hurried adieu was then said, the riders set spurs to their steeds, which started at a gallop. They soon lost sight of the borders of Narbonne, hills, valleys and mountains were traversed and crossed. Where is the city of Brubant? I confess I cannot tell, and I rather think that the poet of the twelfth century was equally ignorant of its locality.

But at length, wherever it was, they came in full view of it, and it presented a grand and beautiful appearance in the eyes of the Narbonnais. It was lighted up by the sun and splendid to behold.

"Oh!" exclaimed Bernard, "what a beautiful city!"

He did not pause long in admiration, but bravely entered the town at the head of his hundred knights. He did not dismount until he had reached the palace gates beneath the olive trees. He then got off his horse and mounted, leisurely, the wide stone steps which led up to the great hall. There sat the duke in the midst of all his barons, just as if this singular visitor had been expected.

"Fair and brave sir," said Bernard to the duke in a clear and steady voice, "the Count Aimeri demands that you give to me your beautiful daughter in marriage."

The duke consented on the spot, and the young lady arrived just at the right moment to give her consent also to this most unexpected marriage.

"My daughter, beautiful and wise, I have given you a husband."

"Blessed be God! Tell me his name, good sir."

"He is the rich Bernard of Narbonne, my daughter."

"I accept him willingly, sir."

Then the bishop was sent for in haste, and Bernard with his blessing was soon affianced to the young lady. Next day the solemn ceremony took place, and there was a grand banquet in the vaulted hall. The match was made, Bernard was married—well married—and the poet adds naïvely: "Of this son of Aimeri I have nothing more to say, neither of his wife—Heaven bless her!" Let us pass on.

This scene which I have just related as described in the old poem —this same scene is almost exactly reproduced two or three times, and what we have just related of Bernard might, with the omission or alteration of a few words, be applicable to Garin and to Hernaut. Nothing is more lifelike or more popular, more truly epic, than these almost literal transcriptions. Thus we see Garin, driven by his father from Narbonne, directing his steps to the town of Anseüne which he delivers from the Saracens, and then marries the daughter of Duke Naimes, Eustache the Fair.

Again we see Hernaut the Red, also driven from home by Aimeri, far from his beloved Narbonne, saving at the lance's point the town of Girone, which was besieged by the Infidels, and behold him quickly wedded to the beautiful Beatrix.

The destiny of Beuves was not so commonplace, for *he* is asked in marriage! The King Gascogne the Great was about to die and had only one child, a daughter, Helissent the Beautiful. According to the strictest canons of the Feudal law the orphan girl sought King Charles and asked him to provide her with a husband.

"My father is dead," she said, "I come to you to find me a husband."

The king, without hesitation, took her by the hand, and, calling Beuves, said:—

"Take this damsel to wife."

"A thousand thanks, sire," replied Beuves.

The bishop was immediately summoned, and the young people were married on the spot. The transaction could not have been more quickly accomplished.

Thus it happened that four sons of Aimeri obtained for themselves fortunes by wealthy marriages: in this manner they acquired the duchies of Brubant, Anseüne, Girone, and Commarcis. And these duchies were equal to kingdoms.

It is true that Arnier and Guillaume, their brothers, were not so quickly made happy: but four *damoiseaux* well married, four out of six, was not so bad, and was enough to satisfy the most exigent listeners to romances in the castles of the twelfth century. We will not be more exacting.

However, the tests to which our *damoiseaux* were exposed may come to an end, and we need only henceforth discuss their virtues —and their failings!

VII.

The *damoiseau* was courageous—that was a matter of course. His greatest desire from the age of ten years was to follow in the train of great knights clothed in armour who went to war on their superb chargers, lances in rest. These departures—when he could not follow them—put him in a rage, and the knights would laugh heartily at the indignation of the "infant" who was obliged to remain at home with his mother and her women.

"This is the manner in which I am dishonoured," said the young valet, gravely, "and I shall be looked upon as base and worthless!"

These were the very words of the young Guibert, the seventh child of Aimeri de Narbonne, when he was a spectator of the departure of his brothers who were going to seek their fortunes. It was in vain that his father promised him, and actually reserved for him alone, all the town and the whole duchy of Narbonne; no, nothing would console him.

In this poem of the Narbonnais it was not only the "infant" who possessed precocious courage. Vivien, the admirable Vivien, of whom we have so often spoken, had a brother fifteen years old, whom they were going to leave within the shelter of the walls of Orange at the time when the great and decisive battle of Aliscans was about to be fought.

"You are too young, and too small," said the benevolent Guillaume to the infant Guichardet, " to go to this battle against the Infidels. You are not capable of beholding the scene of a battle-field covered with dead bodies. Remain with your aunt Guibourc. Later on we will see about making you a knight."

Guichardet wept, Guichardet remained; but he had ideas of his own which he put rapidly into execution. He made his way to the stable and took a horse "strong and swift," saddled it, and went off unarmed. In vain Guibourc, "the countess with the proud face," sent one hundred knights in pursuit of him. The youth returned of his own accord by a round-about road, and begged his aunt to dub him knight.

It is unusual, as we have seen elsewhere, for the order of knighthood to be conferred by a woman, but in this instance nothing could be more natural. Guibourc laced the helmet upon the youthful head, inducted him into his hauberk, girded him with his sword. It is related that scarcely had the young man been knighted than he set off at full speed to encounter the Infidels. But his many emotions mastered him, and he was in tears.

The youthful Lorrainers did not yield to the youthful Narbonnais. They had the same blood in their veins. When the very youthful Hernaudin heard of the death of his father Begon, he exclaimed—

"O! if I had but my little armour that I might assist my uncle Garin against his enemies!"

Garin was present and happened to hear him: he was delighted

with this little outburst of anger.   He clasped the child in his arms
and cried—

"You are too bold, fair nephew, but you greatly resemble my
poor brother, the rich Duke—Heaven rest his soul."   The scene
was charming.

The king's reciters of the poems did not display any less
address than did those of other periods, and put before the
nobles no less worthy models.   Charles alone did not suffice for
them, for these poets one day conceived the idea of re-celebrating
his father Pepin, and of rhyming certain episodes of his history or
legends which had formerly been recounted in fit terms by the
monk Saint-Gall.

To those who joked about his small stature King Pepin gave
proofs of his great courage.   He was present at a combat of
animals, which was then one of the diversions which was most
acceptable to the somewhat brutal tastes of the German race.
Suddenly they saw him throw himself between a lion and a bull
which were fighting in a most terrible fashion.   At one stroke—at
a single blow—he cut off the lion's head, and looked in a defiant
manner at those who had expected a few more blows to be struck
in effecting his purpose.

"David was a little man, yet he slew Goliath.   Alexander was
short, but several of his captains had less strength and less courage
than he."

Thus speaks the writer of the annals, and he is forced to confess
that the poet had embellished his verse in some degree, or disfigured this little bit of more or less apocryphal history.   We read
in the *chanson* of a lion which escaped from its cage and frightened
Charles Martel himself.   Pepin, who was still quite a young man,
seized a boar-spear, and walking deliberately up to the animal,
pierced him in the stomach, and nailed him to the earth.   Charles
embraced the youthful victor, and his mother gave way to tears.
This was a commencement which foreshadowed him as a great
king; there was one example the more for our *damoiseaux*.

But it was young Roland—"Rolandin"—who, in this same era,
that of Charlemagne—was, above all, the perfect type of courage;
the ideal of the noble "infant."   Everyone wished to resemble
him, even in his bad points: everyone copied him a little.

The mind of a *damoiseau* in the eleventh and twelfth centuries was composed, like Roland's, of a number of elements, the presence of which might be easily determined ; but of which it is very difficult to appreciate exactly the true proportions. There was much barbarism and roughness: some little levity, and a great deal of courage.

Picture to yourselves the departure for the army during the heroic years of the Middle Ages ; a departure for the Holy Land, for the Crusades. The clashing of arms, the whinnying of horses, the tearful farewells, the long posse of knights winding, more pensive than cheerful, along the highways, followed by their squires carrying their arms. Here and there a troubadour, who sang warlike songs like those of Conon of Bethune or of Thibaut of Champagne.

Such was the army of the Emperor Charles when he set out for Italy, to wage that terrible war against the pagan, King Agolant ; a war which was destined to culminate in Calabria by the celebrated battle of Aspromonte. Now, one day this grand army passed through Laon, beneath the walls of the castle, and the noise made by the troops arrested the attention of some youths who were shut up in the palace to prevent them from proceeding to the holy war.

As may be assumed, these lads were in a great rage, and occupied themselves night and day with projects for escape. But when they heard the horns and trumpets, and the neighing of the horses; when through the narrow windows, which resembled loopholes, they perceived the squires seeking for quarters for their masters, when they ascertained that this was the army of Charlemagne, and that they might never have another opportunity to join it, they could contain themselves no longer, and made up their minds to try a strange stratagem.

There were five of these sons of barons, but the most determined of all was Roland. This eaglet had been put into the cage, but if he had to break the bars he would not remain there.

Unfortunately at the castle of Laon there was a porter to whom the custody of these youths had been specially confided, and who did not seem to understand their pleasantry. Roland at first attempted to bribe him, and tried other means to win him from his allegiance.

"Let us go and play for a little while outside," he would say in a purposely measured voice. "Let us out for a while." He coaxed him, called him gentleman, even gave him a title. "Do you know what we will do for you when we grow up? We will make you a knight."

But the man was not to be won over by these blandishments. "Knight!" he would say. "What a wretched calling his is! One is sure to receive so many ugly blows. I would rather remain here and sleep." Then in severe tones he would add—

"Go back to your apartment and amuse yourself with your falcons. You shall not go out."

Roland thereupon beat a retreat, but he did not despair of overcoming the porter's resistance, and employed persuasion and force by turns.

"We only want to see the knights pass by, good master porter: let us go out. Come now!"

"No, I tell you," was the reply.

"Ah, then you will not do what we want? Here is what you deserve."

Then they all fell upon the unfortunate man and beat him soundly with sticks, leaving him for dead, stretched apparently lifeless upon the stones. After this they opened the gate and made their escape.

The army of Charles had by this time departed. It had already proceeded some distance upon its way. The five youths were on foot and cut a sorry figure.

"Ah!" said 'Rolandin,' "we ought to have horses, but since we have none we must proceed on foot—or take them."

At this time five good Bretons came by most opportunely.

"Now is our time," cried the nephew of Charles, who as you perceive directed the enterprise. "Come on. Come on."

Then the five fiery young men fell upon the astonished Bretons, routed them, dismounted them, and leaped upon their horses, which proved excellent cattle. But the despoiled Bretons complained to their King Salomon of this impudent band of young men, these unknown youthful brigands.

"Who are these 'infants?'" he cried. It was very important that he should know, and he sent one thousand men in pursuit of them. This band surrounded the youths and closed in upon them,

"LET US GO OUT. COME NOW."—"NO, I TELL YOU."

getting nearer and nearer, and watching the lads with some curiosity.

" Ah, it is Roland ! " exclaimed a loud voice, with a loud laugh, and the voice was that of the King of Bretagne, who had recognised Charlemagne's nephew.

" It is Roland, it is Roland," repeated all the other knights. As for the five youths, they did not know whether to laugh or cry, but eventually they gained their point. The beating of the porter and the robbery of the Bretons were overlooked : the knights feasted them, permitted them to join the grand army, and to take part in the Crusade. Roland had triumphed !

All " infants " had not the impudence of Roland. Some of them at the age of twelve were already grave and steady, and regarded life in its true light. I do not wish to close the few pages which I have devoted to the virtues of our budding knights without having traced, rapidly, a portrait of one of these *damoiseaux* of high lineage and proud air who were devoted to duty and to duty alone. I will call this portrait simply " a son," and I regret very much that Victor Hugo has never found a place for him in his magnificent gallery of his *Legend of the Centuries.* It is more beautiful than *Aymerillot.*

" A son ! " We must first picture to ourselves the authority of a father of the Feudal period. Although he lived with his family every day and all day, he was rather feared than loved, and thus embodied the old proverb, *E longinquo auctoritas.* The children began by trembling in the presence of their father, but subsequently embraced him. All his sons fixed their regard upon him with a view to resemble him, and were ready to take up the sword in his defence. It was a kind of patriarchal life mingled with military roughness, of which there is no need to exaggerate either the beauty or the rudeness. The following tale is authentic and will vouch for this, for it is more historical than many histories. It came to pass at one time that the English people in London were very much interested in a young Frenchman, about twelve years old, who had recently arrived at Dover, and had resided in London for some few days. Everyone was talking of this extraordinary youth. He was very handsome, and none of his contemporaries could compare with him any more than a magpie can compare with a falcon. Who would not have admired him, he was so adroit with the bow, so clever in fencing! But, above everything, so generous! All day he would be giving away rich furs, horses, and falcons.

So one can imagine that it was easy enough to be clothed in London at that time free of expense. One had only to go to the young Frenchman's house, where a number of servants were ready and willing to distribute cloaks, pelisses and other garments to the applicants. All the poor people knew the way to this blessed mansion. The King had taken the youthful valet into his service, and all the *châtelaines* in England united in a chorus in praise of his beauty and accomplishments. His mother, in France, prayed for him!

His name was Witasse. He was the son of the Count of Boulogne, and the brother of that Godfrey who was destined one day to refuse, so piously, to wear the golden crown in the Holy City of Jerusalem.

Now just at the very time when this *damoiseau* of Boulogne was making such a sensation in the city of London, it happened that Rainaume, Count of Montreuil (a traitor), took possession of the territory of his lord, the Count of Boulogne, who was dangerously ill; and whilst his eldest son was in England he invaded the province at the head of a thousand knights, pillaged, burned, and committed sacrilege everywhere. The history of the Feudal period is full of acts of violence of this nature, which should be spurned and held in abhorrence by every honest man.

However, in this instance, a courier mounted and rode in hot haste to the castle of the Count of Boulogne with the news.

"Your territory—your whole territory is in flames!" he cried.

The poor count listened in fear and trembling, but anger overcame him and he essayed to rise from his sick bed to punish the traitor, but alas! he fell back, unable to get up. The countess tore her hair, and exclaimed:

"My son, my dear son, why are you not here?"

It was at once decided that a message should be despatched to the young traveller; and then the youth's mother became comforted, took courage, and supported by her pride became almost sublime.

"I myself," she exclaimed, "I myself will, in the absence of our son, engage in raising an army. I will find the knights, and trust our son will arrive in time."

Four days afterwards the Count's messenger arrived at Dover. He mounted his horse and rode without once getting off the animal's back until he entered London. He took his meals on horseback, and only stopped three times to drink on the road. He flew along the highways, and at length, almost as exhausted as his poor horse, he was fortunate enough to enter the palace of the King of England.

It happened curiously enough that the messenger arrived exactly at meal-time. It was the dinner hour. A very youthful-looking man was standing behind the king's chair. The youth had fair hair and was holding a golden cup in his hand. This youth was Witasse.

The messenger came in without any ceremony, took the lad aside and in a few words delivered his message.

"Your father is ill, and a traitor has invaded his territory. Come!"

Without hesitating an instant the *valet* placed the golden cup in the king's hand.

"I am not thirsty," said His Majesty in surprise: "and I did not ask for wine."

"Take it," replied the *damoiseau*, brusquely. "If you do not it will fall to the ground."

Then, without vouchsafing any further information, he quitted the palace.

People who happened to be travelling between London and Dover that day, gazed in stupefied astonishment at the youth and his attendant who were riding madly along, their horses all covered with foam and sweat. No halting, no pulling up. Quickly—more quickly still. The riders scarcely took time to prostrate themselves before the altar in Canterbury Cathedral when they were away again like the wind. "Faster, faster," was the cry.

At length they came in sight of Dover.

"Who are those sailors?"

"Boulogne fishermen."

"Quick, a boat! More quickly still! Make haste!"

They reached the shores of Boulogne, and then a terrible sight met the eyes of the youthful traveller, who had come with such tremendous haste from London town.   The whole province was in flames.

" Vengeance, vengeance ! " he exclaimed.

Witasse then mounted a horse and went forth to encounter the traitor who had thus devastated the Count's dominions.   The young man proved victorious, killed his adversary, and then without a word returned to England.   He had avenged his father.

Some days afterwards, as mid-day was being recorded by the convent bells, the King of England sat down to dine.   He at once perceived a youth with fair hair and merry eyes, who tendered to him his golden cup of wine.   The *valet* was quite covered with dust, and strange to relate was wearing spurs.

" Whence come you, Witasse ? " asked the king, who suspected his page had absented himself upon some adventure of an amorous nature.

" I come from a certain place," replied the young man proudly, " a place whither none could have proceeded in my stead."

Modestly he remained silent, and rather concealed the facts : he never mentioned his great filial devotion.   The king was not made acquainted with the circumstances till long afterwards, and was full of admiration.

" We must make a knight of him at once," he cried.

Next day Witasse, the model son, was no longer a *damoiseau!*

VIII.

The *damoiseau* was nearly immaculate : he was considered an example of virtue ; but under penalty of being unjust we must remark that the faults and vices of the youthful Feudal Barons did not differ materially from those with which philosophers and poets of all countries have reproached the youths of all nations.   They are common property—current coin.

The *damoiseau* was choleric, the blood quickly flew to his head. When the wife of Charlemagne boasted before the young Aimeri, of having made Girard de Vienne kiss her foot while under the impression that it was the emperor's—when she had the bad taste to tell to Girard's nephew this practical joke, which then was tantamount to a deadly outrage, Aimeri felt very angry; rage gnawed in his heart, he seized a knife and threw it at the head of the empress, who stooped suddenly and thus avoided the blow.

Aimeri was of course immediately seized and carried out, while the furious youth cried, " Let us go, let us go," to his attendants.

But it was over a game of chess particularly that the *damoiseaux* lost their tempers. Why did Charlot son of Charlemagne break Beaudonniet's head with the chess-board ? Simply because Beaudonniet, son of Ogier, had given him check-mate !

Again, Renaud de Montauban was scarcely a knight when, as the result of a dispute at play, he buried the chess-board in the head of Bertolais the nephew of the emperor.

Those chess-boards of the twelfth century were not the thin wooden boards which a child may break, but massive ; their four corners being so strong and pointed as to cut into bone and flesh, and inflict mortal wounds. When the son of Olive and Doon de la Roche, when the little Landri, was obliged to be present at the second marriage of his father, he put himself into a furious passion, and addressing the officiating prelate, exclaimed—

" As for you I will slay you when I am a man."

Then turning to the bride he said, " I will be avenged," and struck down with a chess-board some traitor who had ventured to calumniate his mother. Nothing could calm this little passionate soul—but it was at least furious in a good cause—on behalf of his deserted mother.

The same sentiment and a similar expression of it, somewhat legitimate and excusable, animated the " infant " Gautier in that romance of passion which is called *Raoul de Cambrai*.

" If I live long enough to have a helmet laced on my head, and a sword in my hand, you will dearly pay for this, uncle Raoul."

But I cannot recall any act of violence comparable to that of Renier and Girard, sons of Garin de Montglane, as it is related in "*Girars de Viane;*" violence—inexcusable, reckless, stupid violence —by gross young Germans who were enraged.

They arrived one day at the court of the king, and were very scandalised in the first place because they were not accorded a brilliant reception. They seated themselves at table and were poorly served with a small loaf, and but little to drink.

This treatment exasperated them, but they got into a towering passion when the Seneschal refused them corn for their mules, and when he had the audacity to strike one of them with his staff. Renier raised his fist, struck the Seneschal in the face, broke his nose, killed him, and then threw the body into the granary.

Terrified by this summary action, the attendants and squires fled in all directions; a universal panic ensued, and no one in the whole court was calm or composed except the murderer and his brother. They seemed to be actually delighted. That evening they amused and enjoyed themselves in dancing, and so on.

But next day there was another tale to be told. They were desirous to approach the king, who was in the chapel hearing the Mass, but, as the young men were poorly clad, the usher repulsed them, saying—

"These lads in grey coats really want to enter the palace, when great barons dressed in furs and fine stuffs are obliged to remain at the gate."

The usher would have been better advised to have held his tongue, for he drew this sharp reproof from Renier, a speech which has become famous—

"Don't you know, miserable creature that you are, that—

> " Le cuers n'est mie ne on vair ne on gris
> Mais qu'il est on ventre, la ou Deus l'a assis !"

Thereupon these madman attacked the gate of the palace, that august and almost sacred gate; and Renier first with a kick—Renier the gentle *damoiseau*—broke it in halves. In vain did the porter attempt to resist this brute, this madman who had thrown aside all semblance of humanity. The unfortunate man was struck down in his turn, crushed to death beneath his gate, killed outright; and then the young men, feeling well satisfied with themselves, and laughing at the incident, at length appeared before the emperor who, in fear and trembling, hastened to create them knights !

The *damoiseau* was frivolous like all young people, but in France his levity often took the form of child's-play—a somewhat Parisian practical joking, and this is evidenced by the episode of Roland and the porter of Laon. One cannot be a Frenchman "with impunity," and our race has always relished a good laugh. I do not mean to say that our jokes of the twelfth century were always classic, but they were sometimes quite comic—which was a very natural and bright *trait*.

One of those which may most easily provoke a smile (it incited our somewhat dense ancestors to laughter) is a hit at the story of Floovant and his master. It is true that this fable is borrowed from "*Gesta Dagoberti regis*," and Dagobert himself has hitherto had the honour of this schoolboy incident : but the poet of the twelfth century, to whom we are indebted for a new edition of this narrative, has so agreeably arranged and adapted it to his time, that it may pass for an original tale.

This incident took place at the time when it was the fashion in France to wear beards. Clerics and laymen were all equally bearded, and the depth of dishonour consisted in being hairless. If a robber were taken in the very act, "Let him be shaved," was the sentence.

Now, no one in France had a more beautiful beard than the Duke of Burgundy, named Sénéchal, whom King Clovis had appointed tutor to his own son Floovant. We can just imagine what a beautiful beard it was when it tempted a page to such a strange proceeding—to such a cruel joke. When his master was asleep the youth approached, and suddenly conceived the idea of cutting off that lovely beard. And he did it with his "pen-knife," the small knife with which he used to peel apples !

But we can picture the grief and rage of Sénéchal when he awoke and found his chin denuded of hair.

" Your father shall be made acquainted with this—he shall cut off your head and limbs for this."

In vain the youth pleaded and promised the victim thirty chargers, fifteen castles, and equipments for three hundred knights.

"No, no," replied the shorn one, " your father shall know all."

Thereupon he proceeded to the king, hiding the shaven and dishonoured chin in his cloak, and uncovered his face when he came into the presence of Clovis.

"Look here," he said, "this is your son's doing."

The unfortunate Floovant did not escape with less than seven years of exile. He paid dearly enough for his practical joke.

But it is not Floovant who, as we would say at present, held the appointment as jester: it was not he but Hernaut de Girone, whom they called Hernaut the Red. The brother of William of Orange was a regular practical joker, the "farceur" of our *chansons de geste*. It was his business, so to speak, to make people laugh.

When his father drove him away from home with his five brothers to seek his fortune elsewhere, he started with them for Paris. The way was long, and the journey abounded in adventures of all kinds. They were all young and lovely *damoiseaux* who had no thought of care. They very much resembled children of all nations and of all times who will listen over and over again to the same story, and laugh as heartily at the hundredth repetition as at the first.

The chief and never-failing joke amongst the brothers of Hernaut was to pretend that he was the King's Seneschal. They bestowed this title on him and rendered him, in joke, all the honours which were really due to that exalted personage. Guillaume invested him with mock solemnity—

"Henceforth," said he, "be brave and proud, and administer justice properly."

In this way they reached the gates of Paris, where the King was holding his court. But unfortunately the city was full, crowded, so that no lodging could be found for our travellers.

What was to be done? Hernaut did not lose his presence of mind, nor, like the Abbé of Cluny, complain of not finding shelter, Abbé of Cluny though he was.

"Do not alarm yourselves," said Hernaut gravely. "You now see the King's Seneschal before you in person! Yes, the Seneschal himself. You shall have a lodging. Come on."

It cost Hernaut nothing to make these promises, but he wondered anxiously how he should perform them. He continued to wander about Paris, and in a certain wide street he perceived a very pleasing smell of cookery.

"Ho! ho!" he cried. "Who is feasting here?"

Without more ado he entered the house and found a number of

" bachelors" seated at table. These joyous and convivial gentlemen informed him that they composed the suite of the Duke of
Burgundy.

"What do I care," replied Hernaut. "I am the King's
Seneschal, and am in want of these apartments. Get out !"

As they resisted he attacked them, and finally remained master
of the situation. Then he installed the Abbé of Cluny in a
beautiful chamber hung with tapestry, and left him to chant
matins with his monks.

He now proceeded to find a lodging for the good King of Pavia,
Boniface, who was wandering about the streets seeking for an
hotel.

"I am the King's Seneschal," said Hernaut to him. "You
shall have a lodging immediately."

Thereupon he entered a palace which was ablaze with light—
grant luminaire par leanz esgarda.

"Who are you ?" he asked the owners of the magnificent
mansion.

He found they were the Pope's legate and two archbishops.
He turned them out and said to Boniface : "Go in, if you
please."

He had a similar adventure with some fat Germans whose
lodgings he desired.

He began by complimenting them on their personal appearance.
Like the fox he commenced with flattery, but he did not hesitate to
have recourse to blows after a while. The Germans quitted their
lodging, and complained to the king of the outrage committed by
the strange, too grasping, and interfering Seneschal.

While the Germans were complaining to the King, Hernaut was
taking his ease in the house of which he had dispossessed them,
" Let *jongleurs* come and sing before me," he said.

But this was the last of his escapades. Everything was
discovered, and the king's people were on the point of making
very short work of Hernaut and his brothers who defended him.
But fortunately the particulars of the affair came to the knowledge
of Charlemagne, who was delighted with the impudence of these
fine young fellows of Narbonne, and conferred knighthood upon
them. They well deserved it.

There was besides another species of levity, and Gautier
d'Aupais had not the same character as Hernaut de Beaulande.
Nevertheless he is still a joker, and offers much resemblance
to our modern contemporary " giddy-pates."

His father was a gentleman in the neighbourhood of Beauvais
who would have been very pleased to have seen him succeed in tilt
and tourney : and sent him on a certain day to one of these costly
entertainments.   The young man met with indifferent success, but
compensated himself by dining sumptuously at the inn, not having
a *sou* wherewith to pay his bill.

These were daily adventures.   He played to reimburse himself,
and lost everything, even to his clothes.   His father received him
with blows, and hit so hard that he tore the young man's
shirt.

Humiliated, furious, Gautier swore to quit his paternal mansion,
where his mother and sisters, good souls, in vain endeavoured to
detain him.   He would have gone to the end of the world, I believe,
had not the smile of a young lady arrested him.

She was the daughter of a vavasseur (or under-vassal), and
Gautier was seized with a violent and honourable passion for her ;
and with a view to behold her every day, if only for an instant, he
accepted the humble post of watchman in her father's house.

The occupation is a trying one, and one may freeze up in the
gaite ; but what can you expect ? one can *see* up there.   The young
man was soon admitted to the service of the table ; and then, as he
could see more of the lady, he esteemed himself all the happier.
In order to approach more closely the lady he loved, he determined
to learn conscientiously the business of a *jongleur*, or singer.   He
declaimed, he played his music, he sang ; and by these means
managed at length to penetrate to the bower of his lady-love.
There, terrified by his audacity, and feeling very shy, he fled !   I
may as well state that he became bolder as time went on, and that
this romance (it is always a romance) terminated in a marriage.
This old story has a flavour of novelty about it.

The *damoiseau* was sometimes both sensual and debauched, and,
amongst the youthful nobles of the twelfth century, more than one
could be cited who bore some resemblance to Aubri the Burgundian,
the type of reckless vice and wild brutality.   But at the same time

we must remark that, as a rule, the youthful nobles of the twelfth century were well-behaved, at least so the old poems present them to us, and we have no reason to question their testimony. It has been said, and with reason, that in a man's heart there is only room for one great passion at a time. Our *damoiseaux* loved war too well to love women. I am even inclined to believe that they even preferred their hawks and hounds to the society of ladies.

In all our *chansons de geste* we find that the ladies make the advances (but the records may be less trustworthy on this point), and it would appear that the young "curled darlings" did not always receive the damsels with excessive politeness. They did not yield until they were compelled. It is true the young ladies were very aggressive indeed, and apparently shameless. We find instances of this in *Aiol*, in *Gaydon*, in *Gui de Nanteuil*, in which poems we have striking examples of want of propriety, and plain speaking. The most ardent swains in our day could not use plainer language; the sexes seem reversed. The Saracens also seem to speak in like manner with Christians, and the old poets, sublimely ignorant of local colour, have painted French and Arabian women with the same brush. For instance Salmandrine in *Doon de la Roche;* Malatrie in *Beuves de Commarchis;* Esclarmonde in *Huon de Bordeaux;* Floripes in *Fierabras;* and Rosemonde in *Elie de Saint-Gilles.* These five female pagans have nothing to distinguish them, in our minds, from Isodoré in *Ansëis de Carthage,* and the daughter of Gueri le Sor in *Raoul de Cambrai.* Amongst them all we find the same characteristics, the same effrontery. Esclarmonde sighs to Huon; nor is Rosemonde behindhand. They indeed present themselves to the youthful nobles in such fashion that the poor youths are compelled to consent. We need not quote any references, of which there are many in the old poems.

But, it must be confessed that, we should look with considerable suspicion on these statements of our poets, which cannot be accepted as exact or always serious. The troubadours of the period were more ignorant of the ladies of their day—and especially of the young ladies—than of any other portion of society; and we must reduce to their proper value these highly spiced and seasoned allegations and statements. I maintain, notwithstanding this evidence, that the young noble in those "iron days" was too much of a

warrior and a hunter to have leisure for love-making. Such is the
fact—such is the opinion to which we adhere—at the same time
that we must confess that the Romances of the Round Table seem
very greatly to countenance such a condition of things, making
flirtation fashionable, making brave souls effeminate, and changing
the youthful warrior to a carpet-knight.

We must not exaggerate anything, however, and the natural love
which is inspired in knight and gentlewoman will, we trust, never
cease to exist in, and to illumine, the earth. Our youthful barons
were not unaware of its existence either. One of our most primitive heroes, we read, recalls his first love with delight—" O for the
time when I was a youth," he exclaims. " O, that was a happy time.
Then I preferred a green cap to a hundred silver marks, and did
great homage to beauteous dames ! "

But, as a matter of fact, we find that this affection amongst our
damoiseaux had something violent and brutal about it nevertheless.
Look at Roland beneath the walls of Vienna ; look at him just
when he was about to engage in that interminable duel with Oliver
which has been so well described by the author of *Girars de Viane*, and
after him by the greatest poet of our own country. The scene was
indeed a very animated one, and the ladies—all the ladies of the
city—had assembled without the walls to be spectators of the
terrible combat between Oliver and Roland. Amongst them was
one damsel whose beauty eclipsed all others ; long fair hair
crowned by a jewelled hat, eyes piercing as the falcon's, well-
shaped feet and hands, rivalling the lily in whiteness, a complexion
fresh and brilliant, just tinged with a soft colour : this was Aude
—the beautiful Aude.

She was clad in that charming costume, which our old poets
well knew, and over her shoulders was thrown a most becoming
short cloak. She was charming, and illuminated the scene by her
beauty. At the first glance Roland singled her out from all the
rest. And what did this hero, this nephew of a king do ? Did he
sigh in the fashion of a Knight of the Round Table ? By no
means. Roland rushed towards her, threw himself upon her. He
was a barbarian, and only in that fashion did he understand love.
He seized her and would have carried her off before the eyes of all
those present, that charming damsel, the type in our epic poetry of

all that was truly pure and innocent, but Aude called to her brother
for help :—" Oliver, my brother, Oliver ! " Oliver rushed upon
Roland and attacked him fiercely.

" You are a duke, and I am a count," he exclaimed. " We can
fight on equal terms ; " and without further parley he delivered
some of those terrific blows, of which the secret has died with him.
Oliver, in whom fraternal affection and the sight of his sister's
danger had excited strong passion, felled Roland to the earth, and,
without pausing to see whether he picked himself up again, carried
off his sister, and bestowed her in safety within the walls of Vienna.
She was saved—but she loved Roland !

Notwithstanding the nature of this coarse love of his, I prefer it
to the more romantic and criminal affection that subsisted between
Huon and the beautiful Esclarmonde. There was a refinement of
sensuality about the latter which smacks of the nefarious influence
of the Round Table. Scarcely had the lovers met than a terrible
tempest arose and shattered the vessel in which they had sailed,
and which in consequence of their sin seemed accursed. They
were driven about for a long while, tossed upon the angry sea,
clutching a wretched plank, until they were at length cast upon a
desolate island.

" Ah," exclaimed Esclarmonde, " we have indeed fallen ! "

And her companion replied :

" Tristan died for love of the beautiful Iseult; let us die also,
you and I ! "

The youthful nobles of the twelfth century more nearly resembled
Roland than Huon, and, notwithstanding all reservations, I cannot
refrain from congratulating them warmly on their choice.

The *damoiseau* was not only passionate and sensual, he was also
proud, haughty, quick-tempered, and jealous. Such a character
was Charlot, such was the son of Charlemagne, whom the author
of " *Ogier le Danois*," and more particularly the writer of " *Huon
de Bordeaux*," have painted in such gloomy tones. His father
reproached him most bitterly for consorting with traitors and
making friends of them : " *Miex aimme asés les traïtors laniers
Que les preudommes ; s'en ai le cuer irié !* "

We perceive him one day killing the son of Ogier, and by this
act setting the torch to a train of a terrible war, and then leading

the sons of Duke Seguin of Bordeaux into an ambuscade, in which
he himself perished.   Here is a souvenir of a really historical
personage, and our Charlot is none other than "Charles the
Infant," son of Charles the Bald, who died on 29th of September,
866, under similar circumstances.   The historical personage and
the hero of the legend are about on a par, and when Reginon
accuses the former of "youthful levity" he uses an euphuism
which we cannot apply to either individual, but which can be
applied unquestionably to a certain number of the *valets*—the
youthful barons of the twelfth century.

There is no need to dwell longer upon such a scene, so let us
turn as a last example to the young noble of the time of Louis the
Seventh, or of Philip Augustus, the bold, strong, elegant and
courageous youth launched into the midst of some "epic battle"
and preserving in all his heroism, something humane and charming.
"*Jouenes hom sui, ne vuel encor morir,*" was the cry of the youthful
Ernaut (as we have already perceived), as he fled before Raoul de
Cambrai.   Who would expect to find in that most sanguinary of
our epic poems this cry so natural and so true, this very same
exclamation which André Chenier has put into the mouth of his
young captive—" I do not want to die yet ! "

And now the time of probation is over, and we come—(O !
happiness—O ! joy) to the period at which our *damoiseau* is told
he must prepare himself to receive knighthood—at last !

IX.

At what age were the youths admitted to the eighth sacrament ?
There is no doubt that there existed some connection between the
arrival at "majority," and the period at which one could be dubbed
knight.   But the time when the youth attained his majority varied.

Amongst German tribes it varied.   With the Salians it was twelve
years, with the Ripuarians fifteen.   These different dates obtained
for a more or less lengthened period in the districts inhabited by
the descendants of those tribes, and a curious vein of study is here
opened to us.   But of all the Germans it may be said as Theodoric
said of the Goths, " It is strength that regulates the attainment of

the majority. As soon as he was big enough to fight, the young barbarian came of age.''

However that may have been, thanks to the softening tone of manners and under the visible influence of Roman Law, there has arisen amongst us a more and more marked tendency to postpone the arrival at majority, and to fix the date of coming of age at twenty or twenty-one. This tendency had already obtained to a certain extent in the twelfth century. In Glanville, in the *Très ancien Coutumier Normand,* it is fixed at twenty-one. In the thirteenth century the custom became still more accentuated. It is true that in Beauvaisis the old German custom is adhered to, and fifteen is stated as the period of coming of age ; but the Coutume de France mentions twenty, while the second part of *Très ancien Coutumier Normand,* the *Très ancien Coutume d'Anjou,* and the *Etablissements de Saint Louis* are unanimous in putting the period, thenceforth agreed upon, at twenty-one. In the twelfth century the unanimity was still more striking, and it is best to accept that age here. So twenty-one years was the time for coming of age—not twenty-one years accomplished, but only entered upon.

Well, all these variations regarding the age of majority we find repeated when the question of the proper time for dubbing the aspirant a knight arose. So once again we find an evident parallelism between these two questions. But on the plain of Chivalry the German idea resisted longer, much longer, than on the level of Majority.

In our chronicles as in our *chansons de geste,* which so accurately reflect the Chivalresque life of the period, we find many opinions regarding the age for becoming a knight; and these are not easy to reconcile. They prove to us that an aspirant might become a knight at twelve, thirteen, fourteen, fifteen, seventeen, and nineteen. If I had to give the average age I should say fifteen—the period of arriving at majority amongst the Germans !

But it is necessary to take into consideration the same influences which concurred in pushing back the age for the attainment of the majority, and we must state that the tendency became more and more marked to '' push back '' the age for the bestowal of knight-hood to twenty-one also. But this was no easy matter.

In the thirteenth century twenty-one was the fashionable age.

If Arthur were dubbed knight at fifteen, it was for political reasons.
If Philip the Fair was in after years knighted at sixteen, it was for
similar reasons, for he was actually King of Navarre at the time.
On the other hand, the sons of Saint Louis and of Philip the Fair
were not armed until they were twenty years of age. "One cannot
attain one's majority, nor become a knight, until after one has
entered on his twenty-first year." Such is the present rule, and
we can find very few exceptions to it in France; but we are now
very far from German traditions, and even from the twelfth
century.

In brief, our *damoiseau*, the youth whom we have followed day
by day, is yet only fifteen and will be dubbed knight. It is quite
true; his feathers are overlapping the nest! *Pennæ nido majores.*
He cannot hide his exultation, and he goes about the castle
singing, "A knight, a knight, I am to be dubbed a knight!"

CHAPTER VII.

THE ADMISSION TO CHIVALRY.—ITS THEORY AND HISTORY.

I.

IN our old poets we find many expressions to denote the entry or admission to chivalry. One is girt with the sword or the baldric; one is made, armed, or dubbed knight. The last expression appears to have been the most usual at the same time as it is the most technical, but it, nevertheless, presents to us some little difficulties. That it is derived from the Anglo-Saxon *dubban*, that it signifies to strike, that it carries the allusion to the famous "blow" which the investor bestows upon the shoulder of the newly-made knight, I am ready to admit; but, at the same time, I must say that the meaning is in our language somewhat "pre-historic," for, in the most ancient testimony in our national poetry, we find the word dub is simply used in the sense of "arming."

However, no matter what word was used to signify the admission of the youthful aspirant into the ranks of chivalry, the prospect was equally alluring to our youthful *damoiseau*, who anticipated it with impatient enthusiasm. It was the all absorbing idea, his sole thought. The squire asked himself when should he become a knight; and the wedded knight, some years married, would murmur to his wife, "When shall our children become knights?" The old baron, contemplating with lack-lustre eyes the youngest of his children, would say, "Look, behold, my sons. If Providence will only spare me to see them knights, my heart, my old heart will rejoice!"

Chivalry was then the dream, the end, the regal honour. It has been said, and truly, that our century had the "torment of the infinite." This expression of Schlegel cannot be applied to the Middle Ages because they possessed nothing peculiarly tormenting;

but we can truly say that if our forefathers had not the "torment" of chivalry they had the passion for it.

Scholars have sometimes been wrong in attempting to reduce truths to dry and uninteresting classifications, but their proceedings, even if far-fetched, must not be altogether despised. Apropos of the admission to Chivalry, the chaplain of our future knight proposed to himself a little treatise which he divided into five chapters entitled *Quis ? Quando ? Ubi ? Per quem ? Quomodo ?* He even endeavoured to condense these five questions into a single hexameter verse, but nothing came of the attempt.

Nevertheless we shall follow the chaplain's lead, but for the sake of clearness put our ideas in French (English). Who was eligible to be armed a knight ? When will he receive the order of Chivalry ? Where should he receive it ? By whom should it be conferred ? What are the rites of this eighth sacrament which so many thousands valued so highly ? These are the five questions which we are about to answer in turn.

II.

Who was eligible for knighthood ? If we were to reply "Everybody," we should not be far from the truth. No one could or can say that Chivalry was a "close" institution, or, if you prefer the term, a caste. Only the infirm were excluded because they could not cut a good figure in battle, and the whole of Chivalry is summed up in the word "fighting." The Church very wisely excludes cripples from the altar, where they would be ridiculed, and the warriors of the Middle Ages also very wisely excluded them from Chivalry, in which they would have been useless. Depravity of mind, infamous manners, the disdain which attaches to certain professions, or origin : all these moral infirmities were calculated to close the doors of Chivalry against such base and dishonoured persons. It is true that Richard Cœur de Lion was very anxious to make Mercadier, the bandit chief, his companion-in-arms, a knight, but he could not. It was simply impossible. As he was unable to ennoble this brigand, he enriched him, which was a much more feasible feat.

However, Chivalry was "open."

Yes, it was open to the *vilains*, and our *chansons*, which we have already quoted in this connection, supply us with more than one famous instance which will be useful to put on record here.   The poor woodcutter, Varocher, who devoted himself so heroically to the Queen of France, then so ignominiously calumniated and proscribed, who for her sake abandoned his wife and children to become

Galien created a Knight by the dead hand of Roland (*see* p. 231).

her guide and defender, who led her into Hungary, and protected her infant child Louis, born in exile, as he had protected his mother : this kind of labouring man, whose great shock head of hair made all the passers-by laugh, this *vilain* of *vilains* one day was dubbed knight by Charlemagne himself in person.   Yes, an emperor girded on his sword, a duke actually buckled his spurs, and a queen invested him with the *cirlaton* reserved for the nobility. She did more ; she exclaimed as she thus invested him, " There is not in the whole world a man more loyal ! "   If you give to these words their true significance you will understand that Chivalry was the royal recompense, and that the lowest of the *vilains* could aspire to it.

The other peasant was Simon le Voyer, who so generously received the sweet and innocent wife of King Pepin, Bertha. This man of humble birth was also admitted to the same dignity, to the same honour. A mantle of cloth of gold was cast over his shoulders, the king girt him with his sword, and the Duke Namus fastened his spurs. Both his sons were created knights at the same time, and, like him, received the king's embrace. Such an elevation surprised no one, and the act was less unusual than one might suppose. Our romances are full of complaints against those who introduced peasants into the orders of chivalry. "It is a very ill recompense to a warrior to make the sons of *vilains* knights," remarks the author of *Girart de Roussillon*, and one almost feels that the cry is wrung from the depths of his heart.

The fact is that the privilege was abused. Without taking into consideration those provinces in which the tradespeople arrogated to themselves the power of girding on the sword of knighthood, there occurred a great scandal amongst the true knights when certain *parvenus* bestowed on themselves the *accolade* just as in the present day certain financiers decorate themselves. Take for instance the case of that merchant who is mentioned in *Doon de Maience*. He had never in all his life done anything but money-grubbing; that was his only merit, but he was knighted because of his wealth. "*Mis pour son grant avoir l'ot ou fet adouber.*"

The verse is typical, and might with equal truth be applied to knights of our own day. In fact, the bestowal of knighthood was a very excellent means by which men were bent to one's will, and became the creatures of the great. When the traitor Herchembaud wished to get rid of the children of Gui de Maience, he sought first to corrupt their tutor. "I will make you a knight," he said. This was likewise the promise which young Roland made to the porter of the castle of Laon where he was restrained: but the porter, who was a vulgar-minded man, did not think much of chivalry. "It is a trade," said he, "in which one receives too many blows," and he rudely declined, as we have seen, the advances of the nephew of Charlemagne. But it was different with the two serfs who so heroically refused to desert poor Amis when he was smitten with leprosy, for they joyfully permitted themselves to be dubbed knights. As a last trait, knighthood was accessible to *jongleurs,* and even to comedians! This is saying a great deal in a very few words.

But we must not go too far and generalise, for, however numerous the cases may have been, they were, after all, only excep-tions. The others composed the rule—well, not perhaps the rule, but the custom—and it was contained in the following formula, "Of *damoiseaux,* of sons of knights, of young nobles, came the stuff of which knights are made."

Amongst the candidates for knighthood were those who had to endure the privations, and submit to the rude discipline of an esquire; but this was not an indispensable condition, and noble birth generally was sufficient. It is true that the young noble was not born a knight, but he belonged to a social class in which, at proper age, all the male members were created knights. The man of war made his son a warrior as soon as he was able to bear his armour, and wield his sword. This was only natural, and was the result of circumstances.

III.

At what time of life could he receive the "sacrament" of Chivalry? We need not here again enter upon this question, which has already been elucidated. But were there not certain days which were set apart for this solemn rite? Yes, certainly; and our forefathers, who were religious men, chose the anniversaries of the great church festivals. They were certain on those days of having a numerous audience, and a crowd of spectators! The tradespeople and peasantry who thronged the churches, took intense delight (after mass) in playing at the quintain, which generally brought the feast to a conclusion. It may be allowed that the grandees did not disdain the applause of the populace, and indeed, may be said to have sought it rather too freely. We have noticed in our old poems five days, fête days, which were more especially devoted to the creation of knights. These were Christmas Day, Easter, Ascension Day, Whitsunday, and Saint John's Day.

One only of these festivals falls in the winter, and it was the least patronized, because the formalities of creation required open air, springtime and festivity. To dub a knight in the winter, is almost a contradiction in terms. Easter and Whitsuntide were evidently the favourite fixtures : " *A Pasques en Avril que soés est li tens,*" and elsewhere—" *Ce fu à Pentecoste qu'est plusiers li estes.*" Do not speak of December for the celebration of that beautiful fête —no, give me the months of April, May, and June. The budding knights are then more in keeping with the blossoms of the trees. Our forefathers did not very probably go into it quite so deeply as all that, but they had a very vivid sense of the harmonies of which they did not render exact account. They felt the influence of spring without being able to explain it scientifically. Besides, Easter is really the fête of fêtes, the day of days. It was the first day of the year, the acme of the Liturgical year, and all the traditions of the primitive church were then fresh and living in the hearts of those rough Christians.

It has again not been sufficiently insisted on, that the nights at Easter and Whitsuntide have been, from far Christian antiquity, sanctified by the Vigils, of which the Liturgy still possesses the traces, and in which all faithful people took an active part. Between the vigils of arms—the watching of the armour—of which we shall shortly speak, and the beautiful religious vigils of Easter and Pentecost there is a natural and glorious co-relation. I do not wish to adventure into dangerous symbolism, but I can nevertheless not forget that the Feast of Pentecost is the anniversary of the foundation of that church to which all knights in former days devoted their swords and their lives, and involuntarily there come to my mind the different orders of the Holy Ghost which did honour to the Church and to France. Still more than Easter Pentecost was a well recognised solemn feast-day, and I am not surprised at it. On that morning, at high mass, our young *damoiseaux* were greatly moved while listening to a " sequence " usually composed for the occasion, and which the clergy took pleasure in translating for them. "In toil be our repose, and in burning hardships our refreshment, and our delight." Our future soldiers relished this versicle very much, and they were soon to be called to suffer but toils and privations under the burning sun of Palestine. *In labore requies, in æstu temperies!*

But the church festivals were not the only days on which our newly-made knights were created. Advantage was taken very often of those numerous private gatherings and fêtes which peopled the solitudes of the castle or the palace. On the occasion of a wedding or a baptism of royalties, many varlets were dubbed knights. The creation of the son of a king as knight, was the opportunity for dubbing many less distinguished individuals. It was a great compliment to give to the son of a king an escort of twenty, fifty, or a hundred newly-created cavaliers like himself. This was a delicate attention, a luxury. But all these kinds of ceremonies appear to us, if we may say so, too polite and civil. The function which we prefer to all others is that which is carried out on the field of battle, or in the midst of the fight, without any such " apparatus " or preparation, when the warrior is covered with blood and dust. Notwithstanding the somewhat unpleasant character of such a ceremony, of such an improvised consecration, there is something of an air of triumph in the weird surroundings, something of hope and joy.

There is still one more festival. It happened when the Crusaders were gallantly struggling beneath the walls of Antioch, when, seeing the brilliant exploits of the Squire Gontier d'Aire, Godfrey de Bouillon exclaimed : " We will make him a knight as soon as ever he pleases ! " But the *damoiseau* replied in the true Christian spirit and refused the honour, the offer of which must have been to him a source of great joy. " No," he replied, " no more dubbing of knights; no more chevaliers until we have taken the Holy Sepulchre ! " This refusal is not far removed from sublimity.

IV.

" Where was the knight armed ? "

On the field of battle, first of all, in the hour of enthusiasm and victory after some doughty deed. This grand old custom may be placed very far back into antiquity, and our old poems give us many striking instances of it. In this manner Danois was dubbed

under the walls of Rome after having covered himself with glory
in one of the greatest battles which established the destiny of the
Eternal City. Thus he was made a Knight after having snatched
from Pagan hands the oriflamme, the standard of France.

On another occasion it happened that Bertrand, son of Bernard
of Brabant, presented himself one day to his father in the heat of
battle and requested to be made a knight.

"What do you know about it? You cannot even wield a
lance," replied his father, brutally, as he aimed a blow at the face
of his son, who thereupon dashed into the enemies' ranks and
sought a warrior's death. We can, then, imagine that any creation
of knights on the field of battle was unattended by any complicated
ceremonies, and that the ritual was of the simplest character. In
two minutes the whole business was completed.

Archbishop Turpin "made no bones about it;" he rushed into
the battle exclaiming "*Je suis evesques,*" or "*me fez chevalier.*"
But this was rather a summary proceeding, for a consecrator at
least was absolutely necessary to make a warrior a true knight,
and he could not thus take the matter into his own hands. From
the thirteenth to the sixteenth centuries the fashion of creating
knights on the field of battle only obtained in France, and in
all Christian Europe. It opened the door to abuses. Chivalry as
we have said ought to be the highest form of recompense, the most
noble and the most enviable of all rewards, and it was a great
pleasure to see the young men, pale and wounded, on the evening
of some well-fought day, receiving the *paumée* and fitting on their
gold spurs.

After the battle this was all very well; before the battle it was
unnecessary. Juan, King of Portugal, is greatly to be admired,
when before the Battle of Aljubarrota in 1385 he placed in the
van of his army the sixty warriors whom he had just created
knights, and thus dismissed them proudly:

"Beaux Seigneurs," he said, "I send you into the first shock of
the battle. Do all you can in honour, otherwise your gold spurs
may not sit very comfortably on you!"

This is all very well, but if I rejoice over the four hundred and
sixty French knights who were created before the victory of
Rosebecque, I am not quite so proud of the five hundred who were

dubbed before the defeat at Agincourt. I am not often of Brantôme's opinion, and I may be too proud of it, but I am compelled to admit his reasoning when he states his preference for knighthood conferred after a battle.

Now I will close all I have to say about the creations "in battle" with the relation of the interesting incident which recalls the memory of one of the greatest knights in our national history—I mean Du Guesclin, who has been found worthy of having our latest *chansons de geste* devoted to him.

The scene took place long after the death of this rough but celebrated captain, in 1423, on the evening of the battle of Brossiniere. This was one of those rare—very rare—victories which in some measure consoled France during the Hundred Years' War, as the victory of Coulmiers did in 1870 : a little ray of sunshine in the darkness of our day. The conqueror of 1423 called himself Count d'Aumale, and he was the king's cousin.

He ended the glorious day, as was his custom, in making many knights on the field of battle. The youthful André de Laval was of the number, and the commander girt him with Du Guesclin's own sword, saying, " May Heaven make you as valiant as he who once wore it ! "

If we were a nation of more traditions, if we had a more lively regard for the ancient honour of France, we would guard jealously the remembrance of those proud words. But we are as ignorant of them as of the bond which united the great souls of Du Guesclin and Joan of Arc ; for there are perhaps not ten Frenchmen at the present day—no not ten—who are acquainted with the touching incident of the deliverer of Orleans sending her ring which she wore as a girl to the widow of Bertrand du Guesclin, who fifty years before had worked so hard to deliver France. To have such a story as this in their annals and not to know it !

Notwithstanding the poetic side of the creations which were made on the field, warriors resigned themselves to enter into Chivalry in a more prosaic fashion, for it was in times of peace that most knights were dubbed. This function, like our first communions, re-assembled the scattered family and united it tenderly again. The ceremony took place in a church or castle, according as the family of the postulant or the novice himself had elected the liturgic or the military ritual. The church chosen was generally the nearest monastery, and it was an exceptional case in which the knight was dubbed in the Sanctuary of Saint Catherine or Saint Sepulchre afterwards.

But the lay rites it must be maintained remained for a long time in vogue, and we are compelled to inquire what part of the castle was specially reserved for such an important and striking ceremony? Either the meadows or fields which surrounded the castle, or the open space at the top of the steps leading to it. The first rites of the creation did not require any great space, and that in front of the castle was sufficient. From the picturesque point of view simply, no better place could have been selected, and it may be recommended to decorators and artists. At the top of these steps everything assumed an air of grandeur, and a thousand spectators could easily witness all the details of the ceremony. When, however, the last acts of the military ritual had to be accomplished, when the new knight had to vault into the saddle, to gallop and strike at the *quintain*, neither the terrace nor the step was sufficiently large. He was compelled to leave the castle, he was followed by all his friends, and surrounded by the crowd of spectators. The ceremony was concluded in the open on some lovely spring day amid blossoms and flowers.

I need scarcely add that our *damoiseau* was ever ready to be dubbed in the palace, and at the risk of sounding a sad note in this joyous strain I must add that sometimes a warrior was made a knight on his death-bed. The ceremony was most touching, and eminently calculated to inspire a work of art. But I decidedly prefer the field of battle to all other places.

So we now know what were the conditions on which the College of Chivalry could be entered, the time of year, and the ordinary surroundings amid which the ceremony took place.

But who was the consecrator? To whom belonged the privilege of making knights? It is necessary to ascertain this.

V.

Every knight has the power to create knights.—This is the principle which we must first lay down and which is predominant: it was the ancient and primordial custom, the spirit, the life, the very essence of the institution.

Chivalry was a society in which all members had a right to introduce new members, and as many as they pleased. That is the whole matter.

There is in the hand and in the sword of every knight a power (I nearly wrote "a fluid," but I did not dare) which is really capable of creating other knights. It was the most noble and the most precious privilege of the *miles*. If it were not an abuse of so sacred a term, I would say that he was a military priest. But after all, Chivalry in this, as in other things, has been modelled on the Church. A Christian is permitted to make Christians in some circumstances, and the water of Baptism may in some instances fall from any hand. So in like manner every knight could very legitimately say to himself, "I can make others knights;" and hold up his head proudly.

But of course it must be understood that in practice this was not the case, and the right was not exercised by all knights. The candidate who was very young and inexperienced, cast his eyes round him and debated within himself who should be his sponsor. Now, the first knight who presented himself to his mind was his father. One need not be a profound student of human nature to come to the conclusion that the youth would voluntarily select his father for his sponsor. "Between *pater* and *patrinus* and the chaplain of our château," there is so little difference.

Therefore in our *chansons de geste* nothing is more usual than to find instances of fathers creating their sons knights. Thus Hervis of Metz was one day armed by his father Duke Peter. But I am not acquainted with any more complete type, and any more charming instance of the dubbing of the knight than that scene in Aiol, in which we behold the youthful hero of that charming poem, on the point of starting from home for the Court of Louis, entreating his father to grant him the arms of Chivalry. The poor mother is a spectator of the ceremony which presages for her a long absence from her son.

"My son," she said, "never forget your father who is ill."

"My son," said his father, "never forget your mother who will soon be here all alone!"

Then the old Elias girt him with the steel sword, the *brant d'acier*, and bestowed the *colée* on his son. Aiol could now leave —he was a knight!

It is, perhaps, scarcely necessary to add that when the father of the *damoiseau* was not within reach, the young man had recourse to his nearest relatives, and chose amongst them his sponsor. The uncle is indicated, and it is marvellous to note in our epic poems how paternal the uncle was. There is the admirable William of Orange, one of those heroes—a rare occurrence in our old poems—who had no children. But he was greatly attached to all his nephews, and most of all he loved Vivien. He would never yield to another the delight and pleasure he felt in conferring knighthood, and there came a certain Easter-tide (*que l'on dit en esté*) when William armed Vivien.

"I vow," said his nephew, "I vow, dear uncle, that I will never retire one step before the Saracens!"

Thus spoke the new knight with all the impetuosity and imprudence of youth. Alas! he adhered only too well to his promise. He was slain at Aliscans.

There was another sponsor who was sometimes preferred by the novices to both father and uncle, and he whom custom, morals, and right favoured was their liege-lord. The liege-lord or *a* liege-lord. The young nobles found it to their interest to place themselves under the protection of some rich and powerful baron—it is something of the same kind of feeling which influences our parents at our baptisms. Any Christian can no doubt hold a baby at the font, but the family of the child, in a spirit of calculation not to be condemned, choose in preference those whose means and position are likely to advance the child's interests. Thus it happened that our would-be knights demanded the *colée* from a count, a duke, their suzerain, or, ascending rapidly the social ladder, from the emperor or king.

Our old romances (*chansons*) sometimes enlighten us upon

certain points which history fails to illuminate. This is the case as regards the conferring of knighthood by sovereigns, concerning which we are by no means well informed, and of which the compilers of history have not taken sufficient notice. We are, for our own part, convinced that emperors and kings have habitually profited by the impulse which directed to them so many aspirants for knighthood, very anxious to receive their swords from the hands of such exalted personages, pleased at the idea of obtaining such powerful protectors, and assured under such conditions of having a successful career.

We are convinced that kings and emperors themselves begged for the creation, or at least for the opportunity of confirming all these new knights. It is equally certain that this attempt broke down, and the older custom prevailed. Instead of making a leap over their natural sponsors, the *valets* more often continued to request the *colée* from their fathers, and from their liege-lords direct, from some powerful neighbouring baron, or from a simple knight; and the royal confirmation was very rarely sought. But all this did not happen in a day, nor without many interesting changes of fortune. Our old poems, fortunately, are not so silent on this subject as are our histories.

We can all understand that the squires indulged the wish to have their swords girt on by the king in a marble hall under the eyes of a thousand barons clothed in silver mail, in the presence of many hundreds of beautiful dames arrayed in silks and gold embroidery, and the ceremonial was otherwise imposing, much more so than if it had taken place in their father's castle. That fathers shared their sons' sentiments in this matter, and had voluntarily despatched them to the court, is a fact attested by at least fifty of our *chansons*.

The ceremony was always carried out in the same fashion. The old baron, looking round on his elder sons, would perceive one day that they were strong enough and big enough to wield sword and lance. Then the same words would rise to his lips—

"Go and request the emperor to knight you—to give you lands."

So they departed, meeting with numerous adventures of all kinds, and of which the recital forms the foundation of all romances, until one morning they reached Paris dusty and gleeful, exhausted, perhaps, but delighted with their surroundings; and forgetting all the fatigues of the journey, caused themselves to be conducted to the palace where the king awaited them with open arms.

In our old epic poems, which faithfully reflect the manners and customs of the eleventh and twelfth centuries, the solemn seasons of Easter and Whitsuntide seldom passed without witnessing the interesting ceremony of the creation of new knights; and kings, in order to attract to their courts the *damoiseaux* of all countries, dispensed princely *largesses*. This was good policy, and one is at a loss to know whether they were more generous or more diplomatic.

In one of our chansons, which presents to us the greatest detail of the family life of our ancestors, and which we have frequently utilised for its exact and vivid representation of the manners of the period, we find the recital of one of these functions—the creation of knights by a king. Nothing can be more delightful than the little-known pages of *Godefroi de Bouillon.* We are in spirit at Boulogne, and the son of Count Witasse, who was also called Witasse, was sent by his father to the English Court there to be admitted into the Order of Chivalry. The youthful *valet* is incomparable to any other valet or *meschin*. He took in his train ten other *damoiseaux*, twenty-six squires and *sergents*, four knights and four valuable steeds, without mentioning an abundance of money, furs, and birds of chase. Ah, that was a fine departure! And the crossing was favourable. The young Boulonnais and his train halted at Canterbury and Rochester. " Where is the king?" he demanded. " In London." " Let us make for London then." Witasse reached the city before sunset and established himself within the shadow of Saint Paul's.

Scarcely had he arrived when he displayed his magnificence. His rooms were illuminated brightly and gleamed across the street. " Let all those who are hungry come and dine with me; the table is spread." The poor came in crowds, the officers and knights did not hinder them, and very soon people began to gossip about this young *damoiseau* of France who was more liberal and more regal than the king himself.

" I am the son of the Count of Boulogne," said Witasse to the king, one day as they came from mass together, " and I have come hither to request of you my *garnimens* (investiture)."

Thereupon the king embraced him and fêted him, and dubbed him knight with " most joyous luxury." His clothing was magnificent, he had never appeared so handsome, and the poet naively remarks, as he compares him with the other *damoiseaux*, that this youth of " thirteen and a half years old " was to them in comparison as the gerfalcon to the magpie, as silver to lead, as the rose to the nettle. The king himself girded Witasse with his sword, and the *bachelor*, after a glorious run at the quintain, was nominated Seneschal of England " ere the day was over." My goodness ! what a quantity of furs and cloaks, what presents were distributed that evening in the good city of London. The newly created knight gave largesse to everyone, and would carry nothing back to Boulogne. The troubadours sang ; psalms resounded, and universal joy prevailed. This fête was long remembered.

Witasse's brother, whose name was Godfrey, was quietly knighted by his father at Boulogne. In fact such expensive ceremonies could not be repeated often, and the eldest son was frequently the only one who enjoyed the luxury of investiture. It was rather expensive work being dubbed by a king.

It is very certain that kings themselves attached real value to these creations, which tended to favour their encroachments, and to increase their prestige. They would have preferred to multiply them indefinitely and, at the same time, to have enunciated the great principle, " Only the king can arm knights ! " On this point, again, history comes off second best with the poets, who supply the lapse advantageously. We may, as a matter of fact, divide our chansons into two distinct groups--the Royal and the Feudal. Nor is it in the anti-feudal romances that the pretensions of our kings come out with such a force and audacity, and nothing is more valuable from this point of view than a too little known episode in the *Chanson d'Aspremont.*

At the opening of this poem, which belongs to the end of the twelfth and the beginning of the thirteenth century, we find Charlemagne energetically protesting against any of his nobles creating knights—so that none was rash enough to gird any knight;

and again " Charles prevented all those in his dominions from
making a single knight." " Let the *damoiseaux* come to Court
when it shall be assembled.   There each one shall receive a steed,
a sword, a good hauberk, a closed helmet, and a silken robe, and,
if he pleases, he shall be made a knight on the spot."   Summary
penalties were proclaimed against those who would infringe upon
the king's privileges.   They were liable to be exiled—proscribed !

The emperors and kings of our romances have gone even farther,
and Charlemagne in another version of this *Aspremont* which we
have quoted, gives vent to the almost revolutionary expression—
" Let anyone who pleases be a knight."   He immediately put this
audacious theory into practice and, says the poet, he made knights
of all sorts and conditions of men.   " Those who were serfs have
left behind them their servitude."   This is the very acme of
Cæsarism, and it has never descended quite so far in reality.   But
our *chansons* at least bring into the light an undoubted tendency
of the central power.   It is as well to know it.

Hitherto we have spoken of only one " consecrator," but in time
several were required.   This luxury arose, as may be anticipated,
only amongst sons of kings, dukes and counts, and not amongst
the small fry.   However, these sponsors divided the responsibility
and the business.   One put on one spur, another the other, a third
girded on the sword, a fourth bestowed the *paumée*, while a fifth
brought forth the fine steed on which the newly-dubbed knight was
to display his prowess.

These functions were, fortunately, not always so complicated, and
in lieu of five sponsors our well-born squires easily resigned themselves to having four, even three, or perhaps only two !   There was
a series of ceremonials with which we need not weary the reader,
but the whole was imposing and grand.   All who took any part in
the rites performed their duty with becoming seriousness.   The
spurs were gravely fastened, gravely was the sword buckled on, and
gravely was delivered the heavy blow upon the shoulder (the *paumée*).
The ceremonial was religious, quiet, and imposing.   It is impossible
to mention this military but touching ceremonial without recalling
the beautiful composition in which Simone Memmi has immortalised the creation of Saint Martin.   It is a scene from the Middle
Ages—nay, rather I shall say it is the entire cycle of the Middle

Ages, embodied, living, by the genius and the pencil of a great artist.

We have hitherto only spoken of "lay" ceremonial, but in the twelfth century at certain times and in certain countries, a clerical element was imported into the admission to Chivalry. This may astonish some of our contemporaries who believe in secularising everything, but it must be stated that during the periods in which St. Bernard and St. Louis flourished, souls were attracted by a magnet of whose power we have but little knowledge. There were *damoiseaux* who made the journey to Rome in order to be consecrated by "the Vicar of Christ." Many others cast themselves down before bishops, and begged for Chivalric honours at their hands. Examples are numerous, and the office of the *Benedictio novi militis* came in to triumph over ancient prejudices. The abbots who "illumined" a certain number of castles and strongholds made themselves remarkable, especially in England, for their ardour in making new knights. The Church found it necessary to extinguish this bright fire, and in a council held at Westminster, formally prohibited these irregular creations. In Spain, they did not incline in that direction, and this proud, rather too proud, race one day arrived at the pitch of consecration "by oneself!" Spanish kings crowned themselves boldly with their own hands—they were fond of this swagger—and Spanish knights girded themselves with the armour of chivalry. These exhibitions of pride are marvellously like ostentation, but they are not without some characteristics of grandeur. In France, we were not so grand in our ideas, and many a youthful noble, many a young prince, has thought himself happy as long as he lived, if he had been knighted by a lady. Both history and romance unite in presenting to us cases in which these feminine creations have occurred, and in which truly philosophical minds find a new proof of the elevation to which the Christian Middle Age was enabled to raise the position of woman. Antiquity affords no parallel. When the united voices of Peter the Hermit and Urban II. called the Western barons to the Holy Land, we do not find that wives and sisters sought to dissuade their husbands or brothers.

The daughter of Philip the First, Cécile, wife of Tancred, wished to confer with her own hands the honour of knighthood on several squires who were about to proceed to the Holy Land. There were many other Céciles ; and it is to be regretted that our historians have not left us, as Orderic Vital did, the names of some of these modest heroines. Our romances are here more prolix, and, if I may say so, more historical. When the brother of Vivien, the youthful Guichardet, escaped from the town of Orange to fly to the assistance of his brother, who was so soon to perish at Aliscans, his aunt Guibourc would not permit him to undertake such a perilous enterprise until she had herself endowed him with knightly arms. She inducted him into his hauberk ; she laced his helmet round his youthful head ; she herself girded him with his sword. The lad found that Guibourc was too dilatory : he cried with vexation, and escaping once again, he proceeded, and met in full *mêlée* his uncle William, who did not recognise him, and addressed him as " Brother Knight " (*Chevalier frère*). " You do not recognise me," said the young man. " I am named Guichardet, and am your nephew. Guibourc made me a knight, and I have come to release my brother Vivien." Then William embraced him.

But in whatever poetic garb Guibourc may be arrayed, it would be preferable to see chivalry conferred on a young man with a smile or by younger hands. An aunt is all very well, but a betrothed is better, and we are fortunately enabled to be spectators of another scene which is more romantic. That great giant—rather foolish and very brutal—named Robastre was one day dubbed by the tiny hands of Plaisance, and it was not a sword but a hatchet which she fastened to his side. I must say, however, that as a picture in this style I prefer the creation of Jourdain de Blaives by the beautiful Oriabel, who was destined to be his wife. The young *Valet* was making ready to encounter the terrible Sortin, and there was some anxiety lest he should be vanquished in the unequal duel. Love was active on his side—" Will you swear to marry me if you come off victorious ? " said the lady. " Ah," replied Jourdain naïvely, " I will swear it very willingly, and you make me feel happier than if you had given me all Paris—*but I do not dare to say so !* "

Then Oriabel, radiant, went away to the stable to fetch a splendid horse for her *fiancé*, and the investment began. The maiden herself buckled on his sword, but there was another rite at which she hesitated a little. She did not dare to give him the *colée*. " I am

a woman," she said, " and it is not correct for me to strike a man."
" Yes, yes, strike, I pray you," cried Jourdain.   Then she hesitated
no longer, but gave him the customary blow on the dear head
which was bent before her.   " Be a knight," said she, " and may
God give you honour and courage."   Then becoming all womanly
again, she continued, " If by any chance you would care for a kiss,
take one ! "   He took three, and then leaped on his horse boldly.

We have another incident to chronicle — a terrible one — in
contrast to the last mentioned, a " consecrator " which no historian
has told of who appears only in the legend, viz., *a dead
hand!*

The story concerns the youthful son of Oliver, Galien, to whom
his mother one day disclosed the secret of his birth, and he then
heroically set forth to seek his father.   Few poetic conceptions are
so strong, and none are more dramatic.   After many adventures of
a more or less commonplace character which it is needless to
enumerate here, the young man to his great joy found his father
Oliver.   But in what condition?   On the field of Roncesvalles,
dying !   He had not five minutes more to live when his son at
length discovered him !

The illustrious friend of Roland had scarcely time to say these
few words to his son in almost inarticulate tones : " Love Charles
and beware of Ganelon ! "   The young man lost little time in
barren regrets.   He cast one look at his father's body and then
dashed into the midst of the Pagan ranks.   What exploits he
performed ; what charges he made !   As evening fell the knights
perceived a young man covered with blood, descending the
mountain side.   This was Galien, who had avenged his father.
The hero, however, was not yet a knight, and then they were
spectators of a great miracle.   The inanimate corpse of Roland
was there under the eyes of the Emperor, full in Galien's sight !

In the dead silence of the scene the right arm of the illustrious
friend of Oliver was raised slowly, and extended to Charles the
sword held by the blade.   The king understood, and presented to
Galien this incomparable weapon ; then with a sudden inspiration
the king said : " You shall be made a knight."   But such a hero
must not be conventionally dubbed, so the son of Pepin stooped
towards Roland, took the arm of the dead warrior and with this

cold hand bestowed the *colée* on Galien. Never had it been so administered before, and never since.

This is the only occasion even in romance in which a living knight has been created by the hand of a dead chevalier.

VI.

We now know who were the candidates admitted to Chivalry. We know also where, when, and by whom the new knights were created, and we have replied to the four questions of our chaplain which seemed to us at one time somewhat pedantic and indiscreet. *"Quis? Ubi? Quando? Per quem?"* There now remains the fifth and last question, the most difficult of all, and one which it will be necessary to consider in greater detail. How was a knight created? *Quomodo?*

The majority of writers on Chivalry have on this topic fallen into strange errors, and have unfortunately mixed up the various epochs. They have read and re-read that charming little poem of which we have already spoken more than once, *l'Ordene de Chevalerie,* which they regard as a classic manual, and of which they have attempted a more or less faithful commentary. But as a matter of fact these pleasing and facile verses do not give a correct idea of the Chivalry of the eleventh and twelfth centuries. The *Ordene,* which is a work of the time of Saint Louis, reveals, as we have already stated, a very advanced condition of the subject—a delicate civilization, poetic, refined. It is the same in the case of the *Benedictio novi militis* which we found in the old Pontifical writings. These are only works compiled after much seeking of theories, and well "boiled down" codifications. There is nothing in them original, primitive, nor "native."

Just recall the simple and bald origin which we have been compelled to assign to Chivalry; do not forget that it was the giving of arms to the youthful German. An old soldier presented a hatchet or a gun to a youthful recruit—this was the first and most ancient of all Chivalric rites. There was no other element: that was all!

To this primitive germ all the other elements were by degrees united by the force of circumstances. This development is what we are about to demonstrate.

To present a weapon to a youth who is going to fight is very well, he could not do without it; but since the commencement of the eleventh century the nobles only fought on horseback, and all "cavaliers," as the name indicates, were necessarily horsemen. So it is quite natural to begin by putting the novice in a condition proper for him to spur his steed and rush into the battle. From this arose the investment of the spurs.

Spurs are very well too, but a battle was then only a series of duels. Warriors fought hand to hand, and if a cavalier was not clad in iron or steel he would be incontinently lost or maimed. So before he girded on his sword he clothed himself in a fine shirt of mail, and with a casque on his head with which he protected his nose; then he put on hauberk and helmet.

In order to feel more at his ease, and "fit," the youthful noble would indulge in a bath first. But the bath had nothing symbolic or ritualistic in it. It was not a symbol: it was merely for health's sake.

There then was our young noble bathed, spurred, clothed and in a coat of mail. The solemn moment has arrived. *He is girded with his sword!* This is the essence, and as theologians say, the form of the sacrament of chivalry. The rest is merely accessory.

The *colée* itself—the heavy blow of the palm upon the nape of the neck—was only adopted later, and was not necessary for the validity of the sacrament. We could quote many instances in our old poems in which the *colée* was not bestowed, and in which the knight was dubbed only with the sword. At what period did the blow with the palm of the hand come into vogue? Whence did it arise? What was the real significance of it? We will endeavour to reply to all these questions by and by.

Whatever may have been the object of this savage "confirmation," this *paumée* which the consecrator let fall on the neck of the novice sometimes with sufficient force to stun him, it is certain that the brutality was accompanied by a little sermon or piece of advice which had no Christian germ in it. "Be brave!" Then the newly-made knight was requested to demonstrate his qualities of cavalier.

He took a run and leaped into the saddle—it was considered disgraceful to touch the stirrup—then he dashed away at a gallop, watched by hundreds of spectators who applauded him. But he had still to prove his skill and strength, and to show that he was competent to meet his opponents in battle. There were for this purpose on the *estaches,* on posts, some " dummies " or effigies, and trophies of arms. It was necessary for the new knight to overturn these without pausing in his career. Then there was the quintain which we shall have another opportunity to describe. This joust terminated the ceremony. Then amidst acclamations and joyous cries the young knight dismounted, and went to seek repose, or some other excitement.

Such was the first mode of " dubbing a knight." It is all material, Germanic, barbarous. The Church had no concern in it, and did not even appear at it. The elements composing it are all strictly military, and that is why we have chosen to delineate it as the Military System.

But of course the Church could not remain long an indifferent spectator of such an important institution, and one which tended to rob it of its influence. It is no exaggeration to compare the Church during the Middle Ages to the sun which illuminates everything, and from which no living thing can definitively withdraw itself. Little by little, without any violent transition, without shock, and simply by the effort of social necessity, the creation of knights (*adoubement*), which did not cease to be a lay function, became Christianised. It must be confessed that the evolution did not succeed everywhere, and that the ancient mode subsisted side by side with the new, but the transformation was important, and frequently definitive. Nothing was easier. Many families more Christian than their neighbours began to think that these rites, which were certainly somewhat gross, did not ascribe to God a part worthy of Him, and hastened to repair such a regrettable omission. The future knight hurried to place upon the altar of some monastery his arms, so that the association might give to them an august and sacramental character. Other damoiseaux went farther, and implored the priests to bless their swords. It will be seen that the priest is not here in the character of the consecrator or sponsor. *He blessed the sword, but he did not invest the knight with it!*

But in spite of all a decisive step was taken and the advance did not cease there. What was wanting at the entry into Chivalry was a preparation proportioned to the majestic nature of the dedication —"an avenue," so to speak, and this the Church created. Nobody knew better than she how to make such preparation, and she made it quite evident. It was not much trouble to the aspirants for knighthood to hear on the morning of their admission the same mass which they heard every other day, and which on that occasion only would assume a character of more special solemnity. This was something gained, but it was not sufficient. The Church recalled those grand and solemn vigils which had been held in all Christian churches during the bright nights of Easter and Pentecost, and which terminated at dawn with the baptisms of numbers of catechumens clothed in white dresses.

The "Watching of the Armour" arose from these vigils. It is nothing but an imitation—almost a copy of them. The knight passed the whole night in a church waiting his second baptism, and this was the most Christian rite of a function into which the odour of sanctity was penetrating deeper and deeper. To "Christianize" the creation of the knight it was only requisite to give a religious flavour to the little sermon, a very crude and military address which accompanied the bestowal of the sword or of the accolade. This was easy enough. Instead of saying "Be brave," one had to say "Love God," and the change was accomplished!

Such was the second method of creation. A single epithet fits it, and we willingly adopt it: it was the Christian Method!

The matter might have rested there, but the Church deemed it necessary to proceed farther. In addition to the two former rituals which, we must not forget, continued to coexist during the Middle Ages, she formulated a third. This was one peculiar to herself, it was all her own, it was completely and entirely Catholic; but it necessitated a sort of *coup d'état*. The laity were by it relegated to the second rank, and to sum up in a few words, the consecrator of the new knight was not a layman but a priest. The bishop stepped into the places of the knight, the father, the liege lord, the suzerain, or of the sovereign. It was the bishop who not only blessed but girded on the sword; it was he who said "Be thou knight;" it was he who bestowed the accolade, greatly changed now. It was no longer the heavy blow of the fist; the gentle hand of the bishop could not deliver such buffets. The ecclesiastic did not strike, he touched. Some gentle taps with the flat of the sword satisfied the pacific consecrator. So the mode of entry in Chivalry became unquestionably clerical. It was then no longer the creation but the benediction of the new soldier. It is in the missal and not in the epic poetry of the period that the new ritual will be found.

To sum up: the first method was essentially military; the second was religious, but still of a lay character; the third was Liturgical, and the title will cling to it.

We have thus placed before our readers the "fatal" chain of ideas and of facts which, between the ninth and eleventh centuries, successively produced the three principal forms of admission to Chivalry. We have nothing which we can substitute for the examples, texts, and types. We are compelled to search our old poems and volumes for the scenes of action, so vivid and so warm, of these three methods, of which we, alas! have written so coldly!

VII.

The creation of knights according to the first or military mode is that generally referred to in our most ancient histories or text-books. The rite as therein described is simplicity itself, austere and rough. It is the old German "assumption of arms;" no hand-buffet on the neck, no accolade. This coarseness was still absent, and it is difficult to fix the exact time of its appearance. It is probable that it dates some distance back, and is doubtless of barbarian origin; but, according to the text-books, there is nothing certainly known about it before the twelfth century. When William the Conqueror, in the nineteenth year of his reign, wished to make his son Henry a knight, one of his historians contents himself with telling us in the simplest way that "he assumed manly arms!" This is the usual formula, and in it we perceive a certain savour of far antiquity. This same William had formerly received from the King of France the insignia of Chivalry. But still there was no buffet nor accolade. To be endowed with the arms of Chivalry was still at that epoch a consecrated term, and it is not unpoetic. In Germany the ritual was then the same as in Normandy and England; and the kings themselves, when they were created knights, were simply girt with the sword. Still no accolade! But why need we lose ourselves in this maze of detail? We have in our possession a page of a chronicle, a document almost unique, and full of interest which one might say was borrowed, almost copied, from a *chanson de geste*, and we are by no means certain that the monk Marmoutier, who is the author of it, had not before him some poetic effusion of which he sought to translate the manly energy into classic Latin, though somewhat pedantic, perhaps, and full of epithets. It treats of the "chivalry" of the youthful Geoffrey Plantagenet, and of the arms which this son of the Count of Anjou received from the hands of Henry, King of England. This was in 1129. Listen!

Geoffrey was then fifteen years of age. He was well-looking, and knew how to manage his steed; but these were by no means the highest of his many attributes. "Send me your son to Rouen; I will marry him to my daughter, and, as he is not yet a knight, I will myself dub him at Whitsuntide." This was the message which Count Foulques received one day from the King of England. It was not difficult to obey such a command; he obeyed.

Five barons were selected to accompany the young man, five barons of renown: Hardouin de Saint-Mars, Jaquelin de Maillé, Robert de Semblençai, Jean de Clervaux, and Robert de Blois. Twenty-five pages, of the same age as Geoffrey, rode behind him with an imposing escort of knights. They hastened to depart, and after a rapid progress reached Rouen. The King of England, "who never rose to receive anyone," came to meet the young man, and embraced him; after a while he began to interrogate the youthful baron, and to put him through a kind of examination. The historian assures us that the postulant came out "with flying colours" from his examination. But we may be glad to hear that it was extremely simple, and did not include arithmetic.

Now evening has come! Night—the night of Pentecost, on which, in former times, so many new Christians were baptised—an occasion as solemn as that of Easter. Next day, the very next day, Geoffrey will be a belted knight.

In a private apartment the future knight is preparing for the solemn rites. Custom has ordained that these shall be preceded by a bath. Geoffrey and his twenty-five companions plunge into this water, which has nothing symbolical for them. Then they clothe him in a linen shirt, a robe of cloth of gold, silk small-clothes, and shoes on which lions were embroidered in gold, and a purple body-garment. The other pages are also clad in linen and purple garments. Then the youthful procession file out, lithe, active, superb, brilliant! The young English prince walks in advance of the rest, and one old chronicler does not hesitate to compare him to the rose, and to the lily of the field.

The ceremony was to be performed in the open air, so the steeds and arms had already been prepared and made ready for the young cavaliers. The charger reserved for Geoffrey was a splendid Spanish horse whose paces "were as swift as the bird's flight." This comparison is frequently found in our old poems, whence the historian has probably borrowed it. The son of the Count of Anjou is there the observed of all observers, but he stands motionless, paying attention to all that is taking place. He is then inducted into a hauberk of double plate, which can resist the thrust of strongest lance, shoes of mail, his shield with its device of golden lions is hung around his neck, and on his head is placed a helmet, set with precious stones, warranted to withstand the best tempered swords. Finally, the long and tough lance of ash, tipped with iron of Poitiers, and a sword from the king's own armoury—a marvel of workmanship, a masterpiece of that Galant who is so often mentioned in the *Chansons*.

The preparations are complete; the young man is armed from head to foot; he is a knight. All he has to do is to mount his horse without the aid of stirrups, and to take part in the sham fight which brings the *fête* to a conclusion, though the term conclusion is scarcely applicable, as the historian declares that the festival lasted no less than seven days. On the eighth Geoffrey was married!

Thus Jean, monk of Marmoutier; and whatever may have been borrowed from our epic poetry, the record is worthy of our attention.

Notwithstanding the magnificence of the adornments, the splendour of the costumes, the duration of the festival, this mode of conferring knighthood had nothing complicated in its ceremonial. It was essentially the old putting on of armour preceded by a bath, and a solemn putting on of vesture. There was no accolade, no sermon, not even the quintain. Do not forget that this was a royal act which we have been considering, a ceremony in one of the most considerable cities of France, the centre of one of the most civilised provinces, in the twelfth century. By that we may judge of other ceremonials of knighthood of the same period.

From this point of view, nothing can be less polished than the oldest texts of our Chansons, which ring out the same sound as do the historical records of the time. I venture to say that they are even more truly historical—more truthful. Open *Auberi le Bourgoing* for example. Open this " barbarous poem ! " How did the hero create Gauthier, to whom he owed his life ? He commanded that he should be clad in the richest garments, and armed; then he presented him with a good steed. That was the whole ceremonial, and the poet does not hesitate to say : " *Si li donna l'ordre de chevalier.*" There is nothing complicated about it ! In *Ogier* we find the same simplicity, but the scenery is more imposing than the drama. Charlemagne is before Rome, which he is endeavouring to snatch from its pagan conquerors. Ogier, who is still very youthful, has reddened the soil with the blood of many Saracens, and excited the admiration of the army by his incomparable bravery. The emperor, who had formerly entertained some doubts concerning the youth, dismounts, and in the thick of the fight girds him with his sword. The poem puts it shortly thus—

> " Lors desciendi li rois Kalles à tant,
> La bone espée a çainte Ogier au flanc,
> Chevaliers fu Ogiers d'or en avant ! "

Other poems are more full of detail, but more material. The author of *Garin le Loherain*, when he relates how Aubri was made knight, does not lose himself in the analysis of the rites ; he scarcely mentions the putting on of the armour, but he dwells with some complaisance on the appearance of the strong and rough youth, whose breadth of shoulder excited his admiration. So we may perceive that the taste of the period was in favour of muscular force. "Look at him," said Garin to his brother Bejon; "if he live, what a baron he will make!"

We cannot expect any more delicacy from the author of *Raoul de Cambrai*. The Count of Cambrai, when he conferred knighthood on Bernier, contented himself with arming him. Then Bernier covered his sword with golden bands, seized his lance, the pennon of which was fixed with five golden nails, and galloped his horse round amid the admiring barons, who remarked to each other what an excellent horseman he was.

It would be easy to multiply examples, but it is preferable to condense them into one or two types. To that terrible old poem again—to *Garin de Loherain*—we must go and borrow the most significant and convincing proof. The two principal actors of this strange scene were an elderly knight named Fromont and a very youthful page, his own son, named Fromondin—a striking and charming contrast. At the appearance of the youth marching at the head of twenty other *valets*, Bernard de Naisil rushed towards him, kissed him, and calling Baudouin de Flandre, said: "Look what a splendid nephew we have got. Suppose we go to and demand from Fromont the *poestis* to make him a knight." "I am quite willing," said the Fleming. "Come along!" They went, and were very uncourteously received. In vain did they represent to this brutal father that his son had already reached manly stature, that his chest was broad and his arms strong, and was capable of smashing the lances of all his enemies. "Look how strong, how handsome he is!" "No, he is too young," replied the old man, who did not like anyone to think him old, and who hurled a superb defiance at the heads of Bernard and Baudouin. But at length he listened to reason, and so changed his mind that he wished the ceremonial to take place in an hour!

The baths were immediately prepared and filled with water. Fromondin entered into the first and his companions into the others. Outside, the neighing of the chargers were audible amid the voices of the squires who held the bridles of the palfreys. Amongst all

F. MEAULLE sc

"REMEMBER ME, AND BE VALIANT, AIMERI."

[p. 240.

these valuable animals was one which attracted the attention of all present—it was Beaucent, old Fromont's steed. Young Fromondin perceived it immediately he issued from his bath, and with a headlong bound he leaped right on to the back of the animal from the plain. Then caracolling he ran against Don Bernard de Naisil, whom he nearly unhorsed. It was done for a joke; the lad screamed with laughter, and cried to his uncle: "Old gentleman, I trust you will make yourself quite at home in my house." The other did not smile, but he took occasion to read his nephew a lecture. "I wish to do so," he said, "but on the condition that you will attend to my behests; and there are three things which I would first mention—Learn how to use your spurs, to respect older knights, and to give to the poor!" The ceremony terminated with this little discourse, and a Homeric feast in the open air. The sword had not even been girded on with any ceremonial observance.

The ceremony attending the admission of Godfrey, son of Eustace of Boulogne, to the knightly dignity, represents the last and most brilliant phase of the creation without accolade. Godfrey was dubbed knight by his father, and "never was king or admiral so well armed." His clothing was of the best, his helmet was blazing with precious stones, topazes, emeralds, sapphires, diamonds, loadstones, and others. Then he was girt with the sword, the same weapon with which he fought one of the most bitter enemies of the Christians—Agolant. It is needless to add that it came from the famous workshops of Galant, and only one weapon could equal it—Roland's sword, Durendal. The large shield was hung round Godfrey's neck, the device being two lion cubs, white; and the steed which was brought to him was covered with a white *diaspre* which hung to the ground. Godfrey was a splendid horseman, and looked superb with his stout spear, and his pennon with three flying eagles. "To the field!" he cried, and galloped thither followed by all those who came to be admitted with him, by his father and all the other barons. Then, after the course, the banquet, a splendid repast at which troubadours sang and jongleurs recited, till at length, at daybreak, the festivities came to an end.

VIII.

We cannot fix the date of the poem of *Godefroi de Bouillon* before a period anterior to the thirteenth century, but in certain districts of France for a long time before its issue the *colée* or "buffet" was in general use. I am convinced that it came to us French from the North, and that it was not customary in France long previous to the eleventh century. In the chronicles and poems of the twelfth century we find a large number of cases of this form of "creation," which, just as the former method, was toned down, rendered less gross, and more civilised and graceful by degrees. A historian of the twelfth century who is too little known, Lambert d'Ardres, speaks of the *alapa* in every page of his charming and interesting chronicle. We may almost say that he discovered the definitive formula of this barbarous rite when we read the circumstances attending the creation of Arnoul the Second, the Count of Ardres and Guines. The narrative shows us in vivid terms the father of the young prince who bestowed on him the "military buffet" or *colée* "without the youth being able to return it." *Dedit ei militarem, non repercutiendus, alapam.*

The scene is laid at Guines at Whitsuntide in the year 1181, in full assembly of the numerous spectators who came to "consecrate" the feasts and festivities of that blessed day ! But the historian vainly endeavours to elevate this rite to the level of a sacrament. The words *non repercutiendus* cannot be deprived of their material character, they too plainly characterise this brutal fashion of entering into the ranks of chivalry. We might quote a dozen other instances, but we will transport our readers suddenly into the middle of the thirteenth century and call attention to the prevailing practice of German admission to chivalry in gentler times. The author of the *Grande Chronique belge* says candidly that in order to avoid the heavy buffets of the new chivalry the majority of the knights of his time contented themselves with the *colée*, and the same chronicler relates also that William of Holland, who was chosen King of the Romans in 1247, received on his neck the terrible blow which "created" knights. So between Lambert d'Ardres and the Belgian Chronicle numerous cases may be established.

Our old poems are not less conclusive, and about the commencement of the thirteenth century the brutality of the fisticuff is exemplified in a more picturesque and taking form. The first appearance of Elias of Saint-Gilles is from this point of view a masterpiece of description, rough but true. The father of Elias, Julien de Saint-Gilles, had a perfectly white beard. He was a proud baron, who had never been guilty of a dishonourable action, or of treason; who respected the monasteries, and caused refuges and bridges to be built for the accommodation of poor travellers. It was then a hundred years since he had been dubbed knight, and he felt the necessity for repose and good living. So he summoned his son before him, and in order to excite the young man's anger, he reproached him with never having accomplished any exploit. " At your age," cried the old man, " I had already taken castles, forts, and cities ! " The young man got into such a passion under the lash of these words that the old man inquired satirically whether Elias did not think the cloister or the cell his proper vocation. This was too much. Elias determined to quit for ever the place where he was forced to submit to such insults. " Hold your tongue, you poor thing," cried his father. " Do you imagine you can leave here thus, without arms or escort ? Why, they will ridicule you on the road and say ' Do you see that young man ? He is the son of Julien with the Beard. His father has driven him from home.' No, no, you shall not go thus; I will dub you knight here, this instant." Then turning to his attendants he said, " Let a quintain be prepared, and let them carry my arms out." The ceremony immediately commenced. The old knight girded the sword upon his son : then clenching his hand the vigorous centenarian dealt the youth a blow of his sledge-hammer fist which made him reel again. The new knight felt his blood rush to his face at such an indignity, and muttered no very complimentary epithets. " Ah," he said, " if anyone else had treated me so ! But he is my father and it is my duty to submit." Then he exerted himself to be calm outwardly, raised his head proudly, leaped on horseback with a bound, and raced for the quintain, carrying the apparatus away in a masterly fashion. " He will be a brave knight ! " cried his father, who was delighted. But his mother wept sore for the son who would shortly leave home ! This scene is at once feudal and true to nature.

The *colée* consisted of two acts and an address; to clench the hand and bring it down heavily upon the neck of the postulant, accompanied by a word or two, or a sentence of a strictly military character, was the whole ceremony. "Be a true knight, and valiant against thine enemies!" or, "Forget not to be faithful to thy liege lord!" or more simple still, "Be valiant!" These two words carry great weight, and say everything.

A type less exceptional than that of Saint-Gilles is here worthy of place, and we will borrow it from the fine romance of *Girars de Viane*, which the poet no doubt has resuscitated from a more antique work. "In order to dub the 'damoisel' Aimeri a knight they all proceeded to a rich meadow—Duke Girard with his brothers. There the squire was arrayed in a fine hauberk, and Girard girded on his proved sword. Then with his clenched hand he smote him a heavy blow. 'Remember me, Aimeri, and be valiant,' he cried. 'Great thanks, sire,' the young man replied, 'I will be valiant if it please God that I live!' Then an Arab steed was brought him, and he mounted immediately. Around his neck a circular shield was suspended; he grasped a trusty lance and circled the flowery mead on horseback, while the spectators said to one another: 'Truly he is a good knight!'"[*]

This was the usual mode of procedure, and we need not quote other instances in support of it. It is, however, important to state that the *colée*, which in some places had not formed a part of the old chivalric ritual, in time replaced all other rites—in some instances a knight was created by the "accolade" only. This is strange, but true. Then it came to pass that the heavy blow was considered too rough a mode, and a more pacific and elegant method replaced it. A buffet with the fist! Fie! It is barbarous; rude! A blow with the flat of a sabre is sufficiently military surely, and much more graceful. The merciful Church, which had no love for brutality, voluntarily adopted, if it did not invent, this mode, which was not the last development. For the rude rough *colée*, after being subverted by the more poetic blow of the sword on the shoulder, became in time, by a certain play upon words, the familiar "accolade," which was not too often either a kiss of sincerity or of peace.

[*] *Girars de Viane*, ed. P. Tarbé.

However, we have now said all that is necessary concerning the military mode of knighthood, so let us pass on to the religious method.

IX.

The Religious mode of knighting was not discovered all at once, nor arranged in a day, by some inventive genius, but it is by a process of infiltration, if I may so speak, that Christianity penetrated into the ancient ceremonial of Chivalry. A long period elapsed before faith and piety were imbibed by our military-mannered barons. It came nevertheless, but only by degrees. The greatest innovation was the " Watching of the Armour," and it was really hardly an innovation after all, because, independently of the great vigils of Easter and Whitsuntide, our ancestors were already conversant with " watchings," as we ascertain from a celebrated work in the first years of the twelfth century, in which are sung the praises of the lives of saints and the exploits of heroes.* The Watching of the Armour, then, is only an imitation, or, as we should now call it, an " adaptation." It was customary for knights to hear mass every day. In the placing of the arms upon the altar one sees at once an intelligent copy of the old custom, which dates back to antiquity, and consisted in placing thus on the sacred stone the parchments containing promises, and such solemn engagements.

It was also quite natural that the idea and the name of God should have been introduced into the lay-sermon which accompanied the bestowal of the *colée*, and that, after having said " Be valiant," it should have come to pass that, by various transitions, the formula ran one day—" Remember the passion and death of Jesus ! " There then remained the benediction of the sword, but the Church, the ever-blessing Church, had for a long time been in the habit of blessing the dwelling, the nuptial chamber, the first-fruits of the earth, the bread and eggs, and even more common things in every-day use. To bestow a benediction on the lance or sword which was used against the enemies of Christianity ; to

* *Vita sancti Willelmi.*

bless the helmet and the coat of mail which would render invulnerable the bodies of the friends of Holy Church, was the most obvious of all duties. But here it became necessary to set up a formal distinction between the second and third mode of knighting, and it is not without reason that we have applied to the second method the term *religious*, and to the third *liturgical*. The blessing of the *sword* and the blessing of the *girdle* are very different acts.

In the religious mode the priest contented himself with making the sign of the cross on the sword ; in the *liturgical* method the bishop is the consecrator. It is no layman, it is the bishop himself who, with anointed hands, clasps the sword to the side of the new-made knight, and says to him *Accingere gladio tuo super femur tuum, potentissime.* Another feature serves to distinguish the two methods which no one will have any excuse for confounding in future ; the terms used in the creation by the religious method were always the vulgar tongue of the country wherein the ceremony took place ; the liturgical ceremonial was conducted in Latin !

The second method of conferring knighthood was that destined to live. The military mode died because of its coarseness ; the liturgical because it seemed too *clerical* in the worse acceptation of the term, and some perceived in its adoption an interference of the Church. This accusation, if unjust, was specious, and knights more often preferred to create knights. A sincerely Christian rite was sufficient for them, and they were tenacious regarding their character of consecrators. This rite, besides, had undergone more than one change during the Middle Ages. We are shown in *L'Ordene de Chevalerie* the outlines of a complicated symbolism, and the fourteenth and fifteenth centuries added I know not what subtleties and refinements, which go to make up the Modern Code of Chivalry. Our poets, dramatists and painters are hardly acquainted with any other, and they dress it up in variegated hues, but its origin is that we have attributed to it, and it only remains for us to make clear its historical development to our readers.

Our epic poetry, thank Heaven, is full of instances of the *religious* method, but it is seldom that one can find a really complete description which presents to us at the same time the five acts of ceremonial—the watching of the armour, the solemn mass, the deposition of the arms upon the altar, the benediction of the sword, and the little sermon *à la chrétienne* which accompanied the bestowal of the *paumée*. One need not, however, worry about this, for really one or two of these formalities were sufficient to give scientifically to a " Chivalry " of the twelfth and thirteenth centuries the religious character which distinguished it so clearly from the military method. The eldest son of Witasse, Count of Boulogne, watched all through the night which preceded his admission into Chivalry. He undertook this vigil in the name of the Virgin Mary, and did not leave the convent until after he had heard *matins*. In the same way watched Hervis de Loherain, the nephews of Aimeri de Narbonne, Gerart and Guïelin, Guy, the son of Anseïs of Carthage, and fifty others. As regards the mass *Girars de Viane* states that in his time it was the custom of the newly-made knights (the *custom*, mind), to hear mass piously and to pray to God before receiving their arms. Two cycles which are often at variance, those of the king and of William, agree in narrating the affecting episode of placing the arms upon the altar so that the contact may sanctify them for ever after, and John of Salisbury adds in his Latin, that this was a general custom to which one felt compelled to attribute great antiquity. It is more particularly in Latin chronicles that we find allusion made to the benediction of the sword and the old " Pontificals " give us, side by side with the *Benedictio novi militis*, of which we have already spoken, the *Benedictio ensis et armorum* which gives the layman the right to gird on the sword, and the bishop the privilege to bless it.

There remains the sermon, and it passes through many phases. First it is crude and short—" Be brave ! " but by degrees it assumes more of a religious character and becomes as it were " Christianised "—" May the true God give thee courage ! " Then after a while—not without a struggle—it becomes entirely of a pious character—" If I bestow upon thee this sword it is on the condition that thou shalt be a champion of the Lord ! " There are shades, we admit, but they are historical differences which must be appreciated.

So far we have noticed nothing symbolic, and, indeed, symbolism

did not make its appearance very soon.   Thus before the thirteenth
century the ceremony of creation was religious : it was not
symbolic.   But we have here the *Ordene de Chevalerie*, a little
learned, dogmatic poem, elevating and attractive, in which the
flower of symbolism is fully expanded : a somewhat artificial
flower, but not without its charm.

The *Ordene* is a work of art, a kind of scientific treatise whose
doctrines one cannot find in any of the epic *chansons*, or in any of
the more really popular poems.

The scene is laid in the Holy Land, and the text consists of
dialogue.   The interlocutors are a Christian knight—a prisoner,
called Hue de Tabarie, and the other a powerful pagan prince—a
conqueror named Saladin.   It appears that the conqueror is
attracted to his prisoner as iron is by a magnet.   Now in the
Saracen's mind one single idea is dominant—he wants to be made
a knight.   This is the subject of the poem.

" How are knights created ? "   This is the anxious and sincere
question put by Saladin, and the reply of the Christian is haughty.
The first step towards becoming a knight is to become a Christian,
and in the *Ordene* Hue de Tabarie tells the Sultan plainly that the
Holy Order of Chivalry is not within his reach, for he continues :
" You are not of the true faith, and have not been baptised.   To
create you a knight would be an act as foolish as to cover a dung-
heap with silk to prevent the foul odour from escaping ! "   The
suggestion is not remarkable for politeness, but what does it
matter ?   Saladin insists, commands !   The prisoner is constrained
to obey, and at this point begins the animated commentary upon
all the rites of the ceremonial.   The bath is the first of these rites,
which are at the same time symbols.   Says the consecrating
knight : " Even as the infant emerges without sin from the font
after baptism, so do you emerge from this bath spotless and without blemish."

Here we already have reached a high level of comparison, and
weak indeed is the intelligence which cannot comprehend such
language !   The novice comes out of his bath transfigured and
radiant, and is placed on a couch.   " Win a resting-place in
Heaven ; such is the aim of Chivalry ! "   Saladin, very attentive
and respectful, permits himself to be arrayed in the white

garments of the catechumens of the primitive Church. "It is necessary," continues the knight, "that those who desire to reach Heaven should be pure in mind as in body." After this exhortation to chastity, the Christian envelopes his companion in a vermilion robe and says: "Remember: you must not hesitate to shed every drop of your blood in defence of Holy Church!" Then the feet of the new-made knight are inducted into black shoes in order to recall to his mind the earth from which he came, and to which he must return, and to preserve him from a feeling of pride.

After this the consecrator assumes a more solemn tone and demeanor: the decisive moment is approaching. The *cingulum,* the girdle, is fastened round the loins of the aspirant. This is a white girdle, and once more recalls to the mind of the Christian soldier, the defender of the Church, the importance of chastity. To the dark shoes are attached the golden spurs, and the aspirant is admonished to be in future as obedient to the spur of the Divine Will as the charger is to the material spurs. Now it is time to bestow upon the knight the weapon which is a distinctive sign of knighthood—the two-edged sword. "With one side thou must strike the rich who oppress the poor, with the other punish the strong who persecute the weak!" This is the true idea of Chivalry; it is, as we have already said, the armed Force in the service of the unarmed Truth.

After a little more ceremonial the termination is reached. On the head of the new knight is placed a white cap, which again reminds him of the significance which attaches to it, and to the necessity for possessing an unspotted soul—a mind protected by innocence or re-cleansed by penitence. The ceremony should then terminate with the buffet or *colée,* but Hue de Tabarie does not dare to strike the pagan sovereign in that manner, so he contents himself with preaching him a little sermon which embodies all his former exhortations. He says:—

"There are four things which a knight should observe all his life if he would preserve his honour untarnished. The first is— 'Never parley with traitors;' the second—'Never lead astray dame nor damsel, but on the contrary respect them and defend them against all injury;' the third obligation is piously to observe all fast days and days of abstinence ; and finally, to hear mass every day and to make an offering at the monastery."

Saladin, delighted, listened attentively, and evidenced himself worthy of being a Christian by incontinently releasing his prisoner who had addressed him in such noble and worthy language.

Such is the *Ordene de Chevalrie,* which it is necessary to consider here as a work in which individual fancy plays a certain part. That which is most evident in this poem, which has a distinctly Christian character, is its general spiritual tone ; but we must not take all the refined symbolism literally, nor imagine that this was universally understood and practised in all Catholic countries.

However theoretical, however far-fetched it may appear, the *Ordene* has had an influence on the development of the institution of Chivalry. We may rather say that it is not the *Ordene* itself, but the whole current of ideas, all the system, all the doctrines, which the poem has been the means of expressing in a more or less correct form, that have exerted such influence. Thanks to the number of additional rites and pious excrescences the ceremony of the admission to knighthood ended, in the fourteenth and fifteenth centuries, by becoming something very complex, and necessitated many explanations by competent people. Austere fastings, long nights passed in prayer with priest and sponsors in the holy gloom of cathedral aisles; the Sacraments of Penitence and the Eucharist eagerly sought, and partaken of by the candidate with every appearance of piety and devotion ; baths which had really become symbolic of purity, white robes which were worn in imitation of the early neophytes, and finally the assistance rendered by sermons in which all the articles of belief were reviewed, commented on, and defended—all these constituted the prologue and preliminaries to the grand drama of admission to Chivalry.

But they were only the introduction, the preface, and some may consider that they formed a very long avenue to the palace of the order. But at length the great day dawned. The aspirant entered solemnly into the church, and advanced slowly to the altar carrying his sword slanting-wise. He presented it to the priest, who blessed it (liturgically) and suspended it thus consecrated around the neck of the young candidate. Some of the future knights remained in the sacred edifice to complete the rites, some preferred the open air, or the castle ; but in any case each aspirant approached the consecrator and tendered him the sword.

"What is your reason for entering the order ? Do you truly desire the honour of the Faith and of Chivalry ? " The youthful baron would reply more or less firmly, but in a fashion calculated to satisfy his questioner, who would at length grant his request. Then he would quickly re-assume his arms, and if there were any fair ladies present they would assist him to don his armour. They would first fasten the left spur, then the right, the hauberk and the coat of mail, the cuirass (there were cuirasses then), the arm-pieces and gauntlets. These accoutrements were heavy as well as noisy, as may be judged from our museums. Then the aspirant knelt, and awaited the final act which would constitute him a new man—a knight ! The consecrator did not unduly prolong the attitude : he delivered on the shoulder, or neck, three strokes with the flat of the sword. Sometimes ancient usage countenanced the hand which did not bestow the buffet, but touched the cheek of the aspirant. Everything had been toned down. Then a voice declared—"In the name of God and St. Michael and St. George I dub thee knight." The ceremony was then complete, the aspirant had become a knight ! Nevertheless he had not his helmet yet, but it was soon adjusted, his shield was quickly buckled on, and his lance placed in his hand. Then "to horse ! " was the cry. The knight sprang upon his fine steed ; if he could only mount without the assistance of the stirrups he was accounted perfect. Seated in the saddle—he is superb ! and he "parades his new dignity," executing many grand caracoles before the eyes of the ladies, who admire him greatly. This is the ancient *eslais*, some-what humanised ; and the reader may discern from the foregoing account the forms of the antique ceremonials which obtained in the ritual of the fifteenth century. They are somewhat confused, but there they are !

What a complication it is ! How one regrets the plain savage rites of the time of Philip Augustus ! How one regrets the "buffet" on the neck, the primitive buckling on of the heavy sword, the old-time address, and all the simple, straightforward ritual !

X.

The Church, as early as the tenth or eleventh century, began to find these rites too gross, and had endeavoured to give them a decidedly liturgical character ; and this fact brings us naturally to the consideration of the third and last method of creating the knight, the true character of which is easy to determine.   " It is no longer a layman but a bishop who is the consecrator."   Everything takes place at the altar, and the service is in Latin.

The date which we assign to this method is sufficient to scandalise some very erudite authorities, and makes it older by some centuries than it is usually supposed to be.

What period, then, does the *Benedictio novi militis* actually date from?   On this question, as on many others, authorities are not agreed.   But we cannot leave the matter thus ; we must decide the question, which is really an important one.

People usually, and too frequently, confound the benediction of the new knight with the benediction of the armour, or the blessing of the sword.   These are rites essentially different, which in the Pontificals have sometimes been separated, sometimes united. The bishop blessed the lance, the sword, the *vexillum,* the hauberk, the shield.   So far so good, and this benediction was the proper prologue to the consecration, the " crowning " of the knight.   But this consecration, we must remember, consisted primarily in the girding on of the sword by the hands of the officiating bishop, and in a modified form of *colée* which was accompanied by the words, " Be thou knight ! "

The question being thus stated, we need not trouble ourselves concerning the epoch at which we find the bishop blessing the armour of the knight for the first time, but we must ascertain the period at which a bishop consecrated—we may almost say created —a knight.

In a small library in Rome, to which the initiated only can find the way, at the Vallicellane, is preserved a MS. which many savants have already called to testify for them.   This is what they term an *Ordo Romanus,* or, to speak more plainly, a Ceremonial, a Ritual. The writing bears all the characteristics of the Lombardian small-type edition of the tenth century, or perhaps the first half of the

eleventh century. Mabillon, who knew it, attributed it to the time
of the Ottos, and is of opinion that it was actually written under
Otto the Third, between the years 983 and 1002 A.D. It is certain
that it bears the following distich, which is of great historical
interest, if not of great literary value :—

> " Gaudeat omnis homo quia regnat tertius Otto
> Illius imperio gaudeat omnis homo."

A little higher up there occurs a supplication to the Mother of
God to look favourably upon the people of Rome, and to protect the
Ottos. The book destined to fix the Roman rites was probably
written at Rome, and, even if we admit that it is a copy and not an
original, we cannot possibly date it later than 1050 A.D.

Well, then, if we open this MS. at the first page we find ourselves in the very midst of military devotion : this is the *Benedictio
vexilli bellici;* and then immediately afterwards is the benediction
of the sword, including those magnificent prayers, the *Exaudi* and
Benedic, which still form a portion of the Roman Pontifical, and
they have, as we now see, a very ancient origin. There is nothing
special, so far, except the really ancient forms of these prayers.
Following the benediction of the sword the choir used to intone the
old *Speciosus Forma,* of which we shall also find the greater
portion in other Pontificals, and which marks the exact period at
which the girding on of the sword used to take place. The versicle
Accingere gladio tuo super femur is not less characteristic ; and also
the following prayer, or orison, " 'Tis Thou, O God, Who hast
caused Thy servant to be girt with the sword."

It is evident that, at the time the *Speciosus Forma* was being
chanted, the soldier was not yet girded with the sword, but that he
was armed when the orison was commenced. But who had thus
armed him ? Whose hands had clasped his belt ? That is just
the information which the MS. does not afford us, and we have to
seek it in another *Ordo Romanus,* evidently derived from this one,
which tells us that the Bishop officiated. " *Deinde cingat eum
Episcopus, dicendo: accipe hunc gladium!* " Though unable to cite
positive proof, I am convinced that the bishop most likely did gird
on the sword. But, after all, this is only conjecture, not certainty.

Beyond the text of the Vallicellane MS. we can quote nothing before the twelfth, nor even before the thirteenth century. Martène, who has studied the subject more than anyone, declares that he has "*never* discovered any trace of the *Benedictio novi militis* in any of the ancient Pontificals." And the illustrious Benedictine is not able to publish in his *De antiquis Ecclesiæ ritibus* anything older than an extract from William Durand's Pontifical, which only dates from the later half of the thirteenth century.

It is in vain that people bring forward the authority of another *Ordo Romanus*—a very full one (*Ordo vulgatus*) which was issued in the sixteenth century. It is well known that it is only a rough compilation, a "mosaic" of varied fragments. We may use it as a reference to a later period, and it reproduces the principal features of the Vallicellane MS., but as we are not aware of the exact sources from whence it comes, one is always apt to question its authority.

So there only remains to us the text of the Vallicellane, with all its lights and shades; and I think we may conclude that the *Benedictio novi militis* was probably of Roman Pontifical origin, and that from Rome it radiated over other countries. But I do not think that it was introduced into France before the twelfth century. It was not in common use until the time of Saint Louis.

XI.

In the actual state of the question the *Benedictio novi militis* is represented by three classes of authorities. First comes the famous *Ordo Vulgatus*, which has been published successively by Cassander Hiltorp Ferrari and by the publishers of the *Maxima Bibliotheca Patrum*. It is evidently derived from the text of the Vallicellane. Secondly, there is the *Pontifical* of William Durand, which is conveyed almost in its entirety (its greatest honour) into the official edition of the *Roman Pontifical*. Thirdly and lastly, there is the valuable MS. 4748 in the Vatican, which goes no farther back than the thirteenth century, but which is the most *Roman* of all, and informs us categorically of the special rites performed in St. Peter's at the creation of new knights. It is by no means improbable that some day or other new MSS. may be discovered, and we ought to wish for them as we ought to wish for the diffusion of a beautiful idea, or the reproduction of a fine work of art. After this preface we have only to open the ancient Pontificals and give them life.

Our readers must not be surprised if we give the foremost place to the Pontifical of William Durand, and present it as the most complete type of this magnificent rite—as that which is most completely " French."

The Pontifical Mass is celebrated in the newly-finished cathedral : the bishop is present—the bishop who in the Middle Ages possesses the authority and weight of a crowned king. The last echoes of the concluding Alleluja are resounding through the chancel. At that moment—it is well chosen—the prelate proceeds to the benediction of the swords, which forms the first act of the liturgical drama. To bless this piece of metal, which may perhaps be drawn in the service of and to save the Truth, the bishop reads in solemn tones some of the prayers, so unjustly decried, which are the glory of the Catholic literature. " Bless this sword so that Thy servant may in future be in opposition to the cruelty of heretics and pagans; the defender of the Church, and of widows, orphans, and all those who fear God." Then the bishop adds, " Bless this sword, holy Lord, all-powerful Father, eternal God, bless it in the name of the coming of Jesus Christ, and by the descent of the Holy Ghost. Grant that Thy servant, always possessing thy love as his armour, may tread down his enemies, and victorious may be sheltered from all harm."

It seems to us that the most illustrious philosophers and poets of pagan antiquity would have admired such firm and noble language, but that their ideal never attained such a high pitch. What might not they have said while listening to the words which the bishop borrowed from the Old Testament. " Blessed be the Lord my God who teacheth my hands to war, and my fingers to fight. My castle and deliverer, my defender ! " Then, after a dualogue between the bishop and the choir, the grave slow accents of the prelate are heard once more in the prayer—

" Holy God, all-powerful Father, eternal Lord, who orders and disposes all things, Who, only in order that Justice may be upheld here below, and that the fury of the wicked may be restrained, hast, by a most salutary decree, permitted man to wield the sword. For the protection of thy people Thou hast ordained the institution of Chivalry. To a child, to David, Thou didst in olden time give victory over Goliath. Thou tookest Judas Maccabeus by the hand, and led him to triumph over all those nations which had not called upon thy name. Behold now thy servant, who has bent his neck beneath the military yoke, send him from on high the strength and courage necessary for the defence of Truth and Justice. Increase his faith, strengthen his hope, enlarge his charity, give him Thy fear and love, humility and perseverance, obedience and patience. Dispose him to all that is right, and grant that with this sword he may strike none unjustly, but may with it defend all that is just, all that is good."

Meantime the great sword was lying on the altar unsheathed. At the close of the prayer the bishop seized it, all perfumed as it was and consecrated by the almost Eucharistic contact, and placed it in the right hand of the future knight.

"Receive it," he said, "in the name of the Father, the Son, and the Holy Ghost." Then he sheathed the weapon and—this was the solemn moment—girt it about the aspirant who was kneeling before him, saying: "Be thou girded with this sword, O most powerful." Then the knight brandished the sword, and flourished it with pride and confidence, joyfully. Then he wiped it beneath his left arm as if it were already besmeared with the blood of his enemies, and returned it to the scabbard. Then the new knight and the bishop exchanged the kiss of peace, and the latter said : "Be thou a soldier—peaceful, courageous, faithful, devoted to God." Here the "buffet," the alapa, was administered according to the ancient ritual, yet the blow was not delivered with a brutal fist, but with the fingers, which gently touched the cheek of the cavalier. Then the bishop cried—

"Awake from dull sleep, and rise to the honour and the faith of Christ!"

If any other knights were present they attached the spurs to the heels of the defender of Eternal Justice. The ceremony ended, in the *Pontifical* of William Durand, with the solemn benediction of the vexillum, and in the Roman Pontifical by this rubric, which is not wanting in beauty—" *His dictis novus miles vadit in pace.*"

In peace—and he a soldier !

Very different is the text of the *Ordo Romanus*, which occupies the second, and would deserve the first, place because of the antiquity of its origin, if we were better informed concerning each of the elements which compose it. In it we find once more all the text of the Vallicellane, but singularly augmented, dilated, embellished. It is a long series of benedictions of arms, in the midst of which the girding on of the sword, and the consecration of the new knight, are introduced. The title is significant: " Rite for arming a defender of the Church or other knight." The ecclesiastical idea is here more dominant still than in the Pontifical of Durand. The liturgic function commences by the benediction of the vexillum and the bishop first of all invokes the Deity, " who is the true strength of conquerors," so that the pennon may be in some manner " surrounded by the name of God," and become a terror to all enemies of the Christians. Then the lance has its turn, and here the consecrating prelate does not forget to remind his hearers of the spear which pierced the side of the crucified Saviour. In the name of St. Michael, who is the chief of the Heavenly Chivalry, in the name of all celestial virtues, God is implored to assist the bearer of this blessed pennon ; and the names of Abraham and David, who were formerly great conquerors, are invoked.

The benediction of the sword is much the same as that given in the Pontifical of Durand, and we need not be surprised that it is so, for that was the stock ritual, and less liable to be modified. The future knight now kneels down, and on him descends the episcopal blessing. The sacramental moment has arrived ; the bishop girds the warrior, and says : " Take this sword with the blessing of God, and mayest thou, by virtue of the Holy Spirit, repulse at the point of this sword all your enemies, and those of Holy Church." Then the choir strikes in, and chants the beautiful verses: " *Speciosus forma præ filiis hominum, Specie tua et pulchritudine, et Propter Veritatem,*" which are taken from the forty-fourth Psalm.

Then the prayers succeed, and so far the knight has not secured any but his offensive armour. It is now time to think of the rest, and chiefly to bless the immense shield, which is a kind of barricade behind which the warrior entrenches himself. The service then puts him under the protection of the three illustrious knights, called Saint Maurice, Saint Sebastian, and Saint George, and when the shield is bestowed upon the knight the choir sings : " *Scuto circumdabit te, Veritas Ejus,*" taken from the nineteenth Psalm, and the other, " Thou shalt not fear the arrow that flieth by day." The ceremony has by this time lasted a long while, and is almost at an end ; then the bishop, raising his eyes to Heaven, invokes the joys of this world and the next upon the future knight.

To Rome, to the time-honoured basilica of Saint Peter, we are carried to view the scene of our third and last instance, and we do not represent the magnificent cathedral which all know at the present time, but the old church which Michael Angelo demolished, and which was built on the plan of our basilicas of the early centuries, less vast, more lightly, perhaps as beautiful as the work of the sixteenth century. The *Ordo*—MS. 4748 of the Vatican— commences with this significant rubrical sentence : " How to create a knight in the holy basilica of Saint Peter." In fact the cavalier is here consecrated *vice et auctoritate Apostolorum ;* he is, so to speak, armed by the apostles Peter and Paul, and the whole rite is not only pontifical but liturgical. This form possesses an air of grandeur, and the little address which accompanies the bestowal of the sword is of a proud and stirring beauty, thus :—

" Take this sword, with it exercise justice, and cut down all in- justice. Defend the Church of God and her faithful ones. With it disperse the enemies of Christ. Raise up what is earthly, and what you have elevated, preserve. Put down injustice and strengthen what is of good report. By these means, radiant and proud in the triumph of the virtues, you will reach the Heavenly kingdom, where, with Christ, whose type you are, you will reign eternally ! "

We do not ever remember to have met language more elevating, and it is fortunate that with it we are enabled to bring to a con- clusion all that concerns the august rites attending the admission to the Order of Chivalry. We have reached a high standpoint, let us not fall away from it.

XII.

The road we have traversed has been long, sometimes obscure, and sometimes difficult, but it may prove to be one of those journeys of which one may say hereafter : " I am glad that I undertook it." The halting-places also have been numerous, and it will be necessary to inspect them once again.

A sword is given to a warrior ; such is the origin—the distant origin of all the military ceremonial—such is the first act of the Ritual of Chivalry. Later was joined to this a heavy blow with the fist, which was inflicted on the neck of the youthful aspirant, accompanied by the words : " Be valiant."

Subsequently Christian feeling penetrated, little by little, this primitive savagery, and we have had the pleasure to witness this slow but fortunate emancipation. The youthful noble, moulded by the Church and his mother's teaching, believed that he brought down the blessing of Heaven on his sword, his lance, and hauberk, if he deposited them upon the altar of some monastery. From that to the blessing by the priest is not very far. The hearing of mass was to him not a matter of business, and he would not have wished to omit it. The religious vigils in which he took part with all his family during the nights preceding the great festivals gave him naturally the idea of preparation, by a special vigil, for the sacrament of Chivalry. However irreligious, however brutal, however much of a soldier the knight might have been who admitted the aspirant, he could no longer content himself with, say, " Be a valiant knight ; " he was constrained to say, he was compelled to recognise the Christian spirit, and say to the novice : " Be thou a soldier of Jesus Christ."

Up to this period, however, the consecrator had been a layman, but the time arrived when, by the force of circumstances and in certain countries, the bishop consecrated the knights. Then the ancient form of consecration became the *Benedictio novi militis,* and the old barbarous rite was transformed into a chapter of the *Pontifical.*

This is our last halting-place at the end of a long journey.

CHAPTER VIII.

THE ADMISSION TO CHIVALRY.—THE PRACTICE AT THE END OF THE TWELFTH CENTURY.

Honour doit querre li nouvious adoubez ("The newly-made knight must seek honour"). This is the text upon which for many days the youthful knight used to meditate. True, he pondered it after a rough and ready fashion, but it received all the attention which a youth of sixteen was capable of bestowing upon it. He has even been known to ask his father the precise meaning of the word "honneur," and the latter has replied that honour consisted in fighting well (saying to himself, " Leave it to fate "), and with a little glory into the bargain! These are not the terms he employed : they are in fact very modern, but this is the application of his little sermon. Then the great day approached—the day of admission. For this ceremony, on which his life depended, the young man was obliged to choose either the Feast of Easter or Whitsuntide. " On which was my father dubbed knight ? " " At Whitsuntide," is the reply. Then he no longer hesitates. Later on, when Chivalry became more refined, the aspirants prepared themselves by many days of fasting ; but truth forces us to state that up to the twelfth century our barons were less austere without being less religious, and they contented themselves generally in observing the fasts imposed by tradition and discipline.

Let us look now at the eve of Pentecost.

This vigil was almost as solemn amongst the youthful Christians as was Easter. Numbers of catechumens were baptized ; and this function was as extended and as beautiful as the Paschal feast. The next day was the day on which the descent of the Holy Spirit would be commemorated. The morrow was the day upon which from the top of the Cathedral the priests let fall a rain of roses on the faithful—a ceremony intended to represent the tongues of fire which sat on the Apostles. An important day indeed !

On the Saturday the castle was the scene of much animation, which was easily to be understood. The mother of the aspirant has placed on some piece of furniture in the hall or in his chamber the white shirt, the golden spurs, and the ermine robe with which the young man is to be dressed. It is thus that in our own day

Admission according to the liturgical mode.

the family lay out the trousseau of the intended bride : and as a matter of fact there are several points in common between the ceremony of marriage and the ceremony of knighthood. If some rich person had made the young man a present of some costly stuffs, they were opened out, commented upon and admired. But what is that noise which we hear at the gate ? No, it is not a " noise " —it is something more harmonious than mere noise, it is a small band of musicians and *jongleurs* who have come to wish success to the young knight of the morrow. They will not leave him any more, they will attach themselves to his person, calculating in advance the liberal presents which he will make them. There they are at any rate in the hall playing the viol and harp; the *gige* and the *chifonie*. No one has time to listen to their songs or music, but they come all the same, and they have calculated correctly. The poor people also do not forget to put in an appearance, and receive *largesse*, and this is a practice in which they indulge for several days. But the hours roll on and we see that night will soon come. Let it hasten: it is time it came now.

The attention of the reader should now be directed to two very different places—the church and the castle. The young baron would have wished perhaps to have his arms blessed by a priest according to a then novel form which was beginning to extend itself, but in default of this benediction he would have his good sword consecrated in a definite and almost sacramental manner. At this time his younger brother is carrying his arms to the altar of a neighbouring convent. Yes, upon that altar God will descend, and on it he will place the heavy sword which will one day cause blood to flow. It will remain all night upon the altar.

At the château the scene is more commonplace. In the great hall, whence the minstrels have been temporarily banished, suddenly are deposited a dozen enormous pans or troughs filled with hot water. These are for the baths, which are by ritual commanded for the youthful baron and his companions who intend to be admitted into Chivalry on the morrow.

The hour appointed for the bath was not always the same. Some candidates took it before the Vigil of Arms, others on the following morning. But no matter at what time it was taken, it possessed the same significance and the same characteristics. It was a curious medley of the poetic and the practical, of the ideal and the real, and we need not go out of our way to consider it from either side. I am persuaded that in its origin it had nothing symbolic about it, and that it may be looked upon merely as a sanitary precaution. It is equally likely that the bath was sometimes accompanied with a kind of massage to which our ancestors seemed to have attached considerable importance in more everyday circumstances. But the symbolic was soon grafted on the practical; it was the usual course. As the youthful baron was intelligent and of an inquiring mind he quickly perceived the analogy between the Bath and Baptism, between confirmation and the *paumée*. The churchmen of the period assisted him further, and at the end of the twelfth century this symbolism was definitively constituted. But they renounced the rubbing process, which did not easily lend itself to the symbolical side, and seemed somewhat barbarous. "The bath," the youth would cry, "is designed to efface all the blemishes of my past life, and I shall issue from it, clean."

However, he plunges into it with delight mingled with some gravity of thought. The youths did not chatter in the bath over much; laughing was prohibited, and thought was of an elevating character. Around these rough baths hurried attendants carrying the silken robes and costly furs—a continual bustle and movement are apparent. When the young men emerge from the baths the attendants throw over their shoulders the warm robes of vair or minever, and the bright and glossy silk or samite. Some elderly relatives and friends take advantage of the opportunity to present the aspirants with complete costumes, and the youths emerge from the bath-rooms glowing with health and good-looks. The dresses are rich and beautiful. Now for the Church!

[At Rome in the thirteenth century the Bath had a more poetic character. When a Roman knight was created at Saint Peter's it was usual, *juxta morem patriæ*, to have a bath of rose-water. I am uncertain whence this custom arose, but conclude that it is Oriental. At any rate after the ceremony of the perfumed bath our knight was placed naked on a bed, and obliged to rest for a while. But I prefer the French custom.]

Night is falling on the old castle, and the nearest monastery is a league away. Surrounded by youthful valets, who like himself have been bathed, and who will on the morrow be made knights, our *damoiseau* of France bids a rapid farewell to his mother, his sisters and other relatives. This "farewell" had nothing painful about it; it was only a temporary parting after all, and they would quickly meet again. This custom of watching the armour was a very interesting and touching one, but I do not think that it came into practice before the first half of the twelfth century. The young squire's companions are the sons of his sponsors and his peers. The road is traversed merrily but without any unseemly uproar. In the fading light, along those hedge-bordered roads, amidst the songs of birds and the scents of flowers, the young men speak of the various phases of the approaching ceremonial of the morrow; of the customs in vogue in other countries which they compare with those of their own. The journey is not long, and very soon they perceive in the gloaming the small chapel whose façade is ornamented with symbolical figures of the four Evangelists. Against the pier stands a large image of the Saviour who teaches and blesses all men. They respectfully salute it. Then the heavy door rolls back and the fine sturdy youths enter joyously. They can see nothing but a luminosity which is apparent at the other end in one of the chapels which open from the choir. In this chapel the watch-night ceremony will be held, and it is easy to perceive at the first glance to what Saint it is dedicated, though the stained-glass windows and the mural decorations tell us little in that light. But we can readily recognise the Saint in the panoply of knighthood who is represented as bestowing half his military cloak upon a beggar, the blessed Saint Martin !

The youthful barons make no secret of their preference for the Saint and for his chapel, but in their naïve piety they do not forget the Virgin Mary, and in her name the vigil is begun. The vigil will be long and wearisome, for they are not permitted to sit down for a single moment—standing upright or kneeling they must remain for ten hours in prayer. These devotions are lengthy. "Grant me honour and to my father life," is one petition. Notice that they do not beseech honour for their parent—he in their eyes is already the incarnation of honour, and it would prove them as wanting in respect if they thought otherwise. Then they probably permit thoughts to have the upper hand, and they picture the mighty lance-thrusts they will deliver, and perhaps the individuals to whom they will be dealt. They are not without some solace in thinking of the great day when they will be fully equipped with hauberk blue and helmet, surmounted with a rich sparkling carbuncle; when armed with heavy sword they will deal such cutting blows; of the coming war, of their brave deeds. They will perhaps be preoccupied in mind, but we must give these young people the benefit of extenuating circumstances. Then to escape

WATCHING THE ARMOUR.

from such mundane thoughts they turn again to prayer. At length a pale light penetrates the sanctuary, which gradually increases till the windows become transparent. 'Tis daybreak indeed. Truly the night had begun to feel very long. At length the welcome day has come.

Then the echo of footsteps is heard within the church; the priest is approaching to say mass. For a moment our young aspirant may have entertained the idea that the bishop himself had arrived, but the prelate is then occupied in pastoral visits, of which he keeps an accurate record. He is twenty leagues away and the roads are bad. So he cannot come, and he has appointed one of his canons in his place. No matter who celebrates it this mass is most solemnly conducted, and of very ancient origin. It is far anterior to the Vigil of the Armour which the elders did not know, and which even the father of our youthful knight regards as a superfluity—or at least as an innovation. Later, our aspirant will make confession and take the Sacrament—but we cannot exactly state that in the twelfth century he did more than attend the mass. He conducted himself with becoming gravity, and was probably only disturbed in his devotion by the representation of Saint Martin receiving knighthood as depicted on the glass window. He received the benediction, and then with his companions seeks the portals. It is six o'clock on a May morning: the air is fresh, and the young men are fasting!

Their exit from the church is rather noisy, it is so long since these young people have shouted or sung. They return to the castle —*moult maient grant hustin;* and we may confess that they are worthy of pardon. Remember they had been previously silent for ten hours, and they will be knights before the evening.

At the château the table is already laid, and our future knights eat white bread and venison. They have need to recruit their strength for the approaching ceremony and for the athletic games, the *eslais* and the *quintain.* The day will be as rough as it will be imposing, and they must prepare their muscles as well as their minds.

Immediately after the repast the ceremonial begins.

The youthful aspirant then retires to his chamber, wherein his mother has carefully laid out all the articles of dress he will require.

These are chiefly white, such as the shirt and silk "trunks," the
"chausses" of the period.   The shoes come from Montpellier,
the robe is of linen, and the cloak, which is very expensive, is of
almost indescribable richness.   How well the youth looks in his
gay habiliments, what an air!   Ladies assist him to don the body
garment and cloak, and arrange its folds with practised hands.
No one knows so well how to put on the finishing touches to these
masculine draperies.   The lad has never looked so well, and the
women smile as they feast their eyes on him.   "How like me he
is!" said the father, and he recalls the day on which he was made a
knight.   Such memories make him feel twenty years younger.

The youth leaves his room, traverses the hall and comes out
upon the steps, and the moment he appears in the full light of
morning a general cry of admiration ascends from the terraces for
the fresh-coloured youth, whose fair hair, proud mien and broad
shoulders are greatly pleasing.   The relatives of his fifteen companions in arms are present, and they simultaneously exclaim
"How handsome he is!" as they each think of their own candidate.
Suddenly the shrill trumpets sound, and officially announce the
opening of the ceremonial.   An orchestra or band replies.   This
band consists of *jongleurs* who had arrived on the previous evening.
Their voices mingle with their instruments, as do the acclamations
of the spectators.

But it would require a more experienced pen and palette of more
varied colours to paint the spectacle.   All those ladies with such
long fair hair, clothed in the richest and newest costumes; those
mailed knights in blue, red, or green with orfray embroideries;
those fair and rosy children who cower beside their mothers; the
jongleurs sombrely clad and carrying all kinds of curiously formed
instruments; those priests and monks so friendly with their
neighbours, and so intent upon a spectacle which has nothing
clerical about it; and then the vast open space below the steps
wherein a most solemn scene is about to be enacted—a grave drama
to be presented.   The joyful cries, the sound of trumpets, the
strains of the band, the dazzling toilettes, the enthusiastic cheers,
the stirring crowd, these fine strong youths who advance with slow
and stately steps towards the old knights who are about to assume
the positions of their consecrators and sponsors, the prevailing

ideas of the Church and of the Saviour which dominate all, and tinge all those present with their influence—God and Feudality ; War and Youth ; all elements commingle, intersperse, penetrate, and end in completing and mingling in, an original and curious harmony which has nothing false nor tame about it—but which is all energy, fire, military, manly, French ! Ah ! language fails one !

Then our youthful baron descends the steps and advances slowly across the grass of the open space below. Upon the field the servitors have spread a carpet or some straw, for without this detail there would be no creation of knights. All eyes are fixed upon those few square feet which for the spectators are just then " all the world," so to speak. An air of solemnity obtains. No more cries of welcome, no more singing, no talking even. Everyone is profoundly silent.

The aspirant is placed in the centre of the carpeted space. One of his sponsors then approaches him—an elderly individual is this godfather, wearing a white beard—a knight who in his day had taken part in the expedition to the East undertaken by King Louis le Jeune. He embraces the youth, and with somewhat trembling hands puts on the steel leg-pieces on the sturdy limbs of the "novice," and fastens his spurs—golden spurs—on his heels, saying himself some such words as the following—

" I trust that he will conduct himself in such fashion that his spurs may never be hacked off in shame and degradation." He then retires with measured step.

Then from the ranks of the spectators advance the aspirant's two uncles, who have arrived from the Holy Land, having escaped the disasters at Tiberias. They carry, with a dignity which has something sacerdotal about it, the hauberk and the helmet of the new knight—their nephew. The hauberk is white—a suit of mail without plastron, worn over the other garments, falling to the knees, and divided back and front. The skirt and sleeves are ornamented with rough embroidery of iron or steel wire, but it is usefully furnished with a hood which enwraps the chin, ears, skull, and covers a portion of the forehead, thus leaving only the eyes, nose and mouth exposed. The helmet is an iron casque very pointed at the top and surmounted by some large stone such as a ruby or carbuncle, and studded round and adown the jointures with

smaller stones.   A long strip of metal (like a pot-handle) descends
straight over the nose and protects it from injury.   This appendage
is called the "nasal."

The above is a description of the old style of helmet, and at that
period of which we are speaking another mode was coming into
fashion, which was more irksome and scarcely more becoming.
The helm is heavy and tiring to the wearer.   The youthful face
disappears under such head-gear, all wearers appear to be the same
age.   The hauberk is suspended like a shirt from the neck, the
helmet is attached to it by leathern laces, and it requires some
exercise of patience to fasten.   But at length the task is finished,
and there is our youthful baron encased in iron.   No features of
his face except his sprouting moustache and his bright eyes can be
distinguished.

If one may be permitted the avowal it must be confessed, that up
to this point our young knight has not been greatly impressed by
the chivalric rites.   His sponsors have only bestowed upon him de-
fensive armour, and his youthful courage leads him to disdain such
protection.   He wishes to encounter the pagan hand to hand un-
armoured.   But it will be otherwise when he receives his weapons,
which he will, he hopes, some day imbue in Saracenic blood.   He
is most anxious to obtain his sword of all things.   Already, the
question had been discussed, and he had confessed that he could
not feel himself actually a knight "until the moment when his
hand grasps his sword for the first time."   That was all-
sufficient—the remainder of the rite counted for nothing in
comparison.

We may therefore pardon his emotion when he perceives his
father's liege-lord approaching him carrying the sword—the famous
sword !   The weapon so ardently desired and expected, which is
suspended from a rich baldric or shoulder-belt, is glinting in
the sunlight !   The youth turns red and pale by turns, and con-
gratulates himself that his face is so concealed by his hood of mail.
He trembles with conflicting emotions; he closes his eyes; and
then tries to recover his composure.   When he again recovers himself, O happiness ! he feels the sword pendant on his left side, and
opening his eyes he perceives the noble who has girded him
with it.

" My dear lad," says this fine old warrior, " I could tell you that this weapon was forged by the celebrated Galant to whom we owe ' Durendal,' and all the other renowned swords of which the *jongleurs* have sung and spoken. I might add that it was formerly tested upon the famous staircase of steel leading from the palace of Charlemagne at Aix (though I have never seen it), and where even Courtain, the famous sword of Ogier of Denmark, was notched. I could tell you a long and painful story about it, and make you believe that I have conquered with it a Saracen Emir in a splendid adventure in a distant land. But I prefer to tell you the plain truth. This good sword I forged myself, and have carried it for years. One day it happened—at the gates of Jerusalem—on our last pilgrimage to the Holy Sepulchre—that I was attacked by twenty infidels who seized my arms, and put me in direst peril ; when, suddenly, someone came up, snatched the weapon from the Saracen, killed two of the party, and dispersed the remainder. I was saved ! My deliverer was your father, as you know. Do as he did, and you will do full well ! "

The young baron then regarded the sword with admiration and kissed it reverently : the pommel, in the form of a cross, contained some sacred relics—such as a few hairs of St. Bernard, whom our knight's father knew, and a fragment of the cope of St. Thomas à Becket, who was so treacherously murdered in Canterbury Cathedral. It is true that more valuable relics existed, but none more authentic nor more inspiring. The youth is proud of them— and at length lifts his head.

No longer his liege-lord, but his father stands before him and whispers, " Bend your head. I am about to give you the *colée*."

Now the most brutal portion of the ceremony has been reached, and the part which the youth's mother has dreaded. She prefers the English ritual " *sans paumée*," without the blow of the fist, to the French ritual, to which the *paumée* gives a distinctive character. But she is obliged to bow to the inexorable will of the baron. She is compelled to resign herself to the inevitable and wait the issue.

The father of our new knight is rather coarse and very much imbued with the rough usages of the olden time. It is, therefore, not a gentle blow—an almost caressing movement—which he delivers

on his son's neck, but a formidable blow of his right hand. He
puts all his force into it—he is still a powerful man—and the
youth reels beneath the blow. After a while he falls to the
ground.

"Ah," he exclaims, "if my father had not been the striker!"

His mother had, meantime, not dared to look, and her attendant
had to tell her when to turn her eyes again upon the youth. The
father himself, now throwing off his harshness, embraces his son,
who has become his equal, and says :—"Be thou brave and upright.
Remember that you spring from a race which should never be
false. Honour all knights ; be liberal to the poor ; love God! and
may our Saviour, who was crucified himself, protect you from
all your enemies. Go!"

The youth, in a firm voice, then replies :—"I thank you, O
father, and may the Lord hear your prayer. May I serve him, and
may he love me." That is the whole dialogue, and it is long
enough. Then the young man says to himself :—"I would rather
receive the *colée* from the living arm of my father than, like Galien,
from the dead hand of Roland."

During the centuries which followed the ceremony was not so
quickly disposed of. Before the actual consecration of the new
knight he was compelled to submit to an interrogatory—a regular
examination as to his duties and the aspects of Chivalry : even the
oath of fidelity was imposed, but it is easy to perceive that these
rites have not the antique flavour. They are evidently modern
additions. In the twelfth century the aspirant used to content
himself by mentally devoting himself to the service of the church,
and made some mental vow similar to that taken by the youthful
Vivien, as stated in one of our oldest poems :—"I swear never to
retreat one step before the Saracens!" The Church did not
approve the rashness of such a vow.

The fifteen companions of our young knight were knighted on
the same carpet as he had been dubbed, with the same rites and
the same solemnity. At this period of time the ceremony might
appear to us rather too long, but we should not judge our ancestors
by our present day ideas. I have never seen any complaint of the
length of those twelfth-century ceremonials. The more noble the
youthful knight the more aspirants armed with him. Such was

the rule, of which numerous examples exist. But to return to our picture.

What is the cause of this sudden movement and commotion amongst the spectators? Why all this tumult, these cries? The crowd swings backwards and forwards and forms into line. Why?

The loud whinneying of horses is audible. They come, and, in truth, their presence is opportune. One can hardly be created a chevalier without a horse! These are fine chargers, splendid animals! The young squires who lead them will soon be, in their turn, knights, and we may perceive amongst them the brother of the newly-made knight, who appears as joyous as the elder one, and ruddy with happiness.

The horse of our young knight is a present from his liege-lord. The animal is young but of good breed. When it becomes necessary to name him the youth hesitates a long time between "Veillantif" and "Marchegai." But finally the former is chosen: it was the name of Roland's horse, and the young baron loves Roland. He has already ridden "Veillantif," as all present are aware. As soon as the horse is presented, the youth scans him with a glance. In vain does the splendid animal plunge, and rear, and paw the ground or champ his foaming bit—all in vain his efforts. He has found his master. Amongst the audience gossips whisper and make inquiries of each other as to the young baron's horsemanship, and as to how he will mount. But anxiety and curiosity are quickly allayed. There is an unusual exclamation as the young man, after patting the animal's neck, retires a pace or two and then leaps into the saddle without touching the stirrup. The delighted warriors exclaimed: "He did not use the stirrup," and fair ladies echo the praise throughout the assembly, so the good news is carried through the crowd, "*Sans étrier!*"

The young baron, modest and calm, curbs Veillantif, who stands motionless. The knight is awarding the arms, which are only given to a mounted cavalier, the immense shield and the lance. The former covers his body entirely; the latter is eight feet in length. On the shield are two lions *or* on a field *azure;* and from the lance tip flutters a red pennon with three tongues, the extremities of which just touch the casque of the young knight.

Nothing now is wanting; he has only to prove to the crowd that he
is an accomplished cavalier.   It is all very well to mount a horse,
but can he put him through his paces?   Let us see.   Proceed.
Gallop.

The gallop was termed the *eslais*, and was one of the elements
most insisted on : the most official performance in the long ritual
of knighthood.   The youth is quite contented.   Giving his horse
the spur, he darts away like a tempest.   Cheers are redoubled as
he circumscribes the course.   He, pleased with the enthusiasm of
the spectators, caracoles and makes some people fear for the result
of his showy performance.   Ladies shrink and tremble for the
youth ; the knights laugh at their fears and reassure them ; the
eslais is concluded.

But after the *eslais* comes the quintain.   This is the last test to
which the new knight is subjected, the last pleasure, alas ! in such
an eventful day.

Our young friend is an accomplished cavalier, and has just
furnished proofs of it.   But is he adroit?   Is he strong?   This
lance which he handles so cleverly, can he use it properly ?   If an
infidel were to encounter him, could the knight lay his lance in
rest, aim properly, attack, strike, and overcome his enemy?   That
is just what everyone was anxious to know, and that is what the
tilting at the quintain will show.   Now, to it !

For such play as the quintain a long space is absolutely
necessary.   But there was a large meadow available in which the
inhabitants of the castle used to walk on Sundays.   The fifteen
young knights also made their way thither in single file, singing at
the top of their voices, joyously and with light hearts, seated on
restless and fretting chargers.   All the assemblage follows.   The
meadow is covered with ladies and their cavaliers in striking dresses
and ermine robes, forming a charming "mosaic" on the field,
whence arises a continual murmur of conversation.   Clothed in
sombre garments the lower classes occupy the second rank and
take part in the fête.   The spectacle is really charming.   But
what is the quintain ?

The quintain (or quintaine) is a kind of large puppet or lay
figure, placed on the summit of a post, which was invariably made
up of the following elements: "one, or many hauberks, one, or

several shields." The shields naturally were placed over the hauberks. This very primitive puppet was supposed to be an enemy, an infidel, a Saracen.

At a given signal the attendants raised the post, which had been in readiness on the ground. It was then the custom for the knight to charge, lance at rest, and strike the quintain as he passed. Victory fell to the happy assailant who, with one blow, pierced the shields through and through, and ripped up the hauberks, and finally—this was the crowning achievement, snatched the post itself from the ground, so that only a confused heap of arms, armour, and the supports remained.

In order to increase the difficulties of the encounter, and to impose a more severe task upon the knights, it often happened that two posts, one beyond the other, were set up, both furnished with shields, &c. But in exceptional cases even four or five quintains were erected. This seems almost incredible, but we have it on the authority of the text-books.*

Such was the game which enchanted our ancestors, in every generation less refined than ourselves; this is the origin of our contemporary tournaments or tilting matches. The antique hauberk is now replaced by a head of cardboard or other material— it matters little. It is the same exercise, and the knights of Saumur in 1884 were, without being aware of the fact, only imitators of the cavaliers of the twelfth century.

We regret that, to make ourselves more intelligible, we have likened the quintain to a "game." It was more than that, it was a test—what do I say? it was *the* test; the supreme trial, on which all chivalric life depended. Just think that all his life, so to speak, the old baron had been putting to himself the question, "Will my son be able to accomplish that feat?" And then comes the moment when, thanks to an exercise somewhat savage and puerile, he, at length, sees the question answered. You can imagine his anxiety. We must not after all imagine that the horizon of the feudal existence was a very extended one. The barons were soldiers first of all, and every château was a riding-school.

---

* Two posts, *vide Elie de St. Gilles* and *Godefroi de Bouillon;* four posts, *Aiol;* five posts, for the gigantic *Renvart.—Aliscans.*

At the opening of one of our most curious *chansons*, we are
brought face to face with a scene which, in its intensely faithful,
feudal roughness, brings the importance of the quintain vividly
before us. The old Count Julien de Saint Gilles wished to test
the prowess of his son Elias, whom he intended to dub knight.
He is quite a baron of the old school is Julien, and when he
bestows upon him the buffet (*paumée*), he delivers a blow that would
fell an ox. But he is not satisfied with that: he awaits the
quintain with feverish anxiety, and says to his son—

"Remember if you do not bring down the quintain I will
disinherit you. You may find another home, you shall not live in
mine: be off!"

The youth obeys, curbing his feelings, and it is not without
difficulty that this Roderick submits to the coarseness of this Don
Diego. He charges violently, and at his first attempt—a master-
stroke nevertheless—he pierces the shields, rends the hauberks, and
splinters the posts. Then his father is delighted and almost raves
with joy. "I will give you my possessions," he cries, "they are
all yours!" But the son has not forgotten the parental threats,
and he is proud in his turn. He replies—

"You speak foolishly! I do not want your land. For no earthly
consideration would I remain at your château! I go hence at
once!" Thereupon he bade his father farewell and went forth to
seek his fortune.

Thus we may perceive a successful bout at the quintain was
sufficient to make a man's fortune in those days, just as a
successful book or an eloquent address in these modern times.
When Renaud de Montauban before Charlemagne pierced the
shield and broke the post, the Emperor could not restrain his
enthusiasm, and exclaimed—"Thou shalt be the Seneschal of my
Empire." Prime minister! Yes, for a successful attempt—a
tour de force of which any circus-rider of our own days would be
capable; and such a reward by no means astonished our ancestors.
But we must put ourselves in their place. War was their normal
condition and daily occupation. They most highly valued a brave
warrior, and in their eyes a brave knight was one who could most
easily kill his enemy. From such considerations as these the
fashion and importance of the quintain arose. Some prime

ministers of other epochs attained power by means less worthy perhaps than those lance-thrusts!

The quintain, also, only represented infidels, so it was the visible symbol of felons and traitors. With what pleasure they were struck down! In one of the romances of the middle ages, the old Guy (de Mayence) who lived for a long time hidden in a wood, gave one day his armour to his son—Doolin—who was only fifteen years old. It was a very rustic and incorrect creation. The father had no lance to give his son. "Take this pole," he cried. He had not the proper framework of a quintain at hand, so he said—"You see yonder tree, charge at it at full speed, so that I may see whether you are really expert on horseback, *à cheval pommelé*." The youthful Doon did not need a second exhortation; he spurred his steed, struck the beech tree full at the first attempt and splintered his lance. "Good, very good," cried his father. "Ah," replied the lad, who had already drawn his sword to defend himself against an imaginary foe, "you need not be surprised, father, I imagined that the tree was the traitor Herchenbaut, who persecuted my mother and myself. That is the reason why I struck it so well and truly." *

The youthful baron whose "creation" we have been describing had not met with traitors as Doon de Mayence had. He had only the Saracens to contend against, and he pictured to himself a Turk when he laid his lance in rest, and set spurs to his good steed Veillantif. A silence had fallen on the field; every man's gaze was centred on the quintain, and the ladies' eyes upon the knight (*quintanier*): what would be the result? You may anticipate it, my reader. After the lapse of five minutes a blow resounds over the field, then the clattering of armour is heard. A sudden rush from all sides is made towards the spot, and the ladies can look down upon a small heap of armour; they can distinguish two shields pierced through, two hauberks in rags, and a broken post lying amongst the "ruins." The pennon of the youth's lance is missing; it has been torn off in the assault, but the quintain is down, and our new knight is unquestionably the victor.

They will feast him when he returns, reining his horse backwards.

* Doon de Maience.

He salutes with his sword, dismounts and permits himself to be welcomed and embraced by the ladies, assures his mother that he is in no wise fatigued, drinks a goblet of wine which is handed to him, and endeavours to be as modest as he can.

But do not imagine that it was all over yet. Men were of iron in those days. Our young hero mounts again, for he must now proceed to *behourder* with his friends, even with the squires and pages. *Behourder* is sham fighting, and in this instance it is represented by fencing, or sword-play, on horseback. The young baron is the more disposed to undergo this new fatigue because several of his associates have been unsuccessful at the quintain and hope to retrieve their fallen fortunes at the sword-play. They descend to the meadow and engage in pairs. Around each pair of combatants a circle is formed, while cries and clapping of hands resound in all directions as the adversaries charge, turn, wheel, and attack each other, or splinter a lance against an opponent's shield.

A bright sun illuminates the scene of mimic battle, which after a while threatens to assume proportions and features more serious than originally contemplated, and the sonorous voice of our youthful knight's father is heard putting an end to the engagement, in which several combatants have received wounds. As says the old poem of *Aliscans*—

> " Li cuens a fait le jeu laissier,
> Qu'il ne se blecent as lances abaissier."

In this encounter also our young hero comes off victorious. An enthusiastic *jongleur* declared: " There is no one to equal him in fifty cities! The red shield suits him marvellously, and people declare that he must have been born with it. If he live, what a warrior he will be!" Another rhymer quotes the following couplets from *Garin de Loherain*—

> " In Langres town the King is holding Court,
> From every side the barons have arrived.
> That day bold Garin was created knight
> With Fromont, William, and Begon the Brave ;
> And many more whose names I need not tell.
> Grand is the *fête*, and worthily sustained
> By all the new made knights in their degrees.
> The feast is o'er ! They quit the palace halls ;
> And, mounting for the joust, they snatch their swords !

> Begon is riding his good steed Baucent,
> The which on him the King had just bestowed.
> Begon is brave, he comes of lineage proud ;
> And holding high his wide and gleaming shield,
> Swoops on as straight as falcon unconfined,
> While all the knights of France his prowess see ! "

Thus sang the troubadours, and they but echoed the feelings of the whole assemblage.

Night is now approaching : the shadows fall upon the grass, and people think it is time to return to the shelter of the castle. There is another repast awaiting them and more music, another and final distribution of presents—magnificent gifts to every one of the guests. The *jongleurs* then pack up their instruments and music, the guests take leave, and soon the castle, lately so uproarious, becomes silent and deserted. The newly-made knight takes leave of his mother, doffs his armour, and throwing himself upon his bed, is soon asleep !

The old baron has retired to his chamber, though not to sleep. He, as becomes a man of orderly habits, is counting the cost of the day. Certainly the *fête* was most successful, and he calculates that at least a hundred knights and two hundred pages must have been present. But the expenses ; great Heaven—what expenses ! How well those legislators must have been inspired who decreed that the lord of the castle should be reimbursed by, or should receive aid from, his vassals " for the knighting of his eldest son." There was no better plan. But three other subsidies of the same nature are *still due to him !* viz., " On the day on which he departed to the Crusades." But he has returned long ago ! " On the day when he was taken prisoner ; " but he had been three years in the Holy Land ! and " On the day when his eldest daughter is married." But she is only seven years old ! The ceremony of knighthood is decidedly expensive, and all the subsidies in the world would not satisfy its cost !

Now he begins to admire and approve of the conduct of those who remain squires all their lives, or who are content with a small family gathering at the ceremony, or those who could imitate Rigaud in *Garin de Loherain,* who turned with contempt from the furred garments with which he was presented before he was girt with his sword ! Ah, those were wise men indeed !

The baron could not sleep until he had jotted down roughly the various items of expense. The cost was enormous, and I will content myself by merely transcribing the heads of the principal disbursements.

Horses bestowed on knights — six brown, seven black, two sorrel.*

Falcons and hawks given to same cavaliers.

Dress and arms for my son.

Dresses and armour for his fifteen companions.

Dresses bestowed upon my wife and the ladies invited, furs, &c.

Weapons and golden girdles, &c.

Dinner.

Presents to *jongleurs.*

Destruction of crops in the country by knights and attendants, and moneys paid to servants.

Largesse and alms.

The sum total is so tremendous that I am compelled to withhold it. The poor baron is literally " knocked all of a heap," and endeavours to forget in sleep the terrible sum. He looks at the heroic side of the question and goes to bed !

All this time our new knight is dreaming of his new chivalry. So he has at last the right to carry a sword. He now can enter a church in full armour ; he can wear " the vair and the grey." He can seat himself at table with other knights, and have the pleasure of seeing everyone rise up when he enters. What honours are these ! But he has also his duties to perform. When will the next war be ? So even as Goethe cried " Light, Light," our new knight calls " Battle, Battle ! " Then he goes to sleep again. . . .

---

* A black horse was then worth 12 livres, a brown 14 livres, and a sorrel 18 livres.

CHAPTER IX.

THE ESPOUSALS OF THE KNIGHT.—THE MARRIAGE THEORETICALLY
AND HISTORICALLY CONSIDERED.

I.

It cannot be denied that Feudalism has not had a good influence on marriage. This true statement is made with the object of making clear the following pages, and we are compelled to put it forward at once. We are very desirous not to take up an extreme view either with the enthusiastic admirers nor amongst the fanatical enemies of the Feudal system. It had very considerable influence, as was inevitable, upon all the institutions of the period which it dominated, and we need not worry ourselves more about it than about specific gravity in the physical world.

Everything could be—everything was given in fief—titles, functions, incomes, privileges, costumes, lands! But after a while the Feudal system assumed a decidedly military phase. What most concerned the barons of that rude epoch was the possibility of having vassals who would be actually fighting men who would side with them and for them, helm on head and lance in hand. That is the reason why about the twelfth century women were considered incapable of holding a fief—that is why minors of noble families found their position so unbearable during the first period of the Feudal system. So long as he was too young to engage in battle the youth could claim nothing, his liege-lord could confiscate his possessions or claim his land. This was rather hard upon him, no doubt, and ere long some alleviation was proposed. But that was nevertheless the backbone of the system, and the jurists who defined the fief were not wrong in describing it as a portion of land which was held subject to military service. It was derived from that, and that explains the whole matter.

Now what were the consequences of such a doctrine as regarded marriage? They are easy enough to predicate, and had a fatal effect upon the dignity, as well as upon the liberty, of the marriage state.

A baron died, let us say, leaving his only daughter as heiress of his fief, a child of six years old, a minor. The suzerain hears this, and declares that he is being cheated out of one of the most important of his rights. What good is this girl to him, what can she do for him? If a war were to break out can she assist him, bring up vassals to his ranks, and throw herself into the thick of battle? No. You see that she is useless to the baron, and even detrimental. Such a scandal must not be permitted to continue, and it is absolutely necessary that the fiefs must be occupied and " worked." The suzerain with a very bad grace consents to wait a few years, but as soon as the girl is of a marriageable age—as soon as she is twelve years old in fact—he demands that she shall choose a husband or have one chosen for her, and the poor child cannot refuse. 'Tis true that the baron would probably give her her choice of three knights. But suppose they do not please her? suppose they are all ill-favoured or brutal? suppose that she finally declines them all? It is of no consequence. " Choose ! " She chooses.

It must be admitted that the girl herself has an interest in the possession of a husband as a defender, and in the strict interpretation of her rights could compel the baron to give her a choice of husbands. And again we must not picture the damsels of the twelfth century as innocent and simple-minded as our young ladies now, small, delicate, very youthful in mind and heart. The young women of the heroic age were stout and vigorous in body and mind, and I imagine that they did not think they were very much to be pitied in being thus legally given in marriage. Nevertheless there was nothing of the Christian character, of individual freedom ; and amongst these forced marriages there were many which turned out fatally unhappy. This is what we protest against.

Our old poems are full of such instances, and our *chansons de geste* are perhaps the best commentary on the *Libri Feudorum.* One day in front of the palace of Charlemagne in Paris the attendants perceived a young girl approaching with great self-possession. She proved to be Hellissent, daughter of Yon of

Gascony. She dismounted at the steps, ascended them at a bound, and threw herself at the king's feet, saying, boldly:

"My father died two months ago, I request that you will appoint some one to marry me."

A like instance is that of the beautiful Aiglentine who was to become the wife of Guy of Nanteuil—the lovely Aiglentine, who was "fairest of the fair and whiter than a siren!" She made her

King Yon of Gascony informs his sister Clarissa that he wishes her to marry Renaud de Montauban (p. 294).

appearance in the same way at the court of the Emperor, not to be a partaker in the enjoyments of his state, but to demand a husband! Widows, who were sometimes placed in circumstances similar to those in which minors found themselves, were no way backward in demanding their rights, as we may learn from the history of the Duchess of Burgundy in *Girars de Viane.*

"My husband has died, but what is the use of mourning? It is the dress since the time of Moses in which some have died and others have lived. Find me a husband then who is brave and

valiant, for I am in want of some one to take care of my
land."

The king presented Girars de Viane on the spot, and he,
" looking her over," and finding her to his liking, consented to take
care of it for her !

The privilege of giving their vassals in marriage is one of those
which kings in their capacity of " seigneur suzerains " exercised
with a great deal of pleasure.   There was nothing more agreeable
to them than to take a pretty blushing maiden by the hand and
present her to some powerful baron whom the king wished to
conciliate.   This was neither a lengthy nor a complicated treaty.
He bestowed on his ally at once a fief and a wife.   In this manner
did Raoul Trillefer become possessed of the fief of Cambrisin and
of Alais the Fair—the most beautiful woman of her time—by favour
of the King of France.   Thus also did the Emperor Otho in the
midst of the assembly of his barons confer on Count Witasse of
Boulogne the hand of the beautiful Ydain, and all the territory of
Bouillon.

But sometimes it happened by happy accident that the selection
of the sovereign coincided with the lady's own choice.   One day
the good Duke Milon, who was about to quit the world and retire
into a monastery, entered the chamber in which his two daughters
were seated, and thus addressed them :

" Go put on your most becoming costumes, and come to see the
knights whom I wish you to marry."

Now these young ladies had cast their affections upon Garin de
Lorraine and his brother Begue respectively, but, woman-like, they
had not mentioned anything of this to their father. The elder one
(who was very diplomatic) even then contented herself with
the remark, " The barons for whom you destine us are perhaps false
knights or traitors."

" Not so," replied the good duke, who did not wish to leave his
children in any uncertainty, or to embarrass them, " not so, these
gentlemen are named Garin and Begue."

The young ladies did not require any further inducement.   They
immediately arrayed themselves in their best dresses and permitted
their long hair to float coquettishly down their backs.   The king
welcomed them, and without any hesitation, gave Aelis to Garin

and the beautiful Beatris to Begue of Belin. The damsels laughed and said :

" Sire, we are quite at your disposal ! " Young ladies of our time have more reserve, but, perhaps, less frankness.

But matters did not always turn out so happily, and this giving in marriage was not free from injustice. Kings were too ready to give away fiefs and wives to barons who had served them well, and it was all done in the most natural way in the world. The land and the lady were disposed of together. This feature gives to the opening of *Charroi de Nîmes* such an astonishing flavour of antiquity.

" One of these days," said the king to Count William, who threatened him, " one of these days, shortly, one of my barons will die. I will give you the land and the widow if you will accept them ! " Later on he actually sets forth all the vacant hereditaments. " Take the possessions of the Marquis Béranger who is dying, and take his wife into the bargain ! "

Then William completely lost his temper, and struck the wretched king dumb with his reply :

" You have a very short memory, sire," said he. " Don't you recollect one day when in battle with the Saracens, that you were unhorsed and in imminent peril of death ? One of your barons perceived your danger ; he hastened to your assistance, cleared a space around you with his sword as a wild boar keeps hounds at bay ; then he dismounted, held the stirrup for you and helped you into the saddle. He was the Marquis Béranger—the same knight whose wife you are now offering to me ! He has a son who is still young. I will slay the first man who lays his hand upon the lad ! "

Thus spoke William, but all barons were not so noble-minded. As we advance towards the thirteenth century such scandals became less frequent, but the land and the lady are separated with difficulty, and have but too often the same destiny. It was the force of circumstances and of right. In any case one could not wed without the king's consent. " *A mollier la prendra se le Roi le consent.*" This verse of *Gui de Nanteuil* is extremely eloquent and precise. But, nevertheless, it cannot be said that under such conditions marriage was free or a really Christian rite.

It is quite certain that the land counted for everything, and the consent of the lady very little, but widows had to endure the most under the feudal system.   They were not included in the bargain by those sovereigns who wished a fief to be occupied at once. They had not time to weep, and had to re-marry again very quickly. Scarcely a month had elapsed after Hellissent, a lady of Ponthieu, had lost her husband when her brother Beaudouin of Flanders came to her and proposed to her another husband.   The fraternal argument deserves to be cited. '' This one is richer than the last!'' The widow made some semblance of resistance, but as soon as her brother had mentioned the name of the new suitor, Fromont, '' Sire,'' said she, '' I will do your pleasure.''   Then without waiting a moment her brother seized her hand and gave her to Fromont. The wedding was celebrated immediately, and the poet adds that there was great rejoicing at it. *" Asez i ont le jor gabé et ri.* And this bride was a widow of less than a month!

But this was by no means an isolated case.   Charlemagne in a very arbitrary manner re-married at one time all the widows of the barons who had lost their lives in Spain.   Begue de Belin died, and his brother Garin was in tears.   Nothing more natural, nothing more touching than this expression of grief; but then why did not Garin respect the grief of his sister-in-law, and not seek to console with the coarse statement that '' Another knight will make you his wife! ''   Why, as we see in another place, should a widow have been compelled to marry one of the murderers of her son?   I am of opinion that our old poets were not very exact chroniclers, and that they often exaggerated the conduct of their heroes and maligned them.   But, in any event, we are in these times a long way from the Christian view of widowhood, and from the practice of the Church, which only tolerates—for it cannot entirely approve— the celebration of second marriages.

Other evils accompanied the feudal marriage, and I would refer to the extremely rapid way in which it was solemnised.   In fact, it was hardly solemnised at all—it was hurried through at full speed. To the instances previously quoted we may add that of the departure of Aimeri's children.   The old man wanted to get his sons off his hands, and finding his best chances in marrying them off quickly he said one day, '' You are very foolish to count on my property as inheritance. You won't have it." Then addressing Garin, he continued : " You shall go to Bavaria, and you will say to Duke Nicas that you have come to marry his daughter ; tell him to give her to you with the city of Anseüne, its ports, and its shore. It is true that the land is at present in possession of the Saracens, but you have only to reconquer it."

Garin was delighted with the prospect, and he put himself at the head of a thousand knights. He did not reckon how many days the journey occupied, but it was a long time. At length they reached Bavaria. The young baron perceived the château of Naimes, rode up, and dismounting, presented himself to the old duke in the great hall. Garin saluted him, and explained his mission. " Thou art of high degree," remarked the duke, " and I will give thee my fair-faced daughter." He immediately summoned the damsel, who had fair hair. " Belle," he said, " I am going to give you a husband." " God be praised ! " replied the innocent damsel. The archbishop was summoned at once, and the young people were married. Short and sweet !

No wonder such marriages were the causes of so many great wars, and in this statement our poets are quite in accord with history. Nothing in those days was more conducive to the shedding of blood than all these competitions between wives and fiefs. The King of Moriane, Therri, happened to be mortally wounded by a bolt from a crossbow, by a *quarrel* which the Saracens launched against him. He felt that he was dying, and could only reconcile himself to his fate by the thought that he could leave his daughter well protected by a powerful husband. On Garin, the Lorrainer, he had set his mind, and he sent in search of him without delay.

" I will give you Blancheflor, with my domains and territory," he said.

Garin accepted the terms, on condition of receiving the consent of King Pepin, and the young people plighted their troth.

" Now," said King Therri, when this ceremony had been performed, " who can extract this bolt from my flesh ? " The attempt was made, but when the *quarrel* was extracted he died. Garin hastened to the emperor, who was at Langres, and requested his sanction to the marriage with Blancheflor. But some one present protested against such an union. " You forget, sire," said this personage, "that you have already promised me the first vacant fief; and to me—to me only, does Blancheflor belong." Who was the speaker ? He was Fromont of Bordeaux, who was destined to become the mortal enemy of the Lorrainers.

Garin at first contested his claim temperately and with courtesy, but soon was carried away by his anger, and exploded in wrath. He would have attacked his adversary if the emperor had not himself caught him by the cloak. Garin did not marry Blancheflor, but in this episode was laid the train of a terrible war—that war of savages, the recital of which is sufficient to fill every page of the epic poems of the Lorrains. This is the reason why so many knights were slain, so many châteaux destroyed, so many towns sacked, so many children disinherited!

" Iluec commence li grano bonoflemens." *

While the Church was persuading the baron to regard his wife as his equal before Heaven, Feudalism, so frequently in opposition to the Church, was teaching him to despise his spouse. Knights in those days had no regard for anything but fighting, and the most beautiful woman did not please them half so much as a good lance, or a fine horse. This trait is well brought out by the author of *Girbers de Metz* in a really fine page. It is related that the daughter of Anseis was seated one day at the casement as two knights were riding by. The lady was well-formed, rosy of complexion, her skin white as a lily. The two cavaliers who were passing were Garin and his cousin Girbert.

"Look, Girbert," said his cousin. "By Saint Mary, that is a lovely woman!"

Perhaps you will think that the other knight would have turned round, and even glanced at the object of this encomium. But no; he only replied: "Ah! but see what a fine beast my horse is!"

Garin, nevertheless, persisted, and said: "I have never seen such a charming girl, with such a beautiful skin, and such glorious black eyes." The other cavalier replied: "I have never seen any charger to equal mine!"

The dialogue is continued in this strain for some time; there is

* *Garin li Loherains.*

nothing forced in it; it is an exact picture of the period. In the minds of all warriors there always has been, at bottom, a sort of disdain for woman—who consoles while she subdues them. But the feeling existed, with innumerable railleries and disdainful commentaries upon feminine occupations, and lightmindedness, and dress.

"It is silly to confide in a woman!" say the poets with damnable iteration. "A woman's heart is a very flimsy article," exclaims one of those personages, who in our romances was described as gifted with wisdom and good sense in no small degree.* "Out of seven thousand women," says the author of *Amis et Amiles*, who bases his statement on the authority of Solomon, "there may be, perhaps, three or four who are really trustworthy, whom one can depend upon." The barons were particular, above all things, in interdicting women from interfering with their affairs, and never consulted their wives. "Cursed be the knight who seeks advice from his spouse, when he ought to be in the tilt-yard!" And again: "Those princes are badly inspired who seek counsel in women's apartments."

Then again we may perceive how they repulsed those who wished at any cost to interfere with what did not concern them. "Go back to your painted and decorated apartments, go out of sight, take your ease, drink, eat, work tapestry, wind silk. But bear in mind that you must not interfere in anything else. Our business is ours; it is to fight! Silence!"

If they persisted, their lords and masters got very angry, their savage nature came uppermost. They got red in the face, and trembled with rage; and sometimes, like the brutes they were, dealt their wives a sounding buffet in the face. This hint was generally sufficient, and the lady profited by the lesson, saying humbly, "Thank you" to her lord, while some even pushed their meekness to the extreme limit of adding, "when it pleases you, you may strike me again!" This was perhaps going rather too far along the road to heroism, and I am assured that most of our present-day wives would stop on the way.

* Le Vavasser Gautier in *Gaydon.* "Et cuer de fame resont mais si legier; c'on ne se puet en elles affier."

It is a fact beyond question that Feudal legislation gave a much more extensive power to the husband than our present legislation does. The woman then had to make up her mind to it. She could not, when married, go to court, or make any contract without her husband's consent. He, and this is a serious matter, had the *right* to beat her—yes, the *right!* But there were only two cases in which the legislature actually permitted this personal punishment, viz., for adultery, or for presenting her lord with an idiot child. It is true that the legislature tried to temper this infliction, and we find, in the thirteenth century, the good Beaumanoir, in his *Coutumes du Beauvaisis*, declaring that the husband should only beat his wife reasonably! "Reasonably" is delightful! But when a husband was angry, the temptation was rather strong, the descent to anger steep, and sometimes the fist was harder and quicker than he intended it to be.

II.

So much coarseness was fortunately tempered by natural feelings and rights, but above all by the Church and the canonical law. One can never obtain a true idea of the Middle Ages unless one pictures the Church standing out clear and beautiful behind each individual of this rude epoch, like the superb Muse which Ingres has depicted as standing behind Cherubini. The Church was there, indicating to the recalcitrant barons the good they ought to do, and against which they were setting themselves. She had a decided influence on marriage, and, in order to direct it the better, she took the marriage-state under her special protection, and referred all matrimonial questions, up to the close of the old regime, to ecclesiastical tribunals. This was not a privilege, but justice.

How old are you? Have you parents or relatives? Do you give your consent freely to this marriage? These were the three questions which the Church put first to intending wives. *Ætas, remotio parentelæ consensus personarum*, such were in fact, in other words, the three conditions requisite for the validity of the marriage. Nothing could be more prudent.

"A man cannot marry before he is full fifteen years old, a woman not before she is over twelve." This prudent rule, this formal decision of the Church was evaded by noble families. Feudalism had truly terrible exigencies. In order that the same baron might some day possess two fiefs instead of one, in order that in certain cases he should bear two titles, to increase his surroundings and possessions, there were no sacrifices which they would not offer, and they used most scandalously to marry together babies of five years old! The Church protested, but the laws of the Church were good enough for the lower classes and *villeins*. The barons let her protest, and went on marrying at any age they deemed expedient. One of our poets complains in round terms of these premature unions.

"Ah," he says, "everything is degenerating! Formerly the man would not marry until he had passed thirty years of age and the young lady was grown up. When the wedding-day arrived, they felt so modest and shy that they fancied everyone was looking at them. Faith and loyalty reigned supreme. But now-a-days avarice and luxury are in the ascendant, and two children of twelve years old are wedded! Take care lest they have children!" The troubadours and *jongleurs* used to recite this warning from Aiol before the members of families in which such scandals were permitted, but although they looked down for a moment, they began again next day. What they had refused to a priest they would not grant to a poet!

The question of blood relationship gave rise to many dissensions. Before the Lateran Council in 1215 it was forbidden to marry within the seventh degree of consanguinity. The Council interfered and permitted marriage up to the fourth degree. But remember that connections and spiritual parents were made equal in this respect to true relations—blood relations! If you were a god-parent, you thereby entered into relationship with your co-sponsor, which prohibited marriage in like conditions as blood degrees. But it is true that some people took advantage of this severity of the Church to indulge themselves; the rigorous prohibition opened the door to abuses. After some years of wedded life a husband, tired of his wife, would suddenly discover that she was his relative. Then, "Quick, quick, let us dissolve a marriage so sacrilegious, so abominable, so contrary to all laws, human and divine!"

They were separated, and the husband, this exemplary Christian, threw himself into the arms of another woman! So some people gained their desire for change and novelty, which is the essence of voluptuousness. This was a rehabilitation, a canonical and pious restoration of the old divorce. Bishops and priests, alas! were found ready to countenance such infamy, instead of boldly proclaiming it and crushing it out. Notwithstanding appearances the law was a good one, and can only be regarded as a deliberate attempt on the part of the Church to inspire Christian generations with profound respect for family ties, and a horror more profound still for all that could by any possible means be construed into an act of incest. To this law we owe our present healthy races, whose blood is not enfeebled and vitiated by marriages of close relations, which are now condemned alike by Science and by the Church.

If our barons were six feet high, well set up, rich in complexion, with large hands, and possessed of great muscular force, if they were as handsome as strong, if their blood coursed purely through their veins, and if their children resembled them, they owe all those benefits to the church, which they loved to disparage, and against which they rebelled with the watchword of revolt, the parrot cry of—

> " Maryée en aient li prevoire lisant
> Et li clergie qui la loi vout gardant."

We are not the less disposed to pity the poor souls who " loved each other with a tender love," which the church pitilessly refused to consecrate. The case of poor Rosamond is certainly touching, for when she was on the point of wedding Elias of Saint-Gilles, whom she loved devotedly, she found that such a marriage was out of the question, because of the "spiritual" relationship which existed between the pair. " You have held the same child at the baptismal font; marriage is impossible!" The intending bridegroom wept sore; Rosamond fainted away, and (we must unfortunately be unromantic enough to tell it) then demanded another husband!

It was to the third condition of the three—the free consent of the future spouses—that the church, and with reason, attached the greatest importance. To be sure there was nothing so elevating and sacramental as the benediction of the priest, but it is not the *form* of the rite, it is the mutual consent of both parties which constitutes it binding. They marry themselves, as it were, before the priest. To this necessary consent we now add the benediction of the church, as a useful and magnificent treasure in our hearts, but it is not indispensable. Such is the Romish doctrine which was accepted throughout the Middle Ages, and we find its application in all our epic poetry.

The Feudal law determined that the young man should ask his father's consent to his marriage,—a very useful precaution, and one calculated to prevent awkward complications. The young damsel could not marry without her parents' consent. So the Church, which dislikes any underhand proceedings, decreed that banns should be published in the service three several times, and commanded the engaged couple to make a solemn declaration before the vicar and two witnesses.

But it is the "Yes"—it is always the "Yes" of the pair which is the binding condition of their union, without which their marriage would be null and void. "Wilt thou marry this fair lady?" is the question put by the Abbé to Huidemer in our old poem of *Beuves d'Hanstonne.* "Yes!" he replied, "and I will bestow upon her all Burgundy as a dowry." "And thou, maiden, who art now weeping, wilt thou have this baron for thine husband?" "No!" she answered, "I will not wed with this traitor!" So the marriage did not take place.

Nevertheless, matters did not progress so lugubriously as a rule, and nothing could exceed the solemnity with which the parties pronounced the sacramental "*öil.*" Let us rather look at the case of Aubri of Burgundy, and Queen Guibourc *à la clere fachon.*

"Lady," said the hermit, as he blessed them, "wilt thou have this Burgundian for thy husband?" "Yes, reverend sir, for he is to me good and beautiful" (*bel et bon*). Then the holy man called Aubri by his name, and said: "Wilt thou take Guibourc to wife,

with the kingdom which pertains to her?" "Yes! by Saint
Fagon," exclaimed Aubri, "I have been wishing for this occasion
for a long time." Then they were married!

This excellent doctrine of mutual consent has been most successful in the Christian community, where it has happily counteracted
the grossness and rigour of the Feudal law. Fathers and mothers
consulted their daughters, their brothers and sisters, and evil befell
those who did not do so. "My fair sister," said the King Boniface
to Hermengart, one day, "I have bestowed you on the best knight
in the world!" But Hermengart was not a maiden to permit any
husband to be forced on her. "You must understand that I will
never have any other man than Aimeri for my husband." Then,
with some pardonable coquetry, she enumerated all the offers she
had already refused, the Doge of Venice, and Savari of Germany
amongst others.

We are better acquainted with the charming episode of King
Yon of Gascony when he announced to his sister, the beautiful
Clarissa, that she was to be married. The king entered the paved
hall, where he found his sister seated upon a silken cushion. She
had upon her knees a banner, which she was in the act of illuminating
(for she was educated), and she said in her heart that Renaud should
be her husband.

"Fair sister," said the king, "I have betrothed you."

The maiden listened, while she bowed her head over the banner,
and changed colour rapidly—a prey to harassing thoughts.

"For the love of Heaven, good brother, tell me to whom you
have apportioned me?" she cried, at last.

"You have had great luck," replied the king. "I have betrothed
you to the most valiant of all knights who ever girded sword. His
name is Renaud, son of Aymon."

The maiden heard, and was comforted. "As you please," she
replied.

However, we must not misunderstand the situation. King Yon
only pretended to dispose of his sister in marriage while he really
followed her inclinations, and the princess only yielded so compla-
cently because her heart was in accord with her brother's expressed
wishes. The verse says plainly "*Elle a dit à son cuer qu'a Renaut
ert donée.*" She was consulted and was perfectly free to choose.

The rudest barons objected to take a lady against her will. This Aimeri of whom we have spoken, who was in love with Hermingart, made a very clear statement on this subject. The first time he saw her he approached her, threw his cloak behind him and embraced her. Then they walked together and talked long of love.

"I have come an immense distance in search of you," said he. "But fear not to tell me all your thoughts: for all the gold in the ten towns I would not take you against your will."

But on the other hand I am of opinion that Aimeri was pretty sure of his ground.

The most beautiful episode relating to the freedom of the marriage contract is presented to us in a poem of the decadence in *L'Entrée d'Espagne*. Shamefully treated by Charlemagne, Roland had quitted Spain and had embarked for the East. He arrived at the very time when the King of Persia was about to marry his daughter to a neighbouring king, named Malquidant. The princess was very lovely, and very young ; the intended bride-groom was old and the maiden liked him not. But no one appealed against this forced marriage : the courtiers approved it, and in the midst of this servile silence Roland entered the council hall. He made himself acquainted with all the circumstances of the case, and then suddenly rising he exclaimed indignantly "Know ye why I have come hither? No one dares to say a word; then I will speak! Since chance has conducted me hither, I declare that I am ready to do battle in defence of this great truth, viz., that there is nothing more contrary to the laws of God and of man than marry-ing a man or woman against the will of either of them. I have spoken!" Longer speeches have often been made, but none more to the point than this.

Such were the conditions of marriage which the Church had wisely imposed. By way of clenching the subject as regards consent of both parties, the following language may be quoted—

"Thou shalt not enter the temple on the day of thy marriage until after thou hast expressed thy free consent in the presence of witnesses, in a clear and intelligible voice, publicly." It was *beneath the porch* that assent was given and the Oui pronounced. And thus the charming young couple who entered the sacred edifice were no longer only affianced, but actually married.

III.

We have yet to consider the pecuniary aspect of the ceremony, and this was no small affair, while the system of the *dot* obtained in the countries where written law was recognised; the *douaire,** which is of German origin, was the practice in the countries which observed the "law of custom." *Douaire* signifies the right assured to a wife "to enjoy after the death of her husband a portion of the goods which belonged to him when he married—on his wedding day." In other words it is "a constitution of usufruct to the benefit of the woman."

In our old songs in which the heroes are kings, counts, and dukes, the dower included magnificent presents of fiefs, lands, and towns, which even on the wedding day the husband gracefully bestowed upon his bride. In this way Aimeri of Narbonne endowed his wife Hermingart with the splendid gift he had promised her, which included the Narbondais and the Beaulandais.

So Bernier said when speaking of the daughter of Gueri le Sor whom he was about to marry, "De Ribemont shall be my wife's dower." No wonder that it was a question of dower and not of *dot*, for it was in the midst of Germanic surroundings, and one would have been thrice blind to have contested the barbaric laws of the people.

All is finished and regulated : the law has done its work. But there is something higher than the law—ideas and manners are of a more elevated character. The ideas of marriage and its customs are derived principally from the Church.

The woman, whom the law left in a condition of inferiority, and who in our old poems is represented as ill-treated, seized by the hair, beaten with the hand, and threatened with the stick or the sword, the woman after all began to be considered the equal of the man—his peer. A sacred oath united her to her husband, and she began to delight in reminding him that she was not only his peer but his companion, his "jurée." The word indicates the progress accomplished, and our heroes then called their wives nothing but " sweet friend," " sweet dame," or " fair sister." Finally this

* *Dot* is a portion ; *douaire* is a dowry.

idea obtained everywhere. Hierarchically placed below the level of the man, the woman in all other respects was his equal.

It is true that animated by a salutary terror a certain number of monastic scribes—chiefly in the twelfth century—compared woman to the Evil One, and went so far as to argue the cause of her intellectual and moral inferiority. This is an exception which we feel bound in justice to notice, but it is not the dominant idea of the periods we are studying. Woman as a wife was fenced in with honour and respect : the good wife was everywhere extolled. " A good wife," says one of our old poets, " is sufficient to enlighten a kingdom," and a monk adds "we should love, serve, and honour Woman, for we have all sprung from her."

As she lived all the winter in a château, the wife, by force of circumstances, gained an influence over her husband, which the couples of ancient Greece and Rome never attained, and never could attain. There was an intimacy which was impossible in countries wherein women are relegated to a separated part of the house. There was no gynecium in our châteaux. People lived and moved and had their being in a space a few yards square. The most delicate soon ruled the more heavy minded. The wife ruled, or rather, governed.

While our poets have rather decried the damsels, they often extol the married woman. This is somewhat curious. They have immortalised those incomparable types of the Feudal Christian spouse, Berte, Guibourc, Ameline. But in the sky of the Middle Ages there shines a star, even more radiant, which illuminated not only a kingdom but the whole of Christendom.

The Holy Virgin. One of the terms most frequently applied to the Deity by our old romancists is " God, the son of the Virgin." All women, all wives, looked up to her and made her the pattern of their lives. They all cried with Saint Bernard to her : " Thou art the way for the erring, the pardon for sinners, the life of the world." The men, less mystic, thought themselves happy if they possessed in the pommels of their swords some relic of the Holy Virgin, and they dedicated to her honour the vigil preceding their admission to knighthood. They did more honour to their wives by thinking of her—the mother of God, whom they regarded with a sacred love. In outraging a woman they outraged her prototype—

her heavenly image, and the more brutal would think twice ere they acted so.

Notwithstanding all this poetry, men's passions were not extinguished, and there were lapses from the hum-drum domesticity of marriage: but they found the Church barring their passage. It must, however, be confessed that she did not always prove the stronger, and that there were even in the ranks of the clerical army grave and regrettable defections. Up to the twelfth century we find instances of divorce, but it is not correct to class *dessoivrement* with divorce: they must not be confounded. The former is permitted by the Church: only it is a separation which does not permit either of the parties to contract another marriage.

In one of our oldest *chansons* we find an instance of this cruel but rare separation, which may be quoted here. It was the case of the unfortunate Count Amis, who was suddenly struck down with leprosy as by lightning. His spouse, Lubias, was not one of those good wives; she had a horror of the disease, and petitioned the bishop for a decree of separation which, legally, could not be given until after a regular ecclesiastical inquiry. Two knights carried the unhappy Amis into the presence of the prelate. The lady pointed at the unfortunate man trembling with fever. She was implacable; the sick one had no defender.

"Separate me from this invalid," she exclaimed. "I will give you thirty pounds of Paris *sous*, with my Arabian mule." The bishop replied proudly: "Madam, you are the very last person who should thus promulgate the malady from which your lord is suffering." But the lady retorted angrily: "Bishops are born only to do my bidding. If you will not do as you are bidden, put down your crozier!"

Nevertheless, throughout the town public opinion was greatly stirred: people grumbled about this miserable man, whose condition disgusted everyone. They pitied, not him, but his wife. "She is right," they said, "and is most unfortunately married. In order to encourage this expression of opinion, Lubias skilfully distributed *largesse* amongst the people—nobles and commons alike. So the bishop, who ought to have resisted to the death, was compelled to yield, and appeal fruitlessly to the other prelates. The unfortunate leper did not wait for the consummation of the matter, but himself applied for a judicial separation on condition that he should be supplied with scraps from his wife's table. But he was divorced, hunted from his own city; conducted to a miserable hut at the gates of the town, where no comforter, no friend but his son Girard, a lad of seven years old, ever came to visit him.

Notwithstanding the perfidy of certain ladies of the Lubias type; notwithstanding the complacent culpability of some bishops, in spite of all this, the great principle of the indissolubility of the marriage tie has prevailed in all Christian communities.

CHAPTER X.

THE ESPOUSALS OF THE KNIGHT.—BEFORE MARRIAGE.

I.

In a neighbouring castle at Ferté-Henri lives a daughter of a knight, destined to be one day a knight's wife and the mother of knights. Let us call her Aëlis.

Her life to the age of sixteen has presented no event worthy of record save the occasion of the departure of her father for the Holy Land, whence he never more returned. The girl was then six years old, and her father had had—I know not wherefore—a presentiment that he would never see his child again : a pretty little thing, and more sensible than most others of her age. The poor baron could not tear himself away, but he was obliged to go at last, and on the day he left home he turned to his old liege-lord and to him confided the child. "To you I confide my daughter Aëlis. Advise her for her good." They never saw him again.

It is not necessary to describe the succeeding years of childhood, which were monotonous. Children at that period amused themselves very much as our young people do, playing at housekeeping, or with dolls, particularly the latter, which they dressed and undressed to their hearts' content. This occupation was ever new and delightful as to-day and as it will be a thousand years hence, for human nature does not alter so much as some people think. The young girls of the twelfth century played rackets and battledore just as our schoolgirls do, but they paid great attention to the serious game of chess, and it was extremely amusing to see these fair little things playing against their grandsires, and moving the kings, castles, and pawns so deftly.

But chess was only a portion—a very small portion of the education of those children, and our Aëlis is expert in many other sciences. She does not pride herself upon them too much.

The daughters of the neighbouring knights are far from being so learned, for at that period, nothing was more variable than the amount of instruction of noble ladies or of the baser-born either. Some were perfectly ignorant, and others were almost "blue-stockings." We must not exaggerate anything, but take the medium here as elsewhere—the ordinary routine education.*

Aude dies of grief upon learning the death of Roland, her betrothed.

The very first things to be learned were prayers. The Church was very positive that the child should know the *Pater*, the *Ave*, and the *Credo*, and the Church was not to be disobeyed, nobody had yet suggested that; but the child was not limited to these devotions. She had a Psalter and knew by heart many of the beautiful chaunts which are considered the most natural expressions of

---

* Mr. Ch. Jourdain, in his *Memoir of the Education of Ladies in the Middle Ages*, says that besides the "mother tongue," instruction included the recital of fables and romances, singing, and the art of accompanying herself on the musical instruments of the period—the harp or viols—a little astronomy, falconry, chess and "dice," and sufficient knowledge of surgery to attend to a wounded knight.

humanity in all ages. She heard mass every day, and a still more unusual circumstance, understood it! At the commencement of the service she said the little prayer taught her by the priest, and at the elevation of the Host, she humbly obeyed the terms of the rubric which directed her to "put your head between your hands, and lay bare all your wants to God as your heart suggests." She never went to bed without saying that extremely popular form of prayer to the Virgin for protection.

" Be near me to counsel and support me in all my prayers and intercessions, in all my troubles and necessities, in all my thoughts, words and deeds, every day and hour of my life."

In fact, she knew her religion with which she mingled some superstitions of a very childish nature but harmless too. She confessed and communicated with true sincerity ; she was pious ; she knew and loved God, and that was by no means the least of the elements of her little knowledge and belief.

She was first sent to the nearest school with an alphabet suspended from her girdle, and little ivory tablets, so that she might even learn to write poetry, but this arrangement had to be relinquished because the school was too far off. Some little girls were already at this time brought up by nuns in certain convents, but it was considered preferable to have a governess at the château—an instructress who would remain for five or six years. At thirteen she had to pass an examination, if you please ! She could read and write in Romansh and Latin, could repeat or decipher her Psalter or her "Hours," and she used to read to her more ignorant brothers the romances which had lately been purchased from the wandering minstrels. The last one she had thus read was entitled *Gui de Bourgogne,* which they found so interesting that she had to read it three times over. One morning, a manuscript called Tales and Fables comes in, and this she will immediately commence if the chaplain makes no great objection. He would have preferred the Miracles of the Virgin himself. I will not go so far as to state that our typical damsel is acquainted with Latin, but she knows a few words of it, of which she can almost grasp the meaning. But on the other hand, she is now a ready reckoner ; and on summer nights, when the sky is studded with stars, she can indicate to her mother and her aged grandfather, some of the constellations in the heavens. The "Chemin de Saint Jacques," or "Milky Way," is very familiar to her, and on this subject she can recount many impossible and charming legends. Yet the love of the poetic has not robbed her of her practical good sense; she is something of a chemist, something of a surgeon and a doctor. The sight of a wound does not alarm her, and she does not mind staining her little hands with blood. She is acquainted with the properties of certain unguents, and can bray in a mortar certain herbs which will heal nearly all maladies. She has already in the last war given proof of her skill, and has reset no less than three broken arms. But this little ambulance-nurse is before all things lively, a laughing philosopher —and she excels in singing, preferring it to any other occupation. She sings by herself in the morning; she sings after the grand feasts which her mother gives—she sings always and everywhere.

Neither does she fear to warble the pastorals and love songs, not knowing too much of what she sings, or knowing a little too much. What says the old ditty:

> " Vierge, pucele honorée,
> Vierge munde et pure ;
> Par voz est reconfortié
> Humaine nature.
> Par voz enluminée
> Toute creature." *

Such damsels were not those of the time of Philip Augustus, but they were only apparently bold. Like the youthful damsels of Paris, in the fourteenth century, "they naturally walked with upright carriage, the head erect, the eyes cast down, not staring right or left, nor did they stop to speak with anyone in the street." At church their eyes were rivetted on their missals, or on the face of the image of the Virgin ; but all this did not prevent them from being vigorous, merry girls, nor from practising falconry, which they pursued with consummate skill. They were clever horsewomen, and nothing could have been more delightful than to have seen those pretty young girls on their palfreys, going hunting, laughing frankly ; daring and charming, strong and amiable, something like young Englishwomen of our own time, but more free in manner. This, in fact, was a course of instruction neither deep nor

* Recueil de Motets français des xiie et xiiie siècles.

complicated, but which was calculated to form fine healthy young women—our great-grandmothers, if you please, respecting whom it would be neither fair nor decent to say anything offensive.

Other occupations, more humble, and more of a homely character, filled up and did honour to the lives of these young girls. The damsel of that period could sew, spin, weave, and embroider. As a seamstress she had no equal, and she used to make the clothing and shirts for her brothers. No doubt she preferred to do silver or golden embroidery, but to excuse this preference she might have said of herself—as a heroine of one of her favourite romances did—that she could sell her work, and keep all the family with the proceeds. But she did not wish to be put to the test. What pleased her much less than embroidery was the care of the beds and the table services. Though she was no prude, and even may not have known what prudery meant, she, nevertheless, did not like to receive the guests, nor to disarm the knights who returned from the tourney. She was fond of horses, and would pat them and amuse herself watching them. She had no distaste for the stable, whither she would often go to inquire if Marchegay was properly shod, or if Passeavant had been well fed. There was plenty to do, and the days of our young damsels were decidedly well filled up.

Amongst so much work there was need of some rest. First of all the walk, the promenade to the woods and meadows, occasions which our young ladies, like everybody else in all times, turned to account by gathering flowers and making crowns and garlands of them. Our girl-type did not know how to cultivate roses, nor did she understand gardening. Her chaplet of violets sufficed for her, with some singing and dancing. She may have been rather too fond of the latter pleasure, and, with the view of tempering this taste, her mother, who had been a great dancer in her time, would relate some fearsome stories of which she would dream all night. There was one particular tale, quite authentic, which made her flesh creep, of a certain ball given by a certain count on Christmas Day. He was on his way to the Crusades, and had the idea of giving a ball in one of his castles on the journey, but, alas, the dancing was so fast and furious the floor gave way suddenly. One of the first bodies that the knight found was that of his son. At this the damsel would shiver, but continue to dance all the same,

—no doubt thinking herself and her associates too light to bring down any floor. Moreover, she could sing while she danced, and like an excellent *coryphée*, hummed the tunes which took the place of orchestral music at these *rondes*, with numerous figures in which hobby horses took part. She laughed openly, and enjoyed herself thoroughly, but the chaplain did not laugh ; he pretended that the devil was of the party.

This poor man had many other troubles to fight against, and many like tendencies to oppose, particularly, certain superstitions of pagan origin, absolutely pagan, to which he found Aëlis too much attached. Had he not already warned her against the pernicious practice of drawing lots, which was a very reprehensible practice. Her paternal uncle, on his departure for the Holy Land, had formerly given her a bad example on this point. He had opened at hazard with his eyes shut— the great Bible in the neighbouring abbey, and he said to himself that the first line on the top of the left-hand page would have for him all the significance of an oracle, and would decide his destiny. They called these searchings *Sortes Sanctorum*, or *Apostolorum*, terms explained by the searchings made in the New as well as in the Old Testament. The poor man lighted upon the following text in the book of Job:—

" Antequam dies ejus impleantur, peribit,"

consequently he felt greatly alarmed—an unjustifiable alarm—for he was already nearly sixty years of age. But other *sortes* had been invented still more ingenious, and less Christian if possible. Upon a scrap of parchment were written fifty answers, which corresponded to fifty silken threads of different colours that hung like a fringe from the parchment. The girl blindfolded would touch one of these threads and hurriedly read the response of the oracle, which was generally of a "discouraging decisiveness," *e.g.* : "A great happiness is on the point of coming to you," or " Take care, a storm to-day ; but, have patience, fine weather will supervene to-morrow." " Why do you wish to change your condition ? you have the honey, and you wish the vinegar."

Our young damsel has already begun to ridicule these childish things, for she is not silly, and she has given them up some months ago, preferring now the songs of minstrels, their tales and lays, the grand and heavy poems, and above all these the mysteries and plays. She has been a spectator—open-mouthed and fascinated—of a true liturgic "mystery," which the priests acted at last Easter time in the church of the neighbouring town; but she, worldly-minded, rather preferred the *Play of Saint Nicholas* and *Adam*, which had nothing of a liturgical character. She revelled in the open air, and preferred active life. Her horse, Regibet, was a companion, and they passed long days together in the woods. She was devoted to hawks and dogs, for she was a fearless huntress. Hawk on wrist she was as classic as any sculptured Greek, and I often wonder why our sculptors and painters still continue to represent Diana, when they have models quite as charming in these feudal damsels of fifteen, with golden hair and blue eyes, innocent, happy, impassioned, saucy, charming!

We must paint their portraits somewhat more in detail, but particularly that of our own girl-type Aëlis.

II.

She is a blonde: of that you may be certain; and perhaps in all our romances you will not meet with a single brunette. The old authors compare her long hair to fine gold, to honey-gold, to the gold of cups, pure and delicate. This is not too flattering a comparison either. Sometimes our heroine lets it hang over her shoulders, naturally; sometimes—though this mode was in her time going out of fashion — she plaits her sunny locks and intertwines them with threads of gold. The beautiful plaits thus laced with gold fell thickly over her arms and bosom. She resembles the statue of Saint Lucy which was at the door of the cathedral—or to speak more correctly the statue resembles her. Her colour is that of the blonde. She is white and rose—"*Desur le blanc est le vermeil assis;*" and poets too often employ the same imagery in describing her. We must really excuse these poor people, for similes were not so very abundant as one might imagine. Thus they would declare that her pretty colour gave her all the appearance of a rose in May in the morning when the sun was shining. "She is as white as snow in February; the lily cannot match the purity of her skin," and so on. The Homeric epithet most often employed was that which we may truly apply to her,

"I WILL NOT RISE TILL YOU HAVE FORGIVEN MY MOTHER."   [p. 307.

viz., Aëlis of the fair countenance—"*au clair visage.*" "A throat
like polished ivory"—another old simile—"sustained gracefully
regular and rounded features o'er-topped by a white forehead as
clear and refulgent as crystal." The eyes, like those of the young
man whose portrait we have already sketched, are *vair* (blue),
always bright and laughing, shielded by delicately-pencilled brows:
"no less beautiful (this is a strong statement) than those of the
mountain falcon." The mouth is small like that of a child; the
lips coloured like peach-blossoms, pink rather than red. As for
the teeth they are small, even and regular as if made by compass,
and planted in the gums. This regularity and evenness of the
teeth was regarded as a great beauty. Nor is it necessary to add
that her sweet breath has the odour of incense. I have nothing to
tell you of her nose, which is straight, and her chin, which is
dimpled. Our poets do not minutely describe the other charms of
her person, they seem to concentrate all their efforts on the
features of the face. Long white arms and hands and well-shaped
feet are all the other particulars. She is still slender, and hopes
to remain so always, for in those days they cared only for tall
figures, not greatly developed, low hips and narrow girths.

But I congratulate our old romancists on not going very deeply
into these details which, after all, only savour of excessive
realism. They prefer to compare our Aëlis to "an angel from
Heaven," and though it is rather an old comparison it is not
lacking in grace ; it will be used to the end of the world, and there
is no reason why it should not be. But the most general simile,
that they used most, was borrowed from the light. As soon as our
youthful Aëlis entered a palace, or a hall in it, immediately "her
beauty illuminated it ! '' After all this simple image is true, for
between beauty and light there is an evident and necessary co-
relationship. I only prefer to this the description in *Girart de
Roussillon*, which is the most charming of all the portraits, and
applies exactly to our Aëlis. "She possessed a beautiful and pure
body and a demeanor so dignified that the wisest of men remained
silent astounded by her beauty. The demeanor of her whose
portrait I am endeavouring to paint is to beauty what the soul
is to the body, what style is to speech." Aëlis holds herself
upright, and rather proudly : she is very good style.

Her mind is not so easy to pourtray as her body, and we are compelled to confess that documentary evidence fails us here. Nothing can be more exact than the testimony of our old poets, and they may be implicitly credited on questions of amusement, costume, architecture, furniture, the private life and customs of the epochs in which they lived and the society with which they mingled. We may even suppose them capable (and nothing can be more true) of reproducing exactly the manners and the characteristics of the knights whom they met, and of the military society in which they moved. But we cannot so readily admit that they were equally well acquainted with the manners and characteristics of the ladies young or old. Even at this later period our writers live too often away from family life and the domestic hearth, and so our literature in this respect cannot be accepted as an exact reflection of our society. They ignore all the treasures of humility, devotion, and the high virtues which are hidden in all our houses. Our dramas and our romances do not disclose these, and so we are, alas! judged by our neighbours on evidence which is not strictly truthful, and our portraits which are not really likenesses. Now we have possessed some such delineators ever since the development of our intellectual life, and woe to those who are willing to judge French Society after that depicted in *Renart*, the *Fabliaux*, and the *Roman de la Rose*. Our epic poets were only clever, some of whom were *jongleurs*, half comedians, half poets or "publishers!" I do not think any of them were capable of drawing the portrait of a young damsel correctly.

The greater part of the young damsels of our *chansons* are represented by our poets as dreadful little monsters, such as we would have had great difficulty in finding even in the tents of savages, even in the woods in which these barbarians were encamped. Bold, cynical, and only concerned to know that the eyes of the world were fixed on them, and only obedient to their instincts. Their aggressiveness surpassed all imagination, as it was contrary to all likeness or observation of human nature. I know that we cannot expect from the youthful Christians of the twelfth century, the admirable delicacy and the perfections of the contemporaries of Saint François de Sales, that they had little or no resemblance to Madame de Sevigné and Madame de Grignan; I am quite aware that to chisel out that incomparable statue, the French-Christian wife or woman, to produce this result we must have the workmanship and polish of many centuries. But I can by no means admit that after many centuries of Christianity in the Christian country of France, so many young girls have realised the type vulgarised by our rhymers. As soon as they can produce historical instances, texts worthy of credence, I will give in with all sadness and deference, for as soon as I am face to face with a scientific fact I am convinced and sacrifice my most cherished illusions on the spot. So I await these proofs based not on exceptions, but on the generality of instances of women, and till then I shall, as a critic, reject the suspected testimony of our poets and romancists. These are caricatures, not portraits.

All our poets, however, have not been guilty of presenting types so contrary to truth, and we shall quote one of these.

The liberty of speech, the liberty of manners, are the chief characteristics of her whom we wish to delineate. She is by no means ignorant. Chaste as she is, she has not that "fearing innocence," that blushing reserve which characterises so many young French girls of our day. To move about amid so many dangers it was, perhaps, necessary that she should be acquainted with them, but it must be confessed that she does not exercise sufficient prudence in avoiding them. What would you have? She is curious and resembles those ladies at Vienna, who, when their city was besieged, came without the walls to witness the combat between Oliver and Roland. The duel—the battle—is so fascinating. Aude is there with her friends, in all the sparkle of her brilliant youth, a hat studded with precious stones on her head, a short mantle over her shoulders, and the pink flush on her cheeks. You know that she was punished for her curiosity and that Roland carried her away very roughly. Then she suddenly became more " Christianlike," and cried out to the "King of Majesty " in a very outraged, maidenly manner. It was rather late, no doubt, but the cry was heard.

Our Aëlis would not, perhaps, go so far as this, but she would not be far behind. Like Aude she loves peril, and would adventure it ; like Aude she knows how to defend herself even with her hands and nails ! She not only knows how to deliver the rude *paumée* on the faces of her assaulters, but her ingenuity and powers of trickery are of very high order.   By no means a dreamer, nor a "lamartinienne," she uses readily the right word which is sometimes not the "proper" one, and she can listen without blushing to the light songs of the minstrels, even to some of their "fables" — if they are not of the most advanced type.   Nevertheless her mother one day "showed the door" to one of those gentry who wanted to recite an episode in *Aiol* or the commencement of *Ogier le Danois*.   "Enough of this nonsense," she cried, as she turned out the intruder.

But both mother and daughter had heard too much of it before, and had they not been real Christians, such literature would have affected them unwholesomely.   Romances had not made Aëlis a coquette ; she is that by nature, and was, formerly, fond of ornaments, jewels, and ornamented girdles.   But she was cured of this serious defect by two moralists, a minstrel — of the honest kind — and a poor country priest.   She had one day gone out in full dress, and was strolling near the church in company with several of her friends attired in equally grand style, when she met a minstrel who was greatly preoccupied and who seemed in search of someone.

"Whom do you seek ?" she asked.

"A Christian woman," he replied, regarding the group of ladies with a quizzical look.

The priest, looking at the lions and dragons on the splendid girdle of our damsel, said—"Those are the images of the beasts which will devour you in hell ! "

Aëlis understood and profited by the lesson, and at the time we now meet her she has little to correct, save a taste for what her companions termed gossip.   Without being one of those people who are always chattering and betraying secrets, she did not always put a guard upon her lips, she speaks very fast and very often.   But we have enumerated all her faults and the list, fortunately, is exhausted.   She is also very charming and pleasant, and one could not very well repress those rudenesses and little lapses of courtesy, the angers and tempers to which the daughters of barons in those days were only too prone.   As regards idleness, she only knows its name ; she is up at daybreak, and is not one of those who delight to sing—

> " Li tans s'en vait—Et rien n'ai pait—
> Li tans s'en vient—Et ne fais rien."

BETROTHAL OF ROLAND AND AUDE. [*p.*311.

We said just now that she was a gossip, but as a matter of fact all her words are true and sensible. This precocious wisdom is closely entwined in her with an engaging gracefulness which rather gives a zest to it. "She is wise and courteous," is the general verdict, and they may add, proud, and I do not class this pride as a fault, for there is a proper and an improper pride. This haughtiness of hers tended to make her more masculine and courageous. On one occasion, when returning home with her brother, the pair were set upon by a band of footpads; arming herself with a Danish axe, she laid about her manfully; hewed herself a passage in blood. On another occasion, when her father was taken prisoner and she could not help him personally, she soundly rated a squire—one of her friends—who somewhat nervous was standing there open-mouthed.

"Do you not see that my father, who has loved you and nourished you so tenderly, is in peril of his life? What are you waiting for, fellow? you are not like your brave relations : you will be a coward all your life! Hold your tongue. Be off!"

The young man obeyed this stern command and rushed away. He succeeded in rescuing his lord, or rather it was his brave daughter who really rescued him. There were alarms every day, and the virtue which most became young damsels at such times was not precisely gentleness. One is compelled to defend oneself, and to this explanation all the heroines of our songs seem to invite Aëlis. One day, she was asked which of those heroines she would prefer to resemble. After requesting permission to reflect for a while, she replied in a calm, measured tone :

"I would like to resemble the beautiful Aude, who died when she learned the death of her Roland; I would like to resemble her, on condition that my Roland did not die. Again, I would like to resemble Hermengart of Pavia, who chose her own husband ; to Bertha, wife of Girard de Roussillon, who was such an excellent seamstress ; but above all, a true Christian, so simple and so loyal; and finally, I would like to resemble that Aëlis in the poem of *Aliscans*, whose name I bear, and who had the joy, the ineffable joy, to save her mother's life, and the honour of her house." Then turning to her mother she added, "Fortunately, I have nothing like this to fear, and must be contented with a less heroic affection." Then she embraced her mother—and there I finish my portrait.

This Aëlis, in the poem of *Aliscans* just referred to, and whom our Aëlis wishes to resemble, was a charming and enlightened figure in the Middle Ages, and may be accepted as the true type of the feudal maiden, softening by degrees the rudenesses of the Iron Age, calming the impetuosity of her father and brothers, taking the sword from their hands; charming and civilising them. It is this influence, the true influence of the woman, which it is necessary to know and recognise before we can reach the preliminaries of the marriage state.

William had been vanquished at Aliscans, of which he had the misfortune to be the only survivor. Roncesvalles, compared with this disaster, was only an affair of outposts. The Christians were to be wiped out in favour of Mohamet.

Then, overcome with grief, the old hero, sad and defeated, mounted his distressed steed; and, without pausing to attend to his wounds, all breathless as he was, took the road from Orange to Laon. It was a long journey. At length, he came in sight of his destination. There were the towers of King Louis' palace. The count breathed again; he dismounted to relate the circumstances connected with the terrible defeat to an auditory, which would no doubt demand ample vengeance. In this king, whom he himself had placed upon the throne, whom he had delivered from all his enemies, he would unquestionably find the support of which he—and more than he, the Church—had need. This hope revived his sinking strength, and he pictured to himself full and terrible reprisals. But what does he hear? Laughter and chuckling? What are the passers-by saying in undertones? What! are they pointing the finger of scorn at *him*, William? Does he move their mirth? "What accoutrements!" said one; "look at his beard," cried another. "What a horse!" giggled a third. Then came loud laughter. Passing on, William dismounted at the palace gates, but no one came to hold his steed, or to tie him up to the tree by yonder steps. Everyone ran away and left him alone, while from a distance, they criticised this half-naked warrior. They soon recognised him, however. " 'Tis William," they said. "William, it is William," was the cry which echoed through the palace, but no one was moved by it. "Beaten! What does he want? To demand assistance! To trouble us in our peaceful repose!" Those who fled most speedily, those who mocked him most bitterly, were the very men who owed to him their lands, their fiefs, even the very furs they wore on their breasts! In vain he cried to them in a troubled voice, "I tell you the Christians have been beaten at Aliscans; I tell you Vivien is dead; all the French have been slain!" They would not listen, they fled away and left him alone. Then exhausted, in disgust, and deeply chagrined, this great captain, this hero, felt all his pride, all his strength, abandon him. He gave way, thought of his wife, who was still living, and of his nephew who had perished, and burst into tears.

Still the King remained. But the King found the visit inopportune, to say the least of it. The Queen, who was William's own sister, too readily imbibed the same feelings as her spouse towards the new-comer, and when he entered the audience hall, his clothing in rags, his poor worn mantle soiled and ragged, his chemise blackened, and his head unkempt, she would not approach him. She remained seated proudly on her throne; had neither a smile nor a word of welcome for the grand champion of Christianity, for the unfortunate vanquished knight, her own brother! This was the day of her coronation, and William had chosen an unfortunate time in which to present himself. Truly he was a killjoy, and it was necessary to get rid of him as quickly as possible.

Then terrible in his anger and gloomy scorn arose William, and throwing himself upon this ingrate he seized her by her fair hair, dragged her to the floor, drew from its sheath his great sword, and in another moment would have slain her with a single blow, when suddenly at the door in the stream of light which poured into the hall appeared a very young and beautiful damsel. She was the Queen's daughter—William's niece. Beneath the alarmed and awe-struck gaze of the spectators, who trembled with fear; in the midst of the terrified silence into which she flings a ray of hope, she advanced towards the infuriated knight and knelt at his feet. What could such a suppliant advance? William paused, taken aback, not knowing what to do. At length the child spoke, and said:

"I will not rise until you have forgiven my mother."

The knight at this felt tears rise to his eyes: he kissed his niece, let his sword fall, and stammered his apologies. What would you? It is the old story. He weeps, he pardons, he is pardoned. But the happiest of all was the youthful Aëlis, and the old poet with simple enthusiasm, which we can thoroughly appreciate, exclaims:

" God, how delighted the lovely Aëlis was ! "

But not more than we are.

Such was the influence of the young damsel: but now the hour of her marriage is striking. Alas! sometimes it struck too soon.

III.

She whose history we are relating had a sensible mother, who did not permit her daughter to marry too early. This early marriage was by no means unusual at that period, and we frequently find children married at twelve years of age. We know in what scathing terms the author of *Aiol* speaks of this scandal. But it is probable that this satirist has experienced the same fate as his compeers and made few converts.

Our Aëlis, who would not be permitted to marry before she was sixteen, was then fifteen, and had thought of marriage for some months. She had her likes and dislikes—quite rightly too. She had an ideal of her own as other young ladies have, and said nothing about it to her mother, who knew all. She more particularly disliked old men, and she took an oath never to marry a greybeard like her cousin, and like many of her friends. One morning a minstrel had sung to her a ballad, in which the heroine had expressed just the same horror of aged suitors. " Love not an old man with wrinkled face, do not permit your satin skin to be scratched ; " and also, " Accept not his love nor his companionship."

Aëlis could not contain her satisfaction at hearing such sentiments which so coincided with her own, and at the concluding line : " An old man who weds a young damsel is a fool," she cried, " Oh that is true," when a look from her mother reminded her that she had been too demonstrative and too sincere.

The husband she had in her mind was a young squire whose cheek was soft with downy beard, who was brave, and a fine swordsman. A very young man who had fought well and who loved her tenderly. It goes without saying that he is good-looking, courteous, and well-instructed. Shall I tell her day-dream, which was perhaps not very likely to come to pass? It was that a splendid tournament should be given in her honour, and she would wed the victor. But when she heard one day that the victor in a certain tournament had been an elderly knight, a coarse and brutish warrior, she came to the conclusion that perhaps it would be better to select a husband with greater care and discernment. At any rate she thanked Heaven that she was not a women to take lands or money into consideration. She had a soul above these. "There is not one knight in the whole world whom I would choose for his wealth," she said. "For I attach no importance to fortune, and he is truly rich who has his heart's desire." And again she declared, "Let him possess a good sword, and perform feats of 'derring-do' for love, I hold him quit of all the rest. If he has no land I have enough for two."

The first time that she spoke of *him*—she always would remember it—was one Sunday after mass, and her mother first pronounced his name, that dear name, in her presence. I will not go so far as to declare that the damsel had not thought of him. She was at the time employed in tapestry-work, like *Clarisse* in the *Renaus de Montauban*, and fortunately her head was bent over her task; I say "fortunately" because it is certain that she blushed. "Now," said her mother, "reflect whether this baron pleases you, for I do not wish you to marry against your inclination. Take your time."

Aëlis did not require a long time to make up her mind, because it had been already made up for several weeks, perhaps months, on this very question. So a few days afterwards the mother confided her daughter to the young baron's care with the solemn words, "I confide her to you as Jesus confided his mother to Saint John!" They went out for their first walk together on Easter Sunday, at the end of April. A sweet perfume filled the air, which was merry with the songs of birds, and all people who saw the lovers pass cried out in admiration of their beauty.

I do not know any period more delightful in man's life than the first days of betrothal, which have been well termed "primavera della vita." This is the time of endless hopes, and of facile promises which voluntarily assume the sanctity of oaths. The Church has never refused to bless these open and sincere betrothals, but it has been obliged to put young people on their guard against sudden and impulsive engagements. The simple dialogue "I will take you to be my wife,"—"and I you for my husband," was very near becoming a real peril, against which it was necessary that her legislators should afford some protection. In a moment of passion one might say "I take you" instead of saying "I will take you," and certain affianced couples would then consider themselves actually married. So, at times, betrothal degenerated into a clandestine marriage, from which the parties when they got tired of each other could seek release on the ground of illegality. Fortunately the Church was on the watch, and firmly forbade the employment of the "present" tense in the important sentence; it authorised only the "future." To speak canonically, it forbade in the form of betrothal the "*verba de præsenti*," which it reserved for the actual marriage, and only permitted the "*verba de futuro*."

She went further than this, and surrounded the betrothal with a "useful publicity," giving witnesses of the ceremony; and the day arrived when such vows were exchanged in the parish church of one of the contracting parties. Such excellent rules were not the outcome of a day, and we find very few instances of this in our old poems. But we find frequently the ceremonial of the "pledge"— the "plighting" of two young people—which must not be confused with betrothal. On the table were gravely laid relics of saints, and two men approached them—an old man and a young man. "I swear," says the former, "to give you my daughter in marriage." "And I swear to take her for my wife," says the other. In some cases only one takes the oath, but in no instance does the lady seem to have been present at this ceremony.

Amongst all the accounts of betrothals which we meet with in our old poems there is one which our young "engaged couples" preferred to all the others, and which they wished to write down at the dictation of a minstrel.

In the great hall in Charlemagne's palace in Vienna, where the

Emperor was holding his Court, suddenly there appeared a charming damsel, who remained standing modestly near the entrance. She was the beautiful Aude, the daughter of Renier de Gennes, and sister of the Oliver who, after having fought with Roland that ever-memorable duel, ended by falling into his foe's arms, and crying out " I love you more than any man living " ("*Je vous aim plus que home qui soit né* "). He even added, " I bestow on you my sister."

This was she, here was the lady of incomparable beauty. Charles perceived her, and was immediately seized with the greatest admiration for her. " I demand you for my nephew Roland," he said, rising. Without waiting a moment he sent for his nephew and bestowed upon him Aude *à per et à moillier.* He put the hand of the blushing damsel into that of his nephew who blushed too. The Archbishop was present, who affianced them before all the company (" devant tous les a fait fiancer "); and they were settling the marriage day, when suddenly there entered a messenger, covered with dust, and greatly alarmed. " The Saracens, the Saracens," he cried. " They have invaded France ! " A general murmur arose, " War ! War ! " and still Roland held the hand of Aude, recking not that he would go forth to die at Roncesvalles.

Our two lovers had no need of contract, oaths, or any ceremonial. Their hearts were true and loving, that was sufficient. But one morning the young damsel gave the youth a ring on which was engraven the names of both ; this gage he hastened to place on his finger. It was the true love pledge, the " gage *d'amour* par excellence," and sometimes a pretty exchange of rings was made. The ring, besides, was straightforward, legitimate, religious in its significance, and should not be confounded with those other love tokens which were illicit not to say immoral. No doubt they were very beautiful, such as the blonde tresses which the lady of Fayel gave to the Sire de Coucy, but we know quite well that she had no right to give away such a treasure. Nor do I admire more those pretty embroidered ribbons which some ladies sent their " friends," on which they inscribed those affectionate mottos which they had much better have left unwritten—such as, " *Je sui druerie : Ne me donnez mie : Ki nostre amur desevre : La mort puist receivre !* " Nor, again, can I countenance those ladies " sleeves," which our barons used to wear as a token of eternal love. They were true sleeves, more or less pleated, of varied size according to the fashion of the day. They were fastened to the shoulder or the arm, and being very long they hung down sometimes to the knight's feet and hampered him considerably. The ladies sent them clandestinely to their knights, who occasionally wore them as pennons, and were pleased to see them fluttering in the breeze. At tournaments they wore these sleeves and were recognized by them; they wore their "colours." Fortunately evil sometimes falls into ridicule here below, and the accumulated numbers of sleeves caused merriment amongst spectators. There is a record in *Godefroi de Bouillon* of many hundreds and thousands of knight-bacheliers each wearing one day a lady's sleeve on his arm. This almost constituted an uniform. But all these subtleties and refinements were dangerous. By their aid illicit affection was perpetuated in the Middle Ages as Platonic love, and these symbols and puerilities rendered it more dangerous and hateful. Courage was needed to condemn these practices, that only made those smile whose approval was not much held in esteem. The little gold ring of Aëlis is more poetic indeed than all the tresses of fair hair, and all the embroidered sleeves. Nothing is beautiful but the good: it only is worthy of admiration.

IV.

The betrothals of our young friends soon approached their termination. He came every day to see her at the Ferté-Henri, and she took care to don her richest dress, her ermine pelisse, and on Sundays her most "fetching" sable cloak, over which her beautiful fair hair hung down luxuriantly. One day he surprised her and found her in more simple attire, but with a little blush she resigned herself to the situation. She remarked very wisely : " You will see me like this every day of my life," and she had no wish to re-attire herself. Surprises succeeded surprises, great pleasures succeeded small ones. The young couple had dined together more than once, and wished to sit close together. O, joy ! They had both eaten from the same porringer, and it was interesting to see how he left her the choicest morsels as if unconsciously. I really believe that in those days he really fasted, but such self-denial did not last long. Our youthful knight did not die of hunger.

The days pass rapidly away. Every morning new gifts come in. The chaplain of Ferté-Henri says that this lavishness, this *sponsalitia largitas* was permitted, even recommended to lovers. Amongst other presents the young baron sends to his lady-love the "Saluts" in verse, which are very delightful, composed by himself in collaboration with a minstrel!* The verses given below let us see what a really loving heart can say, and what it might have expressed with a little less rhetorical display.

The days pass away still more rapidly. Then a morning comes when the mother of Aëlis says to her daughter, with tears in her eyes :—"In eight days more we shall be parted!" Eight days which are eight years for the damsel, and eight minutes for her mother.

Those invited from a distance are already on the way; the ladies' dresses are nearly completed; the minstrels announce their arrival; the hall is hung with tapestry; singing, weeping, and prayer succeed each other. . . . .

It is Saturday, the marriage day—the auspicious morning has arrived!

---

* Here is a specimen which requires no rendering into English :—
> "Flor di lis, rose espanie
> Taillie pour esgarder,
> Je vous aim sans tricherie :
> Si n'en puis mon cuer oster."

Here is another :—
> "C'est la rosete, c'est la flor,
> La violete de douçor.
> Sa grant biauté, sa grant valor,
> M'i fet penser et nuit et jor,
> Et tint mon fin cuer en baudor.
> Simplete et coie,
> Blanchete et bloie,
> Dieus vous doinst joie
> Et grant honor."

CHAPTER XI.

THE ESPOUSALS OF THE KNIGHT.—A TWELFTH CENTURY MARRIAGE.

I.

THERE is not a cloud in the sky; the sun rises in a clear blue atmosphere. The bells of the churches are announcing the mass, and seem to ring more joyfully than usual. All is peaceful and happy, no one except at Ferté-Henri seems disturbed. Agitated or, at least, extremely busy, they are there. The bride is being dressed! The damsel is surrounded by ladies and servants, all occupied in decking her for the ceremony. But at that time there was no special costume for a wedding : the bride was merely dressed in all her best. We may reasonably conclude that the costume was perfectly new, but that is all. There was nothing to distinguish this handsome toilette from that worn by Aëlis at Eastertide, or even on the Sunday last past. Our ancestors had not yet invented the charming "colour" white as a costume for brides.

The damsel was a long time plaiting her luxuriant golden hair into two long plaits. Her maid Mahant handed her pretty ribbons and lace of gold, which she dexterously entwined with her fair locks. They called this *crins galonez*. Nearly all ladies supplemented their natural adornment with false hair, but Aëlis was rich enough to do without this addition. In about half-an-hour her plaits are finished, and hang down her back in shining heavy tails. She looks in the glass to see the effect, and is satisfied.

She has no need to whiten her complexion, nor to paint her face. The statues of saints are thus adorned, but no Christian woman should paint or powder her face. A poet of the twelfth century, however, remarks that certain women of his time were powdered with saffron. But Aëlis had no such adornments. She is just as she emerged from her bath; her beauty is entirely and simply owing to nature.

To any who complain of the duration of her toilette she quietly replies that this is a special occasion and not as other days. We must not imagine for a moment that young people of that period were accustomed to dress themselves so grandly every day in costumes which the statues at Chartres reproduce so correctly.

The Bridal Pair coming from Church.

An archæologist of our day justly observes that once bedizoned in this sumptuous manner, a poor woman was compelled to stand stiffly upright all day, like a statue, and she could hardly move her fingers. This is all very well, but you may depend that the ladies of the twelfth century were no fools, and only reserved such stiffness for *fête* days, while on all other occasions their dresses were easy and untrammelling. For a wedding it was different. If a lady could not on that occasion adorn herself to the top of her bent, when could she do so?

So the damsel's apartment—that chamber in which she had slept for the last time, is shining with silk and satin. All her luxurious dresses and habiliments are hung around: all the most beautiful materials then known are fully represented.

There are the *pailes*, by which are understood the tissue of embossed silk, gold and silver brocades, cloths woven with silk and gold. Ladies who wore such expensive dresses were generally very rich: châtelaines at least, almost of the rank of countess. There were also those heavy robes of thick silk, "six thread," white, green or red "samite." This was less costly than the *paile*, but more beautiful than and worth double the *cendal*. The sheath of her husband's sword is covered with samite, so is her only manuscript— a life of St. Thomas the Martyr, in verse and very beautiful—which she will carry with her to her new home.

Again we find the *cendals* or *cendés*,* which are of reasonable price. Some are striped, some plain; those which have the best effect are scarlet, and shine out amidst the other stuffs, extinguishing their hues. With the *cendal* of this kind Aëlis has fashioned with her own hands the pennon which floats from her husband's lance.

Besides these are *ciclatons* which resemble samite; *osterins* or purple-tinted silks, *diaspres* or embroidered silks from Persia, *pourpres*, which are "shot" silks; and stuffs from Mossoul, gold-embroidered, of fabulous lightness, something like our China crêpe, and with which very pretty *bliauts*, (or body-garments) for ladies, were made. The portion of the chamber occupied by these wares looks like an Eastern bazaar, and radiates bands of colour.

However, we must not overlook the more simple materials of the every-day toilette, for she will not dress in *paile*, *diaspre* and muslins every day. So we find woollen stuffs made in the country: in Flanders, Picardy, Champagne, Languedoc: good stout materials, as honest as the men who made them. For winter wear, thicker cloths, blue, brown, green, madder-colour; for summer thinner stuffs, serges, tarletans, druggets. These do not please the eye to the same extent, but they are durable.

Then the linen, the strong and beautiful linen with which the

---

* The existence of velvet is not certain before the fourteenth century.

linings of the pelissons, the chemises, and the under-garments are made. In the face of so many grand treasures, they have the appearance of concealing themselves—like virtue.

With the furs we come back to luxury again. The nobles yielded to the vileins and country people the skins of lamb, hare, fox and so on, and only used four furs for themselves—the vair, the grey, the sable, and the ermine. The grey is the back-fur of the northern squirrel : the vair is the belly covering of the same animal, which is chequered with the grey. The ermine is spotted, and great care was taken to fasten symmetrically on the beautiful white fur the little black tails. There is no need to speak of the marten, whose fur composes the richest sable mantles of earls and kings ; but we remark with surprise that the beautiful white furs are dyed, chiefly red. They were fond of red in those days.

If we pass all these materials again in review we pause to admire the designs of the silks. They are geometrical, as if done with the compass, or of the rose-window pattern : some have animals embroidered in gold on a bright ground, lions and birds *affrontés*, some with quaint inscriptions which a certain priest pretends are in Arabian character, but is not sure. These designs are relieved by fringes, *passementeries* of gold, by orfrays which are themselves ornamented with oriental designs. These trimmings are to be seen everywhere except on the woollen stuffs.

But it is time for Aëlis to make her selection from all these riches. Time flies and only an hour remains before she must proceed to church. She must hurry. The toilette is begun—a great business.

II.

The chemise is of fine linen, white as " the lily of the field," with a light tinge of yellow which is not disagreeable. Its only luxury consists in its pleats or folds, which have a charming, simple effect. Aëlis would not have any embroidery at the neck or cuffs : she remembered the words of a preacher the year before, who denounced the luxury of female dress, exclaiming in a moment of eloquent indignation, " Some chemises cost more than a priest's surplice ! "

Aëlis had determined that she would never lay herself open to any such accusation, even on her wedding-day, and she kept her word. Over her chemise, which falls to her ankles, she hastens to put on the kind of dress which at that time formed the principal element of ladies' costume as it did of manly habiliments—the ermine pelisse, to wit the *pelisson hermin*. A very fine ermine fur had been placed by the tailor within two layers of the material in such a manner as to show only at the borders, sleeves, and collar of the garment. One of the two materials is cloth, and it is next the chemise, invisible. The outer one, which is visible, is of fine silk, a *cendal* of price. Aëlis had for a long time hesitated as to what colour she would wear, but at length she decided upon a deep red as the tint of her *cendal*. A narrow gold border ornamented the ends of the sleeves, which are tight round the wrists, and also the hem of the garment, which falls to the ankles. A pretty trimming ornaments the edge and throat of the "pelisse." This vestment, which is straight and adjusted to the figure, has not, it must be confessed, a light or graceful effect. It does not fine down, but rather exaggerates the form ; and I imagine, for I have no proofs for such temerity of opinion, that in the *pelisson hermin* the fur trimming on the corsage, and even that on the skirt, should have been dispensed with, so as to leave the fur only on the collar and sleeves. In other words, the *pelisson* would become a dress. Besides, Aëlis had to wear her tunic, or *bliaut*, over it, an article of apparel purposely invented to correct the imperfections of the *pelisson*, and hiding it almost entirely. Here luxury ran riot, and Aëlis did not check it. Everything was admissible in this garment, which was the Sunday vestment, the dress for the *fête*, worn, perhaps, ten or twenty times a year. This beautiful tunic, very light, was of green silk, embroidered with gold, falling almost as low as the underskirt. The sleeves, very wide and very long, almost trailed on the ground, and permitted to be seen the tight sleeves of the *pelisson* with their violet and gold trimmings. The upper part of the *bliaut* is cut away a little at the neck, square, so that the throat of the furred robe is visible. The skirt, which fastens at the back, is in pleats. Between the corsage and the skirt the seamstress has inserted a piece of light and elastic stuff, not less fitting than the corsage itself, which very cleverly encloses the hips and abdomen. This middle-piece was laced up the back like the corsage, of which it formed the continuation, and it was laced as tightly as possible, like the cuirasses of the present day. The upper portion, round the neck and shoulders, is embellished with gold lace, and the immense sleeves, also laced, are slashed and curved.

But what chiefly appeals to the eyes is the girdle—the splendid waist-belt, which is thrown negligently over the hips, and falls in front as far as the hem of the *bliaut*. The goldsmith has been employed upon it not less than two months in the chasing, not to mention the fixing of the gems—the topazes, agates, carbuncles, and sardonyx stones. Note that each of these has a special virtue, one as a preservative from fever, another as a light at night, rendering other light needless. Aëlis is very pleased to exhibit it, and regrets to be obliged to wear over it her cloak, which was then the distinguishing mark of a nobly-born lady. But no matter, she will manage to display, somehow or other, her *bliaut*, girdle, and cloak. The last-mentioned she fastens gracefully on her shoulder with an agate and jewelled clasp, and carries it even more grace-fully over her left arm. The opening of the cloak is on the left side, and the girdle, with nearly half of the charming body-garment (*bliaut*), is displayed. The cloak itself is rich, and falls in artistic folds to the knee. It is of *paile*, purple of hue, and embroidered around the borders. Aëlis is quite content with the manner in which it hangs, and we need no other eulogy.

All this time Aëlis has been wearing bedroom slippers, but, pretty as they are, these *eschapins* would clash with her sumptuous garb, and so her feet are now encased in small narrow shoes with pointed toes of Cordova leather, embroidered with gold. Jewels, absolute jewels in their way. On her head she adjusts a small circular veil—it is so difficult to fix it properly, and upon this thin and delicate material she consents that a diadem of gold, studded with emeralds, may be placed. To this crown the damsel prefers the diadems and chaplets of flowers which she used to wear at Whitsuntide ; they cost so little, too ; they were very pretty, and smelt so sweetly. The coronet is most beautiful, but the chaplet was more joyous. But it is only waste of time to think more about it. All is ready : the bridal toilette is finished.

Aëlis is not a coquette, but she understands the art of dressing herself, and makes twenty observations to each of her servants during the toilette as to the fit and set of her dress. She also discovers a hair out of place in her eyebrow, and requests that it may be put straight. Taking it altogether, she is by no means dissatisfied with her little self, and smiles at her reflection in the mirror in a very contented fashion.

"Well, my dear child, you are grandly dressed out!" exclaims her grandmother, who just then enters the room. "If you were always so bedizened you could never stir a finger, and we would have you seated in a chair like a statue for ever, watching other people at work."

"Do not fear, good mother. Rest easy: I confess I do feel a little stiff in this dress, and can scarcely bend myself; but you may rest assured that I shall not wear it except on great occasions, and when the Church ordains holidays. When it is worn out I will give it to some poor monastery, to make into chasubles and copes. This is my grand dress, but I have others for every-day wear: a *bliaut* in one piece, shorter than the robe, and fastened with a simple cord; a whimple on my head, and shoes not even embroidered. What do you say to that!"

"I say that you are perfection, notwithstanding your diadem, which dazzles my old eyes; and I want to kiss you. Come! let us go."

III.

The toilet of a man did not occupy such a long time as that of a young lady, even although he was not conceited. There is no doubt that in the twelfth century there were numerous points of resemblance between the attire of men and women. The chemise, the pelisson, the cloak, and the chaplet present a striking affinity. Nevertheless our youthful knight took only an hour to dress, while the damsel, assisted by her mother and three servants was hardly attired in four hours. It was the fault of those blond tresses, it was the fault of the *bliaut*, whose complicated economy I have been endeavouring to describe, the fault of the servants, who were so slow, and of the mother, who was not satisfied with her child's appearance. But her husband will excuse Aëlis that day. He is quite ready and is scarce less gorgeous than she. His limbs are cased in brown silk shoes which have come from Bruges. He has not assumed the effeminacy of the silken chemise, he prefers a white linen covering—a fine *cainsil,* which is at the same time light and strong. His ermine *pelisson* is much the same as that worn by Aëlis every day, the fur being the lining between two materials, the outer one of silk—a beautiful red *paile* embroidered with gold with ermine on the upper part, round the collar, and "ospreys" at the neck and sleeves. The *bliaut* is something like the garment his spouse will wear on the morrow, a tunic shorter than the *pelisson* of silk, and deep blue in colour. The sleeves are tight to the wrist and wide at the arm-holes—ospreys, much larger than those on the *pelisson,* decorate not only the sleeves but the hem of the garment and the shoulder-piece, which opens vertically. The *bliaut* is slashed (or *gironné*) beneath the lace. The cloak, which is semicircular, is of double furs and indicates great luxury; one is almost suffocated in it with its load of vair and grey ermine and sable. The silk of this mantle is of the same quality as that of the pelisson; same grain and colour. On the front and at the bottom of the cloak are four square pieces, very rich, which are embroidered with gold and studded with precious stones; these are the *tasseaux.* A clasp elegantly fastens this splendid covering at the right shoulder. The baron knows how to carry his cloak and that is an art in itself. He knows how to dispose the folds to the best advantage and how to throw it behind him. Being a man of sense he refuses to wear the ordinary shoes of the day, which are ridiculous. His shoes are pointed but reasonably, none of those great turned up things like curving horns, which a depraved taste has imposed on the knights of the period in certain provinces; thin soles and no heels. A chaplet adorns the curly head—a chaplet which he has endeavoured to make like that worn by Aëlis that is encrusted with similar stones. So he is apparelled and ready for the wedding.

Then he presents himself to his lady-love in all his splendour, but more curious to inspect her costume than to exhibit his own, he approaches her and asks with a smile—" Are you pleased with me as I am ? " She replies only with one word—" Come ! "

IV.

The church is at no great distance and the bells are perfectly audible, nevertheless our young couple will require a quarter of an hour to reach the edifice which they have decided to do on horseback as is customary.   No doubt, like many others who have aspired to be grandees, they could have been wed in the castle chapel, for they have a cousin—a bishop—who would gladly have performed the rite for them.   But they very wisely prefer to do as their parents before them did.   The procession is arranged at the steps of the château.

In front is a group of minstrels—a perfect orchestra of viols, flutes, harps and violins of shapes as curious as the musicians are strange.   The church ordains that the young people shall be married fasting, but the minstrels are under no such restrictions and are in good humour accordingly.

Aëlis has for a long time reflected on the question " Shall I go to church on a palfrey or on a mule ? "   She has decided in favour of the mule, which is the mount usually adopted by the ladies of the time.   Besides it is a handsome mule, black, shining, sure-footed, broad-backed, his ears always in movement.   But his caparison was very striking.

The *sambue*, or lady's saddle, was ornamented with gold and ivory, the saddle-cloth was of scarlet samite, on the forehead blazed a carbuncle, which served for a torch by night and which was said to cure all maladies—but Aëlis's incredulous little pout when she was told so, indicated her scepticism.   The breast-piece was hung with silver bells, thirty in number, and their tinkling was charming to the ears, and the *jongleurs* were not best pleased.

Aëlis's godfather lifts her into the saddle—to-morrow her husband will perform that act—where she sits with pendant limbs, very gracefully, patting her mule, who shakes his silver bells and seems proud of the music.   Grandfather, who is rather serious, places himself at her right hand, for he is acting in the place of her dead father—to conduct her to the church. But the bridegroom is not far off; he is firmly seated on his palfrey, on an enamelled saddle, proud and smiling.   Near him is the mother of Aëlis and *her* mother, the former rather sad, the latter radiant, each on a fine mule. Then, in pairs and threes, come the relatives and friends, magnificently clad in costumes relatively similar to those already described, wearing golden circlets. In a kind of car, painted with flower designs, are seated many of the older guests who can recall their own youthful days, and laugh somewhat dolefully at the recollection.

On each side of the road is a long line of spectators, vassals, and shop-keepers from the nearest town, who seem rather envious at beholding so much magnificence, and regarding in a melancholy manner the habiliments of their masters, become thoughtful. But the moment of departure has arrived. The muscians strike up a gladsome fanfare; the silver bells of the mules' trappings mingle with the strains, and the defile commences, winding amid the trees alive with startled birds. Just as the cortége is obliged to pause at the great gates a clear voice bursts forth in the song of love which the bride most likes. This melody is replied to by another minstrel, who also sings a hymn or *motet*, of which the bridegroom is the author, which compels a smile and an affectionate word from the object of his muse.

The church is at the summit of a hill, and the acclivity compels our friends to dismount from their horses and mules, and here again the grandfather of Aëlis assists her to alight " *en sa brace la prent,*" and she comes lightly down upon the straw which covers the road. A seductive perfume surrounds them; the fifteen steps which ascend to the church door have been strewn with roses and gladioli. The procession walks on flowers. The neighbouring houses are decorated with flags and draped with coloured stuffs; the musicians continue to play and conversation proceeds; rich and merry laughter is heard on all sides. Suddenly the hubbub ceases; the priest has appeared.

The actual marriage takes place beneath the porch, the ceremonial within being only complementary and ornamental. Those at the portal of the ancient edifice, beneath the shadow of the statues of the Saviour and the Holy Saints, the affianced man and maiden give their free and solemn consent to the union, and the sacrament consists in the " yes " they respectively pronounce. Aëlis laughs not now; she has turned pale. The knight is serious, the priest is calm, and proceeds to recite slowly—very slowly—the conditions which the wisdom of the Church exacts from the married. "There are no canonical obstacles? You are of the proper age; you are not relatives; you are both Christians. Your parents consent; the publications have been made, and the banns proclaimed three times in the parish church during service. No one opposes your union. You have witnesses; 'some hundreds' you say? two persons would have sufficed. We are at a period of the ecclesiastical year when the Church permits the celebration of weddings. All conditions are complied with, and it only remains for me to demand from you solemnly your consent to the marriage. This is the moment for you to reflect whether you have any great duties to fulfil, and to think of Him who blessed all marriages in the world by His presence at the marriage in Cana of Galilee. . . . Let us pray!"

In a powerful voice which was audible far and near, the priest demands from the pair their sacramental consent, and then are heard, less distinctly, two responses:—

"Yes; I, Henry, take thee to wife."

"Yes; I, Aëlis, take thee for my husband."

The second reply is even more tremulous than the former, but in no way devoid of firmness and decision. At this moment the affianced pair clasp each the right hand in each other's, and gaze at each other blushing. All eyes are centered upon them. They are married.

We need not dwell long on these heights; stern prosaic facts compel us to descend quickly. At that period there were not the fine distinctions between the civil and religious marriage that now exist. The Church and the Church alone was concerned, and it concerned itself with the temporal interests of the newly wedded pair. If they lived in the "country of the dowry" in districts where the dowry was customary, the priest gave them a lecture on the solemnity of their contract. If the *dot* or marriage portion was usual, then he recited in a loud and intelligible voice the various elements of the portion.

But here again the Christian spirit comes forth. To sanctify these endowments, the newly-married couple and their witnesses, are exhorted to distribute moneys to the poor spectators. The sight of this queenly lady throwing newly-coined money amongst her retainers was a sight to be remembered. It had been told to Aëlis, that one day, when a miserly usurer had been married, a stone statue above the porch had fallen upon him and killed him on the spot! She had no fear of such a fate, because she had no such miserly thoughts, and her purse was already emptied.

The next rite is the surrender, the "dation," of the bride by her father and mother. The giving away to the husband. But alas, on this occasion, the mother is alone, and she, recalling her husband, is choked with sobs. All the spectators are bathed in tears. In fact these French people of the thirteenth century were more sensitive than we can quite credit, and on almost every occasion the water of the heart mounted to the eyes. Aëlis very pale, her eyes fixed on the ground, did not attempt to stay her tears. But at length her mother, by an heroic effort, controlled her weeping, and advanced to the young baron to present to him her daughter. The ungloved hands of the bride and groom clasped each other "For ever on the faith of God and in my own, in sickness or in health, I promise to shelter her." The doubtful words, in sickness or in health, appear rather out of tune with the poetic surroundings: nevertheless, they contain a deeper meaning than the rest, and evidence a better knowledge of human nature. They indicate clearly the ephemeral character of beauty, youth, and strength: they are as good as a sermon.

When the priest came out of the church he carried between his hands a book and resting on it a small circlet of silver which glittered in the sunshine. He must consecrate this ring which symbolised all the engagements which the married pair had entered into. In certain dioceses holy water is sprinkled on it, and in others the priest contents himself with a prayer—as follows:

"May the Creator and Preserver of all men, may the Giver of Grace and eternal Life cause his blessing to descend on this ring." Then the husband took the ring and put it successively, with tender respect, upon three fingers of the bride's right hand, saying each time, "In the name of the Father, of the Son, and of the Holy Ghost." After this he placed it on one of the fingers of Aëlis's left hand, where it will remain until death, a pledge of faithfulness and fidelity. This rite was so "telling" that it appealed power-

fully to concrete minds of the men of the twelfth century who
spoke ordinarily of espousing a "*dame d'anel.*"

It made no difference whether the material of which the ring
was composed was more or less rich, plain or studded with precious
stones or graven with the names of the Creator and the Saints, possessing virtues more or less powerful ; a simple silver circlet was as
efficacious as a regal ring. "With this ring I thee espouse, with
my body I thee honour, with my goods I thee endow." That is all
that the husband said when placing the ring on his wife's finger.
That was the contract.

In the district inhabited by our young friends, the people preserved a lively souvenir of the old law of the Salian Franks which
ordained that the future husband should offer symbolically the *sou*
and the *denier* to the family of his future wife. It was a purchase
—a regular buying—though in the twelfth century it is certain
that there was no such purchase per *solidum et denarium;* but
when the husband said the words, "With my goods I thee endow,"
he placed diffidently and delicately three small pieces of money—
three new *deniers**—in it. Not being able to clasp in his arms his
lands and other possessions he performed the endowments
symbolically.

However, all this time we are standing in the porch. It now only
remains to pay the newly married pair a mark of respect of which
the new sacrament renders them worthy in the eyes of the Church.
It incenses them. Then only are the doors of the church thrown
wide open to receive them. They perceive suddenly the perspective
of the church—the painted windows, the altar. They advance
greatly moved and nervous, amid their friends and the spectators.
But when they reach the centre of the nave they prostrate themselves and remain in this position a considerable time beneath the
extended and benignant hand of the priest. "The God of Abraham,
the God of Isaac, and the God of Jacob cause to spring up in the
souls of these young people the seeds of life eternal." Then
addressing himself to the young couple, still prostrate, he says,
"May God bless you, and Himself teach you to worship one
another in your bodies and in your souls." Then the pair rise and

---

* About $\frac{1}{12}$ of a sou ; two metal discs united by a bar "Deniers pour épouser," on
one side ; and "tournois denier" on the other.

are conducted to the chancel (or choir), where mass is said—the mass of the Trinity—the bride standing close to her husband on his right hand.*

At the offertory, the newly-married couple make their offering which is rich. After the Sanctus they again kneel down to receive the great and solemn Benediction of the priest. Then four young barons extend a *paile* of purple hue above the heads of the bride and bridegroom. This is unique and pretty, and it is hardly necessary to say, that with the old Ritualists this veil expressed the extreme care and delicacy with which the married pair wished to conceal the love which Heaven had blessed. I would rather it had assumed the form of the antique veil, and that it had actually enveloped the young couple.

However, the sublime blessing descends on the pair, and it is almost textually the same which the Roman Church has inserted in the Œcumenical Books. " May the woman be as worthy as Rachel, and as wise as Rebecca, as faithful as Sarah." *Sit verecundia gravis, pudore venerabilis doctrinis cœlestibus erudita.* If these brilliant examples ornament the ritual of some antique paganism, we cannot have sufficient admiration for such elevated ideas, nor enthusiasm enough for such a grand form.

The mass is over : the *Agnus Dei* is chaunted. A pretty scene concludes the striking series which our grandees have ignored and which I would wish them to learn. The bridegroom advances to the altar and receives from the priest the kiss of peace. To whom will he transmit it ?—it is needless to inquire—To his young wife whom he embraces chastely in the middle of the sanctuary at the foot of the cross !

Leaving the church, they find a compact and noisy crowd, the musicians as before heading the procession. For nearly two hours this assemblage of relatives and friends has been gathered together, grave and silent. Some relief is necessary. The ladies begin to chatter.

At the base of the hill the horses and mules are waiting. Ladies and knights mount while they talk. Then the cavalcade starts back to the château.

---

* Introductis illis in chorum ecclesiæ ad dexteram partem, et, statuta muliere ad dexteram viri, incipiat missa de Sancta Trinitate.

Many of our old poets have left vivid descriptions of this return from the church. They have painted in glowing terms the appearance of the road carpetted with green, the incense and the perfumes which filled the air ; the groups of minstrels looking on or singing in the procession of the married pair, and, further away, the flowery meads and country all in festal array.

At a cross road there is quite a commotion. Quite a troop of friends on horseback has come to meet and congratulate the bride and bridegroom. They embrace each other cheerfully, and then the two cavalcades unite and proceed leisurely in the direction of the castle, where everything is ready to receive them. It is in the great hall, the paved *salle,* that the grand reception is held, and for many days previous preparations have been made there with this view. It has been whitewashed and painted anew, the walls have been clothed in tapestry, and the river banks and gardens have been scoured to supply wild flowers and roses. It is superb even when empty and naked, but it has never appeared so resplendent as now, with all these mural and floral decorations. A solemn entry is necessary here. Wait a moment. . . . .

The cortége has entered the courtyard, the minstrels pass aside, and there the bride and bridegroom dismount. Two by two their relatives and friends advance and mount the staircase. A beautiful gleam of sunshine at this moment lights up all their costumes, the silk and the gold, the fair hair of the multitude of ladies and knights. It is a magnificent spectacle.

They do not dine in the hall, but in the neighbouring meadow in tents. It was then the correct thing to invite grand personages to weddings, a custom that still obtains, and it was a point of honour to invite as many as possible. The more the prouder the host. This custom even gave rise to rivalries, competitions, and jealousy. " I have had so many earls at my wedding party ! " " I had quite as many ! " The mistake was that, in imitation of royalty, these personages considered it necessary to make presents to the guests ; cloaks, garments, &c. Each of these gifts was accompanied with a kind word and a smile, and it was seldom that the knight found a moment to seek the room where his brother was awaiting him. On this occasion they had to negotiate an exchange of fiefs and submit the arrangement to Aëlis. The exchange is made without any difficulty or question. In order to confirm this act Aëlis kisses her brother-in-law, and her husband too.

Then the clear-toned clarions announce dinner. The tables are loaded with gold plate. The most beautiful of the tents, which is covered with blue silk, is set apart for the newly-wedded pair, their near relations, and the most important guests. Preceded by the equerries, the immense concourse hurries towards the tents in some little disorder. Everyone is anxious to learn where his or her place is; so they push, and cry out, and laugh as they go. There is little quiet, save in the upper tent, where the bride is seated beside her husband. Around the guests the seneschals pass and repass, carrying roasted peacocks on golden dishes. Behind the wedded pair, two knights—barons—stand gravely, deeming themselves honoured in waiting upon them. The bride-groom says to them, "I am not able to bestow upon you two *chateaux*, as a hero of romance would, for the trouble you are taking, seeing I have only two myself, but I would pray you to take wine with my wife and me." The baron addressed bows, accepts the golden jug, and fills the cups presented to him. The lady with the fair countenance touches one with her lips as her husband drinks deeply. They scarcely eat anything.

I am not disposed to detail the hundreds of dishes which are served. They will be remembered long in the district, but the memory of the wedding will remain particularly with those who partook of the festivities. The lower class of spectators will not say, "the wedded pair were charming," but "what a number of dishes they had at dinner!" The minstrels, grouped in a corner, are somewhat more dignified and more deserving of attention. During the repast, which was long, they contented themselves by playing their most beautiful pieces. Some—but these were of the lower order juggled and "walked on their heads." It was not until the close of the repast that they sang and recited. Let me relate what they chaunted.

The first performers sought to be realistic, and recounted the love of Oriabel for Jourdain de Blaives, her husband. Jourdain had to go away, and she did not wish to be separated from him.

"Let me go with you," she cried. "I will be your housekeeper and economical. I will be your squire; yes, I will saddle your horses, and shoe them myself. When you mount I will hold your stirrup, when you return, I will take off your spurs, and assist you to disrobe! Let me go with you! I will lie beneath your stair-case, glad to see you go in and out. I will be your servant, and that will console me, for I love you dearly!" Jourdain let himself be persuaded, and they went forth together.

The second *jongleur* is more military. He relates the history of that wonderful army corps of women who fought so valiantly under the walls of Antioch and Jerusalem against the Infidels. "See them," said he, "going out to fill their wide sleeves with stones, and to bend over the wounded, while their husbands followed them with eyes suffused with tears. The poor wounded men turned to them, crying for water, and the women comforted them in body and soul. Their shoes were worn out, their feet were bleeding, their hearts were heavy; but they never despaired, and deserved equally with their husbands the name of Crusaders and knights.

The third *jongleur* told of Berte who espoused Girard de Rousillon as follows: "The more Girard saw of her the more he loved her. He had never seen anyone who equalled her wisdom and good sense." The singer afterwards showed how the hero fell upon evil days, and how his wife had to become a seamstress, and he himself a charcoal burner. Beneath the dust and grime she remained still beautiful, and young men would stop to look at her, and agreed that if it were not for her position as the wife of a charcoal burner, no lady would be more *gentille*. She spent two and twenty years in this retirement, pure, good, resigned—a Christian. At the end of this period, Girard could no longer remain in seclusion, and went one day to see a tournament. Girard, like everybody else, went to the jousts assisted by his wife whom he held so dear. The lady beheld the vassals jousting, and the sight of the games brought to her recollection the time when her husband used to ride a joust. She felt so affected at last, that the tears ran down her cheeks and fell upon Girard's beard. The count stood up, and said, "Lady, I perceive that you regret you are not in France. Leave me, and go." "No," she replied. "Please God, I will never quit your side alive. I would rather pass through a fiery furnace than leave you." At this avowal the count embraced her on the spot.

GIRARD DE ROUSILLON AND HIS WIFE IN RETIREMENT.

If truth must be told, beautiful as these songs were, they were too lugubrious for a wedding-day. The audience had by this time become grave. The ladies were weeping, some for Oriabel, some for Berte. The men began to speak of war, *àpropos* of Girard, and became somewhat too demonstrative. It therefore became necessary to throw some festivity into this unseasonable gravity. So a reciter told the amusing story of Renart, and how he put Ysengrin into a well. A singer trolled out a lively ditty. Then love-songs succeeded, of which the greater part were of a warm character. Our ancestors did not object to calling a spade a spade, and the ditties would be "taboo" nowadays. But, nevertheless, they did not wish their wives to resemble the wenches which these impure pastorals pictured. These follies exasperate us, and, I have no doubt, they irritated Aëlis also.

At other tables in other tents there is more noise. Joking of a very coarse kind here assumed all the strength which it lost in the presence of Aëlis. It raged rampant, and triumphed over all else. Then, again, the guests drank heavily, and the wine gets into their heads. These knights are soldiers, who are apt to become riotous when in their cups. A terrible quarrel arose in one of the tents. Two barons were at loggerheads. One of them snatched from the other the golden cup which he wished to present to the bride; the other repossessed himself of it, and, furiously tipsy, dealt his opponent a terrible blow on the forehead. The skin was cut, the bone damaged, and blood flowed in streams. Each combatant had friends, who defended their man, and they were divided into two parties, who quickly encountered each other, and many a knight rolled on the ground. Fortunately the young couple were ignorant of all this. The dinner came to an end, and the wedded pair strolled, side by side, through the meadows. This repast had not lasted less than three hours.

Then the convives divided into two groups, squires and bachelors on one side, the ladies on the other. We can anticipate the amusement they would seek. They organised jousts, and set up the quintain in the field. Being slightly upset by the wine they had imbibed the young men did not perform their parts so well as usual, and the quintain was not upset at the first attempt. On the other hand, the young gallants struck themselves very hard, and some will be lame for many months. But these were regarded as accidents, and laughed at accordingly. They were still a "material"—almost a savage race, and we must take them as we find them.

At some distance away there is dancing. The dances of those days were not complicated: *rondes*, singing *rondes*, in which the ladies themselves sang. When they were out of breath the minstrels took up the strain, and the knights joined in, some singing, some playing instruments. There is a tent specially reserved for dancing, but the lovely *saraband* would not be restrained within such limits, and the couples came out under the trees. For a moment everyone ceased, to watch Aëlis dancing with her husband.

Subsequently they refreshed themselves with supper. Night is drawing on now.

But who are these new-comers at the door of the hall, whom everyone respectfully salutes? A priest, accompanied by two acolytes, one carrying a book, the other a censer. They enter the hall, and are thence conducted to the bridal chamber, which is strewn with roses and painted with floral decorations, and a rich bed provided with a counterpane. The husband and wife were kneeling down and very serious. The priest, now in his stole, made the tour of the bed slowly repeating benedictions, making the sign of the cross, and saying: "Bless this nuptial bed, O Lord, so that Thy Christian children may repose in Thy peace, and wake in Thy love." Then, after a pause, he continued: "May the hand of the Lord be upon you, and may He cause his angels to descend from Heaven and guard you during all the days of your lives."

Then he took the censer from the hands of the acolyte, and again went round the apartment, using the incense after the manner in which an angel incensed the wedding couch of Beatrix and the Chevalier au Cygne.* The priest then advanced toward the door, but paused on the threshold to say a few parting words to the kneeling couple: "Peace, and the presence of the Lord be with you." The baron then arose, and accompanied the churchman, while, according to custom, the women put the bride to bed. They then retired, and finally the husband and wife were left alone. . . .

* Li Angles a le lit de la chambre encensée. (*Le Chevelier au Cygne.*)

Next morning at daybreak they attended mass in the chapel. Far from the noise and tumult and really alone, Aëlis could at length for an hour enjoy the luxury of introspection, and arrange, prospectively, her future behaviour.

"I want, above all things, to be a prudent woman ('*prude fame*'), for I remember the verses of the poem which was sung yesterday :—

> ' La prude fame doit-on chière tenir :
> Et la mauvaise vergonder et honnir ! ' (Aspremont).

I want to deserve this praise bestowed on some heroine of romance. ' Wise in word and deed ; Humble to the great as well as to the lowly.'

> ' Sage en fais et en dis.
> Et humles fu as grans et as petis ' (Auberon).

"It is too much to hope that I shall surpass all other women, but with God's help I will be wise, agreeable, simple-minded, gay. I will not go so far as to wear a hair-shirt as the ancestress of Godfrey de Bouillon did when she lost her husband, the Chevalier au Cygne (I hope I shall not lose my husband) ; but I esteem it highest of all the virtues to be cleanly and delicate in mind and body. The woman ought to have a soul as pure and a body as clean as the most delicate samite and the finest silk. I will love no one but my husband, and I will permit myself to be hacked in pieces ere I swerve from my faith and loyalty. Even if he love me no longer, I will love him always. But it is by my respect that I wish first to display my love. I will be humble, and as a servitor. I will call him ' my sire ' or ' my baron,' or, as he knows a little Latin, ' *domine.*' It does not become a poor woman such as I am to have the air of the countess Yde, who one day did not rise before her husband—telling him that she was of superior lineage, for ' at her breast she held, under her cloak, a duke, an earl, a king ! ' * But I will always stand before him, and willingly do his bidding.

"Humility is only a part of my task, and I must shut out from my heart all malice and pride. I am, unfortunately, like that

---

* Yde was the mother of *Earl* Eustace of Boulogne, Godfrey, *Duke* of "Bouillon," and Baudouin, *King* of Jerusalem.

Berthe who 'spoke like a preacher,' and ended by converting her husband; but then my husband is very different from that terrible Girard, who had a passion for blood and who loved evil. I hope, I am sure, he will spare me such anguish; it nevertheless becomes me to remember '*Damedieu*,' and at least to be in accord with him. Not only with God should I be at peace, but with neighbours, and relatives. It rests with me, I think, to prevent any quarrels, and I will do my best to avoid them. I know that I could not find courage to say to my husband as Beatrix did to Hervis de Metz: 'Rather than see your family irritated against you I will leave you.' But without going so far one can do one's duty: I will fulfil mine. I have heard lately of a new Crusade, and ought I to be so weak as to retain him here, or should I have the courage to bid him go? . . . No; the struggle is ended in my heart, I will not be one of those who fall at the feet of their lords and pray them to stay at home. Rather will I say, as I restrain my tears, ' When the great war is over, when you have seen Jerusalem, when you have kissed the Holy Sepulchre, you will then remember me, and think of coming back again.' I have no need to tell him to be brave, but I should wish him to fancy that I was looking at him in the midst of the fight, and that he would do his best. He fights, while I shall pray.

" But perhaps he will permit me to accompany him, and this will be my greatest joy. What delight to be near him, to know from hour to hour that he lives; to nurse him should he be wounded, and if he die, to die with him. It seems to me that I am quite capable of emulating those women who followed Godfrey of Boulogne to Antioch and Jerusalem. I think I am of their race. I could assist the wounded and dying, encourage the knights, and point out Heaven to them, even under the showers of the Infidel's arrows. I could thus perform my part in the encounter. No doubt many women have thus died, but what would that matter to me if *he* were there ! Should he think fit to leave me at home in our beautiful France, I will obey his orders, and defend his fief in his absence. If his castle be attacked I will mount the walls, and defend it with missiles and stones, as Gibourc defended Orange. He sometimes tells me of that heroic woman who became a seam-stress in order to assist her husband, and who, even in the midst of

GIRARD EXHORTED BY HIS WIFE WHILE RECEIVING THE MESSENGER OF CHARLEMAGNE. [*p.* 342

her troubles, was always gay and sweet of disposition. I hope the Son of St. Marie will give me strength and amiability for a like sacrifice, should it be necessary. Besides, I can sew very well. All the same, I hope that *he* will not be compelled to turn charcoal-burner as Girard did. I prefer him as he is—no, I prefer nothing. If only he love me the rest may be as it will !"

Such were the reflections of Aëlis during the mass (the first after her marriage) until the elevation of the Host. After it she resumed her train of thought. Perhaps she might have children—sons. Yes, sons certainly. She would love them all with equal affection, but she would be strict and severe with them. Perhaps, though, she might have to intercede in their favour with their father, who would be still more severe. She would not hesitate to despatch them to the Crusade ; but how delighted she would be at their return ! If anyone outraged their father they would avenge him. If they should be killed—— But this last idea aroused her from her reverie, and she smiled at the thought that she was picturing the deaths of children yet unborn ! Then glancing towards the altar she perceived that the mass was over, and she and her husband returned together by the long avenue to the castle.

V.

We would pause here at this spectacle of the two handsome young people emerging from the chapel and united in spirit, hand in hand, traversing the flowery meads. But we feel that we may be accused of embellishing their portraits, and invented many traits or described others falsely. A large number of French people cannot bear to hear any praise of France before the period of the serment of the *Jeu du Paume*. They wish it painted as barbarous and unpleasant. They are delighted to persuade themselves with certain historians that our male ancestors were poor wretches, and our lady grandmothers certainly not respectable. The impudent author of the " *Romance of the Rose* " did not feel ashamed to write that prudent women were as rare as the phœnix ! He says :—

" Preude femme, par Saint Denis,
Il en est moins que de fenis ! "

Look at the " classics " of the old French society—the Rose, the Fables, the Renart, and the thousand pastorals and *chansons*, the love-songs of which the monotonous impurity revolts and wearies the most indulgent critics. There are some disgraceful pages in these old romances, in which the writers describe French women, Christians, of the twelfth century, in terms which they would not paint the girls of Madagascar or the daughters of the Sioux Indians.

Well, then we once more affirm that the poets had no idea of the beauties of the mind, nor of the characters of those virtues which shrink from displaying themselves. We affirm that this testimony is unfounded and iniquitous. To these classics of our adversaries we oppose our own, which disclose the exact portraiture of the Middle Ages, as it really was with all its virtues and its vices. These honest writers are historians like Villehardouin, Joinville, and later the familiar treatise of the Chevalier de la Tour-Landry, for the information of his daughters, and the excellent incomparable " *Menagier de Paris,*" the most delightful and the most exact of all, in which we find the invaluable advice given by the husband to his young wife regarding the ruling of her household, and which reveals to us the secrets of the domestic life during that period of our history. " That is a work of the fourteenth century," you will say. I am quite aware of it ! But will any historian maintain that the fourteenth century was not, in comparison with the twelfth, a period of corruption and decadence ?

Aëlis, whose portrait I have sketched, was no doubt superior to the majority of the women of her time, but there was a certain number who resembled her and were worthy of her. Besides, it is from our poems themselves that I have extracted all my colouring, and in my picture there is nothing unwarranted or fanciful. At that period I knew quite well many women were sensual and guilty; many struggled against their passions and fell while endeavouring to rise, or having risen fell again. But the poets too frequently excited them to ill-deeds and then laughed sardonically at their fall. The poets are really to blame.

But, after all, the women of the fourteenth century were Christians, and if, in imitation of that Messire Geoffrey, of whom the Chevalier de la Tour-Landry speaks, we proceed to mark with chalk the doors of those who deserve to be blamed, I am persuaded that a great number of doors in houses, and even in castles of the period, would not have deserved to have such an affront put upon them.

All this while Aëlis and her husband have been wending their way to the château, where the *fêtes* will continue for eight days.*

* Sometimes the festivities continued for fifteen days.

CHAPTER XII.

THE DOMESTIC LIFE OF THE KNIGHT—A DAY IN THE LIFE OF A BARON AT THE END OF THE TWELFTH CENTURY.

I.—FOUR O'CLOCK A.M.

IT is July, and four o'clock in the morning. The sun is trying to penetrate the mist. Below, at some little distance, through the rising mist, we can perceive the château of Plessis, which we shall enter very soon. It is a confused mass of building, and only appeals to the eye by reason of its magnitude. It is imposing but vague.

Writers of poetry have always liked the morning, and that is a feeling to which the contemporaries of Philip Augustus and Saint Louis have always adhered. "There is the sun which God causes to rise;" "there is the sun which disperses the dew!" The spectacle has moved more than one of our knights, who have been struck with the appearance of the sparkling dew upon the grass, and "then they sigh." But they do not sigh long—it is not in their nature: they rather prefer to enjoy themselves during life. "Greeting—all hail—to the Summer, when the days are fine, and long, and clear!" Then the barons heard what the author of Renart calls "Chanticleer!" To this cock-crowing they do not apply a holy sentiment or anything symbolic as Christians at present do, and which the Romish Church has preserved in her liturgy. The people were "material" and gay. They would stop to listen to the lark, or to examine a flower; these were for them the indications and the embodiment of the Springtime and of the morning. But let us accompany them to one of the castles, which we will describe. Larks and thrushes and flowers were no longer the chief objects. They had no place there—the ideas of battle were only acceptable to these warriors.

At the summit of the keep was a watchman who, considerably chilled by his nocturnal vigil, made up for it by saluting the rising sun by sounding a horn or other musical instrument—the tabor or *chalimaiu.* When the tourists of our days ascend the Rigi they are awakened by the Alpine horn, but the scene is unpoetic and is laid in a comfortable hotel. A very different effect was produced

Rosamunde at the Window.

by the watch-horn of the feudal age. "Ah!" the baron would say, "I am well guarded; the enemy cannot take me at disadvantage."

Again from all the neighbouring churches and chapels arose the joyous pealing of bells, which rang for matins. At the elevation of the first mass the bells again sounded, and the lords of the castles never heard them without profound respect and a *naïve* faith. But these did not render the châtelains any more devotional. They attended mass every morning, but when they quitted the sanctuary

they inhaled the fresh air with great enjoyment, and exclaimed
what a lovely day it was! To quote the old poet—

> " Chevalerie quièrent torneor
> Dame qui aime a plus fraische color ! "

This was the effect of spring-time.

To each hour of this day as spent by the baron we wish to attach
one or more examples extracted from our old poems so as to illustrate the true character of feudal life without any exaggeration of
tone or colouring. The brother of Garin de Loherain—Bègne by
name—was once besieged by the Bordelais in his Castle of Belin,
and it came to pass one night that the besiegers, alarmed by the
approach of succour to the garrison, raised the siege and fled towards
Bordeaux. At the first dawn of day the watchman ascended the
keep, but no enemy was visible; they had all disappeared. With
the familiarity then usual the watchman hurried down and burst
into his lord's chamber, where Bègne and his wife, the beautiful
Beatrix, were reposing. The servitor shook his master rudely by
the shoulder and awoke him.

" What do you want, my good friend ? What is the news ? "

" My lord, they have raised the siege ! "

" Sound the horn, my friend, for my people to go forth."

At the very first notes the castle was all alive, and townspeople
as well as knights rushed to the defences. " The assault," they
cried, " it is the assault ! "

Bègne did not delay to undeceive them, but he thought that he
might as well pursue the enemy and quickly too. He laced his
small-clothes, and buckled on his spurs, and donned his armour, and
called upon his wife to gird him with his fine proved sword
Floberge. Beatrix was greatly moved at this, and prayed Heaven
to defend her husband from danger and from death. " That is
well said," replied the duke. Then and only then he cast a
tender glance upon his wife who had but lately recovered her
strength after her accouchement. " Lady," said the baron with
trembling voice, " take good care of my child." So he hastened
away, and she remained in the castle.

Another scene which also occurred during the first hour of the
day. This relates to one of the Saracen princesses, who conceived

such violent affection for a French knight, and who for this love sacrificed her country, her family, her faith. Thus did Rosamunde one day fall in love with Elias of Saint-Gilles; but in the conversion of this youthful pagan there was considerable impulsiveness and sincerity. She would rise early and listen to the matin-songs of the birds, and these carollers reminded her of her love for Elias of Saint-Gilles. She apostrophised the trees and flowers, and the corn, "which spring from the earth in love." Then she knelt before the figure of the Virgin, and exclaimed: "The law of Mahomet is a bad law—I renounce it!" It is true she imposed certain conditions on her acceptance of the Christian religion concerning the protection by Heaven of her chosen love. But Rosamunde at her window was a charming figure to contemplate; and by her presence she completed the beauty of the aspect of the Spring morning.

We must not exaggerate, and so attribute to our knights a very high intelligence, and a very profound love of nature. To put it tersely, we must say that they only cared for spring and light, for some few birds and flowers. This is about all that one can expect from soldiers who never went into subtleties, nor plunged themselves into the profundities of symbolism. What they wanted was "go," *élan*, the upward soaring which carried to Heaven the souls enamoured of Nature, of *all* Nature. Our barons were in this respect far inferior to the incomparable poet of the twelfth century, who traversed the roads of Italy declaiming this inspired canticle—

"Praise to Thee, O God, for all Thy creatures, and chiefly for our brother the Sun, which gives us light and life, which is beautiful shining in such splendour, and which bears witness unto Thee, O God. Praise be unto Thee, O God, for our sister the Moon, and for the stars which Thou hast placed in the heavens so clear and bright. Praise to Thee, O God, for our mother the Earth, which sustains and nourishes us, and brings forth fruit, flowers, the grass and herbs." Thus Saint Francis d'Assisi, and you will perceive how far he is beyond our *chansons de geste* or epic poems. I could leap over several centuries and compare them with another writer whom one would hardly dare to name in conjunction with Saint Francis. Jean Jacques communicated to his own time and has left to us a love of nature which is sometimes feverish and sickly, but which is frequently also delicate, profound and living. Read a page of Lamartine, his pupil, and afterwards, if you care to, endeavour to wade through the formulas in which our poets of the twelfth and thirteenth centuries have condensed their love—their monotonous love for the month of May !

The forest which we must traverse to reach the castle of Plessis in truth contains the spectacle which our barons loved best to contemplate—for there they hunted ! There you might have beheld them in full career, shooting with unerring arrow their quarry. When in the virgin forest, sometimes through a leafy glade, one might get a peep at the massive keep of the castle on its rocky foundation, and beneath the walls the silver ribbon of the river. In the depths of the wood where no openings existed one had to console oneself by listening to the call of the birds and the notes of the songsters. In the mighty wood clothed with verdure the heat was tempered by the shade, and there charcoal-burners plied their trade. Yonder is the high road, the grand route whereupon one may have seen the "little people" bent on business, and the proud knights seeking adventure. The latter carry flowers in their hands and sing as they ride on. Nature is fresh—this race is gay.

The last traces of the morning mists have now disappeared, and at length we can contemplate the château in all the majesty of its surroundings.

The first portion which claims attention is the keep—the donjon —which is perched on the hill upon an artificial eminence. What a height it is ! How massive, too ! We should estimate it a hundred feet high. The general appearance is heavy and ungraceful ; but the eye has not leisure to examine details : the synthesis of the fortress, the knight's estimate of it, is what we must seize.

Now what strikes us most in the general disposition of the castle is its separation into two clearly distinct courts. One of these is smaller than the other, but how much more important ! It contains many dwelling-places and a chapel, but above all, the keep, with its moat or ditch—for it has a fosse all to itself—and with the stout wall which clothes it, as it were, in a body-garment of stone. The other *baille*, which was sometimes many acres in extent, presents the aspect and the animation of a small-sized town. A church dominates it and turns our thoughts to Heaven; a stream runs through it and makes it lively. But look well once more, look at the two courts and remember their simple plan: that is the whole *château!*

These two courts are separated by a crenelated wall, in which are a postern and a door. We will knock at it very soon.

Both courts are surrounded by walls and turrets, which are generally flat on the inner and rounded on the outer face. Those of the upper court, near the keep, are stronger than those below, for the keep, as we shall see presently, is the ultimate aim of besiegers, and its defence must be carefully undertaken and considered.

In front of the walls which compose the general *enceinte* of the castle runs a road or pathway, in which in time of siege the "rounds" are made by night and day: this is termed the *lists*.

In front of the lists a row of heavy stakes forms a wall of wood, like a second wall of defence. It is certainly low, and less solid than the masonry "curtains;" but nevertheless it is an obstacle to be reckoned with. This palisade is termed in Latin *murale barrum*, and in French *les barres*—the barrier. Between the walls of stone and the palisade, the lists form quite a promenade.

At the foot of the palisade the greater part of the castle is defended by a moat, which is designed to render the operation of undermining impossible. Our castle of Plessis is thus fortified and defended. But how can we gain admittance to this vast fortress? Well, do you perceive yonder two turrets—twin towers, between which runs a well-protected and defended passage? This gives access on one side to the surrounding country, and to the lower court on the other by a strong door. In front of it is the deep, wide moat.

But, however deep and wide it may be, I fancy that our typical baron would not sleep very tranquilly if the outer entrance of his castle were not better defended. Over the moat is thrown a drawbridge, which can be raised and lowered by chains at pleasure. But this is not all.

In front of the gate and the bridge, on the opposite bank of the moat, is a square tower, not nearly so high as the others. This advanced work is loop-holed, and is called the *barbican*, entrance to which is gained by a small concealed door on the right side. No important castle is without its barbican, and as early as the end of the twelfth century these works were built of stone. First of wood, but subsequently of stone.

At the base of the slope was the river, which completed the defences. It was navigable, and heavy barges ascended it, whence the cries of the sailors were frequently audible. The surrounding country was featureless, and the river animated it.

So much for the castle!

II.—Eleven a.m.—Outside the Castle.

Now let us come out of the castle for a while, and inquire when it was built? How? By whom? Does it resemble those which preceded it? For how long a period have castles existed? Who invented, and who brought to perfection this mode of defence? It is so much the more important to examine these questions as our knights lived in such castles as this, and that Chivalry itself was, so to speak, nursed there. We cannot thoroughly understand Chivalry if we are not acquainted with the fortress, its walls and its towers, within which it lived and breathed.

Let us now spring back over many centuries and boldly return to the Roman epoch. In fact, let us transport ourselves to the end of the third or the commencement of the fourth century.

The extensive Empire is still majestic, but there is something menacing it in the air, and around it are pressing new races who are demanding their share of the sun. Rome till that time had withstood these incursions of races. On her frontiers, at the openings of the wide valleys, at the fords of great rivers, successive emperors had constructed enormous permanent camps which two legions held or could hold. These places were called *Castra stativa*, and for a long while they sufficed for the defence of the old Roman Empire. They could easily be reconstructed in the square form, their *prætorium*, their roads which intersected each other at right angles, their *via principalis*, their *via quintana*, their forum. The day came, however, in which even such an ingenious system was found insufficient. No matter how well the passage was guarded the barbarians forced it, and some other means of defence became necessary.

The Romans retired, but very slowly. While they thus fell back in the interior of Gaul, they cast their eyes around right and left, everywhere. At the entrances of defiles, at the fords of rivers, on the heights which lay near their road, and which they judged favourable for the protection of Roman territory, and equally when there were no heights, their engineers piled up mounds which were defended by a ditch and a rampart. That was all: there were no complicated works. To these earthen ramparts, which were of varied forms and proportions, were added some fortified posts and, perhaps, a look-out tower. Such were the original castles.

As they did not cost much to construct they were built in all directions. In the fourth century there was a great number of them in Gaul, which was being overrun more and more. In the fifth century the country simply bristled with them.

Nevertheless, the Barbarians continued to advance. They had no castles and did not understand the mode of fortification, or of encampment. True savages as they were, they camped in low places, in meadow-land, or in pastures where their horses were in clover. If it be true, as some allege, that we owe some of our civilisation to them, the castle certainly is not one of those elements—it is decidedly of Roman origin.

The more they advanced the more castles were erected, and one could follow the tract of the invaders by the clue of castles which had been constructed to meet their approaches. First, these *castella* were erected on the frontiers, then in the more central provinces, then in the very heart of the country and, in fact, everywhere. The peoples of the Middle Ages were considerably surprised at the sight of so many ruins, and attributed the castles to the Saracens or to Cæsar.

Those small defences could avail nothing against the fierce German attacks. Pebbles opposed to a torrent! The torrent flowed on and the Gaul became Burgundian, Goth or Frank. The Franks—we will speak only of the Merovingian Gaul—had no opinion of these *castella*, which did not impede their march. The fortifications of the towns surprised them more, and they did not disdain to repair them; but the earth-mounds only aroused their contempt. The Gallo-Romans, however, did not so disdain them, and they sought to preserve themselves from the fury of the conquerors by utilising the old *castella* as refuges. Fortunat has left to us a description of one of these castles of the sixth century, a not very precise description of the *enceinte* (which enclosed the crest and sometimes the slope of the hill) with its palisades, its ditch, its thirty towers dominated by a lofty tower or keep of many floors, of which the ground floor was used as an oratory, while the platform was reserved for the catapult and other machines. Making allowance for all exaggeration it is certain that the fortress described by Fortunat is more complete than the Roman *castella*. One may even believe that it had an influence on the feudal castle of the future, for all the Gallo-Roman castles had disappeared in the sixth century. That was an epoch of relative security from more than one point of view.

The first Carlovingians were Teutons who were fired with ambition to imitate the Romans, and in everything. The force of circumstances demanded it, and they adopted the old system pure and simple, which consisted in defending the frontiers of the Empire only. Two tribes, restless and dangerous neighbours, disturbed Charlemagne more than all the others. These were the Gascons and the Saxons. He constructed once more the *castra stativa*, really fortified barracks; some along the Oder to keep the Saxons in check, and along the Garonne to hold back the Gascons. But this was the last outcome of the old-world strategy. Events precipitated themselves to a conclusion, the idea of authority faded away, the notion of centralization was wiped out; the power declined into the hands of numerous petty sovereigns.

Then we meet the Feudal System, and the Castle was born.

Those Dukes and Earls who created themselves kings—those men-at-arms who protected the weak and timorous, those lords (since we must call them so) were violent, wild, pushing, and all the more jealous of their rights as they rested on a precarious footing. They were menaced by their neighbours, whom they also menaced. Everyone was fighting, or about to fight, somebody else. So it came to pass that one day iron armour was invented to defend the person of the soldier, and then a defence for the family and retainers in war time was initiated—so there arose those castles of the ninth century which so suddenly sprang up in all directions. This is one of the most curious events which History presents to us.

The barons, having inspected the locality, would in most cases choose the very same spots which had been selected four centuries previously when the Romans were struggling against the Barbarians. Nothing could be more natural and legitimate than such a selection. The Romans had generally made a very excellent choice, and it was only a proof of intelligence to follow their lead. Besides, the baron was enabled in many cases to utilize the ruins of the old defences, and the wise man should take all the advantages he can obtain. In short, the castle was begun.

Thus we are compelled to put aside all the ideas handed down to us respecting the grand architects and designers of these castles which ill-informed romance-writers would present to us, and which still find place in the minds of ill-informed readers. We must not expect anything so graceful or so imposing. The first castles were built of mud and wood—not of stone.

The first operation in connection with the defences of this simple building was the elevation of the mound or *motte*. This high accumulation of earth served as the basis of the celebrated " castle." Upon it was erected a great square wooden house as lofty as possible—three or four storeys high—with underground chamber practically in the thickness of mound, where a well is generally found. These wells were dug in anticipation of long and trying sieges. With a supply of water the occupants were invulnerable— without water they were lost.

We must now remember that this wooden house was erected on the mound of earth. Picture it ; it was the germ of all the castles of the Middle Ages : the abiding place of the baron, the *dominus*, the *domino*, the *donjon*.

But wood burns. How was this primitive donjon to be protected from fire ? By means equally primitive. Upon the platform were extended the skins of animals recently flayed. An expedient worthy of savages !

But were not there some outward defences around the donjon as in the case of the ancient *castellum*, some advanced works, some exterior fortifications? Yes, indeed, and these defences would increase in proportion to the wealth of the baron. Some poorer lords could do little in this way beyond a thick-set hedge or a palisade. Such " castles " were known as "la Haye," "le Plessis," just as others were called "la Motte!" But we find superior castles to these, for some barons went so far as to construct an *enceinte* or enclosure of fine stout planks, with wooden towers at regular distances apart. These more solid refuges were termed in bad Latin *firmitates*, in good French *fertés*.

The door of the donjon—for it is very necessary to ascertain the mode of entry—was at the elevation of the first floor just above the summit of the " mound." If anyone wished to come out he let down a ladder, which was easily drawn up again if the enemy appeared. The exterior enclosure was also furnished with a door which originally had no special defence and might pass for a postern. That was all.*

We can now picture to ourselves the manner in which one of these castles would be attacked at the end of the ninth century. The assailants would climb to the assault, cross the first ditch, scale the palisades, but then would find themselves confronted by a huge wooden edifice placed on the summit of an artificial hill, surrounded by a second ditch, with no means of access, as the drawbridge had been pulled up or the planks removed. In those primitive castles the enclosures counted for little : the donjon for everything. It was the inviolable asylum, the unassailable refuge, the last and supreme resource.

Let us now use the magician's wand and see by what means a " castle " of the ninth century was transformed into a château of the twelfth century.

The great point is that *stone superseded timber !*

The square wooden donjon is transformed into a stone keep, which was at first square but subsequently assumed other forms.

---

* A very interesting description of the old " castle " is given by Jean de Colmieu, about 1130 A.D. He mentions the mound raised with earth carried to the spot, a deep ditch was then dug around this mound, a palisade like a wall was constructed with towers of wood at intervals. In the midst was a " citadel," whence a view was obtainable in all directions, admission to which was only gained by a bridge over the deep moat, and by ascending the hill.

The enclosure of planks has become a wall, crenulated, loopholed, and encircled by a roád.

The wooden towers are changed into stone towers, flat on the inside, rounded exteriorly, let into the walls, and supplied with similar means of resistance.

The ancient ricketty bridge or ladder has given place to a flight of marble steps which lead easily to the courtyard of the donjon. The true door is at the exterior of the castle, like the doors of old Roman towns, less elegant, and stronger, placed between two towers supporting a crenulated bastion, and including both portcullis and drawbridge which can be lowered or raised.

Again, instead of one fortified court-yard there are two—the donjon court with its stone wall, which protects the great tower and the exterior *baille* or open space, which is occupied by the inhabitants who, in fact, are numerous, and constitute a regular village.*

The magician's wand has performed wonders. No two buildings can (outwardly) less resemble each other than the castles of the ninth and twelfth centuries ; but, nevertheless, they are composed of the same elements—they are virtually the same edifice. We wish we could have depicted them more vividly, and, with the facile pencil of Quicherat, transfer the successive changes from his sketching-board to our pages. But who can do this in a sufficiently realistic style ?

Our baron thought a long time about rebuilding his castle, and did not make up his mind for five or six years. It is at the confluence of two rivers in a somewhat wild spot upon a rocky eminence which the people call a mountain. The two rivers which flow into each other are of different hue, one being as white as the Garonne, the other as deep blue as the Rhône. They are both—and a great advantage —full of fish. The architect of the castle is a clever man whom the baron has sent for to the neighbouring town—a layman, but full of "clerical" ideas.† He sets about the work resolutely after having made a careful survey and drawn plans which he has submitted

* Travellers by the Stelvio route to or from Nauders will notice an excellent specimen of a fortified place in the small town of Glurns, on the Adige.

† M. Viollet le Duc mentions the twelfth century (?) as the period of the "laicisation of art"—the transfer of art from the monasteries.

to the baron. For three days the man of war discussed with the
man of design these drawings. The parties agreed, and the
labourers were set to work. That was a fine workshop! ten stone-
cutters, twenty-five masons, and in all one hundred and sixty
labourers. They were paid "by the piece" not "by the day." It
was no easy task to build the castle, and on more than one occasion
the master-mason had a tiff with the baron. But all's well that
ends well.

This is a fine sight this workshop, this building of the castle
which tends more and more towards the high-class form. No more
of the simplicity of the Roman period, no more of the *opus spicatum*
or *reticulatum* of the Barbarian epoch, no more bricks: the
"middle style" is merging into the grand. As in former days, the
two revetments of the walls are filled in with solid matter. The
master-mason has his eyes everywhere, and causes the walls to be
strengthened with iron bands when necessary. One day it was remarked that the Flemish towns, even Ypres itself, were only
defended by hedges. He had shrugged his shoulders and exclaimed,
"How behind the age are these Flemings!"

It must be confessed that the building cost a large sum. Very
fortunately stone had not to be carried a long distance, as the
quarries were near, and carriage was therefore saved. The serfs
who attended to these conveyances were not paid certainly, but they
did not suit in other respects; and free labour was not abundant.
In the ninth century there was no need of free labour to build the
castle: the *mansionarii* sufficed. But by dint of money earned
there, worthy folk were enabled to free themselves from their
heaviest burdens. In the eleventh century the "working-man"
was born, replacing the serf. He was employed in castle-building
after terms had been made with him. He is no longer of the dregs
of the population: he is a member of a corporation and holds up his
head "like a Christian!"

People all round about are discussing the building of the castle and
watch its progress with interest: all classes, even priests and monks,
are present, and most of all admiring the activity of the architect
with his rules and measures. This little man whose name is Simon
seems to be everywhere at once, giving his orders and withdrawing
them, raging against the bad workman, praising the industrious,

vaulting over stones, leaping, running, shouting. In order to excavate the ditches, he had to cut away a portion of the adjacent wood, and it was pitiful to see the timber felled—such fine trees fall beneath the axe. The people of the country were indignant at this course, which seemed to them criminal and almost as wicked as killing human beings. Fortunately the finest and shadiest oaks were preserved.

Though the weather was hot and the men were rudely treated by their employers, they perspired and bore it all gaily enough, laughing and chattering loudly. I do not maintain that their anecdotes were always in the best taste, but they served to lighten the labour.

The building of the castle occupied three years. At the end of that time a cry of admiration went up throughout the district. The donjon upon the summit of the rock shone forth " like a flower in summer : " the moats were filled with clear water which sparkled in the sunlight ; the wood was shady and full of flowers ; the meadows extended in the distance. Here and there some smoke was already rising from the roofs of houses ; the towers and crenulated walls formed a white girdle around the courtyards. Hidden within the keep, the chapel tended to elevate the soul from the somewhat material and brutal world around, and seemed to say " Remember thy Creator." Everyone—tradesmen, servants, clergy, and other spectators—declared with a profound air and with many sagacious nods that " no one living could ever take possession of such a castle ! "

But as we have no intention of taking it, let us pass on and visit it.

We once knew a traveller who, with the view to obtain a correct idea concerning a town, always circumambulated it carefully. This is a good plan, and we will adopt it. Let us make the tour of our new castle.

The advanced work, which protects the grand entrance, is not, at this time, in general use in France, but our architect Simon is a master and keeps himself alive to all improvements. So he has built a barbican, for so the small wooden bastille is called. Very soon it will be built of stone, but at present wood is considered sufficient. The barbican is of quadrangular form in this instance, but there are rounded specimens which are even more common perhaps. With planks three small " curtains" have been constructed and two small turrets. These works are of less elevation than those of the main castle, but they conceal the entrance, which the architect has ably succeeded in hiding. But then it is on the left side. When the enemy shall have arrived they will lose some time in seeking the entrance, which will, later on, be furnished with a drawbridge. For the rest, every provision has been made here to resist a possible, and by no means improbable, siege. An enormous barrier is thrown across the road—a barricade. While the enemy is spending his efforts in breaking through it, the garrison will have time to come to the rescue. Should the barbican be taken they will retire into the castle over the great drawbridge. After this point has been passed the besiegers will have to cope with an enormous and massive iron-bound gate—after that the portcullis, and after that another door. They will then find themselves in a courtyard full of every possible pitfall, snare, and danger to them. If after overcoming this resistance they manage by a supreme effort to gain and pass another door which is also furnished with a drawbridge and portcullis, they will find themselves confronted by the donjon ! This is defended by the garrison, well victualled, impregnable ; and there the occupants calmly await the end of the attack.

Now, having glanced once more at the wooden barbican, let us follow the winding course of the moat, above which we set the squared planks, firmly fixed together, that form the *murale barrum:* the barriers. This first defence is to the castle walls what the barbican is to the entrance (the "port"). It does not look nice, this palisade; and it prevents our seeing the lists as well as the basis of the curtains and towers. The moat at any rate is pleasant enough : it is fifteen or twenty fathoms wide, furnished with boats, and abounds in fish. Fortunately the barrier has been broken down for some considerable distance, and we can look in and see the road, called the lists, and the walls.

The lists are plainly visible, and we perceive a guard making his rounds. The wall is also visible, and as we have watched its development for months we know of what materials it is constructed. As in the time of the Romans it is made up of two surfaces filled in with "rubble-stone." The piece of the wall which is contained between two towers from the ground to the battlement is called a curtain. In a church it is a good thing to study a bay; in a castle, a curtain. Let us do so.

It was in 1180 A.D. that in the north of France builders began to slope the bases of their towers, and subsequently of walls. This sloping gives solidity to the fortification, but it has not the same charm as the small square stones of the Roman period with its pretty mixture of red bricks. It is cold and naked in comparison, and we see nothing on it but a few lizards basking in the sun; it is absolutely monotonous and sad. But its height redeems it from the commonplace, and it is moreover crenulated.

If there is one error more difficult to eradicate than another it is the antiquity of crenulation. People, particularly those who live in the charming country of the Comic Opera, think that crenulation is of the middle ages—but it can be proved that it existed in Roman and Gallo-Roman defences, and is a notable element in their construction. Again people are continually confusing the *merlon* with the *créneau*. In a system of crenulation the *créneau* is the opening, the *merlon* is the solid portion. The *créneau* is placed between two *merlons*, and a pretty face might sometimes be placed there too, though generally the stern visage of a man-at-arms was the only one visible.

The *merlon*, then, is the portion of the parapet between two embrasures, and it was devised for the protection of the defenders, and consequently it is six feet high or thereabouts. In Roman architecture it was very small, but later it was properly enlarged. The ancient *merlon* was finished off by a projecting tablet, but in the middle ages the projection was suppressed and the parapet covered with lead. The usual terms employed to describe the crenulation are "embrasured" and "battlemented."

We cannot speak of this subject without recalling the touching and interesting history of Ogier the Dane. The Emperor Charlemagne—indeed the whole empire laid siege to this hero in his castle of Castlefort, but he did not despair, and resisted bravely. One by one he saw his brave companions die; he saw Guielin yield up his spirit as he prayed, Guielin's brother Benoit, Ogier's own squire—fell another day before the lance of the terrible Raimbaut de Frison : the brave Dane remained alone, but in spite of all he resisted : he resolved to hold out ! He ground his corn, warmed his oven, made his bread ; he was his own cook, servitor, squire and cup-bearer. He laid the table ; when the meal was ready he ate it alone ; sadly he thought of Guielin, of Benoit and of all his other late companions. Then he would go to the stables and talk to his horse *Broiefort*, the only living creature within reach. He lifted his feet and shod him, and then cried "Here, *Broiefort*, here are plenty of corn and good fodder—eat ! "

But all this while the siege continued, and it was most necessary that the emperor should not become aware of the terrible extremity to which the castellan had been reduced. Then Ogier conceived an idea which he presently put into execution. He formed "dummys" out of wooden blocks : the hairs from the mane and tail of *Broiefort* served for moustaches ; on each block-head he stuck a helmet ; clothed his puppets with shining hauberks, and armed them with enormous shields (bucklers), and gave them axes. There was his garrison ! Then he took up these "dummys" and placed them on the battlements : they had a marvellous effect. How was it possible that Ogier had still so many companions ! whence come those men-at-arms ? Charlemagne was surprised— furious. He called his archers and said : " Shoot me those devils yonder ! " The archers took aim, and shot truly. Ogier's men-at-arms were struck, were pierced through, but they never budged an inch !

Then the emperor took a supreme resolution. He armed himself, and advanced as closely as possible to the walls of Castlefort, and made a long speech to Ogier's friends.

" It is I," he cried, " I the king of the great realm of France, to whom belong Gascony, Bretagne, Anjou, the Maine and Romain. Now remember, and remember well, that if you do not deliver up to me Ogier, alive or dead, I will burn every one of you ! "

The speech was fine, but, somehow, the defenders of Castelfort were in no degree moved by it. The poet who describes the incident seems to have had his doubts of the intelligence of his readers, for he adds, "How could they reply ? they were only wood ! "

But we have already mentioned the real men-at-arms, and the beautiful women who appeared at the embrasures. These people were not suspended in space, as may be supposed; they trod on solid platforms, which were also of Roman origin. We must not forget that, with their two facings and interior rubble, the walls were very thick, and the *merlons* small; thus there remained a considerable space in the thickness of the wall, on which the defenders stood, or could walk comfortably: these were called the *alveirs*. In Renaud de Montauban we read of the hero going up to the *alveirs* to hold converse with his brothers; but, of course, the primary use of the platform was to put all the members of the garrison in contact with each other, in communication, and they permitted the archers to stand behind the parapets to take aim or prepare their arbalists. When an enemy came in sight, the cry throughout the castle was, "*aux alveirs,*" (to the ramparts). "Garrison the ramparts!"

By what means were the arrows launched from the arbalists? Through the loopholes in the *merlon*. The archers on the ramparts defended the curtains with arrows from the long and the cross-bows. The ramparts were then no longer used as a promenade.

These ramparts or "round roads" have often been the scenes of terrible battles, of which painters rather than poets have realised the horrors. The castle has been forced, the besiegers are within, full of ferocity, and we find them chasing the defenders around the ramparts. From time to time pursuer or pursued may make a false step, and fall down from the platform several feet above the roof. He is incontinently slain. Sometimes a dull heavy thud is heard; a soldier has fallen outwards to the earth in a pool of blood. These combats are epic.

That this "round way"—this platform, was absolutely necessary no one can doubt; but it at times served the assailants, as well as the defenders of the place. Suppose, for instance, that the enemy had penetrated into the castle, and had gained possession of the ramparts. They were then masters of the situation. Our ancestors had provided against this emergency; at intervals small drawbridges had been placed which could be raised at will: so, when the attacking party expected to find footing, they only found space, and fell into a snare. Many other plans were devised and carried out by the defenders or their architects. The rampart platform was continued into a tower, through a door up conveniently disposed steps, and then the enemy was kept at bay for a long time, and the besieged had time to rally their spirits, and prepare for further resistance.

The rampart, however, was greatly exposed, not only to the shafts of the assailants, but to the weather. Many men have been frozen to death on the battlements, and they remained unsheltered until a very simple contrivance was invented—simply a penthouse of timber, which extended from beyond the wall over the rampart, forming a kind of gallery or galleries within and without the parapet. Loopholes were pierced, and slopes provided whence heavy stones or other missiles could be discharged upon the besiegers. This wooden construction still retains its name "hourds," or hoarding.

These hoardings were only erected at first when a siege was feared, or in time of war; but, after a while, they became permanent, as it was found easier to let them remain than to reconstruct them. But then the beams which had been pushed out from the battlements to support the hoarding, gave the architects another idea. They renewed the supports *in stone;* along the top in front was the crenulation, all the system of *merlons* and *créneaux*, and loopholes on the *corbels*. These projecting galleries were called *machicolations*. They hardly appeared before the end of the thirteenth century, and were not covered in until a later date. They need not be described more in detail; they were actually the wooden hoarding or shelter turned to stone-work, through the apertures in which missiles were discharged on the enemy.

The monograph on our " curtain " is finished, and we will now explore one of the towers, one of the thirteen on the exterior of the castle. The crenulation system is applied equally to them, as well as the other means of defence already noticed.

These towers were sometimes square, but another shape, viz., rounded outside and plane within, was generally preferable. Interiorly they were divided into several storeys, which, after the monastic architecture, were vaulted in stone. The vaulting was sustained by arches abutting on a common key, compared by Quicherat to the framework of an umbrella. The staircases were contrived in the thickness of the walls. The art of the engineers consisted in concealing these as much as possible, and to render the ascent difficult by sudden interruptions. These fearful openings did not exist for the garrison who contrived the staircase, but the unfortunate besiegers were sometimes compelled to retrace their steps, or in the darkness they sometimes fell through the holes and were dashed to pieces below. The Romans, who had adopted the tower, did not devise these ingenious traps; but they knew the value of moveable planks, which were taken away on the first appearance of the enemy. On the other hand, we cannot credit them with the idea of the wonderful loopholes of our towers of the Middle Ages. Outside only a chink is perceived, but within it is quite another matter; the loophole is wide, and well suited for the protection of the archer, who is well placed to see and shoot from any point he pleases. This is a masterpiece of design.

Let us continue our progress, though we shall not encounter any novelty. Nothing is more like one tower than another tower, and curtain is similar to curtain. Were it not for some *eschangaites* intended for posts of observation which break agreeably the regularity of the lines, the promenade would be monotonous. It is better for us to go to a little distance, and admire the building as a whole. The effect produced is very good, and can be realised by a visit to Coucy and contemplating the magnificent castle of Angers which is far too little known and admired.

But here we are before the gate of our castle. This is the time to paint it.

At the first glance we recognise the origin of the architecture. The entrance to a grand castle of the twelfth century is derived from the gate of a Roman city of the third and fourth centuries.

Nevertheless, there are departures from the resemblance. The plan is almost the same: the features have nothing in common. There are two races, two civilisations which have not the same character, and do not comprehend life in the same way.

The Roman gate is a triumphal arch flanked by two towers. It is light and luminous, it testifies to safety more or less real of a

great people who do not believe themselves invulnerable, but estimate themselves invincible.

The Feudal gateway between two tall towers is made in a small
archway beneath a fortified position in a narrow alley. There is no
triumphal arch here, it is a corridor. Everything is therein disposed in anticipation of an attack which may be delivered this
evening, to-morrow, any time! We have to do with people who
are continually on the alert, waging war unceasingly, who do not
believe in any safety except behind stone walls with the smallest
possible openings therein. Ah, if we could only pass that door!

Well, however plain and ugly this twelfth century gate may
appear, it nevertheless attests a considerable advance. It has proportions, style, and a beauty of its own, and in no other direction
have the architects of the Middle Ages brought their art to such
perfection; but we could not say as much for the architects of the
first Feudal period, if these people are worthy of the name of architects. Just look once more at the heavy donjon of wood perched
on the mound with its door on the first floor. How on earth were
people to descend from it; we must surmise that the inhabitants
of these towers did sometimes want to breathe fresh air, and to
hunt in the woods. From the threshold of their only door beyond
the moat, on a slope more or less inclined, they built, upon piles and
wedges, a wide swinging bridge which, as we said before, looked more
like the ladder leading to a mill. This *pons lignens* was solid and was
sufficiently firm to bear the passage of horses, but its most valuable
quality was its mobility. From his position on high the watchman
signalled the approach of the enemy: in the twinkling of an eye
the tower was isolated by raising this famous bridge. If it were
but a false alarm the bridge was replaced, but if the enemy really
advanced, they found to their disappointment a wide ditch and an inaccessible tower beyond it. Granted that the tower was only wood,
the bridge of wood was invaluable.

To this bridge, more or less improved upon, our poets gave the
name of *plancher*. When the employment of such primitive means
was abandoned, when our castles were defended by more scientific
bridges, the name was preserved in the first staircases, the steps of
which were of wood, which led from the grand hall to the interior
of the keep. It is the *pons lignens* of the ancients reduced to its

smallest proportions, but still itself, and we are unable to review the beautiful improvements of the twelfth century without recalling their humble origin.

The *pons lignens* was at a certain period replaced by the steps at the base of the donjon, but it was much more urgent to replace it by a proper bridge of a strategic character. Over the wide moat was flung a stone bridge, but the builders took care to leave a gap in it which could be crossed by a moveable plank. At the first intimation of danger the plank was raised, and the enemy was "left out in the cold." This was certainly an improvement upon the mill-ladder system, but it was still only the infancy of art, and it became necessary to find something else. After the inevitable experiments which our poets hardly notice people came to, or rather reverted to, the drawbridge which had been known to and practised by the Romans. The more we consider the question, the more we shall become convinced that there was no other way, and the drawbridge became very naturally a feature of the fortifications of the Middle Ages.

If we may be permitted to go into dry details of technicalities, we may remark that the drawbridge of the Romans was a moveable bridge which sprung from the very threshold of the gate, and fell into its place on the opposite side of the moat in place of a fixed bridge. It was moved by means of pulleys "mounted on axles fitted into the wall." The architects of the twelfth and thirteenth centuries did not generally employ a system so complicated, but simply used the bascule (or counterpoise) bridge.* Long grooves were made on both sides in the masonry over the entrance— through these vertical grooves heavy beams were thrust and maintained in equilibrium. From the extremities of these arms outside the gate hung two stout chains and to these the moveable bridge was fastened: this apparatus is essentially our drawbridge or *torneïs.* If you desired to raise the bridge you had to hang on to and pull the chain in the archway of the gate inside. Each beam had a chain attached to it which was looped on a ring and hung on

---

* There is a difference of opinion between Viollet le Duc and Quicherat on this point. The former says the drawbridge was not in use until the beginning of the fourteenth century when the bascule went out. The latter maintains that it was deviated from in the thirteenth century, and the bascule adopted.

the side wall. A good pull was sufficient to raise the bridge, the beams working in the high grooves on each side. When the chains were loosed again the bridge fell into its place.

This is the kind of bridge which is always referred to in our old poems, and described clearly enough by the writers. In some of our romances, and not the most ancient either, pulleys are mentioned but rarely. I am convinced that *levis* and *torneïs* express the same kind of moveable bridge. It was called *levis* or drawbridge because of its mechanism : and *torneïs* because of the curve it described. The two words do not cancel each other : on the contrary, one is the complement of the other.

At the side of the principal gate there was frequently a postern for the convenience of the garrison. This *postis* had also its drawbridge, a very light construction which one chain was sufficient to raise, as one beam controlled it. A woman could raise and lower it.

Now let us suppose that instead of being welcome guests at this castle we came as enemies, and began to lay siege to it. We have, let us say, carried the barbican and burned the advanced works ; we have ventured upon the stone bridge and find ourselves halting before the gap in it—for the drawbridge is up.

But we need not pursue the hypothesis. Let us fancy that there are spies in the building—a very common feature—and that one of these traitors has lowered the bridge. We rush in headlong. But all is not yet gained, the defence of the besieged is only beginning. They have executed justice on the traitor who had betrayed the bridge ; and we find ourselves engaged in the vaulted passage between the two towers under the central work. Who can estimate the torrents of blood which must have flowed in those corridors in the combats of the Middle Ages, or the thousands of knights who bit the dust! Never mind, we must push on. The first obstacle that meets us is the barricaded door. Some vigorous strokes of the axes will clear away the barrier and the iron-bound folding-doors, and then, perspiring, bleeding, and dusty, we press on further along the fatal corridor. We imagine that the way should be more free and open. Not so. A rattle of chains is heard and another door falls down in our faces! It is not like the former one—it is a kind of grating, composed of iron bars running in a frame vertically in grooves. In ordinary times this portcullis is retained up in the roof of the vaulted passage, in a special place called the portcullis-room; it is moved by windlass and pulleys. This formidable "gridiron" falls down before the astounded besiegers. Yet it is not a new invention. The honour of it belongs to the Romans, but it plays a more important part in the castle than in the Roman city.

As in the case of the door we must hew our way through the portcullis, and then we encounter another door and another portcullis. So many attacks on these obstacles occupy many hours, and the slaughter is terrible.

You fancy now that you are acquainted with the gate of the castle with its two flanking towers, its central bastion, its vaulted gallery, its moveable bridge, it postern-gate, its inner door and portcullis. But you cannot in the confusion of the battle grasp all the details. For instance, you did not perceive beneath the gallery the small door and its stairway which leads to the platform of the central bastion. You did not remark the window over the gate which lights the work, and to which under the name of *bretèche* will one day be applied the "hoarding" already mentioned. You did not remark that plate of copper on which a hammer strikes such a resounding blow, in lieu of a bell of our own time and of the old "knockers" to be seen in ancient churches. Finally, when a conqueror, you have penetrated into the courtyard, you did not notice the singular effect produced by the architectural ensemble of the gateway as seen from within. Without, the towers give it a rugged outline; within, the towers are flat and everything is rectilineal. There are no useless ornamentations here, the architecture has no need of it. It possesses a severe and practical beauty; everything serves some purpose, and nothing is ugly.

The guardianship of the gate is confided to an important personage, one already ridiculed—the porter to wit. He has a lodging in the central work over the gate or in one of the towers—apartments even at that time known as the "lodge," into which he ascended by a staircase. His duties were many and important, and it will be interesting to pass them in review.

His prime duty was to raise and lower the drawbridge; and

nothing could be more important, when war with all its surprises
and tricks was rampant, and spies and traitors to be encountered.
The porter's "pass-word" was very simple. "Let no one come
in!" Nevertheless at every hour of the day or night someone
would hail the porter from without. Sometimes it was the baron
himself who was returning from some joust, or the sentries who
had completed their rounds, or perhaps guests seeking admission.
"Hi, porter, let us in!" In those castles which were furnished
with copper basins or plates a continual din was heard like church
bells ringing, and the porter had to rush out of his lodge to
answer. But whither did he run? At times he hurried up and
looked through the embrasures over the gateway, at others he spied
from the turret placed between the large towers, but in either case
if the bridge was down he would go to his small wicket or opening
in the gate and question the new arrival through it. "Who are
you?" "Whence come you?" And if the reply is not satis-
factory, he shuts the slide again, and calls out "you cannot enter."
At times the new-comer begs him to wait, or to run into the hall
and acquaint the baron of the presence of the visitor; or the chamberlain may give admission. "Must I open the gate?" he asks;
he never fails to ask this question, it is imperative, and if permission
is granted, he raises the bridge first, opens the great gate or the
postern, removes the bar, and bows more or less obsequiously,
according to the rank and importance of the new arrival. In some
castles the porter acted as watchman and usher, and he was
required in cases of attack to manipulate the complicated
machinery of the portcullis. He was a busy man.

That the porter had his failings it is impossible to deny. He
was lazy, indolent, and basked in the sun like a lizard. We may
without calumniating him, state that he was a coward, very fond of
his ease. We have already seen how the porter of Laon castle
received Roland's suggestion to create him a knight. "I am not
fond of fighting," he said. But the porter had two faults which
overshadowed all the rest—he was extremely insolent and very
corruptible. He began by being impudent, and finished by being
venal: a very instructive instance of these ruling traits we cull
from an episode of *Moniage Guillaume.* Bernard du Fossé wished
to enter Paris, but the porter resolutely refused him admittance.

"If you will open the gate I will give you six sous!" This removed the obstacle, and Bernard entered.

The porter to whom Renaud de Montauban offered one night a gold ring, finally resigned himself to the gift, weighed it in his palm, and when he perceived that it was heavy felt greatly pleased. I cannot, I regret to say, mention all the insolent porters; they are too numerous.

There might be written, under the title of "Legends of the Gate," some long stories of heroic tendency. One is forced to choose amid so many gems, but the following little known tale is from *Renans de Montauban,* in which the hero of the fine poem, after a severe retrospective examination of all his past life, takes the resolution to quit "the world," and devote himself to Heaven. The dominant grief is that he has slain a whole troop of men in his time.

"*Par moi sont mort mil homme, dent j'ai le cuer dolent,*" he cries.

War, which formerly seemed to him so grand and beautiful, in such radiant colours, now appears either brutal or criminal, and he only thinks of saving his soul, he wants no more,

"Se puis m'ame salver, plus ne demant noient."

The time too is well chosen for such an eminently Christian resolution. Renaud has made his fortune, he is overweighted with happiness; his children have vanquished the traitors who had opposed them and were in possession of their fiefs; his brothers lived in peace amid the glories of former exploits. All was well: Renaud wanted no more here below save to live amid his friends and relatives and do penance. He resolutely proceeded to carry out his plan.

In the middle of the night when all was silent in the castle he rose, dressed in beggar's clothes, and with naked feet silently descended the stairs. The porter awakened was very much surprised to see his lord and master at such an hour and in such a costume.

"I shall go and call your sons and brothers," he said.

"Do so; but only tell them to pray for me, and that I send them greeting."

" What more shall I say ? "

" As my last advice, my latest wish, I leave them these words.
' Let them seek to do good ! ' "

" And whither goest thou in this condition ? "

" I go to save my soul, and to live a holy life."

On that the porter permitted him to pass out, and the great
Renaud, the conqueror, the hero who had held Charlemagne in
check, and delivered Saint Sepulchre, fled like a thief across the
fields, wrapped in his capote, with his eyes fixed on the ground,
not daring to look behind him. He ran away seeing safety far
away from his home which contained all that was dear to him on
earth.

But soon the day dawned, and Renaud's sons awoke and went to
chapel. On ordinary occasions Renaud preceded them thither and
heard matins with them. But on that morming they did not see
their father, and they began accordingly to feel uneasy. "Renaud,
where is Renaud ? " They searched for him in all directions, they
ran to his chamber, the bed was empty ! the baron's armour, his
sword, lance, and accoutrements were all there, and his horse was
in the stable.

" Renaud !   Where is Renaud ? "

Then the porter came and informed them of what had passed
during the night.   " You will never see him again," said he, " and
listen now to what he bade me tell you."   Then he delivered the
baron's message, exhorting them to love one another. The young
men wept and bemoaned themselves, and after a while they
mounted their horses and, proceeding to the sanctuary, beat at the
gate until eventide.   In vain !

Yet while they were thus seeking him whom they regretted so
dearly, a man of giant stature, all in rags, was hiding himself in
the thick forest, eating wild fruits and debating in his own mind
in what monastery and in what form of religion he could expiate in a
worthy manner his sinful life. This man was Renaud, who had
rushed away in a hurry to save his soul, and scarcely paused until
he reached Cologne, where he died, a poor workman, a worker in
the service of God—one of the masons of Saint Peter's.

However Christianlike such an individual may be, he did not
reach to the elevation of the dramatic scene which, ever memorable

RENAUD, A WORKMAN AT COLOGNE. [p. 372.

in history, occurred at the gate of the town of Orange. It was on that celebrated day upon which William gave battle to the infidels at Aliscans, a battle on which hung the fate of the Christian world. That evening it had to be decided whether Jesus Christ or Mohammet should be master of the earth. In Orange and around the town all was quiet. One might search in vain for a soldier in the fields or in the town. Everyone was fighting. A death-like silence reigned around, and few, if any, felt the solemnity of the hour. Our modern engagements—our artillery duels especially—are noisy, but in the Middle Ages even the grandest *mêlées* were comparatively noiseless. There was another kind of fear that was keenly felt that day at Orange, some leagues from the battle-field.

There were only two men left in the town—a porter and a priest, the porter to look after the drawbridge, and the priest for the care of souls. In the great hall of the castle, and in every chamber along the walls, everywhere, were mute and anxious women, the wives of those who were engaged in the cruel strife at Aliscans. The children, who comprehended nothing of the trouble, climbed upon their mothers' knees and laughed. But the women did not respond to their childish gaiety; they were all mournful and anxious. How will the battle end? Will our side be victorious? Will our husbands, and brothers, and soldiers return?

Gibourc is amongst these ladies, more manly than they, and thinking more of her William than they all think about their fathers, brothers, and husbands. From without no sound comes save now and then a distant echo from the field of battle. Heavens, what a waiting!

Suddenly the porter enters the hall, and looking round in affright upon the assemblage of women, he exclaims—

" There is a man at the portal who desires admittance ! "

" Who is he ? "

" He pretends that he is William," is the reply.

A shudder pervades the assemblage, and thrills Gibourc. She hurries up, restless, incredulous, defiant, and presents herself outside on the small turret between the two great gate towers. On the opposite side of the moat is a knight of commanding form seated motionless on his horse, and curiously enough he is accoutred in Arab fashion, wearing infidel's weapons.

He is a Pagan, thought Gibourc, and we must close our gates against him. "Ho, Infidel," she cried, "thou dost not enter here!" But the horseman replied in quiet tones, sadly: "I am William!" He had not time to tell her how, in order to escape trom the Saracens, he had assumed the Saracen dress, and how this trick had saved him from massacre.

"I am William," he repeated, as great tears rolled down his cheeks. His arms were red with blood, his eyes swollen with sorrow. "Twenty thousand Turks are in chase of me. Open, open the gate for me."

In fact at this moment the thundering tramp of many horsemen became audible; but Gibourc was by no means satisfied of the knight's identity.

"Your tones resemble William's, but many people's voices sound like his," she said.

The Count heard her, and for all reply unlaced his helmet and revealed his face, which was covered with blood.

"Look at me," he cried. "It is I, indeed!"

She leaned forward, shivering; she at length recognized him, but at that moment loud cries of distress became audible. These emanated from the Christian prisoners, whom their Saracen victors were driving before them like a miserable herd. The unfortunate victims were loaded with chains, and were being beaten and terribly illtreated by their captors. At this fearful spectacle the blood rushed to Gibourc's face, and she cried to the new-comer—

"What, do you pretend to be William, the proud baron who has covered himself with fame and glory, and you support the sight of such a spectacle as that? No, no, you are not William. He would never, were he living, have permitted Christians to be treated in such an infamous way! You are not William! No, not William at all!"

At this the valiant baron could have excused himself by explaining how he had fought for sixteen hours and had already lost much blood; but silently he closed his helmet, grasped his spear, and heroically dashed down upon the Saracens in a fierce and unexpected manner. One against a hundred he assailed them, put them to flight, and released the Christian captives. Then he returned to the castle and cried: "Now am I William?"

WILLIAM OF ORANGE RETURNING FROM ALISCANS. [p. 375.

The gates were opened and the unfortunate count was permitted to enter his own town. It was about time. Gibourc, who should have credited him, doubted still! What astonished, even stupified her, was the fact of his returning vanquished. She was so accustomed to a brilliant victory that she could hardly credit the circumstances. Certainly he would not have been displeased if she had played nurse and bestowed all the care in her power upon the beaten warrior. His fifteen wounds, his body hacked and bleeding, the heavy tears which fell from his surcharged eyes, might have touched the hardest heart with pity. But no ; she held back, she stood aloof, the idea of his defeat absorbed all other feelings. "No," she murmured, "it is not possible that you can be William, for if you were you would have returned the victor."

This is truly a feminine argument, and is not far from being sublime in its magnificent illogicality. At length she asked him a question or two.

" Where are all the French ? "

" Dead ! " " And the barons ? " " Dead ! " " Where are your nephews ? " " All dead ! " " Where is Vivien whom I love so dearly ? " " Dead ! " And thus amid his tears and sobs he could but murmur, " Dead, dead, dead ; they were all slain at Aliscans ! "

Then Gibourc drew herself up to her full height, and, as if inspired ; almost fiercely she said, as she restrained her natural grief, " There must be no reposing here ! God and the chivalry of France must be revenged ! Go ! Begone, and solicit in Paris the help of the emperor ! "

She did not consider his wounds, the blood with which he, her William, was covered, in his sixteen hours' fighting. " Go, go ! " she cried.

" Cannot I despatch a messenger instead ? " he pleaded.

" No. Go yourself," was the reply.

" But, if so, I leave you quite alone."

" I quite understand that, and alone will I sustain the siege against the Turks. I will mount the ramparts, and will slay them from above. Go ! "

The husband and wife then fell into each other's arms, but it was only at the very last moment, when William was about to repass the gate which had been so tardily opened to admit him, as he was about to leave his home on his long journey across France, then only did Gibourc become, for a moment, a woman again, and she whispered, as her eyes were fixed tenderly on his, " You will see many more beautiful women than I am yonder, and you will forget me." He, with the splendid austerity of the Feudal baron, dominated and transfigured by Christianity, replied, " No, no, lady. I swear to you that my lips shall touch no other mouth but thine ! "

The " water from his heart " rushed to his eyes, he clasped Gibourc in his arms, covered her face with kisses, and steeling his heart while she clung to him, crying, " Do not forget this unhappy woman," he heroically mounted his horse, bent down to bestow upon her one last kiss, set spurs to his steed, and rode away weeping. May Heaven and the Virgin guide and protect him !

The " Legends of the Gate " would furnish matter for many other narrations, but we need not say more ; so let us proceed, and enter the courtyard of our castle. We first enter the exterior *baille* in the outer *enceinte*, and it is very large. There is quite a little village there under the shade of the walls. In the centre is a church, whose steeple ascends high in air, and round it stand groups of houses, from which smoke ascends, and in which the anciently designated *mansionarii* are at work. Here during the day the sound of agricultural toil is mingled with the clang of iron or wood working, forges, carpenter's shops, mills, millers singing as they transport the sacks of corn and flour, donkeys braying, dogs barking, men shouting, labourers working.

For several years serfdom has been abolished, but the lot of the labourer is not a happy one. " A colourless life " as the poet says. You may perceive them coming out to hoe the fields beyond the walls. Near the mill is a primitive bakehouse, from which issues the smell of new bread. In front of the church a pretty fountain plays into a basin, where woman do their washing, and gossip ; and not far off is a fish-pond, a great resource in times of siege.

Near the great gate is a charnel-house, established during the last war, and Christians who pass it cross themselves devoutly. At the first alarm all the inhabitants of this little world rush into the upper court and into the donjon itself, so as to be quite safe. We will do the same, though there is no danger now, and enter boldly the interior court, which is divided from the exterior *enceinte* by a crenulated wall and a fortified gate. Still another portcullis. Let us pass it. But we are greatly deceived! We had expected to find the keep close to us, and the door near at hand. Nothing of the kind. Buildings are scattered in all directions, outhouses of all kinds. The stable; the *mareschaucie* of the baron, which in some castles is relegated to the outer court, is here inside. Against the walls are the storehouses and cellars. Further on is a bear-pit with a couple of bears, and very near it is the falconry, where, carefully tended, are the hawks, waiting for the baron who visits them twice a day, but more particularly expecting some nice hot meat, or some dainty living prey.

It must be confessed that there is nothing majestic or graceful about these buildings. There are two, of which we have not spoken, which dominate the rest; one is the chapel, with its single nave, and bell-less; the kitchen, however, first claims our attention, and it almost resembles a small church. Picture to yourself a great bell surmounted by a chimney. It is rather curious than ugly. In large monasteries, where there are many hundreds of mouths to feed, the number of hearths and chimneys are multiplied; for instance, there are five shafts at Marmontier, six at Vendome, and a greater number at Fontevrault. But in our castle the central shaft is sufficient, and in the kitchen, which is well-built and well-ventilated, a sheep can be cooked whole, or an ox may be roasted. The baron does not condescend to come here and give his orders, to see that the service is properly carried on, or to reprimand the *keux*.

The kitchen has only one fault, it is very far from the dining-hall; and so the servants are obliged to carry the roast peacocks and other viands across the court and up the steps before reaching the board. Some barons sought to obviate this inconvenience by building the kitchen below the keep; but the old system generally was maintained, and it is the better, after all.

In the *palace*, magnificent buildings extend between the chapel and the keep, but in the simple *castle* there is only the donjon.

Now in a castle the donjon is all in all; the rest is nothing.

All that we have hitherto seen and examined are *bagatelles* in comparison, of no value whatever. But the donjon is still, in the twelfth as in the ninth century, the last refuge, the last resource of the Feudal baron driven into his lair. This word is not too strong; the donjon often was a den as much as, or more than, a house. Sometimes a cave in which the " wild beast " used to defend himself. The hunters had to cross the moat, pass the bridge, break down the door, carry the walls and towers of the two *enceintes*, occupy the courts, burn the houses, the church, the chapel, and even the kitchen. Still the donjon remained, huge, inaccessible, underground ! It possesses all means of dominating the besiegers, and its strength is in its height. Long ere this the donjon has been made of stone; the wooden structures have been destroyed; those towers of the ninth century, with their wooden platforms covered with skins, are nothing !

Some poets declare that the donjons were constructed of marble, but they exaggerate, the *tors marberines* were simply *tors perrines*, stone towers. The material is the same as that of the walls and fortifications. But it is to the height and bulk of the donjon that we will principally call attention, and the reader, in order to understand these things, should picture to himself an immense mass, a high tower, perched on a hillock, or on a rock, overlooking, not only the fortifications of the castle, but all the surrounding country for miles.

The keep of Beaugency was 132 feet high and 72 in width; Loches, which is perhaps the most beautiful donjon in France, is only 100 feet high, but is 67 feet in its widest measurement; Chateau-sur-Epte, 18 métres in height, is 11 métres wide. I do not intend to jump into the thirteenth century and speak about the giant donjon of Coucy, that remarkable keep, 64 métres (about 200 feet) high and 31 métres (some 100 feet) in width (not circum-ference. Our own particular donjon is only 60 feet high and 38 feet in diameter; its walls are 6 feet thick. The architect who built it had some notions of his own, and did not give it the same square form as the others. It is certain that this form is that which the twelfth century more particularly delighted in. There was no need for excess, but the brains of architects must have been exercised considerably in the time of Louis VII. and Philip

Augustus. At that period they attempted, as at Étampes, the *quatre-feuilles* design; the octagon as at Provins, the donjon there being flanked with towers, and surmounted by a sloping, pointed roof. At Gisors a polygonal tower was grafted on a square donjon.

The square form is seldom very pure: the donjons are more often rectangular, with large counter-forts and with turrets at the angles. But our own architect did not care for all these expedients and compromises, but going ahead of all his contemporaries he resolutely as at Châteaudun adopted the circular form which was to be the chief characteristic of the military architecture of the thirteenth century. So the formula is square donjon in the twelfth, round donjon in the thirteenth century. This rule is absolute, and we must insist upon it somewhat.

The beautiful new tower is there before our eyes, surrounded by the wall which is called the " chemise " of the donjon, below which is a deep ditch. It contains three floors above ground, but underground there are two more. These different storeys are connected by a staircase which is contrived in the thickness of the wall.

On each floor are one or two vaulted chambers with beautiful arched windows; delightful from without, these artistic bays are somewhat gloomy within. In consequence of the thickness of the walls these windows open at the extremity of a kind of corridor about eight or ten feet long, and are sometimes so lofty that a staircase is needed to gain access to them.

In the palace the great hall—the most important apartment of the princely mansion—occupies the whole of the first floor of the vast rectangular building which is independent of the donjon : but in the ordinary castle the hall modestly occupies the first floor of the keep itself. Here the vassals pay homage, the troubadours recite, the musicians play : games of chess are also played here, and here dinner is served. If the baron and his wife do not sleep in it they occupy a chamber on the second floor, their children and guests are lodged on the third floor. In the basement are other guest-chambers, badly lighted, but convenient for invalids. Descending some twenty or thirty steps farther, with a candle, we shall find an iron door of very lugubrious aspect. If we turn the heavy key we shall find ourselves in a badly-lighted, loopholed chamber with earthen floor only; this is the prison (the dungeon).

Poets delight in giving descriptions of these places—descriptions which make one's hair stand on end! They delight in strewing the earthy floor with snakes and toads, thorns and briers which tear the clothes and the flesh of the unhappy prisoners. Those were barbarous times if our *chansons* are to be credited. The barons of those days seem to have blindfolded their prisoners as if there was too much light in the prison: they tied their hands behind their backs, placed them in the pillory or put iron collars on their necks, and loaded them with chains. They tortured them in every conceivable way, permitted the rain-water to accumulate in the dungeon until the poor victim was half drowned, and threw them only a crust, or some dried meat, to sustain their miserable existence. They were guarded by a warder who seldom permitted himself to pity them, or to accept a bribe. We referred just now to the legends of the gate, but what are we to say of the legends of the prison! They are no less heroic or touching. Let us see.

I am no admirer of the sensual and silly romance of *Fierabras*, and it makes one angry to think that its foolish, even disgusting, verses were chanted in honour of the relics of the Passion during the celebrated fair of Lendit at Saint Denis in France. But there is a picturesque scene in which Floripas, the beautiful pagan woman, is described as descending into the deep dungeon in which the French prisoners were incarcerated. To reach them it was necessary to kill the warder: she killed him, and the unhappy wretch fell heavily to the ground. Then she lighted a taper and hiding her head behind a pillar conversed with the prisoners regarding their escape. For a painter here is a splendid effect of light and shade.

Ogier is perhaps less poetic when sketched in his dungeon in the prison at Reims, he has terrible combats "with rats and tortoises." At length people believed him dead, and menaced by the Saracen Brehier they cried "O! if Ogier were only living now! If he were only amongst us." Then all the squires went about, even to the tent of the emperor, crying, "Ogier, Ogier, Ogier!" He had previously condemned the knight, and he released him. Ogier conquered Brehier, killed him, and saved France.

But after all to Remir and his wife Erembourc must be attributed the most heroic endurance of all the prisoners in our national epics. A traitor, Fromont by name, tried to compel these faithful vassals to deliver up to him the youthful son of their liege-lord, Girard de Blaives, who had died. The pair firmly refused to do so, so the traitor flung the husband into prison on a bed of thorns, where his wife was soon compelled to join him.

"Now will you render me the child? Give him up and you shall be free."

But they refused, so he devised a horrible torture. He gave orders that the husband only should receive food, and that the wife should be starved to death before his eyes. Nevertheless, their souls never wavered, and Erembourc assumed an attitude worthy even of the mother of the Maccabees. "For Heaven's sake," she cried to her husband, " do not betray the son of your lord."

When Fromont found that he could not prevail he let them lie in prison for a year. Then, believing that they would think better of his proposal after such an experience, and that at any rate they would be greatly weakened, he sent squires to beat them if recalcitrant. Remir, however, was still strong enough to kill three of his assailants, but this final effort exhausted his energies.

"Suppose we make a truce?" he said. "Let us agree with Fromont. Then Erembourc was angry, and said: "What do you say? What are you thinking of? You are mad! You are forgetting God! If you commit such a crime as that all Christians, young and old, will point at you saying: 'There goes the man who, for fear of death, betrayed his liege-lord. Look at him!'"

Then in a solemn tone she continued—

"The day of judgment will surely come; do not forget it! On that day all traitors, *all* traitors, will be condemned; for, on high, remember riches and fine raiment count for nothing, and happy will he be who enters Paradise!"

Subsequently this heroic woman—heroic beyond humanity— proposed to her husband that they should deliver up their own child instead of the son of their lord. We can find nothing more noble than this sacrifice and devotion of Erembourc. . . . .

The prison is underground, but it is not the only subterranean place mentioned in our poems. Even to this day, when tourists visit an old castle, the cicerone hardly ever fails to point out "that people do say that there used to be an underground passage here, which communicated with the open country, only we cannot discover the entrance!" Here we may recall the celebrated remark of Bossuet, "that every error is only an abuse of the truth." It is quite certain that these subterranean passages exist, or did exist. Viollet le Duc has proved their existence at Arques, which is a building dating from the eleventh century, and at Coucy, which is of the thirteenth. "At Coucy the foundations of the castle are traversed by numerous and vast subterranean passages, which appear to have been arranged systematically in order to provide for communication between all points of the defence, interiorly and exteriorly. Tradition says that one of these concealed passages leads to the Abbey of Primontré."

Note the word "tradition." The popular imagination clings to the subterranean passage. We find it everywhere—in the Tuileries, which the people invaded, beneath the churches which they desecrated, and they have made it the scene of crimes as abominable as mysterious. Our poets on this point share the prejudices of the populace; they have used and abused the underground galleries. In them they find the *dénoûement* which they have long been seeking. Shut up in some castle with some lovely fair-haired princess, besieged, blockaded, lost, apparently, our hero suddenly discovers the door leading to an underground passage, and thereby escapes. He marries the princess—and there the romance ends!

These *boves* of our poems are supposed to be very ancient: they are said to be a thousand years old, and are attributed to the Arabs. Here the scientific research of the Middle Ages is again shown to be very small. Any monument, the origin of which could not be traced, was then attributed to the Saracens or to Julius Cæsar. At Orange there is one of these subterranean passages which extends as far as the Rhône; at Castlefort there is another very much of the same character which serves as the communication between the castle and the town. At Montauban there exists a "bove" which leads from the donjon far into the fields. This last gallery has a history, and is worth exploring and explanation.

The sons of Aymon had been for a very long while besieged

in their stronghold. The assailants, not being able to force an entrance to the castle, determined to starve out the garrison, and famine would then overcome the obstinate resistance of Renaud and his brothers. There was no more meat, no more wine, the bread was made only of vetches and lentils. The children grew pale and wan, and the seniors began to think of killing the famous charger Bayard! This seems almost incredible, does it not? But they only bled him, and for fifteen days they existed on the blood of the noble steed. After that time the horse was merely a mass of skin and bone. The majority of the besieged were dead, the charnel-house at the castle gate was full of bodies. Renaud's wife could see her two children dying in her arms, and she cried, " I will eat my hands, for my heart fails me! " Death, and what a death! stared them in the face.

In this extremity Providence came to their assistance, and sent to them an aged man, bent nearly double, who showed Renaud the entrance to the secret passage which would lead him and his companions to the borders of the wood of Serpente. The good duke uttered a cry of joy, and began his retreat, putting Bayard foremost into the cavern, he thought of his steed first, then his wife, his children, and his brothers. They lighted tapers, and this illumination of the thick darkness put some spirit into the poor people, who had thought all was lost. Suddenly Renaud halted, and said :

" We have forgotten the traitor, my brother-in-law, King Yon, who is in the prison yonder."

" Let him stay there," replied the duchess, who was the prisoner's own sister, and by no means sentimental.

" No, no," exclaimed Renaud. " Whatever his misdeeds towards us, I am none the less his vassal, and, so long as I live, I will not consent to let him die in such a manner! "

With that he retraced his steps, descended into the prison, and released the captive King Yon, who was in dire extremity. He pushed him before him along the passage, and rejoined his wife and brothers, who declared that such a good man as Renaud never lived. Some time afterwards a ray of light broke into the passage; it was the daylight, and they managed to get out in the early morning. They were saved!

Now, as they have emerged in safety, we may come out also, and return once more to our donjon, for the last time. We have made ourselves acquainted with it all except the summit.

On this platform the architect has built the watch-tower, which commands an extensive view. This stone sentry-box dates from the twelfth century, and was called the *eschangaite* or *gaite*, and the builder derived it from the donjon of Provins. Other architects have disposed the *eschangaites* in other fashions in other situations. They have built them out, along a " curtain," so as to facilitate surveillance from the flanks, and give them the form of elegant turrets, sometimes square, sometimes rounded, jutting out from the main towers, and overlooking the highest points. In important fortresses a special watch-tower was erected, as at Carcassonne for instance. But, wherever the watch-tower was, the duty of watchman was heavy, and one of the greatest hardships which castellans could impose on their retainers.

On the corporation seal of Rochester we shall find the representation of a watchman blowing the horn, for by that means he had to announce daybreak and curfew. When people went out hunting and when they returned, he also blew the horn. They were very fair musicians, and it was pleasant to hear them morning and evening. But this is the poetical side of the business, the utility was somewhat different in kind—thus :

To signal the approach of the enemy as far as he could possibly see, was one duty, and that was a great deal. A good watchman was bound to have a quick ear and good eye. But what did it matter? Notwithstanding all precautions, the shutting out of air, the provision of warmth, the watch-towers very quickly "took it out " of the unfortunate men who had to remain on duty on winter nights, and it was considered a signal mark of devotion towards a damsel if a knight like Gautier d'Aupais " watched for love."

There is nothing particular on the summit of the tower except the banner of the baron which floats proudly in all winds and dominates every other pennon. When the baron is obliged to capitulate he ascends to the tower, and with tears in his eyes snatches the flag from the staff and casts the banner into the ditch. But the platform of the donjon serves another purpose ; people are hanged there. Yes, when Ogier, at Castlefort, inflicted punishment upon the traitors, he hanged them first, and then he swung them on gibbets, so that people could behold the bodies swinging to and fro in the air from a considerable distance.

The banner, however, always floated on high, a bright banner pleasant to behold, which, in a measure, consoled us for the sight of the pendant corpses. But this banner is not the golden eagle, for it appertains chiefly to the *palace*.

Few historians have drawn the proper distinction between the castle and the palace, and to Viollet le Duc the honour of confirming this distinction is due. He has put them in the proper light. The most modest of knights may have a donjon, the most humble of seigneurs may possess a castle, but the palace is the Royal, the sovereign residence. " *It is the place in which the sovereign administers justice,*" and all rulers possess in the capitals of their kingdoms a palace, " the essential part of which is always the *great hall.*" This distinction cannot be better expressed than by our eminent archæologist. The difference is immense. The castle is above all things military, it is a lair, a refuge. If luxury finds its way thither, it is very slowly, and, besides, wrongly. But the palace is the open symbol of power and authority. Before Feudalism was born, kings and emperors only possessed palaces. Dukes and earls of the ninth century robbed them of this and many other privileges, and these impudent usurpers claimed the right to have *their* palace and *their* carriage. A robbery sanctioned by time, but robbery all the same !

The Suzerainity is confused with the Sovereignty, the authority with ownership. Justice which ought to be rendered in the name of the king is improperly rendered in the name of these ancient functionaries of royalty—of those dukes and earls who, under Charles the Bold and his successors, illegitimately usurped the central power and put themselves in its place. Now the palace is first the " Palace of Justice," and it behoves us to understand the significance of these words. There is a palace, where was formerly a *moll* presided over by a Merovingian or Carlovingian court, surrounded by his *rachinbourgs* or his *scabins.* Everywhere else it is a castle.

Such is the true, the real definition of the *palace*, and, by this, we can interpret the term *principal* which is so frequently united with the word palace. The *palais principal* of our songs or poems, in the *palatium principis*. But the sense has lost something of its strictness and has undergone inevitable deviations and extensions. Every marquis wishes to have pages; every petty prince wants ambassadors : so in time it came to pass that simple castellans wished to give themselves the luxury, in their inner courts, of the beautiful rectangular hall which is the characteristic of the palace. On the other hand, and more frequently still, the suzerains felt that their palaces required to be fortified, and they furnished them with the keep which characterises the castle. These applications caused considerable confusion, but the primary idea is none the less certain, and must be retained.

Nevertheless, it is necessary to cite one or two examples, and we will select, if you please, the palace of Wartburg in Germany, and the beautiful palace of Troyes in France which ceased in 1220 to be the abode of counts, and it is at present writing non-existent. We can picture it as a rectangular building, attached to the church of St. Stephen, which served it as a chapel, with a square tower which served as treasury and donjon, bounded by a garden on the south, and by an open square on the north side, and including above the ground floor a whole line of chambers which flanked one of the sides of the great hall, and looked upon an arm of the Seine. But these are mere details, for the most attractive part of the palace was the great hall itself with its beautiful staircase. It seems as if the palace had been built for the hall. It was not less than twenty-four métres wide, and fifty-two in length : about seventy-five feet by one hundred and sixty feet.

At Poitiers the palace, which displays all the characteristics of the twelfth century architecture, is also in the form of a parallelogram, and has three vaulted floors.

At Wartburg palace there are only two stories, but there is also a kind of gallery on the ground floor like that described by the author of Girart de Roussillon. "When you enter Roussillon there is a staircase and a gallery all round, of which the pillars, the columns, and even the joists are studded with sardonyxes! " I do not think that any one would have invented this characteristic. It is a striking comparison.

If we would picture a great hall we must carry our thoughts back to the beautiful hospital halls of the twelfth and thirteenth centuries. The hall was generally a rectangular space divided into two or three parts lengthwise by one or two ranges of pillars, at once bold and elegant. The hall was vaulted like a church, with a flat, gilt and frescoed ceiling. But we need not discuss it further here; we shall have occasion to return to it.

The roof is of slate or enamelled tiles, surmounted with a crest of lead, and, symbolical of jurisdiction and power, the grand golden eagle sparkles in the sunbeams.

The flight of steps is common to both palace and castle, and we must examine the exterior stairway which gives access to the great hall of the palace, and to the hall of the castle.

The origin of the stairway is well known: it is a transference into stone or marble of the primitive wooden bridge, of the moveable gangway which was sufficient for the castellan of the ninth and tenth centuries, and led him from his donjon, over the court and the walls, to the open country. The flight of steps retained the title of plank, (*plancher*) for a long time; the first *planchers* were virtually wooden staircases (or gangways).

The word itself signified merely a block of stone at first; in this sense the word "*perron*," is used in *Roland* and in other poems. This single or double or triple flight of steps was furnished with balustrades and shaded by trees, pines, olive-trees, and twining vines. Its proportions also varied considerably. At the palace of Troyes it was very wide, at Wartburg it is narrow, but whatever its dimensions, it served many purposes which it will not be out of place to detail. Whoever is not acquainted with them cannot comprehend the Feudal life. It concentrates itself on the steps.

On the "*perron*" the lord of the castle sometimes administered justice, and its fine platform was then regarded as a continuation of the great hall which was at once the symbol and the home of seigneurial justice. It was no unusual thing to hold on the steps one of those courts, in which the vassals were solemnly judged by their peers; but in summer the baron was pleased to seat himself on the top of the steps, and arrange any little disputes which may have arisen amongst the inmates of the castle. These steps have even been the scene of more severe and important decisions than these, and one day an officer having maladministered justice to a *vilein*, the baron from the top of the perron admonished him severely, deprived him of his charge, and expelled him from his fief. The man died of shame.

From these steps solemn addresses were frequently delivered. The clergy would carry thither the golden reliquary from the neighbouring monastery, the beautiful shrine which in miniature represented the chapel of the castle, in which was enclosed one of the fingers of the apostle and patron of the whole county. One day when our knight was starting on a lengthy pilgrimage, he convoked his vassals, and made them swear that they would be faithful to his wife and children during his absence. That great day is still remembered at the time we are supposed to visit the castle, and the appearance of the golden shrine illuminated by the brilliant sunlight, at the moment when the priest was administering the oath, is an incident not to be forgotten. None of the vassals broke their pledge.

Within the shadow of this monumental flight of steps new knights were created, and when the words "Be brave" were pronounced the horn was sounded from the summit of the steps to call the men-at-arms, and to assemble the body of defending troops. On the same place in times of war the enemy's envoys who came to treat with the baron were disarmed, and here the baron himself delivered to his own messengers, or perchance to his son, his final directions, pacific or warlike, as the case might be.

But the flight of steps not only served for these judicial, clerical, or military uses, it had another object which was less official. The baron would seat himself there on the fine summer evenings and enjoy the fresh air with his family under the great elm tree, which formed a verdant tent overhead. There he received his guests and embraced them on their arrival and departure. What laughter, what kisses, what tears were there! There were witnessed the sadness of leave-taking, and the gladness of meeting again. At the bottom of this fine marble staircase were the squires and officers appointed to receive the guests. They hastened to meet them, assisted them to alight from their palfreys, took their steeds to the stables, if the visitors intended to remain, but merely tethered them to iron rings if it was only a short visit. Flesh is weak, and the attendants were not perfect men, they usually attached themselves to the best dressed of the new comers. You remember when William of Orange came to beg the Emperor to have pity on Christendom and France, how he was received because he arrived unkempt and in torn vestments. They fled from him as from a leper and ridiculed him. So he remained alone, abandoned by all at the bottom of the steps, he the liberator of the Church, the prop of the Empire, the King-maker; William himself.

Our typical knight is aware of this incident and has had it engraved on the exterior face of the steps. It is somewhat coarsely executed, but quite understandable, and the baron shows it to all his guests. The intention is very praiseworthy, but the baron is somewhat mistaken if he imagines that he has inflicted a mortal blow on human ingratitude!

But however great may be the beauty of the architecture, " superior to all that the architect has produced in the Middle Ages," we are compelled to admit that a sojourn in the castle was not free from weariness. I am aware that the great hall had been sumptuous, and that, as we shall see later on, the other apartments have been well arranged, decorated with paintings, &c. But these thick walls—eight to ten feet thick, these windows made in the anticipation of a siege, which admitted a very small amount of light, the prospect of " curtain " and turrets—all these elements of a life, principally military, were not calculated to impose rest upon our barons, to please their wives or to amuse their children. They quite understood it too, and without the castle, beyond the fortifications, under the castle walls, they planted pleasure gardens wherein they breathed the fresh air and listened to music. This was the orchard.

That orchards were so planted we have abundant evidence in our *chansons de geste.* According to local circumstances they were planted near the donjon, sometimes near the barbican or bastion. We must not imagine that these were gardens in the modern sense of the word, but simply enclosures filled with fruit trees and a few flowers and shrubs. Birds came there gladly, and there the baron learnt to distinguish between the different songsters. They called them *ors* and *abresses (arboritas).* All around, save where the castle stood, were fields and meadows, and the planted garden.

The descent from the castle to the garden was through a false

postern.   By this passed out the mother of the four sons of Aymon
when she bade adieu to her children who had been abandoned by
their father in a cowardly manner.   By the same means did
Rosamond, the beautiful, descend to succour Elias of Saint-Gilles
wounded, insensible, half dead: and the poet adds that through
this same gate that "young pagan" went out in May to gather
flowers with her daughters.

In such a monotonous existence the orchard occupied a considerable space : but not always for amusement.   In summer time
councils were held there instead of in the great hall.   The *chanson*
of *Roland* opens with two admirable scenes both of which are laid
in the orchard.   There one day did Marsile decide to send
messengers to Charles : under those fine trees did the emperor
receive the ten ambassadors of the last pagan king of Spain.
This picture is imposing.   Fifteen thousand Frenchmen in satin
tunics are stretched upon the white carpet.   The king is seated on
a massive gold throne, from which he overlooks all the barons with a
gravity almost priestly: then suddenly the ten infidels enter the
garden and make their way slowly through the crowd; they are
mounted on white mules the bridles of which are of gold and the
saddles of silver.   They carry olive-branches in their hands, Eastern
fashion, as a token of peace.   It is a scene worthy of Virgil.

But the orchard recalls to us other incidents—touching or sad ;
and, since before entering the castle it is best to be well acquainted
with its surroundings, we will pause for a few moments to consider
these original and charming scenes.

It was in the orchard that the prologue of the popular drama
Macaire was played.   This drama is now known as the "Dog of
Montargis."   It happened some days after Easter, at a feast of the
good baron Requier in the full spring-time.   The pure and beautiful
young Queen of France, whose character was as spotless as her
name, Blanchefleur, was in the garden with her ladies, and a
minstrel was chanting a song to them.   Suddenly comes the traitor
—a kind of Don Juan of the period, who desires at any risk to
triumph over such innocence.   "There is no one," whispers this
Macaire " so beautiful as thou art.   But how unlucky you are in
having such a husband ! "

He continued to make love to her, to flatter and to tempt her ;

Blanchefleur began to think that the baron only thus addressed her to try her powers of resistance, but she soon understood his real drift, and replied in indignant and scathing terms. "Rather than harbour a single thought against the king, I would be cut in pieces or burned alive. My lord shall know all, and will punish you as you deserve. Begone from my presence!"

The wretch hurried away, but that same day he formed the resolution to ruin the queen.

It was also in an orchard that one of the early adventures of that savage hero, Aubri le Bourguignon, occurred. It was at the court of King Orri that Queen Gibourc took a fancy to him; she and her daughter quarrelled about him. The two sons of Orri made up their minds to revenge their father's dishonour, and prepared an ambush for Aubri; they proposed to cudgel him first as an appetiser. At the first blow, one of them deluged Aubri in blood, but he, seizing the cudgel, drove it into his adversary's brain with terrific force; then the giant stretched Congré, that was the name of Orri's son, dead on the sward. The brother fled panic-stricken, but Aubri followed him and cleft him to the breast-bone with his sword. Gasselin, Aubri's nephew, was the only witness of this butchery, and in vain endeavoured to calm the giant's rage. The sward of the orchard was steeped in gore.

It was in the orchard that Jourdain de Blaives, one morning, called to mind the death of Girard, his father, who had been assassinated by the traitor Fromont, and made a resolution to avenge him. In another meadow, Gilbert, a prisoner of the Saracens at Orange, found William there, recounted to him all the wonders of that incomparable city, and gave the "terrible count" the idea of taking possession of it. It was in an orchard that the Count Amis, who had been separated from his wife for seven years, suddenly took it into his head to go and see her again. "Amis heard the *noise* and the cries of the birds. They reminded him of his native place, of his wife and infant son; and he wept tenderly."

Before entering the castle, we had only to see the orchard, and we have now done so. We have only now to knock on the loud-resounding copper-plate at the baron's door. Let us, however, take one last glance around on the donjon and its two courts; on the walls and the towers, on the lists and the palisades, on the gateway and the bridge.   For the last time let us grasp the whole of this picture, and engrave it on our memory.

Such as it is, the castle is the object of a great love! All our knights resemble, more or less, the great Joinville, who, when starting for the Crusade, had not courage to take a last look at the dear walls within which so many happy years had been passed! (*"Je ne voz onques retourner mes yex vers Joinville por ce que le cuer ne me attendrisist du biau chastel que je lessoie!"*)

The eldest of the sons of Aymon, had the same tender feelings when he quitted the paternal dwelling; he wept : " *Quant Renaus s'en parti, de pitié a ploré.*"   In the Holy Land these men thought of the great donjon at home, and their eyes filled with tears.   To all the leaders of the first Crusade the beautiful crown of Jerusalem was offered in vain : everyone thought of his castle, and refused the kingly dignity.   The beloved castle!   It was to them almost a sentient thing, an animated object, they spoke to it and commended it to Heaven!   " *Casteaus, je te comant à Dé!*"   So said Ogier, and Renaud de Montauban is not a whit less tender.   "*Chastiaus,*" said he, "*vos soiés honorés.*"

What grief there was when the knight felt he would never see it more! What joy when he did return! When the sons of Aymon attenuated by hunger, pale with misery and in evil case, made up their minds to seek a resting-place near their mother in the castle of Dordone, they arrived at length, after a long journey, within sight of the dearly-loved donjon and towers! Then their hearts gave way: they recalled all the ills through which they had passed, all the troubles which they had endured; then in pity and in sorrow they fell fainting to the ground!

Now let us enter the castle.

CHAPTER XIII.

THE DOMESTIC LIFE OF THE KNIGHT.—A DAY IN THE LIFE OF A BARON AT END OF THE TWELFTH CENTURY (*continued*).

SIX O'CLOCK A.M.

THE first gleam of dawn is peeping through the shutters of the room in which the knight is sleeping.

Our baron is an early riser, and without flattery we might apply to him the praise bestowed on Charlemagne by a musician of the thirteenth century. *"De main lever estort acoustumés."* There was a curious proverb circulated about early rising : " He who sleeps long in the morning grows thin and lazy." Thin ! We have changed that !

The Seneschal in Courts, the Chamberlain in baronial halls, awakens the ruler—his master. This he accomplishes by beating the pillow on which the sleeper's head reposes. This, and in assisting the baron to dress is his daily duty. It is almost needless to remark that many barons preferred to dress themselves, and to dispense with the services of the chamberlain. They got out of bed, and went at once to the window, opened it, and let in the daylight : then they put on their shoes and dress. This is the usual routine.

The appearance of the room must be sketched. The bed claims our first attention : it is low and wide, the head against the wall; it is shaded by curtains, which run on iron rods. It is rather too luxurious, generally, with its embroidered silk pillows, its ermine counterpane, its three or four feather-beds, its sheets of linen or silk, which the sleeper may tuck round him so as to have some trailing on the stone floor. This floor no doubt is very cold for naked feet, but skins and furs have been laid on it—fox-furs, and such like. Such carpets are more pleasing to the occupant, as they remind him of his exploits in the field and in the forest. Besides, he does not want his well-laid and enamelled bricks, with their quaint designs altogether hidden : he is very proud of his tiled floor as he is of his pictures, in red and yellow ochre, touched up with dark blue and black, which cover the walls of the vast room, &c., and represent all the birds of the air, and all the fishes of the sea. "It is quite a Noah's ark," he will say, smiling.

There was little or no gold in the twelfth century, but the metal had its revenge in the following cycle. There are seats along the walls of the chamber, curtains on moveable screens in front of the windows; near the bed a great candlestick, in which a big wax candle burns all the night. There are other objects, such as rails on which the articles of clothing or accoutrements are hung, and an image of his patron saint completes our cavalier's decorations. A lighted taper illumines the features of a Saint Peter, who invites to repentance and faith! while a gigantic figure of Saint Christopher is painted at the right hand side of the bolted door. The knight is pleased when this painting meets his waking eyes, as he knows that "when one sees the image of Saint Christopher in the morning no ill shall befall him during the day. So I am safe for another day!"

Most of us are aware that during the greater part of the Middle Ages people went naked into bed. This is attested by our chroniclers, our songs and our miniatures. We shall not be surprised to learn that our barons began to put on their clothing in bed, and this was not from laziness but for modesty's sake.

We have not said anything about their ablutions, nevertheless washing was not such a small thing nor so indifferent to them as one might suppose. It has pleased a great historian (Michelet) to pronounce a judgment in a few words, "not a bath in a thousand years!" But passion is always a bad counsellor, and it has inspired that writer with wrong notions altogether. As a matter of fact our ancestors were very fond of water; they were passionately fond of bathing, and in fact used baths more than we do. Hardly had the baron inducted himself into his shirt and his shoes than his pages entered, carrying fresh water in a metal basin and a fine white towel. Before and after each meal there was more washing, and we may affirm that both knight and townsman of the twelfth century washed their hands five and six times a day. This was something.

As regards the bath it was more than a custom—it was a passion. Mind, I am not now speaking of the bath which was one of the sacramental rites of Chivalry, and which the newly-dubbed knight remembered all his life. No, I am merely referring to the ordinary daily life, not to the symbolism of Chivalry. In the donjons were underground chambers which in a few minutes could be transformed into bath-rooms; but we must not expect anything refined or luxurious there. The baths were only tubs or troughs, but the "bath" itself, the bathing, was refined. It was replenished, and "aromatised," all sorts of herbs and scents were

The Morning Prayer.

introduced. These elegant dips were taken under all conceivable circumstances, and when there were no extenuating circumstances at all—merely for the pleasure of it. After illness a bath was used, and after a journey: for journeys in those days were both long and laborious, and in a bath one first found rest.

When the unfortunate mother of the four sons of Aymon met her children emaciated with hunger, and shivering in misery, she said, "I will go and prepare the bath; the first thing for you is the bath;" and she made it ready in her own room. I am most surprised about the after-dinner bath which is so frequently mentioned in our old poems, and I leave to physiologists and

physicians the question of its healthiness or harmfulness.   But as
the reader will perceive, the bath was in use everywhere.   Women
took it as well as men, and the most solemn were those baths on
the eve of, and on the morning after marriage.   They even went so
far as to indulge in the wicked luxury of bathing in company with
their husbands, with the chaplets of wedding flowers on their
heads.   This was a dangerous and evil innovation, and tended to
revive the detestable abuses which had formerly furnished the
church with so many weapons against the practices of the Romans.
But it seems that the later imitations were yet far from such
excesses, and that they had the sense to stop in time.

But however that may be, our baron takes a safe middle course :
he neither abuses the bath nor uses it too sparingly.   He does not
wish to be classed with the individual of whom Aye d'Avignon declared " He has not bathed for a year," and still less does he desire
to be compared with the page mentioned in Garin de Loherain—
" He was unshaven, with a face black as coal, and the only water
with which he was acquainted fell from Heaven."   This very gross
caricature was drawn purposely to excite the indignation and ridicule of the majority of the castellans.   They did laugh heartily, and
bathed all the more assiduously.

We have already described the toilette of our baron, but let us
not leave him now : Let us witness the most significant and the
most noble act of the day—of his life !   Scarcely has he performed
his ablutions when he prays.   The attitude and posture of prayer
was not then the same as at present.   We kneel down—our ancestors prostrated themselves.   This was the adoration of the Eastern
peoples, the grand character of profound humility, the entire and
voluntary surrender and abrogation of self.   Our liturgy still retains
traces of it.   The knights of the twelfth century, in their most
simple devotions, lay down on the ground with outstretched arms,
their heads to the East.   It is true that they were then beginning
to exercise a semi-adoration, and adopting a very humble kneeling
position.   This was the transition to the ordinary kneeling which
has come into vogue, and remains in our daily practice.   But the
proudest barons of the time of Louis VII., or even of Philip
Augustus, kings, emperors, &c., prostrated themselves and wor-
shipped with their hands extended towards the East: " *lor manis
vers Oriant.*"

The magnificent attitude of prayer of the early Christians, the attitude of *orantes* praying standing, their arms extended to Heaven —this traditional posture was still adopted in the twelfth century, and in these circumstances the prayer was necessarily shorter, without being less fervent or less solemn. Again, we find in our old poems examples of the present attitude, the man on his knees with bent head and clasped hands. All these positions are equally sculptural, equally beautiful, and recall the grand sentence which states that " a man is never so great as when he is upon his knees." *

But after all, when praying, the attitude is only a secondary consideration. How did our knights pray ? That is the real question, and one not easily to be solved. I am convinced for my part, that there were two styles, one which I will call the " clerical " the other the secular, or, if I may say so, " laical." These were equally Christian methods, but not of the same fashion. The clerical prayers were theological, exact, often mystic. The " lay " prayers consisted chiefly of a string of facts—historical or legendary, which were culled from the Bible or Apocrypha, and amalgamated without arrangement or order. " If it be true that I believe all these miracles grant me, O Lord, the grace for which I pray " they would say. The clerical prayers have been preserved to us in French or Latin, in those Books of Hours of which millions of copies have circulated from the thirteenth to the sixteenth century. The " lay " prayers have been preserved in our epic poetry. A certain number of our knights prayed like the heroes of these poems, others prayed like the clergy—that's all.

So our baron plunges into prayer, and he is one of those, if you please, who are not inspired with the science of their chaplains, but by the memories of childhood, the familiar teaching of their mothers, and the poems which they have heard. There is nothing of the philosopher in the orison in which he endeavours to sum up all the religious history of the race. He begins by saluting the Glorious Father who created the world, and fashioned Adam of clay, with his spouse Eve. Then he recounts after his own fashion, the drama of the Fall, and how our first parents were thrown into the pit of Baratron with the fiends Berzebu and Nero. He pauses a moment on the murder of Abel, who's blood " reddens

* The word "grand " in the original, meaning (equally) "great " or "tall," gives the sentence greater force.

the waning moon" to this day, and contemplates for a longer
period the face of "Baron Abraham," whose son was raised up to
Heaven "amongst the Innocents," at the moment when he was
about to be sacrificed by his father !

"'Tis thou," cries the knight to his Creater, "who didst deliver Jonah from the whale which had swallowed him. Thou
who didst save the King of Nineveh, with the city and all its inhabitants. Thou didst deliver Daniel the Prophet from the den of
lions, and didst preserve the "three children" in the fiery furnace,
and didst defend Susannah against the false witnesses." Then our
baron made a leap from the Old into the New Testament, and
stopped piously at the manger at Bethlehem. He rapidly reviewed
the visit of the Angel and the birth of the Saviour; of the ox which
bowed so gently and profoundly before the Christ-child; of the
three kings, the wise men, who came from the East; and of the
woman without hands who came to the assistance of the Virgin in
the stable, and who by a miracle immediately became possessed of
beautiful hands. "It is thou, Lord, who raised Saint Lazarus, and
established Saint Peter as sovereign in the gardens of Nero."

Then, as the baron has committed some gross sins—not to men-
tion small ones—he never forgets to name in his prayers the
Magdalen who is the patron of all true penitents. "She approached
Thee softly, unobserved, and in default of any other water bathed
Thy feet with her tears." Then he passes on to commemorate the
Passion, which is the corner-stone of his faith, and follows the
incidents from the entry into Jerusalem "in great humility," to
Golgotha. A personage to whom the Evangelists accord only an un-
important part, the Centurion, Longinus, now becomes the subject
of a stupendous miracle which occurs in most of our epic prayers.
"When the centurion struck Thee with his lance he became blind,
but the blood, flowing adown the lance-pole, reached his eyes and
straightway he saw again."

After this little remains to be added. The knight speaks briefly
of the resurrection and of the breaking of the Gates of Hell
"whence He will deliver all His friends. Thou didst ascend into
Heaven, but Thou shalt appear at the Judgment. Then shall
princes and dukes tremble like leaves. In that the father shall be
no more than the child, nor the priest more than the acolyte,
neither the archbishop greater than the lad." Having thus

finished the theoretic exposition of his creed, our baron begins to think of himself. " I cast myself on Thy bounty and protection," and then he adds with a certain satisfaction which might easily become pride—" I confide also in the heart which Thou hast given me, in my good sword, and in my swift steed." He closes rapidly with the following—" If what I have said be true ; if it be true, O Lord, that I believe it loyally and faithfully, hear those prayers which are offered up for me by our Lady in Paradise ! All glory to Thee, Father ; my arm and my heart I consecrate to Thee."

We have condensed into a couple of pages more than one hundred prayers of our epic poems. It must be added that these " epic orisons " are very brief—shorter than our *précis*, and that our barons generally only took a single theme—the Nativity or the Passion : the Fall of Man, or the incident of the Magdalen. From this point of view it would be easy to draw up a classification which would be very curious and truly scientific.

Such were the lay prayers, but the " clerical " devotions which were recited after dictation by a priest, or read from the missal— were of a much more elevated character. There was less of superstition and more of theology in them ; less fact, more doctrine ; less legend, more learning. But we must not confound the somewhat simple prayers of our poems with the beautiful *Pater*-noster in verse (12th century), nor with the *Obsessio*, which from the thirteenth to the sixteenth is met with in the hundreds of " Books of Hours." No, the two currents flowed side by side. The knights could choose either style of prayer, but it was not given to anyone to mingle them.

When his devotions were finished, the knight, whose feelings of piety were not satisfied by his orisons, proceeded to attend mass. He went every morning without distinction, and recalled his father's injunctions in this respect, to hear mass daily in the morning. Most frequently he went to the nearest monastery, but even at that time many castles possessed chapels of their own. This chapel was in the upper court ; it was small and low beneath the donjon. In the eleventh century it was erected against the wall of the great tower, or rather it was situated, as at Falaise and at Loches, in one of the buildings—one of those towers which formed the antechambers of certain donjons.

This arrangement possessed the great advantage that the baron was not compelled to go out of doors. But in the twelfth century these humble chapels were not approved of; the barons wished for churches in miniature, not rooms appropriated to devotion, to which they gave a character of great simplicity. Seldom were there any ornaments or luxury as in the chapel of the Castle of Montargis. Such a simple chapel our typical baron enters hand in hand with one of his guests. On fête days he went, in greater state, to the neighbouring monastery-church preceded by minstrels.

The castle mass seems to have been chanted generally, but we must not suppose that the church possessed a choir and choristers. The chaplain chanted the *Gloria,* the *Preface,* and the *Pater ;* no more on ordinary occasions. I do not believe that the baron made a daily offering at his own chapel. These offerings in money or in kind, which are so frequently mentioned in our songs, were made in the parish churches, the convents, and "pilgrimages," Sundays and fête days, or on certain solemn occasions. It is likewise an error to represent the knight and his spouse holding some beautiful Books of Hours, "ornamented with costly miniatures." In the twelfth century, and at the beginning of the thirteenth, these "prayerbooks" were very uncommon in the hands of the laity ; and besides, the few and narrow windows of the chapels gave too little light for reading ; so the barons listened to mass, their eyes fixed on the altar, with only their hearts' enthusiasm to carry them through the service.

Sometimes it seems that the daily mass was followed by a sermon, but this was only in the monasteries. One of these very sermons gave rise to an adventure which is very well described by one of the troubadours. It refers to the wild Aubri the Burgundian, who wedded the widow of King Oui, Gibourc. It seems that one morning, awakening very early, the baron missed from his bed his wife! He was in a fury and madly jealous, and in this latter characteristic he resembled all other "Don Juans," he could not bear any interference. He raged and swore that women were at the bottom of all mischief; but these more or less philosophical reflections did not suffice. He dressed hurriedly and went out by the banks of the river. It was a lovely morning, the birds were singing and all was joyous. The miserable Aubri recalled his youthful days, his boyish loves, and the time when he laid his lance at rest for beautiful dames, and when he preferred a pretty green hat or a new girdle to a hundred marks of good French silver. The blood coursed hotly through his veins, and he spoke out like an idiot to the fishes which swam in the stream, and to the birds which flew around him. He compared their lot with his own, their loves and that of his wife Gibourc, who was, no doubt, favouring a new lover—" the wicked, abandoned woman ! " As he gave vent to these expressions of rage he quite forgot that he was leaning against a tree on the brink of the river ; the branch snapped and precipitated him into the water. He scrambled out as well as he could, grumbling.

Meantime his wife, who with two attendants had been to early mass, was quietly returning home. She reached the sleeping-chamber. No Aubri ! A new scene of jealousy began immediately. " He has gone off to amuse himself with another ! I will seek him out." She rose, re-dressed in haste and in anger, went out of doors, and the first person she encountered was the wretched Burgundian, dripping wet, but still in a terrible rage. Each abused the other roundly for a while, but an explanation quickly ensued.

" I only went to mass," said the lady, " and I did not think you would miss me. The preacher was excellent, and discoursed concerning Saint Lawrence, who permitted himself to be grilled for the faith. I waited for the sermon, and this is the cause of all our mischances. You can inquire the truth from the priests at the monastery ! " This explanation was sufficient for the baron : he smiled, and embraced his wife. " Which," says the poet, " is the best thing to do under such circumstances." We do not wish to contradict him.

Now the mass is over, and our knight has come from the chapel, and has returned to his chamber. But he has been up an hour and is hungry. People in those days ate a good deal. Three meals were necessary to our baron. In the morning after mass, in the middle of the day, and before bed-time. The principal meal was the midday dinner, a heavy repast consisting of many dishes, lasting more than an hour—more than two hours sometimes. The little breakfast was not grand but cheerful, and it was fully enjoyed. A proverb says, that to eat in the morning is a sign of good health. The baron could fully endorse the saying without any effort, and without claiming any merit. Let us wish him a good appetite !

CHAPTER XIV.

THE DOMESTIC LIFE OF THE KNIGHT.—A DAY IN THE LIFE OF A
BARON AT THE END OF THE TWELFTH CENTURY (*continued*).

BEFORE DINNER—THE MORNING.

NOTWITHSTANDING the occupations with which people tried to render it endurable, life in a castle in the twelfth century was extremely monotonous, and terrible *ennui* fell on the knights. The thick walls, the narrow windows, the military solitude of the fortress, became wearisome and trying. The wet, cold wintry days seemed interminable to the ladies and children. But they kept up their spirits, and resolutely battled with weariness. The race was vivacious and cheerful.

The fifteen amusements of the knight in time of peace are less known than the fifteen joys of marriage by Antoine de la Salle. But they deserve at least as much publicity, and, besides, they have nothing in them tending to raillery and paradox. These diversions were :—

To go to all tournaments at any cost ; to hunt, to fish, and walk about in the orchard ; these were at least the amusements which attracted the knight from home. But there were others which did not compel his absence. He sat warming himself in the chimney-corner in winter, or, to get the air, in his orchard in summer. He opened his house to all wandering minstrels, heard all their songs, and formed an orchestra. He gave or took lessons in fencing, and enjoyed the luxury of the combats of wild animals—contests dear to all primitive peoples—fights of wild boars and bears of a sanguinary character. He would play twenty games of chess, interspersed with *tables* and dice. But particularly our baron enjoyed his food, of which he ate heartily, and quickly disposed of his store of wine. These were the amusements of the baron who was forced to remain indoors. They were not particularly refined, as you will perceive, but they were better than flirting with the maids. We cannot help admiring the manner in which the baron regarded as an amusement the obligation of holding his feudal court, and the habit he had adopted of entertaining as many guests as possible. The fifteenth and last relaxation consisted in looking

Arrival of Guests at the Castle.

out of window at the passers-by! That was a delight which never palled.

It was particularly in the forenoon, before the midday meal, that the châtelain found it so difficult to amuse himself, and so these "fifteen joys" found their place in that portion of the day. One of our old poets does not scruple to make an addition to these pleasures, an addition which tends to his credit: "The greater number of our barons did good, voluntarily, by distributing alms—doing the work of Jesus Christ." This pleasure—for it is one—outweighs all the rest. Let us depict faithfully the appearance and the incidents of the castle-life during the time from 8 A.M. till noon.

Firstly, the poor people who are in the habit of coming every morning to the castle as well as to the neighbouring abbey, are relieved by the wife of the baron herself, who is anxious to merit the splendid eulogy bestowed upon the mother of Godfrey de Bouillon : "*Ele revesti povre, et autex recovri.*" The chief patient of the baroness is an elderly woman, bent nearly double. The poor creature's lot is a very hard one, for she has little food and a very wretched home. Nevertheless, no sooner does she receive a small coin from some good man than she purchases tapers to burn in honour of God and Our Lady. But the baroness has many other clients, and she supplies them liberally. Upon her purse she has embroidered the beautiful line of a poet of the period : " The more I give away the richer I become ! "

Then, perhaps, after this will arrive some long-expected guests, who are joyfully welcomed. Scarcely have they crossed the bridge when reverence is done them ; hardly have they dismounted when they are kissed on mouth and chin, for kissing was common with both sexes in those days. If the dignity or the age of the new arrivals demanded more respect, then the people were satisfied with kissing their feet and spurs. After all these embraces, the company approached the steps, talking. Then the travellers were conducted to the vaulted chambers where their beds had been prepared. If there were more guests than beds, some others were fixed up in the dining-room. The new arrivals were assisted to undress and to disarm, they were clothed in new dresses and cloaks of splendid quality, their nether limbs being encased in silk stockings, and their feet in fashionable shoes. If the guests were fatigued they had baths prepared for them. Their horses were led to the stables, and were as well attended to as their masters ; they had no lack of corn, and were even shod—in fact, the castle and stable were equally full. The hospitality was prodigal in its generosity. On certain feast days our barons would throw all the gates open and admit the hungry and the poor, who were all entertained and assisted liberally. Hermits and pilgrims were especially welcomed. " Come in, good people, come in ! Do you require clothing or food ? My seneschal shall serve you, or rather wait, I will serve you myself, 'for the love of God who will judge the world!'" In some such way as this did the mother of the four sons of Aymon receive her children, whom she had not seen for many years, and whom she took for pilgrims at first. But when she at length recognized them, what joy it was !

All mornings at the castle were not so cheerful, though, and, if a battle was proceeding within reasonable distance of the *château*, it frequently happened that a wounded or, perchance, a dying man was carried thither. Sometimes the owner of the castle was himself struck down, and esteemed himself happy if he died in the arms of his household. Everything meanwhile is done to alleviate his condition, the doctor is summoned, unguents, bandages, splints, are prepared, and the external plaister is applied. Some vegetable potions or sedatives complete the primitive treatment, and, if he is to take some beverage, they force open his teeth with a dagger. The women are told to depart, and the patient is encouraged by assurances that he will recover by-and-by—he will be all right soon —just as doctors tell us in the present day, and, as in the present day, sometimes a man recovered. We can instance a very pleasing case in which Girard de Roussillon, after he had been wounded by Charles, was forced to alight at Avignon, under the care of a monk doctor. The room is darkened, silence reigns, no one dares to speak. The light is excluded, the curtains drawn, and Girard, lying on his bed of pain, only thinks of the time when he shall be able to resume the combat. " Let everyone prepare for battle," he cries. This in a few words is the character of the Middle Ages.

It is before the mid-day meal that the baron and his wife have most opportunity to regulate the housekeeping and the arrangements of their large establishment, quite a little world in itself. Every castle represented the palace in miniature. There were the same officers and servitors, charged with the same duties, called by the same titles. This will be clearly seen by the following quotations from two most learned students of the Middle Ages :

" In the castle," says Lacurne de Saint-Palaye, " are offices like those at the King's court." " Every baron," says Quicherat, " had his court." And he adds, "Even if his donjon was only built of wood, the owner lodged and kept there a numerous company of servants, vassals, and domestics."

Feudal France, no doubt, included many of these second-class castles, many thousands of these fire-sides, more or less luminous, of which royalty extinguished or modified the light. Nevertheless we must not be general, the historian must be precise and truthful. Let us suppose, then, that the knight assembles all his household two or three hours before dinner, and passes them in review before him. There they are in line, the "retainers of the castle," as they are called.

The most important of all is the seneschal. He is above all. Nothing is more interesting than the history of the seneschal of our kings; we may recollect that in Latin he was called *dapifer*, a modest and significant name. Ah! here is a functionary, or rather a function, that has made a way in the world. He was first, amongst the Romans, a simple table attendant, perhaps a slave, lately freed. He rose higher in the scale, and was charged with the service of the royal table. Now the Merovingians were in the habit of eating much, and dining in a numerous company. No doubt their rich *prædia*, their fat *villæ*, furnished them with provisions necessary for such a state of things, but it was equally desirable that an able man should administer their resources, and act as Comptroller of the Civil list. This personage was the mayor of the palace, and under him the happy *dapifer*, who in the nature of things succeeded to his office. Then the feudal system was introduced; land was everything, and the administration of the land equally important. The former intendant, the seneschal, became the factotum of the king. Over all the kingdom he maintained the sovereignty, administered justice in the king's name, and assembled the Ban, and lower Ban-royal. He was, in fact, a viceroy, of whom even the king was afraid; so much so that the office was suppressed in 1191, and thenceforth no more mention was made of this other "mayor of the palace," whose authority had at one time alarmed the Capets, then not firmly established.

The seneschals of the barons were less formidable, but they had grown up in office in the same manner, and had the same authority respectively. Sometimes the baron confided his pennon to his seneschal, and their duties got mixed with those of the standard bearer, but even so they had precedence of all the intendants, and that was apparent at dinner, the service of which they had to direct and control. Beneath the master-seneschal came in order the various functionaries of the castle, *longo proximi intervallo*. The marshal was charged with the stable duties, transport and tents.

THE MOTHER RECOGNISES HER SONS IN THE CASTLE.

The chamberlain, or ancient treasurer, was often merged in the chamberlain of the interior; he had charge of the furniture, the supervision of the hall and apartments; there was the butler, or "bottler," whose duties were connected with the vaults and cellars, and a degree lower the "dispenser," who purchased provisions and set out the table. After them came the maitrequeux and the sorqueux—the cooks—who had the control of the kitchen. Still a lower grade were the serjeants and boys, who filled the inferior parts, then the hound-tenders, &c., and the watchman.

But we must not overlook the important personages who often assumed grand airs, the porters and the ushers. The former kept the exterior gates, and the others the interior doors of the castle. It is true that their duties were not always the most agreeable, that they sometimes had to put up with personal chastisement, as in the case of the unfortunate wretch who endeavoured to interfere with the terrible Ogier, who "broke his bones." But they were nevertheless servants of the baron, and must be mentioned if one wishes to know the practice of the middle ages.

Around the lady of the castle were assembled all the chamber women, Aiglentine, Jeannette, and twenty others. They were clad very simply—at least they were in the twelfth century, had no cloaks, nor sleeves hanging down low, but aprons, long and narrow, of embroidered cloth. Coquetry and luxury did not reign in this department until later. These ladies must not be confounded with the damsels (*pucelles*), who dressed the ladies and went with them everywhere. These ladies-in-waiting or maids of honour bore the same relation to the lady as the pages to the knight; they were supposed to be of noble birth; their service was voluntary and transitory; they married early. These two classes must be kept totally distinct.

Amongst all the members of the baron's household there reigned the most complete and charming familiarity, tempered with fear and respect. The servitors spoke to their master with a liberty which required no rebuke. From this point of view I know nothing more striking, nothing more beautiful than the terms of the remonstrance addressed by the Seneschal of Raoul de Cambrai to his brutal master after he had destroyed the convent of Origni, and burned the nuns alive. The wretch did not appear to have any remorse for his acts, and he seated himself at table delighted with the prospect of the dinner which he expected to enjoy. Now this of all days was Good Friday, the most solemn fast-day.

"Bring me roast peacocks," he cried, "swans, *au poivre,* and venison in plenty!"

Then the Seneschal, utterly scandalised, boldly cried out, "What are you thinking of? Is it thus that you deny Christianity and your baptism? This is Good Friday, a day on which all sinners worship. Miserable wretches that we are; we have sinned deeply, terribly; we have burned the nuns, and violated the convent. We shall never be reconciled to God! His pity cannot excuse our cruelty."

The retainers were blindly devoted to their masters. They never argued with him, they loved him. We are all aware what a high place the family servant occupies in Christian families, and we have only to recall our own youthful days to be reminded of those old servants who were so excellent, grumbling occasionally of course, but so proud, and willing to stand by us to the death. There is much simplicity mingled with the savagery of the feudal domestic. When the youthful son of Pepin—he who was subsequently Charles the Great—when this child was menaced and compelled to fly, and conceal his identity, even his name, he had one friend who braved fortune and did not despair, followed him like a faithful dog, protected him, defended him, and procured him food. If Charles quitted France, David would also go; if Charles went to Spain, David also went. If he begged a refuge amongst the infidels, David would even abase himself to that extent, with a view of saving his young master. Over the lion's cub he watched with the tenderness of the lioness: he prevented the young eaglet from roaming too far from the nest; but how he was surprised when he perceived the youth growing up a hero and a knight in defiance of all his care. Charles's first escapade rather troubled poor David; but they did not estrange the old man's love, and he was very proud of the exploits which he only wished had been postponed. David is the type of the feudal retainer.

Even the serfs were capable of devotion which is rare in the present day. Is not the history of those two slaves whom Amis purchased a touching narrative? They did not recoil from the leprosy which was eating away their master. His wife actually turned him out of his castle, when his slaves took him in their arms, and constituted themselves his guardians and guides. We read of the three men crossing the whole extent of France, and arriving at the shrine of St. Giles; then at Rome. The slaves there interceded for their master whom Providence had struck down so terribly, and he could not help feeling better when he beheld such devotion.

But I perceive that amongst the retainers of the baron I have omitted those who in some castles ministered directly to the pleasure of the master. The minstrel or *Jongleur*. Amongst all the domestics he was not perhaps the easiest to control, but he was by no means the last one to devote himself to his employer. We need only turn to Daniel, who substituted his own child for his master's when the traitor had decided on the death of the heir. Daniel witnessed the sacrifice of his own son, whose head was dashed against a pillar. What cruelty, what bloodthirstiness! But he only murmured " My son is dead, but my master's son is alive! " This is of course only a romance, but we must not forget that it was read in every castle, and that the poets usually took their characters from life. Poor Daniel!

After the domestics we should describe the family of the baron; but one of our old poets had done this a hundred times better than we can attempt to do. Here is the picture. " One day Begue was in his castle of Belin; to him his wife, the beautiful Beatrix, came in. The duke kissed her warmly on her lips and cheek. The duchess raised her smiling face and meek. Around the hall the children came and went, and laughed and chattered to their heart's content."

The feudal father was a king, but one who governed his own kingdom with a gentle hand which one would scarcely have expected from a giant cased in steel. It is with a sympathetic tenderness that he looks around on his family, and reads the old poem about Doon to his children—of whom he had twelve, sons, like our typical knight; and it was somewhat difficult to bring up such a large family, but the more there are the more he loves them. Victor Hugo has said that the lion-hearted are fathers. We may apply this saying to our knights, who were tender as brave. When they set off for the far-distant Jerusalem they desired to see their children at the last, and cried with the afflicted Amis: " Show me my son Girard once again."

If their lords are away the ladies weep when they think of them:

DOMESTIC LIFE IN THE MIDDLE AGES.

hold, here is a message from him! The woman, it must be confessed, takes it to heart more than the man; between her husband
and her sons she has always been a mediator and intercessor.   She
would beg money for them when their father was angry, something
in this way: "Pity, in the name of all the saints.   He is our heir.
If we ever go to war with our neighbours, will not he sustain for
our sakes all the fighting and battles?"   The husband always
ended by pardoning the transgressor, for he respected and honoured
his wife, his equal, whom he loved.   No doubt he often has terrible
fits of anger, but he never forgets his marriage.   She is still
beautiful, and her good looks quite illuminate the palace.   One day
the baron met his minstrel, and ordered him to compose a verse
upon the baroness's portrait.   "Ah," replied the minstrel, "you
might well have asked for two."   "Let us have them, then."
"Here they are."   "I am all attention!"

> "La Dame est bele et sage; plaisans, et simple et gaie.
> Nule à son tans; n'est mieudre, blonde, brune, ne baie."

"I prefer the former," said the baron, "and I will keep it.   You
can have the other; it may do for another time."

Around this fine couple the children formed joyous groups.   The
daughters were the honour and the joy of their mother, whom, with
the exception of the eldest who was married, they had never
quitted.   Even now when the married daughter hears her mother
mentioned her heart bounds with joy.   The girls, however, are
somewhat nervous in the presence of their father.   When he
returned from hunting they would kiss him respectfully, even
submissively, "foot and heel."   They never addressed him save in
somewhat trembling tones, and one of them being one day rather
disrespectful in speech, he exclaimed: "By the duty I owe my
mother, that is not the way to address your father!"   There was
at that time a popular proverb which inculcated perfect obedience
to one's father: ("*Au bien, au mal, doit-on son père aimer.*")   In
those days they did not argue about the parental authority—they
submitted to it.   Only the youngest members of families exercised
then as now their privileges; they laughed and chattered, and
consoled their parents too at times.   The elder girls would work,
sew, make clothing, embroider, &c.   A great dog in the circle
would complete the scene.   On him, on this typical occasion, is

bestowed the name of the traitor who was compelled to encounter the dog, which had belonged to a good knight whom the ruffian had killed—he is called Macaire.

You will, perhaps, now understand why they loved the old castle, which shielded so many affectionate hearts—somewhat rough, perhaps, but sincere and faithful. You will now understand why the poor Huon of Bordeaux regretted his mother, "the beautiful," from whom he was about to part in search of so many and such perilous adventures, and why this parting should have made him so sad. You will now understand why the Crusaders cast so many and longing glances towards that beautiful France where they had left their wives and children. But I do not wish to get sentimental with them, nor, above all, to exaggerate the facts. Feudal life in no particulars resembled the little idyllic shepherd life of Florian or of Bernis. Those big boys were choleric, rebellious, sanguinary; the daughters were passionate, and possessed tastes which required the refinements of Christianity to temper them; the fathers carried severity even to bloodshed and crime; the castle in some instances was still but the encampment of the barbarian; and the blood of the Christian knight still was mingled with the taint of savagery.

In one scene of the twelfth century, in a Homeric episode, we should like to condense the true picture of those times, so hard to convey in description. Let us transport ourselves to the town of Narbonne, at that period a great fortified city. Like all towns, Narbonne was built around a great tower or castle concentrated in a heavy donjon. Let us go there. The palace is of marble; the chapel adjoins it. It is morning, mass is just finished, and we perceive a procession of twenty-four knights, clad in silk and furs, slowly defiling from the portal. One old baron is in front: he marches with firm tread. He is their lord, Duke Aimeri. His wife, the beautiful Hermengart, is close by with her seven sons. What a sight! But listen to these strong tones.

"Dame Hermengart," says Aimeri, "look at your sons, look well at them. Ah, if I could only see them knighted ere I die!"

Aimeri was destined to be quickly satisfied. A messenger is perceived approaching in a cloud of dust. "Whence come you?" "Charles has sent me!" "And what wills the emperor?" "He desires you to send him four of your sons that he may knight them!"

This was excellent news : the baron was delighted, but he had
not counted on his son William, on that indomitable nature, which
was at times even savage. This youthful hero suddenly turned to
his brothers, and exclaimed :

" You ought to have been knights long ago ! Wretches that
you are, how is it that you have not yet warred against the
Saracens ? How is it that you have not already retaken from them
twenty castles and towns ? As for me, I do not wish to go to the
emperor yonder. Demean myself to the duties of a page or squire !
Nonsense ! *I* take care of the dresses and arms of barons ! I make
their beds ! No, no. But I will take with me a thousand knights,
and I will exterminate the Saracens. I will go ! "

The eldest brother, Bernard, remonstrated in vain against such
presumption. William insulted him : " If you were three hundred
it is I only whom you would obey. I only ! " The brothers got
angry, and bit their lips, " champed their bits," but they submitted
to the yoke of William, who was not their eldest brother either.
Nevertheless, it all ended in their starting for the court of the
emperor, who was the magnet of attraction to all true knights.
They left Hermengart with her youngest sons and her five
daughters, and one hundred knights in Narbonne. A very small
force to resist the Infidel, who came down on the devoted city, on
which he had set his mind. Poor little Guibelin, the youngest of
Aimeri's sons, said to his big brother William as he was going
away : " Brother, if only in my shirt and hose I will go with you—
if I may ! " But his appeal was useless. The lad stayed with his
mother, and the whole strength of Islam fell upon Narbonne !

Well, this scene is true ; it is in no way exaggerated ; and as it
occurred between the hours of eight and mid-day we will leave
with our readers as a remembrance—as a living type of those very
busy hours which extend from dawn to dinner-time.

We must not picture to ourselves a castle of the twelfth century
in the pleasing and luxurious guise of the modern château, nor even
of one of your contemporary houses. A great hall in which the
inhabitants ate and sang and played games : one or two bed-
chambers on each floor ; some smaller rooms : in one of which the
armour of the knight and his followers was kept ; the other a
work-room in which tailors and dressmakers worked, and in which

the linen and the clothes were kept in perfumes and spices. No antechambers, no boudoirs, no studies; according to the wealth of the castle the chambers are more or less grand. They are all alike save that the apartment of the baron and his wife is more highly decorated and better furnished than the others. Let us enter.

The room appears to be generally vaulted, and such is the usual character of circular chambers. Nothing has been easier than the application of the ogive window system to civil and military architecture, scarcely recognised and little used by the Romans, but which, remember, was adopted and brought to perfection by the architects of the twelfth century. It was easy to arrange and multiply the ramifications of this admirable arch, and to make it include round, rectangular, or square spaces. The system is marvellously simple, and lends itself to every kind of combination. If the baron is not sufficiently wealthy to have a vaulted ceiling he contents himself with the under surface of the floor above, a wooden covering supported by heavy beams. But architects are clever fellows, and they took advantage of these great beams to apply some charming decorations. They painted them like the mouldings of the arch in red and yellow, with leafage and black decoration which gave them lightness. Later—in the thirteenth century — they adopted more vivid tones, and even employed gilding. Nothing can be prettier.

To possess a " painted chamber " was the acme of desire, and the advocates of the polychrome architecture easily found adherents and arguments in their favour amongst our forefathers. They would willingly have painted inside and out in subdued and tempered colour. In this too the twelfth century is "the great century of the Middle Ages," and it certainly can claim the most correct intelligence in architectural painting. It would appear that all the artists of that strong period had the same disdain for gold as a great architect of our times has expressed in picturesque and stirring terms. "Gold is a flavouring, not a meat." What we say of gold we can as legitimately say of all other bright colours, and particularly of the vivid blues which are its necessary accompaniment. Just look at the artist who is at work as we enter the castle chamber. He says he is "only a humble assistant," and seeks only to preserve his master's work, instead of obliterating it. " He only leaves me the mouldings of the arch, so that I may bring them out. But on the other hand all the walls are mine, and they constitute a fine domain. I am contented with them."

Our painter—look at him—first executes his pictures on a surface of fresh mortar. He begins by tracing in red ochre, mixed with pure water, the forms of his characters; then he puts in the "local colour" which is destined to form the mezzo-tinto, but he puts it in in successive layers, and mixing with lime, to the required tone : afterwards he models the salient parts, adding more lime as he reaches the later coats; then he redraws with the reddish-brown mixed with black, the contours, the folds, the creases, and the interior features of the forms and draperies. He must be quick—very quick; he must not permit the first coats to dry. Great practice and speed are necessary, and the operation is somewhat complicated.

There is another system which the Gallo-Roman artists at one time practised, but which the twelfth century has not abandoned, which is the only one applicable to the painting of sculptured stone capitals, and polychrome statues. The painting is not traced on mortar but on a layer of " stone-colour " of white or yellowish-white. The red ochre and the black serve as well in either, but the artist only permits himself to use reddish-browns or blacks which he relieves by some yellow or green or white. These are the general characteristics of the paintings of the Louis VII. period. No staring colours—no vivid reds, blues, and no gold. With a few pots of red and yellow ochre, a little black, white or dark blue, the painter produced all his most stirring scenes in fresco; and in this way our chamber was decorated. Look and decide for yourself.

But gold was not banished for long, and even then painters were unconsciously preparing for its approaching triumph. So much colour was thrown into the windows that our poor decorative artists were forced to harmonize their pictures with these brilliant designs. Thenceforward was the fatal mastery of blue and gold. The castle of Coucy is still very simply decorated, very soberly painted : but the Sainte-Chapelle not far off is brilliant in vivid colouring, the reds and blues and gold which have been so abused, and which are so astonishing. We prefer our twelfth century tones of the room.

This chamber, like most others of its period, is chiefly painted with floral decorations; conventionally treated, not copied from nature; the acanthus and scroll, the origin of which is really ancient, but which are alas! degenerated and corrupted. In the rooms on other floors the decoration is limited to the painting of the jointures and the dressings.

Our knight however is ambitious, and he seeks something better than mere ornament. "What shall I paint? A Christ crucified between the old and new dispensations? The Last Judgment? A Saint Peter or Saint Martin?"

"No, no;" replies the baron, "I want something of a more military character, something which will recall my profession. Ah, I have it! Paint me a tourney." "Very well," replies the artist; and he sets to work. He rapidly draws the outline of two knights on a white ground; all the forms and draperies are put in with the same tint of brown. Then he lightens it up; the colours employed are red and yellow ochres, the brown more or less deep with different shades of green, even the rose violet and blue. Between each juxta-imposed colour is a brown streak. The projections are indicated in white. There is no perspective of any kind. The "hieroglyphic" style is still in vogue. If a palace is required, we have a frontal supported on two small pillars. A tree is a stick surmounted with five leaves. The figures are stiff, the ensemble is cold. In fact the work is done conventionally, traditionally; Byzantine. Very architectural but not sufficiently natural. The thirteenth century altered all that, and was inspired by nature. Villard de Honnecourt, the great architect of the period of Saint Louis, went so far as to reduce to geometrical figures, all the forms, attitudes and movements of the human body. Then the ancient Byzantine figures began to live and move. There comes a Giotto yonder and Art itself, the grand Art, makes rapid strides.

Sculpture has a small place in the castle, and then it is only ornamental. The capitals of the pillars of artificial foliage, the antique Corinthian combination disfigured, mingled with monsters, but still imposing and noble. Sculpture as an art is essentially French, and it never hesitated to free itself from foreign trammels. In the twelfth century this freedom took place, and then the last bonds of Byzantinism were broken.

This is not the place to inquire if the victors over the antique traditions were monks or laymen. Suffice it to say that in my mind the artistic clericalism of the twelfth and the lay artist of the thirteenth century are exaggerated. I agree that there were before A.D. 1100 five principal schools of sculpture : the Rhenish, the Toulouse, the Limosian, the Provencal, and the Cluny Schools : and this last named, I am of opinion, is the most original, the most "natural" and that which possessed the best possibilities for the future. But knowledge is not yet complete ; the history of the sculpture of France has yet to be written ; and I imagine that there is less subtlety than propriety in this grouping all the sculpture-schools into eight distinct classes. The Provence school is as Byzantine as Gallo-Roman ; the Toulouse with its flourish and its outrageous animals is only Byzantine ; Cluny submits neither to the influence of the Gallo-Roman nor the Byzantine ; it clings to the Greco-Roman, but with so much force and vigour in imitation that it will eventually become original. On the schools of Saintonge and Poitou the Norman and Saxon influence is exercised. The Venetians who imported so many objects of art to us from Constantinople, Damascus, and Asia Minor, have influenced by these means, the Limosian school ; that of Auvergne remains undecided between neighbouring schools : that of Berry is divided between the traditions of the Byzantine, and the memories of Gallo-Roman art. But the eighth school to which the future really belongs is ours, that of the royal domain, the Isle of France, or rather of France itself. It is eclectic and intelligently so. It mingles and combines all the elements—Gallo-Roman, Byzantine, Norman : it has a freer style and bolder aims than the provincial schools ; it has also a more delicate sense of proportion and of the "ladder of ornamentation." Viollet le Duc affirms that at the end of the twelfth century this "happy school" had become a lay institution. That is no matter, but all this classification seems too obscure and fine-drawn. I prefer the statement of our old master Jules Quicherat, who contends that the *Romansch* ornamentation is only the deformed *Roman* ornamentation. Up to the thirteenth century ornamentation was derived universally from antique artificial foliage ; and since then it has been copied from nature, as on the capitals in the palace of the Doges of Venice, which reproduce in "living stone" the vegetation of the country.

As for the statuaries of France whom we must not confuse with he ornamental sculptors, they stand apart, having cut the cords which united them with the ill-understood traditions of ancient art. Not to Oriental, but to French workmen do we owe the sculptures of Vézelay, Autun, and Moissac. All is Western. More than a century before the painters these bold artists felt their way in the imitation of Nature; imitation still incomplete and awkward, but synthetic and forcible and intelligent. The statues of Chartres had, in 1140, more life and animation than (even the Italian) pictures of the fourteenth century. Thus is united the long chain of sculptors which commences with the pious artists of Chartres, and is continued to the present day by the Guillaumes, the Merciés and the Paul Dubois—pending successors. It is truly our national art !

But our baron of the twelfth century knew nothing of all this ; it was enough for him to admire the pretty capitals of his columns. Let us admire them with him, and halt before one which represents Æsop's fable of the wolf and the crane.

Then let us make a little tour round his room. Two halting-places may be indicated, the chimney and the bed. Let us go from the bed to the chimney, and from the chimney to the bed again by different routes ; the journey is not long.

The chimney is enormous, and has nothing in common with our poor fire-places at which three people can hardly seat themselves. The old chimney is placed between two windows, so that the baron can warm himself and gaze out of window at the same time. If he is curious and chilly he can experience a double pleasure ; and is it not delightful to watch the snow falling while we warm our feet. A mantel of arched design, finely carved, is supported by two *colonettes* or small pillars. But the most striking part of our chimney is its cowl or hood, of conical shape, that looks like a cylindrical tube, and stands out from the wall; it is terminated by a chimney-pot. It lends itself to painting, and, as a matter of fact, it is decorated with floral designs, like those on the walls of the room, perhaps a scene from " The Table Round."

In this chimney, whose proportions were always increasing from the twelfth century to the end of the Middle Ages, were burned whole trunks of trees. Wood was not then wanting in France, which has been so criminally de-forested. Timber was not spared, and the fire was lighted with " flint and steel." There were no fire-

irons save a bar with which the logs were moved, but strong and-
irons were then necessary. They were very tall, and surmounted
by small chafing-dishes. The bellows had also its use, and we now
know what appertained to the twelfth century fire-place. Wicker
screens protected the baron's face from the excessive heat, and at
either side of the chimney were stone brackets on which a candle
was placed, fixed by an iron-pointed tip. The room was, in truth,
badly lighted.

But these hearths, plain and almost barbarous, were cheerful and
charming. There people sat, laughing loudly, hospitably treated,
good and pious. I may venture to say that there was made and
moulded the grand French race. Remember that by the chimney
everyone met, all the representatives of that youthful society encountered each other in process of formation. There was much
roughness, superstition, and ignorance, but faith, good-will, and
bright honest spirits. I am aware that the pleasantry was not
always in the best taste, but it was so frank, and so soon retracted.
The women were present, spinning. The servitors were not excluded
from the general familiarity. Guests were present and well-placed,
describing their troubles, small and great. They pushed against
each other, rubbed shoulders, and told tales, even sang songs, not
so loudly as to awake the children who were asleep near their
parents' bed, quite at the other end of the room. One would relate
the fable of Reynard and the grapes, or a miracle of Saint Anselm,
and so on, or chant the ballad of Doette and Doon.

In this manner they amused themselves, and never felt bored,
around the chimney. Let us proceed.

In our course from the chimney to the bed we shall meet nothing
but furniture, chairs and benches of all shapes. But people did
not require to use them so much as we do now, for they sat on the
ground voluntarily. Even ladies would carry cushions to church
to temper the severity of the cold pavement, and with the same intention the floor of our chamber is covered with a thick carpet, and
rich cushions, new cloth of gold and silk. The knights, in proper
fashion, seated themselves on the flags or bricks. This custom
obtained for a long while, notwithstanding its primitive and
Oriental character, and we find confirmation of this in the poems
of the thirteenth century. But it could not continue in vogue with
a manly and civilized race. No doubt it was a pretty sight to see

the knights and dames in brilliant costumes reclining about the floor on brilliant-hued stuffs from Eastern looms. But it was only pretty to look at. Our baron prefers benches, solid and commodious seats, moveable and placed by the walls, covered with quilts and cushions. Other benches, called "forms," are furnished with backs, and divided like "stalls." They are solid, immoveable, and their workmanship is concealed beneath coverings of wool or feathers, beneath double and quilted rugs.

These seats must have been uncomfortable and hard, but our ancestors managed to soften the asperities. Every baron did not indulge in the luxury of a *faldesteuil*, but, in a large number of castles, there were, in metal or gilded wood, some seat which more or less resembled a throne, and was reserved for the head of the family. A footstool was added to support the dangling legs. The seats themselves were covered with tapestry or cushions. When dependents spoke to their masters, and when they had permission to seat themselves, the servants took a footstool and seated themselves on a level lower than their superiors. The footstool was a sign of inferiority, and of dependence. For familiar and family conversation, between husband and wife, engaged couples, friends, they eschewed the footstools and chairs, and sat on the beds, which were very low.

The bed is on a large plan; it is immense. Placed opposite the spacious chimney it seems so much larger, inasmuch as it is surrounded by curtains, hung crossways : a small room in the end of a large one. Our fathers liked to sleep with their heads very high, almost in a sitting posture. As the bed was upright, the person in it could easily see the fire, and watch it across the room as it crackled in its expiring efforts. Married couples always occupied the same bed, the idea of separation never entered their heads, so the bed was an object of considerable attention; it was the cherished piece of furniture, and was at once an object of art and comfort. They assured the comfort by suspending the bed on cords, which were similar to our straps, and so they formed what was termed a "cordeïs" bed. These were multiplied into feather beds, and so by degrees our ancestors produced quite sudorific effects by the manipulation of materials and arrangements. The luxury of these was excessive; the bed-posts were gilt, and the minstrels hyperbolically declared that they were of gold, for as a rule you may read gilded for "gold" in the old romances. The bedstead was carved, gilt, inlaid with ivory, or ornamented with precious stones or glass-work. During the day a rich quilt was cast over the cloth of gold or linen, and permitted the golden tassels of the feather beds to be seen, with the pillows, which cost fifty marks. This quilt was itself of silk or cloth of gold, or ermine, or marten fur, fringed with gold. Superb and brilliant in the extreme.

I am not quite prepared to give my adhesion to the "musical bed," which is mentioned in one of the old romances. If touched this bed would give forth most musical notes, with which no musician and no bird could vie. The author of *Elie de Saint-Gilles* attributes this marvel to necromancy and magic. We have musical boxes, but I do not know that the Middle Ages could have applied the principle to the bed.

The bed recalls more noble and tender memories. On the occasion of the knight's marriage the priest blessed it, as we have already seen, and repeated Latin prayers. His wife was there then, grave and silent. How well thay remember it! A minstrel one evening recounted how an angel appeared to the grandmother of Godefroi de Bouillon on her wedding-night, who piously scattered incense on the nuptial couch. Near the bed is the cradle with the great object of the parents' love laughing and crowing in it.

But unfortunately many sad memories cling to the bed of our knight, for in it his father breathed his last. The baron was then very, very young: his father had been wounded in battle. They had somehow transported him home, where he lived for three days.

"I wish," said he, "that you would bury me in the costume of the White Friars; I wish to die a monk." They complied with his request; he was robed as a Cistercian, and nothing more com-forting can be imagined than this soldier attired as a monk. He first confessed and got absolution; then he bade good-bye to his little Anseis, who was present, but he understood nothing of what was passing.

"Ah," exclaimed the knight, "if only I had lived, what a knight I would have made of you!"

He thought of his horse *Fleuri*, of which he was very fond, for it had carried him through many a battle. He paused a long time thinking of his wife, the charming Clarissa, with "the beautiful and gentle soul." "You will see me no more, sweetheart : may God guide you!" Then he fainted; but when he revived he only thought of God and the Virgin. "If anyone have any cause of complaint against me I beg his pardon in the name of God." Then he cried—"Protect me, O Lord, protect me from the felon enemy!" These were his last words; his eyes closed, and with a gentle sigh he ceased to breathe.

They watched him all night. The neighbours came from castles near at hand and seated themselves on the carpet round the death-bed. The censers were arranged; there were numerous candles. Next day the knight was buried, but all who attended his funeral were full of hope for his soul. "Let us not mourn," said one old knight, "our friend died absolved and with the sacrament." Then all the rest exclaimed—"His soul has gone; may God receive it and console him!"

So you will perceive that a bed may awaken sad memories and austere thoughts.

The remainder of our little tour will not present so piquant nor so vivid an interest. Here is the immense wardrobe painted vermilion, with white, black and red ornaments, and studded with gems. If you open this piece of furniture you will find belts, armour, clothing, and what not besides. Farther on is a trunk or chest, low, heavy, imposing, well fastened with three locks, enclos-ing the goblets and vessels. Prettier, far, are those small coffers of figured and gilt leather. They came from Constantinople. What do they contain? The lady's jewels and the baron's ornaments. Nothing else? Do not we perceive some long fair tresses carefully wrapped up? When our knight went to Germany he was engaged to the lady who is now his wife. She cut off some locks of her beautiful hair, and there they are. But what is this, a pulpit? That is the " scriptional," the writing-table, and here are the waxen tablets which are used every day by the knight and his dame.

"But," says the chaplain, "turn your eyes from these profane things and look at this shrine, in ivory, of the Virgin, which can be opened and closed at pleasure. The interior represents the Crucifixion, the Resurrection and the Ascension of our Lord. Now look at this little reliquary; take it in your hands and kiss it.

Our baron wore it during his last campaign, and he found the benefit of it. It is, so to speak, the guardian of the room, and of all the castle. Just think what it encloses! a portion of St. Martin's cloak; a tooth of St. Peter, and some hairs of Monseigneur Saint Denis! These are the three patron saints of our land: St. Martin, the defender of the race of Clovis; St. Peter of Charlemagne, and St. Denis of Hugues named Capet. So offer a prayer," continues our chaplain, "to one of these soldiers of God, and kiss once more these glorious relics!"

Our journey is over. It only remains for us to take a comprehensive glance round the room. The general effect is harmonious. We have mentioned the sober colouring of the vaulting, and the fine enamelled brick flooring which is rather inclined to scale off. One is almost afraid to walk upon such a delicate and fragile enamel. These beautiful bricks are all very well for places where there is little traffic, and our baron has made up his mind to replace them by strong stone flooring of white slabs incrusted with black mastic, such as he has already adopted in the great hall, and to cover them with a thick eastern carpet.

These carpets are made in France, and they lead us to speak of the hangings with which our ancestors covered their walls. This was their little luxury, and they, as a rule, only enjoyed it on feast days; but during the year they had so many feast-days. They had solemnities of the Church, weddings, baptisms, churchings, &c. On the mornings of these days, or on the previous evening, the servants would go in with ladders, and drape the walls from top to floor, with beautiful cloth of silk and gold; in fact the whole of the interior was curtained. At the present day we can have no idea of such magnificence. Scarcely had the visitor ascended the steps when he entered the great hall, which was fully decorated, as were all the other apartments. He walked on silk and between silken walls—and such silk! *Pailes*, which as we have seen, is the superb embroidered material; the samite, the brocade called *ciglaton* and the taffetas known as *cendal*. Some of these materials were the same colour, others of different shades. All came from the Orient or from Sicily. It was all splendid, magnificent, surprising!

Again, on these feast-days, the rooms were prettily decorated with leaves and flowers; roses, lilies, jonquils, herbs, gladioli, &c., in poetic and picturesque plenty. Picture the genial, joyous, beautiful French people filling these rooms, laughing, chatting, happy ! This is not an everyday instance I admit, but it is sufficiently well authenticated, and is a reasonable description. Proofs abound.

This chamber which we are about to leave is beloved by our baron more than all the rest of his castle. It conceals in truth, noble existences and rare virtues which are mingled, I do not know how, with the brutality and savagery of a primitive race. Nevertheless, honour is present ; its portal is never open to cowardice or treason. One day in the castle of a neighbour, some traitors had assembled in the bed-chamber, plotting the murder of an infant. Then a great miracle happened. The chamber, which had been till then perfectly white, suddenly turned black as coal !

Our knight is somewhat sceptical, and does not very easily credit such legends. Nevertheless, when such tales are related, he does not laugh ; he thinks he will tell them to his children very gravely. For it is above all things necessary that they should detest treason and love honour and truth.

CHAPTER XV.

MID-DAY—DINNER.

IT is the dinner-hour; twelve o'clock. From the basement of the donjon resounds the sound of a horn; sometimes many horns or trumpets are blown. If there are no musicians present, the summons is made *vivâ voce*, a less effective and certainly a less poetic means of announcing the meal. But at any rate, it served its purpose. " To table, to table," is the cry. We have long superseded the horn by the clock, and cannot imagine the delight with which our forefathers heard the call to dinner, especially when a keen morning had induced a keen appetite.

But the horn of the Middle Ages had a more precise meaning. It not only conveyed the summons to dinner—it also gave the signal for washing the hands—a prosaic but necessary function. This is what is indicated in many poems as " Sounding the water," " Come and wash!" (the " watering horn," in fact). Everyone of high and low degree demanded water before dinner, and they came from all sides; from their rooms, from the orchard, to wash their hands.

All this merry company met on the steps, and prepared to enter the hall, seeking the lavatory. This washing of hands was an indispensable business for those people whose fingers played the part of forks. If one did not wash, one was considered in a very bad way. No doubt when the unfortunate Elias of Saint Giles, who had eaten nothing for three days on one occasion, met with some robbers whose dinner he ate, he did not pause to wash his hands; but then it was excusable.

The lavatory was placed at the entrance of the great hall of the castle, and so arranged that at small jets of water the guests could wash two or three at a time. In some French provinces this custom

still obtains ; the fountains are still to be seen, though I will not
venture to say that they are relics of the twelfth century. We may
conjecture that these old fountains were of metal, marble, or terra-
cotta, furnished with taps &c. ; but this is only hypothetical.

Well, the guests press merrily forward to wash, but then arises
the terrible question of precedence, this question which has given
rise to so many disputes, even to so many wars. This had been

The Lavatory.

foreseen and provided against. The highest of the guests were first
admitted to the lavatory ; clerics had precedence of laymen, both
according to rank. This ceremony was regulated, and almost
official. But outside of these lines of etiquette many very pleasant
meetings took place. On one such occasion did Jourdain de Blaives
meet Oriabel to whom tenderly he tendered the towel.

The custom of washing hands was not less esteemed amongst the
lower classes than amongst the nobles, but the rich " gentlemen "
soon found out that the method lacked dignity and was somewhat
inconvenient. In the twelfth century it became necessary to devise
some other mode, and it was discovered without much difficulty.

Near each guest at table, the pages respectfully placed basins of metal, more or less rich, in which the members of the company dipped or washed their hands. The host was first served, then the lords and ladies highest in rank, and so on. One basin for two persons was the general allowance. So the ancient washing fountain was forgotten, and those who are most conversant with the "local colour" now only represent the basin presented gracefully to the baron by a handsome youth, who is poetically termed a page, but who was scientifically known as a damoiseau or "sergeant." The lavatory was more patriarchal.

As soon as the guests had completed their ablutions they returned towards the hall, where a very striking spectacle met their gaze. A succession of marvels on every side, from entrance to the opposite extremity.

There were, as we have already explained, two kinds of halls. Some square or round, forming an integral part of the donjon, of which they occupied the chief floor; the others, rectangular, constituted the ground floor—often the only floor, those dependences of the donjon which extended into the upper court. Of these, the former was not the more beautiful. It was neither so spacious, so commodious, nor so healthy; one might even declare that it was somewhat oppressive and heavy in character. Only a small number of guests could be seated under the eight arched vaults. There was a want of light. In winter this stone hall was too cold; in summer it was too close. These are the objections, and they are justified; but then we must remember that most of our old-time barons could not afford the luxury of another hall nor yet build fine extra-mural rooms at the foot of the donjon. The existence of the large rectangular hall always indicated considerable wealth and rank, and everyone could not play the duke. Nevertheless, the poor round or square hall of our old castles, was really capable of enclosing great beauty. It only wanted finer proportions.

But in the early years of the thirteenth century, there arose an architect who at once gave the hall the extent and beauty required. This change was made at Coucy, and the donjon there, is unquestionably the most beautiful construction of the Middle Ages. But nothing is more remarkable than the famous hall on the second floor which is capable of containing a thousand men, and is not less than thirty métres in diameter. Beneath the twelve arches of this vaulted chamber, which spring from a central key-stone like an eye, at more than nine feet above the floor is a dodecagonal gallery, a regular triforium, around which hundreds of knights can circulate. I can quite understand the admiration of Viollet le Duc for this audacious work of which an ancient Greek architect would have been proud. And what dinners could have been laid in this splendid hall—what guests might be received there !

Ogier's Revenge.

The exterior halls were of no military value. They were used as halls of justice, and a place of reception and doing homage. The great halls of the hospitals of the twelfth century, mostly resemble these dependences; and this comparison is in no same derogatory, for the hospitals were regular palaces in which the poor were treated like kings. Whether the hall sheltered the sick or the sound, the plan was the same. It was generally a long parallelogram divided into three parts by two rows of semi-circular arches supported on cylindrical columns. The light was admitted by plain semi-circular windows. Of this style is the splendid hall of Angers hospital, and on a less degree its dependences—such is the hall which we are now about to enter in the castle.

The proportions of these halls varied, and we shall be mistaken if we imagine them all like that of Troyes, 160 feet in length and 60 feet wide. Our castellans were more modest in their aspirations.

They were not all princely barons. But even if the hall were not large, and only divided by a single row of pillars, it is still imposing, vast, beautiful. It is built of hewn stone, specially selected and well dressed, for it was never dishonoured by material or workmanship of inferior kinds. Our poets, who were fond of giving therein to their imagination, do not fail to assert that these halls were built of marble. They do not exactly tell a falsehood, but they exaggerate.

It would be difficult to describe the materials of the walls, because they are nearly always concealed by hangings and tapestry; for the hall is as well curtained as the upper chambers. Mosaic work was rarely employed save in pavement, and our castles, notwithstanding some spurious testimony, do not pretend to present to us the rich and curious appearance of St. Mark's at Venice. Artists, on the other hand, had full scope; but there was no scruple in covering their pictures on feast days and gala days, with rich and gaily-coloured hangings. Besides, the original military decorations used by all warlike people were pressed into the service. Along the walls were suspended swords, lances, shields, and other arms. What grand exploits did not these recall! What struggles, what grief! With yonder lance our baron's brother killed a Saracen Emir ten years ago; with yonder horn the valiant Amaury endeavoured to rally his companions to the assistance of the unfortunate Gui de Lusignan, who had been taken prisoner. With that sword he had to preserve and protect the holy wood of the true cross, around which were assembled the last remaining battalions of the Christian host, which the Bishop of Acre, wounded and bleeding, handed with trembling arms to the Bishop of Lydda. But all in vain; the true cross fell into the hands of the infidel. The fortunate Amaury was present after the battle, when Saladin delivered the French barons to his knights to be slain one by one by their captors. Amaury beheld the head of his best friend roll at his feet; but the pagan at whose mercy he stood, had a generous heart, and would not stoop to the office of executioner. Amaury was permitted to live.

The arms and curtains, however, do not satisfy our baron. He must have tapestries, and we must explain the true significance of this term, which were of not the high-class warps. We here protest against an error common to many historians. As a matter of fact, we had none of the high-class tapestry before the close of the thirteenth century, for it is only in 1302 that we find it first mentioned. The Orientals imported in the twelfth and thirteenth centuries velvet carpets, carpets of price, and this manufacture of

Oberon the dwarf and Huon of Bordeaux.

Saracen carpets was very skilfully imitated by the French weavers. But these are a long way apart from our high-warp tapestry. The products of the national tapestry-workers, or *nostrés*, were only woollen stuffs, and we may so assume them.*

Like the Bayeux tapestry, which dates from the eleventh century, and certain church tapestries, which are attributed to the two following centuries, the tapestry which adorns the hall of our baron is only needle-work, embroidery on linen or cloth, and not

---

* Besides the Saracenic tapestry-workers there existed as early as the time of Philip Augustus an industry of *Tapisseur Nostrés*—or native tapestry-workers. The *haute-tisseurs* or high-warp weavers did not appear until 1302.

woven at all.   One of our poems confirms this statement as regards the needle-work.

Between the pretty flowered borders of roses and lilies what histories may not be read?   On two sides of the rectangle may be seen the "history of Ogier, who is at the point of killing the son of Charlemagne, notwithstanding the protests of the French barons, when his arm is arrested by an angel," and "the tale of the dwarf Oberon, before whom Huon of Bordeaux is flying in terror with his thirteen companions."

But all the remainder of the tapestry is devoted to the touching legend of Amis and Amile, those two incomparable friends whose devotion to each other delighted the Middle Ages as Pylades and Orestes had charmed the Greeks.   Some inscriptions in capital letters gave the explanation of each piece, but the guests needed not these descriptions to understand the pictures.   They had learnt them from infancy.   The first tableau represented the baptism of the two friends who resembled one another so closely that no one could distinguish them apart.   This was certainly a miracle!   However, poor Amis became a leper, and was turned out of doors by his wife; when his youngest son, Girard, alone remained with him.   Now, an angel appears to him and says: "You will never recover until your friend consents to wash you in the blood of his children!   You cannot live unless they die!" His friend slew them, and this is the subject of the third picture. The leprosy departs at the first contact of the blood-stained Amiles.   But God, who did not accept Abraham's sacrifice of Isaac, did accept and recompense the faith of Amiles by restoring to him his children, who were given back to their grief-stricken mother.

Then the heavens become once more overcast.   The friends on their way home from a pilgrimage to Rome are met by the terrible Ogier, that ferocious enemy of Charlemagne, who, out of spite against the emperor, slew them in a most cowardly manner.   They were buried in two tombs at a considerable distance apart, but lo and behold! the two bodies began to approach each other and placed themselves side by side!   The Greeks did not think of this! This tableau, at the same time lugubrious and vivid, forms the fourth of the series of tapestry pictures.

With his double embellishment of curtains of Eastern silk and historical tapestries our hall is sufficiently charming, but it is also,

THE RESTORATION OF THE CHILDREN OF AMILE.　　　[v. 432.

like the sleeping-rooms, strewn with flowers and leaves; we perceive the odour of mint, and we walk on blossoms of gladioli and roses. Our knight is not yet contented with such pretty accessories, he wishes to realise a desire which his wife has long entertained. Hitherto he has been satisfied with white window-glass, but now he wishes to rival the neighbouring monastic church, and wants stained glass, blue and red and green. His casements represent St. Peter with two enormous keys; St. Stephen crowned with stones, indicative of his martyrdom; St. John holding in his hand a chalice, from which issues a small serpent, the imagery of the poison with which the high priest of Diana would have killed him. Those three windows project beautiful coloured rays into the hall; but there is still a fourth dedicated to St. Martin, and the decorator has requested permission to continue his work during dinner. He is now at work on his subject—the bestowal of his cloak by the saint on a poor beggar-man.

We are now acquainted with the whole of the hall. Let us look at the table.

Since the sixth century, since the triumph of the Barbarians, the ancient *triclinium* has died out. The Romans reclined at their meals; the conquerors sat.

They were, however, great eaters, and remained at table for a long while in the company of many friends. In these points they were like our feudal ancestors. But the castles unfortunately could only accommodate fixed tables of certain dimensions. Their halls served for many uses, and so moveable tables became necessary. The Romans had quite enough, or too much space; our ancestors had not sufficient.

On the evening preceding, or on the morning of the great dinner, the sergeants or valets carried into the *salle* the trestles on which the long boards were extended covered with fine cloths. There were several tables; though at times they were juxta-posed so as to form apparently a single board. At times round or oval, sometimes rectangular according to the shape of the hall. The upright rims were only seen on the fixed tables, for moveable tables were only set up on grand days; in some castles, the master's table was left day after day.

In spring-time, when the flowers bloomed, in fine weather, the inhabitants of the castle dined in the open air, when the tables were of course "moveable," and the author of *Garin de Loherain,* indicates two hundred tables (!) laid out. The aged Fromont was radiant in the midst of the guests.

"This is the time to have your son made a knight," said Bernard de Naisil to him; "you should rest a little," he added.

"I rest!" exclaimed the old man. "I challenge you to the tourney to-morrow!"

"All his friends wish it," insisted the other.

"Well, be it so," replied the knight, who was not very energetic after his meal—a not uncommon fact, and after his little explosion of anger. So the young man was called and knighted, as elsewhere described, bathed and dressed; he came out on horseback and rode up and down. Afterwards he assumed his place at the board with a hearty appetite. Never has there been another such hasty knighthood.

Let us go inside the castle again.

No matter how many tables had been laid, there was always one higher than the others. This was the "master's table;" the high table for the supreme individual present, who was accompanied by a few privileged persons, who contemplated the other, and palpably inferior, guests. The high table was in evidence, and the cynosure of all regards.

Small and great lords and vassals were seated on cushioned benches, which varied in style at the different tables, the high table having the best seats. In front of the high table was the high daïs, the "maistre dois," the others were of less consequence. This "dois" was not a daïs in the modern acceptance of the term, it was not even a platform as some writers have supposed. It was a backed seat more or less raised—a seat higher, heavier, more ornamented and less mobile than any of the others. We cannot state positively, that the *maistre dois* was partitioned off into stalls; it sometimes contained only two seats. Of the other benches some had backs, some were mere "forms," the greater proportion were ordinary seats, light and easy to move. The upper table dominated all. The *maistre dois* dominated the high table itself, and one day the terms became synonymous.

If we penetrate into the hall two hours before dinner, we shall find twenty or thirty tables on trestles, each supplied with a bench with or without a back, according to circumstances. At this time, the prospect is somewhat meagre and poor. But wait until the cloth is laid : until the " covers are laid." As soon as the guests arrive, the viands are uncovered. The covers had been retained till then. This explanation will account for the modern phrase, which is used in ignorance of its origin.

The tables were laid by the valets or pages, according to the rank of the castellan. By non-nobles and by nobles to be exact. The latter, the " *demoiseaux*," were youthful knights, young men without fortune, without fiefs, who were called bachelors ; and from these aspirants to chivalry were nominated the squires and the " varlets." The non-nobles were the dispensers, the butlers, and " sergeants." The last individuals were the only quality of servants in the families of small knights and those who possessed no sovereignty. The two groups of servitors were employed together, and in this instance the *demoiseaux* directed the *sergeants*. The first thing was to lay the cloths, a more delicate task than may perhaps be imagined. Then the napkins were placed on the cloths ; these were called *doubliers*. Then the various paraphernalia of the meal were laid ; each guest having put by his side every necessary article. Let us see how it was arranged.

Before each guest was placed a knife and spoon. These were indispensable. The spoons were of gold and costly withal. The chamberlain took care to count them when the meal was finished. This was the wish of the baroness, and she had reason to enforce it, I assure you. The knives deserve a passing word ; they were of Poitevin steel with gilt handles. No forks were used before the end of the thirteenth century. There were no serviettes ; they were in the lavatory. If it is necessary to wipe your lips at table, you must do it with the small corner of the cloth, but take care that you are unobserved. You must dine with the most scrupulous propriety.

Each guest is also supplied with a loaf or cake of fine white flour bread. No barley or rye-loaves. They are for the poor. This provision would ensure their not dying of hunger, but they would be thirsty and continue thirsty until the end of the meal and after. So a goblet or *nef* is placed before each one, and it will be frequently emptied. Our host possesses a rich collection of cups of gold and silver of splendid workmanship, which sparkle on the board like suns. The porringers, no doubt, are not less useful, but they are less elegant and less showy. One of them is put between two guests, and they will have the pleasure of eating from the same dish. We notice these with the vast expansive plates—and now we have an idea what each guest is furnished with.

There remains to be mentioned the general table-decoration, which we find somewhat tasteless, for the greatest artists of the period did not see any necessity for it. On our table are placed, in a somewhat irregular and confused manner, ewers of yellow copper, great jugs of wine in lieu of bottles, cups with lids, and cups without lids, goblets of metal and of wood, salt-cellars, and sauce-boats. At dinner, dishes of gold and silver will be put on the table supporting roast swans and peacocks. At grand dinners, a swan or a peacock is served for each two guests! But this is extreme luxury, and does not generally obtain.

This general pell-mell arrangement of plates and goblets, jugs and porringers, was not disagreeable to the eye. The jugs were designed in all kinds of forms, some very quaint—lions, birds and other animals, men and monsters, all vigorous, "living" models. As regards the cups and goblets, we must humbly confess that we are not able to distinguish one from the other. The "cup" was a wider vessel than the goblet, had a higher stem, sometimes shaped like a chalice and serving for two convives; the term "nef," seems to have been applied without distinction to both cups and goblets. Amongst these vases, the one corresponded to the antique *crater*, into which was dipped the *cyathus* which filled the *pocula* and *chalices*, the others resembled the latter vessels, and varied from the open form of the chalice to the clumsier shape of the goblet; the former were of gold or silver, the latter in *madre*, more or less ornamented or mounted. What is *madre?* That is the mystery. It is certain that the term signifies the root of certain woods, the heart of certain species of trees; it is equally impossible to deny that one might have obtained *madre* goblets very cheaply, and this cheapness can only be associated with the small cost of the material. All the value lay in the mounting, but the *madre* was generally spotted, veined, or rayed, and that has been given as the reason why certain stones marked in the same way—the onyx for example —had the same name applied to them. This is rather a far-fetched supposition, and rather too ingenious to be true. It is better to stand, in the twelfth century, by the goblets of real wood, by the goblets of *madre* or of *fust*. To drink good wine out of good wood is not a very great trial, after all.

So we may imagine that nothing could be more varied and sparkling, or cheerful-looking than a dining-room of the twelfth century before the arrival of the guests. On the tables the cups glittered, and could be reckoned by hundreds in the mansions of kings and emperors. There were *nefs* which had a history of their own. It was pretended that the service of Charlemagne came from the treasures of Constantine. The majority of those beautiful vases recalled victories and exploits more or less legendary. When Naines, Ogier, Turpin, and Estous were received at the castle of Montauban, Maugis did not fail to give instructions to the effect that " Before Naines you must place the great cup which I won at Rome, and which holds not less than a *setier;* * before Turpin you shall put the cup of Geoffrey of Bordeaux ; before Ogier that of Didier ; while Estous may have King Yon's cup." But now the tables are laid and the covers put on. The chatter and mutterings of the vassals cease for a while, the guests hurry in, amid a babel of talking and laughter.

It was one thing to invite guests, but quite another matter to place them at table ; the question of precedure was a difficult one. In France there has been a code, a legislative order, for a long while, but theory and practice are very diverse !

The hierarchal order was most natural at a period when rulers were placed so regularly one above the other. The first place in good houses was reserved for the ecclesiastic of the highest position in the church, and the second place to the most elevated layman. The host conducted them, respectfully, to the upper table where all the other guests could see them. If he had not at his table a bishop or an abbé, a suzerain or baron, who was manifestly superior in rank to him, the baron himself would occupy his upper seat, and would place his wife on his right hand. Then all the other barons in order of seniority would group themselves around him. The seneschals and chamberlain no doubt presided over these arrangements, which otherwise might have had some unpleasant consequences.

This hierarchal order, which is by itself somewhat dry and weari-

---

* An ancient measure which varied in different localities. It was a land measure, of about three acres, nominally ; and applied to the extent of the cup not its contents, we suppose.

some, was very luckily for the general amusement tempered by two principles, or, if you prefer the term, by two pleasant and quite "modern" customs. Between two barons a lady was placed, and in this arrangement a nice contrast and continued gaiety were assured. Then between two invited guests a place was reserved for a son or daughter of the house, to whom were entrusted the honours of the table. This was a good arrangement, and the fact that the guests were compelled to associate in pairs enlivened the repast. "To drink from the same jug, to eat from the same porringer" was very "picturesque." A knight and a lady were frequently compelled to eat their dinner in this way, and it gave rise to many acts of politeness. It was a question who would leave the tit-bits to the other—the partner. It is not too much to say that, notwithstanding the realistic side of the question, and the "faces" made while eating, more than one marriage has come from this partaking of meats. This mode of arrangement was called, "*Service à la Française.*"

There were some castles to which only the aristocracy were admitted to table. This is a pride of caste which I can understand, but cannot admire. I prefer the arrangement which excluded children under seven from these long and rather too lively meals. The poor people were really first thought of by the diners as they seated themselves. Above the high table was an inscription in bold letters; the verses were the composition of the baron's chaplain, and the knight voluntarily translated them to his guests—

> Cum sis in mensa, primo de paupere pensa;
> Nam cum pascis eum, pascis, amice, Deum!

However, to suit ladies, he had painted underneath the two following lines, the work of a certain Walter, prior of Vic-sur-Aisne :—

> "Cil qui por Dieu le suen depart ;
> Tout tens en a la meillor part."

As she reads this noble admonition the young lady who is seated below at the second table calls the seneschal, and, demanding another porringer, she places therein the wings of the peacock which had been laid near her, and calling the servant, whispers to him :—

"My friend, carry this to the first poor man you see; I would willingly give him more. Hold! hand him also this cup of wine from my goblet, and tell him to pray for me."

By this time all the convives are seated, and they eat with good appetite. This is the time to find out of what the banquet consists.

The meal will be a long one, and the bill of fare is varied. We know the length of those Norman dinners; these great repasts of the Feudal period (and we are only speaking of them, not of the " every-day" meal), resembled them greatly. " The dinner was not short, it lasted as long as a winter day," says the poet. Eight hours at table ! That is rather too much, and we think that our poet exaggerated. But it is beyond question that dinners extended to six, seven, or ten courses, to fifteen, or even to eighteen, and these only meat and fish ; chiefly meats. Vegetables and fruit did not count with such appetites as these, and this great and substantial supply of food was necessary if the host wished to hear his guests declare that " they had never been seated at a better table. Blessed be our host ! Excellent ! Excellent ! It must be confessed that these rough fellows ate a great deal. The gigantic Renoart devoured five pasties and five capons which he washed down with several quarts of wine. We need not speak of Ogier who disposed of a whole " quarter of beef," which Turpin sent him. Putting these romances aside, we know for a fact that Guy of Burgundy astonished the Saracens by the display of his appetite ; they declared that he ate more than four other cavaliers together. " Well," he replied, " that proves that I am a good and 'well-filled' knight ; a man who eats so well will never be a coward ! "

This appetite never deserted the young knights even when in love. During Doon's courtship of Nicolette, he " never stopped eating ;" nor did she, a child of eleven, neglect her food. When Regaut had the misfortune to lose his uncle Begue he could not at first touch anything. But the empress comforted him and begged him to " try and eat a little. If you would only just taste something !" she cried. He consented to oblige her, and tasted a light repast which consisted of four loaves and a whole roasted peacock, with a small cask of wine. He disposed of all this in a few minutes !

We can picture a dinner of fifteen courses. There was no soup nor fish, nor any trifles, such as we designate *hors d'œuvres*. Our friends in the castle began with flesh—generally venison. It is remarkable how seldom " butcher's meat " figures in their bills of fare. The sportsmen liked the produce of their sport, and they did not draw any distinction between the fowls and game—our first dish is venison—"*Cerf de craisse au poivre chaut.*" It was quite possible to cook the deer whole after having carefully scorched and larded him. It was served in quarters at the various tables in splendid dishes. The "*sauce poivrade*" was served hot in a tureen, and poured over the food. "*Poivre chaut,*" or "*pevrée,*" of the period means only this hot pepper sauce. It was served with all meats. Sometimes a few cloves were thrown in and then it became "*sauce giroflée,*" but the difference was very slight. Butter was almost ignored, and oil was seldom used except for some fritters. Pepper, pepper everywhere: from first to last spices—always spices. This assisted the digestion, and made guests drink! Long live the pepper!

The second course of meat was something substantial to satisfy such capacious stomachs—viz., the shoulder of wild-boar, but at the upper table was set on a rarer animal—namely, a quarter of bear stuffed and roasted. The perfume of the spices is pleasant. Everyone sniffs the savoury odour, and cries of admiration ascend with the steam. By the time these viands are helped, as the guests are not absolutely dying of hunger, conversation becomes general. Old sportsmen like killing the game, but they also like to tell how they killed it, and the poet puts it philosophically—*Assés i mentent li plusor!*" To accuse them of lying to their heart's content is pretty strong—let us say they embellished their narratives. For instance—

"Ah, that wild boar you are eating gave me some trouble, I can tell you. I came across him near the Castle of Motte, five leagues off, in the woods under a great pine tree by the lake. I saw that he was resting near the water, so I cut myself a thick club, and awaited his attack. The moment he perceived me he came rushing towards me at full speed. I gave him a blow which threw him on his haunches, then another on the head which blinded him, but unfortunately my club was broken by this stroke and I had to use my sword to finish him. I wanted to carry him home but I was too exhausted. Ah, he was a fine fellow!"

Again we listen and hear the tale of the bear.

"This bear they are handing you," says the host, "was a bold fellow. I never saw a beast defend himself so well! He killed

two of my hounds and stifled Pierre." Then follows an "interminable" narrative which is interrupted by the arrival of the third
and fourth courses—the peacocks and the swans. These are the
favourite dishes. The birds are kept in great numbers, less for
ornament than for use.

Their appearance gives rise to many reminiscences of the Swan-
knight—whose mother had seven children at a birth, one a girl,
and six boys who were turned into swans—they were restored to
human shape all but one, who remained a lily-white bird and
guided his brothers to Jerusalem. The swan-knight was an an-
cestor of Godfrey de Bouillon—and various other narratives of
Charlemagne, Pepin and others, which more or less refer to the
eating of peacocks and swans, are related. These caused much
laughter; one in particular, in which Maugis the magician per-
sonated a beggar, and induced Charlemagne to put the food into the
suppliant's mouth, caused great merriment.

Then follow all kinds of fowls—capons roasted and fried fowls
—these are the fifth and sixth courses; the seventh and eighth
consist of water-fowl and small game—rabbits, hares, &c.—and
subsequently the waterfowl—herons, cranes, divers, mallards, &c.
The ninth course consists of pasties—venison, pheasant, pigeon
pies, plover pasties, and many others; all kinds of game pies. But
a last pasty is placed before the master. He cuts the thin crust
and out flies a flock of small singing-birds which perch around the
hall. Immediately the doors open, and a number of falcons are
admitted which make short work of the unfortunate little birds.*

Fish comes next, and is not well received; the tenth course
is not so successful as its predecessors—mullet, bream, shad,
barbel, salmon and trout are all disdained by our barons. But they
manage, nevertheless, to find a corner for an eel-pie. After this,
conversation waxes fast and furious. It is a regular Babel, and
repartees are exchanged with much gusto; these "jokes" were of an
ordinary kind, and scarcely interchangeable. " Of what land (*terre*)
are you ? " " Do you want to make *pots* ? " "I was asking where
you were born ! " " I have never been *nês* (*nef*-ewer) nor ship."
The play in each case being on the signification of a word which
has many meanings, as *nef* is "boat" or "ewer."

During these pleasant exchanges a dog, perhaps, will come in,

---

* No doubt the immortal "song of sixpence" is based on this Feudal habit.

and while munching a bone his presence will recall the incident of Macaire and the dog of Mondidier, which found his enemy at the banquet. In the "man and dog fight" which ensued, the quadruped came off victorious—he had avenged his master whom Macaire had assassinated. Sometimes the conversation gets noisy and two knights get to dangerous words, but the host or the ruler of the feast puts a stop to this, and the eleventh and twelfth courses make their appearance.

These consist of confectionery and pastry of all kinds, but the barons do not much affect it. They are waiting for something better. What? You will never guess, you delicate feeders of to-day. You may suppose that fruit, or something equally refreshing, will follow the viands, served with hot sauces and spices! No, by no means—no luscious cool fruits, but spices; hot, burning ginger, cloves, and such-like are eaten freely. Their palates are on fire! so they must drink—that is the idea. At that time certain spiced drinks are also handed round, called *laituaires*. They indeed thirst!

Now what do these barons drink? Wine, and plenty of it. They dislike water greatly. The cups, or goblets, are of immense size, and it is customary to empty your cup during each course. The wine is "heady" stuff. Some have received distinct directions from their doctors to mix water with their wine. They have begged to be permitted to drink the wine first and the water after. But as soon as they have swallowed the wine they declare they are thirsty no longer, and they refuse the water! Well, suppose they drink the pure vintage wine; but they do not, they make up horrible mixtures. If they condescend to drink pure wine it is only at the family table, at the humble daily repast. But their grand feasts! Fie! To the pure juice of the grape they prefer the *piment*, the *claré*, the *bouglerastre*, and *hyssop*. All these beverages are only horrible drugs. The *piment* is a spiced and perfumed wine, *claré* is a composition of wine and aromatic herbs and honey, *bouglerastre* is only a kind of hydromel and wine mixed; *hyssop*, concerning which we have no details, is no doubt an infusion of herbs. I pass by *moret* and other liquors of the same class. In fact, in nearly all wines, honey or spices were dissolved or mixed. Honey and pepper, pepper and honey; they could not get out of that groove. Nevertheless it is pleasing to know that our ancestors left some small space for the old grand brands of Beaune, Auxerre, Burgundy, Anjou, Cyprus, and Malvoisie. I hope they did not ruin these fine wines by such sophistications as we have named above.

The attendance was specially remarkable. Two armies of servitors were employed. One set, youthful, proud of their youth and good looks, splendidly clad in ermine and furs, sons of counts and princes, squires and pages to-day but knights to-morrow! The others, soberly clad, really servants, *meschins*, serfs. As the knights form the first line in battle, and the squires the second, so at table the pages form the first and the valets the second line. There was perpetual hurrying to and fro between the hall and the kitchen. The more guests the more waiters. When counts are at table, knights bachelors only wait on them; but if the king be present he is served by counts, the emperor by kings. The various grades are fixed in almost mathematical order, and our *chansons* show that Charlemagne was waited on by three kings, one to pour out the wine, one to hold the dish (or plate), and another to present the goblet. This might serve as an inspiration for an artist.

All this time it is merry in the hall: the noise of hurrying feet, the aspect of the table, now disordered, the laughing, chattering, drinking crowd of guests, and the somewhat thoughtful smile of the host, who is satisfied with the result, are something to be remembered.

"The dinner is a success," mutters the host, but to whom is the success owing? To that stout man yonder; who is moving around the tables, ordering the attendants hither and thither in a loud voice, who sends messages to the kitchen; who sees everything, the viands, the wines; who thinks of everything, and seems to be everywhere at once. This person is the seneschal! Everything depends on him. The head cook is, so to speak, the *letter* of the repast: the seneschal is the spirit of it. He is only too well aware of it, and is too self-satisfied. Gross, important, superb! He values himself highly, and our ancestors did not spare laughter on this semi-comic personage. They caricatured him, and very well too. You remember that Hernaut the Red, son of William, disguised himself as the seneschal and played his *rôle* marvellously. He was even more gross, vain, and insolent than the true Simon Pure.

The duty of the seneschal is heavy, particularly when the dinner is long; he then becomes flurried and irritable, angry with his inferiors, but even-tempered with others. The meal is approaching its conclusion; the noise is deafening, no one can hear either the music or the singing which has been provided, for our ancestors liked music at dinner, and prefer it to the gymnastic exercises on the tight-rope, which proceed during dinner-time. Music is preferable, and sometimes the guests themselves sing. These exhibitions give rise to remarks more or less proper, which make the elders smile and the young people blush. One youth volunteers a song, but he can only sing in Latin, as he is preparing for the Church. "Go on, we will translate it." Then he begins the famous song:—

> "Meum est propositum in taberna mori."
>
> "Let me die in a tavern with my dying lips steeped in wine!"

Subsequently someone chants the remaining couplets:—

> "Potatores singuli sunt omnes benigni."

"All drinkers," he says, "are famous fellows!" and so on to the praise of good wine.

> "Vinum super omnia bonum diligamus."

Those who understand applaud loudly, and those who do not applaud more loudly still.

Perhaps someone who is about to proceed to the Holy Land will take up a lugubrious tone, but he will be out-voted by some manly neighbour who provokes enthusiasm by describing the glory of the expedition, and even of death under such circumstances. Some ladies weep, others grow pale, a thrill of enthusiasm pervades the company; but then come jokes, and conversation, and pleasantries to remove the sadness, and still enthusiasm for the present.

Music continues for an hour, and as the company has been at table three hours, it is time to leave it. The master of the house gives the signal; the attendants, at a sign from the seneschal, whip the cloths off. The dinner is at an end!

We have, in the foregoing pages, endeavoured to describe a real banquet—a grand feast; the ordinary daily dinner was a very small affair, and there is no need to describe it. Small repasts resemble happy peoples—they have no history.

CHAPTER XVI.

THE DOMESTIC LIFE OF THE KNIGHT—A DAY IN THE LIFE OF A BARON AT THE END OF THE TWELFTH CENTURY (*continued*).

AFTER DINNER.

THE guests rise from table rather tumultuously, and go to wash their hands once more. They then disperse through the rooms and stroll into the open air. Groups—sometimes noisy ones—are formed. The older people seat themselves, the more youthful make up parties in the field for fencing, or games at the quintain, &c.

The lady of the castle is surrounded by male guests who pay her many compliments, but not solely on account of her beauty do they thus attend her. She is dispensing pretty gifts amongst them, and these girdles, furs, and other presents, account for some of the attention she is receiving. Perhaps just then, a hoarse growling is heard—one of the baron's pet bears is half suffocating the other in his embraces, and the knights shout with laughter as they crowd around, and endeavour to separate the infuriated combatants. Their cries and shouts attract all the guests save some few angry ones, who are playing backgammon or chess, and who do not wish to be disturbed, so intent are they on their games. They play for high stakes, too—for money, or, as in one case, for a mule.

There are besides "parlour games." After "hide and seek" comes "confession." The young men amuse themselves with a game called "gabs," or a game of bragging. For instance, one will say : "Give me three shields, I will climb a tree and knock them together. By this noise I will kill all the game in the forest."

"I," says another, "will merely whistle in the direction of Paris, and cause a terrific storm there—won't the citizens be frightened ! "

"I," cries a third, "will turn the river aside and inundate the whole country—won't the people be alarmed ! "

But this nonsense does not last long, the young people are too full of life, and by the time the lasses have finished their confes-

sions the lads leave their " gabs." What should follow but dancing? And they do dance. To stimulate themselves the pages and
squires take to wine again, as if they had drank none for days.
Then they set to dancing a " singing *rondo*," in which the damsels
hold the men's hands, and you may depend on it they are not in a
hurry to let go, or to cease dancing.

Then the musicians, ten in number, with viols, psalteries and harps,

Round the Fire.

play to the elders, who listen gravely; but the young people prefer to
dance. However, to all save the dancers, the greatest pleasure of the
evening is to hear the *jongleur* recite some epic poem in the great hall.

At weddings, as already remarked, three musicians (jongleurs),
were invited to recite. Now there is but one. 'Tis true he is the
best in the country, and in his life, as in his recitals, he differs very
greatly from the others. He is a Christian, and this explains everything. He regards his vocation almost as a sacred mission; he
cares only to recite the lives of the saints or the exploits of knights.
He likes these grand epics, and he loves the Church more, holding

in small esteem all the petty singers of impure ballads which had already begun to pollute castles and towns. He called all such " lustrions," and treated them with silent contempt.

" What shall I sing for you this evening ? " he asks as he strikes the first chord on his viol. The host reflects for a moment and then replies, " I have a suggestion to make ; instead of singing us an entire song, which may to some appear too long, suppose you chant to us some of the most beautiful passages from our old poems. So shall we have the pleasure, in one hour, of going through all our most heroic poems. It would be a perfect treat. Let us hear them."

Then the musician tunes his viol, and begins by imposing silence on his auditory, which is somewhat noisy. " Barons," he cries, " listen to me, and keep quiet ! " Then wishing to compensate his auditors for so prolonged a silence as he requires, and for interrupting so many pleasant discussions, he announces his intention to sing some verses in which those grand subjects Chivalry and Grief, are worthily celebrated. " I commence my lord, with a song of vassalage—of high chivalry and of great toil."

> " Il commence, seignor, chanson de vasselage ;
> De grant chivalrie et de fort ahannage ! "

He has the frankness to confess that these recitations will last until sunset perhaps ; an announcement which causes some dissatisfaction amongst the younger members present, but he adds that he will be perfectly " historical " in his selections. It has all actually happened ! and he does not hesitate to promise an eternity of happiness to his hearers for their complaisance !

After a preface laudatory of the Deity and the Virgin, our *jongleur* commences his actual recital with Charlemagne. " I am not going to tell you of the youth of Charlemagne," he says, " nor of all the troubles which Heaven heaped upon him before he was called to the throne of France. If anyone here complains of his life let him think of the son of Pepin ! I question whether he ever had one hour of real repose. Forced to reconquer his throne before he actually could occupy it, he did not triumph over his enemies except in the matter of the restoration of the Pope to Rome. 'Ah,' he said, ' now will I repose me a little.' But almost immediately he learnt that the Saracens were once again threatening Italy. He at once set out against them, and pursued them as far as Aspremont. He returned victorious, but then Ogier revolted ; the sons

of Aymon did likewise, so did John of Lanson.   Charles quelled all
these rebellions, and when victorious, only thought how to deliver
Christendom from the Infidel.   To bring a very perilous enterprise
to a right ending : to supply himself with the necessary strength
he proceeded, attended by a dozen peers, to kiss the tomb of the
Holy Sepulchre, and bring back to Constantinople the miraculous
relics of the Passion.   At length Charles was ready.   Saint James

Thierry accusing Ganelon.

appeared to him in his sleep, touched him on the shoulder, and
pointing to Spain, said—' Go !'
    " He went ; and at the end of seven years of campaigning he had
but one enemy, and one town before him—Saragossa.   He had his
nephew Roland with him, and feared no defeat.   But there was a
traitor in the camp ; Ganelon sold Roland to the Moors.   I will not
now relate the circumstances nor the death of Roland amongst the
archangels, Raphäel, Gabriel, and Michael.   You have it often
times, and I am sure many of you know by heart the poem.   But
I will tell you how Roland was avenged.   There were two traitors,
and two punishments.   Listen—

" The Emperor caused his clarions to be sounded,
Then he sent forward the baron with the grand army—
They found the track of the Infidel ' Marsile,'
And ardently pressed on in quick pursuit.
But Charles perceived that daylight would him fail,
And, kneeling in the grass, in meadow green,
He prayed, supplicating the great God
To cause the sun to stop and night to wait !
The angel, who was guardian to the king,
Gave order promptly, and he cried to him—
' Press on, Charles ; on, the daylight shall not fail ! '
For Charlemagne did God perform this wonder !
The sun in Heaven halts, immovable—
The pagan flies, the French press in pursuit."

The Punishment of Ganelon.

The traitor Ganelon remained to be dealt with, but his punishment was not less severe than was the Pagans. Charles, on his return to Aix, had him brought before him chained like a wild beast. They bound him to a post, a prelude to his punishment. Before the king's tribunal, where all stood in fear of the prisoner, there arose an implacable accuser, Thierry. He stood up among all those cowards and traitors, and, with a terrible gesture, pointed to the accused, who had been brought in—

" ' Ganelon is felon ! Roland has he slain,
  I to death condemn him ! Let him hang !
  Cast his carcase to the dogs for this,—
  This is the punishment of traitors !
  Should any friend of his give me the lie,
  With this good sword, which hangs upon my hip,
  Am I prepared to meet him, and sustain
  The words I speak ! '   ' Well said,' replied the Franks."

It is sad to think that the most unrighteous causes can sometimes find defenders. Pinabel took up Ganelon's cause. Pinabel,
a baron brave and true; tall and strong. He accepted the challenge,
confessed and received the sacrament. The great duel began;
Pinabel was vanquished, and the death of Ganelon was resolved
upon. The judges had no fear of the accused. The time had
come—

" Then four chargers were brought forth :
  And to them tied the writhing traitor's limbs,
  Wild were the steeds and foaming : at their heads
  Stood four grooms, who led them to the field.
  God ! what a death for Ganelon !
  All his nerves were wrenched, his limbs
  Torn by the horses from his trunk by force.
  The life-blood reddened all the sward around.
  He died a traitor's and a coward's death.
  It is not just for traitors to boast treason ! "

When the minstrel had pronounced the last line " *Ki traïst altre,
nen est dreiz qu'il s'en vant,*" there was a death-like silence. Then
a child cried out against Ganelon. Women wept and barons
pondered. The singer requested permission to repose himself, and
permitted a cup of wine to be presented to him. Meanwhile the
audience resumed the conversation, and the *jongleur* could not
afterwards obtain a hearing for some time. No one seemed
inclined to ask for the next recitation, but everyone desired it.

The *jongleur* then transported his audience into a very different
sphere, and showed them Charles the Great before Roncesvalles;
tears are in his eyes as he murmurs the names of Ganelon and
Roland, Roland and Ganelon, and says aloud: "Four hundred
years after my death people shall still speak of my revenge ! "

The king, a hundred years old, was the only person in the army
who was really energetic. Behind him marched his knights, panting, pale, emaciated, worn out, and only wished for one thing—
bed! This march of the grand army across France, so well

THE GREAT DUEL BETWEEN THIERRY AND PINABEL.   [*p.* 450.

described by our musician, might tempt a painter to depict it. One day I actually shed tears while regarding Meissonier's "1814," but it seems to me that this poor, ragged army, with hanging heads and fallen features, might well provoke pity.

Charles halted, and between the mountains he got a glimpse of a beautiful city. "It shall be mine!" he said, and he began to propose the conduct of the siege to his captains successively.

Charlemagne before Narbonne.

They all being lazy and sleepy, declined; and then the emperor, worthily enraged, insulted them with scorn:—

"Seigneurs, barons, who have served me well,
I tell you now in faith to get you gone!
Return unto your native lands once more.
But, by the Heav'n above which never lies,
Whoever of you goes I will remain.
Begone then French, Burgundians;
Angevins and Flemish, get you hence!
Full thirty months, if need be, I rest here!
When you return to Orleans or France
And people ask 'Where is the Emperor Charles?'
By God, seigneurs, so then shall you reply—
'We left him to besiege Narbonne alone!'"

The reciter ceased to chant, and paused after striking a few chords. As an elderly man who fancied he had a right to preach, he then exclaimed, "Ah! Charles was a hundred years old when he spoke thus. Which of you would be as bold?" Then, perceiving that his remark was very coldly received, he continued:— "Barons, knights, listen to me; Charlemagnes, alas! are not often to be found, more's the pity, for if we still had a Charles with us, we should have a Roland. It is certain that this son of Pepin had no son worthy of him, and who, without William, without that Ameri who took Narbonne, he would never have worn the crown of gold which the angels placed on the brow of the first king of France. But, unfortunately, gratitude is even more rare in the palace of the king than in the castle of the vassal, and Louis soon forgot his deliverer William. Even when rewarding his other barons with states and fiefs, he forgot the very man to whom he owed everything. He was out hunting at the time, but, when he returned, he was justly incensed, and I will tell you of the grandest exhibition of anger which history relates. Clerics would have us believe that we should never remind one reproachfully of the benefits which we may have conferred on him, but in truth this was too much to expect in this instance; the scandal demanded vengeance:—

> " Count William returned from his hunting
> With four arrows in his belt,
> His bow in hand ; and met Bertrand who said,
> ' Our Emperor has bestowed on all his knights
> Lands and fiefs, my uncle ; but on us
> Nothing at all ; we are clean forgotten ! '
> ' Nephew, I will quick unto the King
> And speak with him on this.'
> Then Count William to the palace strode
> And mounting up the marble steps in haste
> With heavy tread upon the palace floor,
> And not a baron heard but felt afraid.

" Then, white with anger, William presented himself before the poor little, trembling, king, and reminded him of all the benefits which he (William) had bestowed on him—of the battle under the walls of Rome where he had saved the king's life, and of his services at Pierrelatte. But he soon took higher flights to the supreme service which the bold count had rendered to the weakling king.

> " When Charlemagne desired to make you king,
> The crown upon the altar was deposited.

Count Hernaut supported by his clan
Desired it, and wished to take it up.
But I saw him ; and, indignant, flung
My hand upon his neck, and threw him down
Upon the holy pavement of the church.
Advancing then the marble steps I scaled ;
Beneath the gaze of Pope and Patriarchs
I seized the crown to place it on your head.
Can you forget such service as was this
When you apportion out your lands and fiefs !

Count William hastens to the King.

"But," continued the reciter, "let us not dwell upon such a scene of ingratitude. Let me then conclude—as it waxes late—with the recital which will please and enliven you. Be silent pray. I am going to speak to you of Ogier. The great Ogier. After the epic of the king, after the epic of William, it would be unfair not to include the epic of Doon, of which Ogier is the glory. Listen, then, gentlefolk, and think not that I sing for your rewards, but to celebrate prowess and chivalry, the best in the world ! "

Then he recounted all the great deeds of Ogier during the siege of Rome, and his double duel with the pagan, Caraheu, and with Brunamont who had defied the Deity. Then our singer described in glowing terms the entry of the Pope into the Eternal City. Behind him rode the emperor, and a young knight very tall, very fiery, very handsome, who was Ogier of Denmark.

But as he was speaking of the Pope, and of the love which Charles entertained for him, a voice cried, " Our King Philip does not love Innocent ! "

" Well, at any rate," remarked the castellan, " he has been re- conciled to him ; the Interdict has been removed, and Agnes has retired to Poissy.   Ingeburg has resigned."

This concluded the afternoon, which had been a long one.   The singer, very much applauded and feasted, received from the baron a present of a Spanish mule, and a tunic of red *paile*.   The epic recitation thus came to an end.   Darkness was setting in.

No matter how sumptuous had been the dinner, our barons had supper before they went to bed, and even this supper did not put an end to drinking, for they demanded wine when they were going to bed.   It was carried in with some solemnity and largely par- taken of.

The chamber was lighted by a large taper which burned in a tall candlestick as high as itself.   Kings and grandees treated them- selves to two torches or tapers.   It was not much of a light after all, but better than " carbuncles."

Around the baron were collected the squires and chamberlains who disrobed him ; around his lady were her maidens, who, behind a curtain, performed the same offices for her.   Beneath the baron's pillow are placed his shirt and breeches, then the pair go to bed naked under an avalanche of bedclothes.   On the pegs are hung their garments for next day.   The taper burned all night.

Frenchmen were accustomed to " gabble " when they retired for the night, and when several slept in the same hall the laughter at the ridiculous boastings and " seasoned " tales was loud and long until sleep overpowered them.

During the winter evenings they did not go to bed until after they had sat for a couple of hours round the fire.   The narratives of sportsmen then succeeded to the tales of pilgrims, who came to beg a corner of the chimney.   Hospitality was freely exercised, but to none so freely as to pilgrims, who were received with open arms and treated to the best.   Refuges were established, and comfortable quarters too, but nowhere were pilgrims, or " penitents," so well treated as at the castles. They were assisted to change their garments, and not till they were comfortable and rested were they questioned as to their journey, whether from Jerusalem, or Rome, or from Saint Martin of Tours, or Cologne, or Compostella.— " Come, tell us, and we will sit up an hour later with you."

Entry of the Pope, escorted by Charlemagne.

When the baron retired he had all the keys carried to his room, and he inquired concerning the watchmen and the defences. " Was the drawbridge up ? Were the watchmen at their posts ?" The eschangaites sound their horns. The night is clear and moonlight.

All is quiet. Sleep then falls upon the castle.

CHAPTER XVII.

THE MILITARY LIFE OF THE KNIGHT.

I. BEFORE THE WAR.

WAR, sport, and tournament; these three words describe the whole existence of the baron, and the two latter should be regarded as a kind of apprenticeship to real war. Every military nation ought to possess "war schools" in some form or other. The Feudal Middle Ages had two of these schools, and we will look at them more closely.

The Tournament is the first of those institutions which was in olden days destined to inculcate the military spirit and military usage. Those who defend this terrible amusement do not forget to make use of this argument against all those who assail it, and even against the Church which has so absolutely condemned it! "How do you imagine that our young knights can meet in any real battle without such training?" they ask. "No," they add, "in order to throw oneself confidently into the *mêlée* one must have seen the blood flow, the teeth give way, and have been unhorsed many times. That is what one may term a school, and Sainte Palaye, who was clear-sighted, was quite right in comparing our tourneys to the Olympian Games.

I confess that this apology seems to me the only possible one, and certain arguments, which are chiefly due to the author of the *Roman de Hem*, appear simply ridiculous. He argues from a very low standpoint, as concerning the means of existence of those who cater for the tourneys; and his reasons seem about on a par with the argument that, if the Church did not exist, how would the beadles live? We need not take more account of those who liken the tourney to the modern steeple-chase.

Those sanguinary exercises were of such importance, that in the admirable poem recently discovered by Paul Meyer, which is dedicated to William the Marshal, Earl of Pembroke, Regent of

England, who died in 1219, a good quarter of the twenty thousand verses are devoted to the tourney. A quarter! That is just the place they filled in the existence of the Feudal knight.

One would naturally wish to go back to the origin of such an important institution, and here the most contradictory opinions have been successively ventilated. The Germans may claim the origin, but the famous text of Tacitus has no weight here. Between the

Going to the Crusade.

naked youths who threw themselves into the *mêlée*, and the *torneors* of the Middle Ages, there is no point of resemblance whatever.

Many chroniclers do not hesitate to state that Geoffrey de Preuilly invented the tourney, but we shall see that there is no need of any elaborate proofs to confute this statement, as Ducange does when he maintains that tourneys existed before the supposed inventor of them. A custom so universal and so complicated in action did not spring one fine day from the brain of any single individual, and spread over the world. Such things are not *invented*.

The fact is, that the Tourney is a French institution. It was born in France, and was imported into England and Germany, and it is with reason that these encounters have been called *conflictes Gallici.* But we think that with the aid of our old poems we can carry the argument further than this.

We believe that the earliest tourneys were real battles, and to borrow a childish term we may say that they were "battles for the good." But this is not all. We are persuaded that in the early tourneys—very terrible and very bloody as they were—was the form of civil war : feudal, private war. The primitive tourney then, is simply a battle like any other. The term tourney, you must remember, was distinguished from the word *joust.* A tourney was always a combat in troops ; a joust on the contrary was only an isolated encounter of two individuals.

But from other points of view the tourney is only a battle like another, and we must explain its various characteristics. The primitive tourney, or *cembel*—I was nearly writing the first style of tourney—was a real battle preceded by a defiance, and was engaged in upon a day and at a time which had been agreed upon by common consent. There was no strategy, no surprises. At the place agreed upon the two armies in the presence of their commanders at the first signal engaged each other. The tourney was a military encounter, in which many thousands of men met at a given point and slew each other.

Such is the tourney as we find it described and coloured in the old romances. It is difficult to say that it is not a faithful picture.

One thing is certain, that even in more civilized times the tourney was still a general encounter—a *mêlée.* Tourneys were distinguished by a certain courtesy in fighting, but they were earnest, bloody, and often mortal. At the once-famous tournaments of Chauvenci, after many days of exercise, the knights voted them "slow" and demanded a "tourney." Then the day and hour were fixed and the meeting became the ancient *cembel* without the number of dead. But how about the wounded and the half-dead combatants, and what bloodshed before so many ladies too !

If one reads carefully the gory pages of *Garin* and the milder records of the *Tournois de Chauvenci,* the resemblance between the "battles" will clearly be perceived. And yet more than a century elapsed between the production of these works.

It is true, also, that tourneys were the origin of the battles to decide which was the best side—and during the Middle Ages duels with this object were fought—always sanguinary and often deadly. *Torneamentum hostile,* says Mathew Paris ; *joustes mortelles,* says Froissart.   Cannot we perceive here the trail of the ancient and sanguinary tourney.

Even the most delicate and graceful encounters have been spoiled and saddened by deaths, which did not surprise nor scandalise our ancestors.   Learned writers have enumerated these fights, and the lamentable accidents.   Such a tourney occurred in 1240, in which sixty or eighty combatants were slain.   This is rather too large a number for simple amusement.   In the most harmless tourneys at Chauvenci there were none but cut and slashed faces and carriages full of the wounded.   So the ancient *cembel* still animated the knights.

But it may be said that in these savage encounters of the Feudal Age there were no spectators, and no ladies looked on them. This is a mistaken idea if entertained, for the old romances describe the maidens and damsels going out to see those barbarous games.   These *cembels* were at once a butchery and a spectacle.

Now how did the primitive tourney assume the second style ? Well, after all, no great change was necessary.

In the old tournament there were two opposing armies, and these dwindled to two parties, two groups ; always two camps ! A defiance was given, but a defiance hedged in by politeness, by formal and even gentle courtesies.   The date and place were fixed in advance, and the knights met but by *invitation !*

In the former great encounters each knight selected his adversary, one worthy of him, and these battles were composed of several elementary jousts.   They gave way gradually to the new system, and the personal element became stronger, which succeeded each other for hours under the gaze of spectators who were interested— or who, at any rate, did not permit themselves to appear bored. But the *mêlée* was preserved, and it was specially known as the " tourney."

In the antique *cembels* sharpened weapons were used, as against infidels.   In the later engagements these were blunted as arms of courtesy.

Ladies, being naturally curious always, determined to satisfy their curiosity in a fashion worthy of themselves and of their cavaliers. Instead of letting them remain standing in the meadow or by the walls, they constructed elegant pavilions of wood, which they called *eschaffaus*, *hourds*, *loges*, or *beffrois*. In these they displayed their pretty faces and magnificent attire. Perched in these buildings they encouraged or commiserated the knights. They tended rather to embitter than to soften the amenities of the tourney, for these ladies liked to see the blood flow, and were more coquette than humane.

The influence of poetry then made itself felt, and songs were sung of the fray which were certainly not canticles. The gallantry of Love Lyrics and Pastorals by degrees invaded the tribunes where the ladies sat. To these songs, which occupied the evenings between the jousts, succeeded dances and " cards." To fight all day and dance at night was rather hard for the men, but the women did not trouble themselves about that !

We are now far from the rude encounters of the early Feudal period, but the grand ornamental tournaments of the fourteenth century were the outcome of the old rough and sanguinary tourneys in which the lists were strewn with the dead and dying.

It was owing to the advance of Christianity that this softening influence occurred—a work of many centuries it is true, and a slow advance of which one would have hastened the progress—an insufficient work which one would gladly have perfected. That the Church bravely struggled against this no person whose opinion is of value will deny. Popes condemned the tourney as " accursed." From Innocent II. to Clement V. we can trace a sequence of anathemas and thunderbolts. The former condemned them and forbade them because they cost men their lives, and the Fathers in Council decided to refuse the rites of sepulture to those who died from their wounds. They would not deprive them of confession nor of the viaticum, but they would deny them ecclesiastical burial. The Lateran Council emphasised this on the 4th April, 1139. Eugene III., in 1148, renewed the same maledictions, and Alexander III. and Innocent III. and IV. followed the same lead. But Nicholas III. in 1279 displayed more energy than all on that date, memorable in the history of the Tourney.

The King of France, having been weak enough to permit what he had previously condemned, the Pontiff called the cardinal, Simon de Saint-Cecile, " over the coals " for not having prevented such a scandal, and commanded them to excommunicate all those who had taken part in those jousts. The poor king had been already cruelly punished for his laxity; his younger brother, Robert of Clermont, had become absolutely imbecile from the effects of a blow he had received in a tournament in that same year, 1279, in honour of Charles, son of the King of Sicily. The poor young man had come to be dubbed knight, and died an idiot in 1318. What a lesson! Clement V. long afterwards confirmed his strictures in a solemn "bull" in the sixteenth year of his pontificate, when he declared that the tourney was fatal to the Crusade, as in the former men, money, and horses, were uselessly squandered! We might pass by the money and the horses, but the men! the men! All the noble blood of Christendom to be shed for nothing!

To the denunciations of the Popes the learned doctors lent their voices. Saint Bernard and Jacques de Vitry, Humbert de Romans, and others took up their parables against the practice. Royalty also chimed in. Philip Augustus made his sons swear never to take part in a tourney. No one would be surprised at Saint Louis detesting it, and Philip the Fair condemned the tourney many times, and he was no coward. The Valois did not sufficiently imitate him.

We need cite no more cases. The popes and the kings could do nothing after all. The French nobles would not hear of any interruption to the course which they regarded as a "school." They continued to break each other's bones to show there was no ill-feeling. Grave writers celebrated the *cembels* in verse, and even dragged in the Virgin as an accessory.

In fine, tourneys have given rise to scandalous excesses, but they have contributed to preserve a brave and manly tone. Between those who have defended and those who have condemned them so boldly and harshly, we may find a middle course worthy of France and Christendom. This is the position we would fain assume. Now, let us describe a "tourney."

The "invitations" have been sent out broadcast thirty leagues round. "To the tourney!" cry the messengers. "The Saturday before Easter Day at Montigny." The news spreads everywhere— to castle and house and manor. The emotion is universal. The ladies prepare their most becoming costumes, and deliberate concerning new ones.

Defiances and challenges are exchanged from town to town, and from castle to castle. Some affix a parchment to a tree on which is written this :—"At the castle of Hayes there are seven knights who are ready to encounter all comers!" This is fixed upon a tree by the roadside.

At Montigny the excitement is much greater—it is feverish. The list of knights is made out in advance, and at least a hundred workmen are engaged upon the barriers and galleries.

The Easter festival arrives. This year it falls on the 20th of April, when the verdure and flowers are blooming, and though no one will travel on the Sunday, next day the jousters are all on the way. People crowd to see them pass, some singly, some in company. One, decked out with money borrowed from a Jew, and behind him an earl escorted by fifty knights and as many squires. The magnificence of their dress is somewhat tarnished by the dust; but wait till you see them next day.

There is a tremendous uproar at Montigny, and even more at Villeneuve, where everyone seeks a lodging. Many houses are improvised as hotels, and the guests are welcomed. But the number of arrivals exceed all preparations, and tents are set up around the little town. Nevertheless from every avenue new arrivals debouch, each one singing his favourite song, as our regiments play their own marches or "quicksteps." . . .

The departure will be less joyous.

On the first morning, at the earliest possible moment, everyone goes out to inspect the lists. We need not represent them as being more elegant than they actually were. Picture to yourself, reader, strong wooden barriers enclosing an immense square or oblong piece of ground. A second interior barrier, less high and not so strong is separated from the former by a regular road or path, along which the footmen, who have to go to the assistance of discomfited tilters, take refuge. Here also are stationed the men-at-arms, who have to prevent the crowd from entering the enclosure. In this "lane" also favoured spectators are permitted to move about. The others essay to see what is going on over the pointed palings. The ladies are better provided for in tribunes, resembling the "stands" erected on modern racecourses. The first places are reserved for the judges or referees, but the ladies occupy all the remaining space, and their costumes are resplendent with silks and precious stones; their fair beauty, blue eyes, and blonde tresses are fascinating, and it seems almost a pleasure to be slain to win such smiles.

Now, ere the tournament commences, glance around and note the multitude of tents which cover the fields; see the banners flaunting everywhere in the town, over houses in which eating, drinking, and enjoyments of all kinds are in full swing. The lists are as yet deserted. They resemble the bull-rings in Spain; and there will be plenty of blood flowing to-morrow.

Though the sun rises betimes at the end of April, the tilters are up before him; indeed, they have scarcely been in bed after the night's festivities. Solemn individuals, heralds, go through the streets and tents calling upon the jousters to prepare for the fray. They are already preparing; half clothed, they show themselves at the entrances of the tents; arms are looked to, horses neigh, song of martial deeds are sung in chorus. Then every youthful knight goes to mass, for they are pious these bachelors, notwithstanding all their love-songs and pastorals.

By the time they come from church the sun is already hot, the tumult increases apace, the roads are crowded; ladies mounted on white mules are already threading their way to the pavilions. The tilters stand aside, forming a lane for these magnificent dames who parade their beauty before their anxious eyes. The jousters arrive at the lists alone or in company with the ladies, who bestow upon them gages to wear in their helmets. The knights sing again. The minstrels have arrived, and begin to rival the barons in melody. The trumpets sound clearly, and penetrate to every ear. The jousts are about to commence!

But we must now introduce the heralds, who are the "living rules" of all such entertainments. They are the guardians of order. No tournament would be possible without them.

Their calling is a strange one. They have risen from small beginnings, but have managed to swell themselves into a very comfortable position, and to make money. At first they were simple *commissionaires*, who announced the tournaments about to be held; "travellers" for the tourney, in fact. They were glad to announce the names of the combatants too, and this was always their principal function, and gave them some importance. With the name of each challenger they shouted his battle-cry, and from that they hired themselves to the jouster who paid them. They thus proffered their services to all knights, and each one had his little circle of "customers." These messengers, who for two months before the tournament went about the country, were then heralds, and the men who announced the names and titles of the combatants with so many flourishes, were heralds! Those comedians in short, who pretended to be greatly moved, and who with tears in their voices implored the ladies to bestow some reward or even their pity on the knights, were always heralds. They were very busy people, very important, very solemn, and very smiling! They were paid well. Robes or steeds—nothing came amiss to them. The minstrels only caused them any uneasiness, but our heralds bravely learned the business of the minstrel, and actually gave their rivals cause to fear.

There were heralds *and* heralds—grades just as amongst minstrels. Some were mere charlatans, but others looked upon their profession as a serious business, and thought themselves invested with a certain authority. In consequence of having attended so many tournaments they had the laws at their finger's ends, and people consulted them and listened to their opinions. They then altered and modified the laws and inscribed them on parchment, so they became scribes. Majestic and cold in demeanour, they eventually were selected to accompany princes and ambassadors to foreign courts, and believed that they actually represented the king their master. Once accustomed to writing they never lost the habit, so they became historians, and our literature of the eleventh century owes to them some of its most distinguished features.

Nine o'clock! 'Tis the hour appointed for the "tourney;" a striking procession is seen approaching, heralds leading, minstrels on the flanks. All the jousters are there riding in twos and threes, the majority glancing upwards at the ladies in the "stands." The march past continues for an hour, and the last in the procession are still at Villeneuve when the advanced members have reached Montigny. Their entry is splendid, trumpets are braying, ladies singing, the sun illuminating all with his beams. The barons display their horsemanship before the ladies in the galleries, who admire their apparently simple evolutions, while some of these fair spectators send sleeves to their gallants to make into pennons, and throw them other love gages, such as gloves, ribbons, or necklaces, until they have nothing left but their dresses and their hair. These incidents show to what a pitch the tournament has been carried. The men give their blood, and the women, more foolishly, their hearts.

Now the latest jouster has arrived in the enclosure, and the tournament is about to commence.

The jousters are all present awaiting their turns, weapons in hand, but these weapons do not resemble those in use in real battle. They are blunted and almost wooden-y, but such is the force with which they are wielded that they inflict mortal blows. At any rate, they wait impatiently the moment of combat; but they may be compelled to remain under arms till nightfall and not secure a challenge. The test is rather severe.

Sometimes in ordinary tournaments, nearly two hundred jousters will engage, and the sport will last several days. The same scene is enacted over and over again—" two combatants will endeavour to vanquish each other with heavy sticks ! " The game may appear monotonous, but to our ancestors no one tourney resembled another. There was a never-ending variety in the wounds and manner of attack. Sometimes both combatants would be slain, sometimes one only—or only one wounded ; and our great-grandmothers were never bored by these sights.

Besides, all tournaments had not the same " style." At some, three lances were shivered—neither more nor less ; at others, one adversary must be unhorsed. But this was frequently the case, and it really seems to us that if we describe one tournament we describe all !

Night is closing on. People are beginning to fear that there will be no more jousting, and that the combat will fail for want of combatants. The heralds are rather nervous also, and cry out for jousters ; but they think it is late, and that they will not be able to see any longer. Suddenly two knights present themselves who have been defying each other for a month past. They are Hervien de Montigny and Jean de Dampierre. Each one has retained a herald in his pay, and these men shout out the name of his baron until the welkin rings. " Dampierre : to the knight Dampierre." " Montigny the chivalrous," replies the other. They rival each other in their acclamations. Both jousters are young, and both handsome. One is clad in ruddy armour, the other habited after Lancelot, the hero of the Table Round!

They are ready at length, and waiting in the centre of the enclosure face to face on their sturdy steeds. At the same moment they lower their enormous lances, and clasp their shields to their chests. Then they spur their horses, stooping their heads, and rush against each other. It is necessary neither to aim too high nor too low, but as nearly as possible in the centre of the body. Each one must calculate his blow with precision, so as not to strike on one side nor in the empty air; for the ladies would laugh at them, and all would go badly with them.

In about ten minutes it is all over. One of the two has had his teeth knocked out, the other has a broken arm. Both have fallen, and their horses have run away. The heralds implore pity and assistance from the ladies. If they dared they would approach, but meanwhile they are content to send messages of sympathy and affection, which are probably insincere. Then the esquires remove the unfortunate jousters, who are half dead, but quite unconquered. This is the last joust that day. The damsels declare that they will dream of the combatants all night, and the heralds pretend that they will talk of the encounter for ever! The ladies now descend from the galleries somewhat saddened, but the feeling of melancholy wears off, and in an hour they are all dancing within, without bestowing a thought upon the broken teeth of Hervien de Montigny, or of the broken arm of Jean de Dampierre!

The first day's jousting is over, but it is succeeded by many others, for a tournament occupies many days when some two hundred combatants are engaged. We would be speedily bored by such displays, but our ancestors liked them; and then the evenings were delightful, the nights were passed in singing and dancing, and at times the jousting was even postponed for other enjoyments for a day. It was a continual intoxication of pleasure.

But after many days of inoffensive engagements, and when scarce twenty knights, more or less wounded, remained, the young cavaliers demanded a tournament, and excited others to seek it. A general tourney was now the cry, and met with no opposition. It was fixed for next day—defiances were exchanged, man against man, province against province, clan against clan. Germans against

Frenchmen, Burgundians against Hainaulters. Heralds went hither and thither announcing the "grand tournament." On that evening there was less dancing, but more play and conversation, while the ladies laughed a little less too : there was something serious afoot, and the bravest were thoughtful for the morrow.

The day breaks clear and fine upon the men who overnight were so joyous, and who may in a few hours be no more. They attend mass, the ladies likewise attending, and I fancy they require the divine blessing as much as their male friends.

The lists are not, on this occasion, the place of meeting. It is the open fields ; space is required for this little war. All the country-side has assembled, and the *vileins* appear in force, but terrified by the knights, who gallop amongst them laughing at their fright. Now the combatants await the signal. It is given !

Picture to yourself, reader, two regiments of cavalry charging each other. The shock is terrible. Every knight seeks out the adversary he has challenged, and if he cannot find him, he attacks somebody else. Disorder is rife, and so this engagement has been called a *mêlée*. If anyone is unhorsed he is trampled under foot. The dust is the great plague of the jousters : it penetrates to their eyes and nostrils, and those who are dying are more quickly suffocated by it. However, the fight becomes more and more animated and furious, more indiscriminate. The combatants began with a smile ; they continue angrily, blindly, and no longer recognize each other. This is so far excusable, as they are fighting hand to hand, and nothing is more likely to engender hot blood than those brutal encounters : they fight as against Infidels !

Now the uproar grows greater, the dust thicker, and the combatants are veiled in an almost impenetrable veil. The squires hasten to the assistance of their masters : the heralds, who do no fighting, but have an eye to the perquisites of the *cembel*, encourage the combatants by voice and gesture : then, turning towards the ladies' gallery, they call upon them for God's sake to stop the *mêlée*. They may request as much as they please, but it is no easy task to accomplish. Swords flash unceasingly, falling on neck and shoulder ; night comes on, the battle continues. The knights no longer know each other, but they continue to fight at random. Darkness falls : the clashing of steel and armour continues ; the cries of the wounded, the shouts of the victors, the neighing of horses resound on all sides, mingled with the pleadings of the vanquished. The day is done: the stars shine out. All is over: the combat is at an end! Then swords are sheathed, the two parties reform, friends again mingle together, the ladies turn homewards, the heralds chaunt the praises of those who have paid them, and think of taking care of the wounded. There are about one hundred and fifty in sad plight.

Such was a tourney of the twelfth and thirteenth centuries, and it will be perceived that it bears little resemblance to those presented on the stage in opera.

The barbarity of these encounters was not their greatest vice, however. To brave death even so was something brave and noble. It may be chivalry in a mistaken sense, but it was at least chivalrous, and there was some heroism in it. But, unfortunately, disinterestedness was not a great virtue of our knights, and tournaments were, with a certain section of the barons, matters of speculation. They took prisoners, and fixed heavy ransoms upon them, and took a number of very valuable horses. The victor took possession of the horse and arms of the vanquished, which the latter had to purchase at a high price. Thus it became a commercial transaction. In less than a year, two knights, by associating together, might capture a hundred knights and steeds. This was lucrative sport; and our horse-racing is preferable to it, for there we do not find the abominable mixture of "business" with prowess—the weight of the sword with the weight of the purse!

Now the fête comes to an end. It has been very costly, and many a baron has been ruined by it—he and his wife too. Her costume and her husband's equipage cost many a broad acre; but perhaps the most ill-advised individual is the baron who has given the entertainment. Of course I know that the expenses should theoretically be shared amongst the jousters; but suppose they forget to pay! Then the dinners, and largesse, and the presents which must be bestowed! Ah, well might the critics say, "They are useless and costly exhibitions!"

But that evening they all put a good face on it. Time enough to think of the expense to-morrow. The question now is, how to bring the tournament to a worthy conclusion.

The assemblage returns to the castle by torchlight; the wounded are attended to : the ladies compliment them in a manner which never cured or hurt anyone : the heralds sing their praises or make them laugh. Those who are uninjured hasten to the baths, and dinner will surely restore them fully. They will even be present during the long evening afterwards, and play in drawing-room entertainments or dramas. Those brave knights who have been hacked and bruised all day are willing to listen to these trivial comedies or play games! Nothing can be braver.

The prize of the tourney is then proclaimed, but it was not so valuable as in after epochs—in the fourteenth and fifteenth centuries. The victor received a falcon or a girdle ; or perhaps a shield ornamented with precious stones and banded with gold. These, offered by the hands of beautiful dames, were I admit worth having; but the best prize of all was the hand of a lovely damsel—and her territory!

The day after the grand tourney the guests separate. The ladies mount their palfreys and ride away with sleeveless robes, ere they can repair the damage they have voluntarily done to their dress. There are sad partings and leave-takings. But at length all are on the way : a knight rising in his stirrups trolls out a love-ditty. The rest listen to the close, and do not spur their steeds until the cadence of the last verse has died away. Then adieu!

The "tourney" was a school of arms, of war; but it was not the only one : the chase has, perhaps, as useful an influence. There were no such expenses, no such amorous enterprises, no such foolish women to be reckoned with as at tournaments. Man warred with the wild beast—so much the better.

There was hunting every day, and when the baron was not thinking of battle you may be certain that he was thinking of stags and wild boars. Every winter morning he donned his hunting dress, his great boots, to which he attached big spurs ; if very cold he put on a mantle of fur. His costume was simple : luxury was only apparent in his ivory hunting-horn, very beautifully carved and ornamented, suspended round his neck by a silken cord of some bright hue. Large buck-skin gloves covered his hands, his bow and arrows were carried by his beaters ; and his Danish axe, and his hunting-knife by himself for close quarters. The hounds gambolled around him. He starts : the morning is delightful. He enters the wood, and seeks the wild boar of whose presence therein he has been informed. Never has such a monster been tracked, and happy indeed will the baron be if he can present its head to his wife. Come on! Come on!

The hounds are put on the scent, and go baying through the wood startling the birds. Where is the boar? At length the peculiar cry of the hounds indicates the spot, and suddenly the game is discovered. He is surrounded by the hounds, but he exacts a severe penalty. The baron's favourites are slain and wounded : their master will avenge his faithful dog. He pursues the boar alone, only a few hounds accompanying him : he comes up with the boar—one, two, three dogs roll helpless on the earth— then the baron approaches, brandishing his boar-spear, and plunges it full into the beast's chest. The blow is fatal : the blood flows in torrents, and the hounds lick it up greedily. Then exhausted, lolling out their tongues, they lie down beside the enormous brute like dwarfs around a giant. The hunt is over.

We need not detail the incidents of the triumphal return, and the delight and terror of all at the castle as they inspect the fearful quarry, and touch its enormous paws and grinning mouth. In such a manner our ancestors hunted—the chase was the great passion of their lives, and no one will deny that it was a good school for a military career.

Thanks to the tournament, thanks to the chase, the man-at-arms was never taken by surprise nor deceived by misrepresentation. He could always proudly declare that he was prepared for anything— "I am ready."

So when a new Crusade was preached he had only to don his hauberk, take leave of his wife and children, embrace the cross, and mount his charger Passavant. He was ready.

Let us now watch him in his career.

CHAPTER XVIII.

THE MILITARY LIFE OF THE KNIGHT.

II.—A SIX MONTHS' CAMPAIGN.

RETARDED by the political egotism of kings and emperors, the Crusade is at length preached. It is decided upon: our knights depart. What way will they travel? Will they go direct to Jerusalem? Will they proceed to Constantinople, or will they adopt a new plan of campaign and commence by clearing the Infidels out of Egypt, and marching more safely into the Holy Land? No one can tell, and really nobody cares. Assume the cross and go: that is all one thinks about. Vainly do the elder ones recall to the too ardent spirits the dangers of the campaign, and the trials which the former Crusaders underwent—the horrors, and hunger, and thirst, when they had to drink the blood of the slain! All these fine descriptions had no effect. "Let us only see Jerusalem," say the knights. "Let us only sing our hymns before the sacred walls, and kiss the spots where Jesus stood!" Well may the modern writers and politicians have affirmed that the Crusades were only acts of faith. To cause the law of God to triumph, and to gain Paradise, were the motives of the barons of the twelfth century. This simple faith explains why, putting aside all pettiness of human policy, these brave men quitted their homes to undergo hunger and privation in a far-distant land, to die miserably alone, with their expiring eyes turned towards Jerusalem, calling on the name of Jesus. These men believed in God, and died for him, hoping for a humble place amid the saints and angels. Some may rail at such blind faith, but it will compare favourably with the contemporary formula :— "Live in comfort, and trouble about nothing."

Then the knights loved fighting for its own sake. They entered into a battle as into Heaven: the longest days seemed too short, if they only spilt their own blood, or someone's else ; as one baron remarked :—"If I had one foot in Paradise, and the other in my own castle, I would step out from Heaven to fight!" Even the glories of Paradise weighed little against the plumed helmet, the cuirass, and the good sword, a broken head, or a man slain in battle! So they went forth to war, the cross upon their breast!

In ordinary wars there were solemn declarations and defiance. This challenge in private wars assumed a strange form. The challenger took two or three hairs from his fur robe, from his ermine pelisse, and threw them proudly before the challenged. But the messengers who more often bore the defiance, put it into practical shape, and more eloquently. "My master demands satisfaction, and if you do not make amends for the wrong you have done, I defy you honourably in his name." These ambassadors did not want for insolence, and silence had to be imposed upon them. The few hairs were better. It is seldom that the embassy of peace succeeded ; but our admiration must not be withheld from those brave feudal messengers who rode with the olive branch, or pine branch, in hand, according to the country, furnished with an order and a glove of defiance ; but being careful, when they had delivered their message, to hold their sword by the blade in token of peace!

In the Crusades there was nothing of that kind. Those wars had no beginning ; the defiance was unlimited, perennial.

Nevertheless, it was necessary to train into regular men-at-arms those youthful "bachelors" who had amused themselves too long with the cross of leaves. The king alone, or the ruler of the country, had the right to proclaim the "ost" or assembly. So the "small people," the commons, were summoned by sound of bells ; but the barons could not be so called out. They were assembled by letter, and the messengers were constantly running about.

The moment the baron received his missive he was delighted, and rushed to his armour closet. Many an engagement, many a tournament had he fought : he had battled against the English, and had campaigned along the Loire, in Normandy, Main, and Touraine. But all these past joys are nothing in comparison to the present : "I am about to proceed to Jerusalem!" His wife and children are pale in fear and anguish, but they do not dare to dissuade him : they even essay to smile.

The knight's arms are of somewhat ancient pattern, but if anyone ridicule them, woe to the jester! He proceeds to the stable to caress his good steed, and to tell him whither he is bound. "Courage, my poor Passavant, we go together." Then he inspects his accoutrements and trappings, and if he finds them in good condition he praises his squires.

Our baron then calls for his chaplain, and makes him commit

The Mêlée.

his last wishes to writing. He bestows fifty livres on each of the neighbouring abbeys, of which there are three; he founds in each one an annual mass to be said during his life, and a requiem after his death. But he wishes to be buried in the chapel of his well-loved Templars, as close to the altar as possible.

Though many others proceed to the Crusade leaving numerous debts, or with heavy engagements and mortgages on their lands, our baron will not leave a single creditor behind him. His wife, who is a true Christian, loudly approves his action, and feigns to be courageous in preparing for a parting which is killing her. She would, on the morrow of their wedding-day, have cried to him with her weak, brave voice :—" If you wish to go to the Crusade, I would say, go !" But this is not now her cry—it is "Remain !" she would say to-day. However, she has faith in God, though with choking tears she remembers that out of twenty who depart scarce one will return. These farewells are usually for ever ! Farewell : embraces which are prolonged, and which all wish to be longer : eyes which can weep no more, so sadly have they wept : mournful resignation, which is akin to despair : the cries of women, with which are mingled the neighing of horses, the champing of bits, the clang of arms : a last embrace, a last kiss, a last look ; the last sound dies away in the distance : those dear ones fear to turn round lest they should retrace their steps. Speech dies on their lips : there is no vent for their thoughts !

It has been decided that the subjection of Egypt shall initiate the Crusade, and to Damietta the Christian fleet proceeds. Our Crusader had to embark at Aigues-Morte, and the scene at the port was calculated to affect him powerfully. Thousands of glistening points of light were scintillating in the harbour on the evening of his arrival : these were the lanterns on the transports. But he had to wait until the next day to become acquainted with the appearance of that sea which he had never yet beheld. He was pleased with the blue waves, but the ships disillusioned him terribly. He had founded his expectations on the old romances : had pictured vessels of ebony and silver : cabins filled with roses and women, fitted¦ with ivory and silken hangings. These ships which he sees are more numerous, but more vulgar ; but they are well-planned, and suited to the demands of war. The idea which the sailors had was that ships were to be floating fortresses, and they should be armed in like manner. The "castles" established on the ships were small wooden towers, squared and "embattled," generally three in number, one at each extremity, and the other on the mast. At the time our Crusader embarks (the middle of the thirteenth century) it is not scientifically certain that this system of castles has been perfected, and all that can be affirmed is that the summits have been crenated as the towers, or curtain, of a castle. Those vessels were very curious :—crescent-shaped, with one mast, or perhaps two masts, bearing flags, with their shields, their small boat, and their barge ; a dozen anchors : their sails white, or emblazoned with a golden cross. On board the braying of trumpets is heard: the bare-headed sailors are seen rushing hither and thither, their hair shaved from their foreheads, clad in two short-sleeved garments. The prow of the ship is furnished with a dragon or other image. Store-rooms are filled with wines and provisions : fodder, arms, lances, and shields. They have even space for the fine horses, though these were generally conveyed in specially-fitted vessels. Such is the appearance of a ship of war in which our Crusader may have embarked. An excellent and spacious cabin is prepared for him and his friends. Some have been so foolish as to bring their hawks and their hounds! As if there were any other game to hunt yonder save Infidels !

The voyage has been long owing to contrary winds, but at length the sandy coast is reached. As they have embarked to the sound of musical instruments, so do they disembark, and the fanfares of trumpets make them forget the tedium of the voyage. They disembark gladly, with a sense of relief, and run about on shore gaily. Then they remember the steeds. Poor brutes! They gladly rush from their stalls and gallop over the sward. How delighted they are: neighing and bounding with joy. The first hour is charming!

The Crusaders are faithful to the rendezvous, they continue to arrive daily from every port in Christendom. The chiefs of the hosts—unfortunately there are several—are called upon to organise the encampments which we will endeavour to describe.

The material for the camp has been brought in barges, and there is no difficulty in unloading them. Should volunteers fail, the Crusaders have no difficulty in persuading the natives, by force or by entreaty, to assist. The transport animals are "requisitioned," and, in default of these, the mules and horses of the army are laid under contribution, and all the necessary materials for tents, &c., are carried up along the sand to the selected site; sinking at every step, and bathed in perspiration, men and beasts of burden proceed to the place where the engineer has roughly drawn the plan of the encampment. In the centre are the tents of the chiefs, and the chapel of the Deity, who is there installed as the true general and guardian of the army. Around these are a series of concentric squares, regularly arranged. Only the knights are considered in these dispositions, the common people are lodged without, but, nevertheless, the camp is vast and consists of two species of tents, pavilions and conical tents, with double or single spaces. The latter are the more common, and extend from a central pole which is often an article of luxurious and costly make; it is called the *estace* or *colombe*. It is made of valuable woods, inlaid with gold or ivory. All around it are fixed the tent-pegs for the cords, and poets have written of silken cords and silver or coral pegs. But in reality the ropes were of hemp, and the pegs of oak. The tent itself was of cloth of a more or less impermeable kind, but luxury also entered here, and we read of tents of staring silk materials, gaudy in colour, and "frivolous." On the top was placed a ball of gold, the chief's pavilion being surmounted by eagles. But the banners are preferable to my mind, and have a fine effect. The interior of the tent is more ornamental than is necessary, historical tapestry representing scenes from the Old Testament are frequent in the large tents. Simple knights are content with silk hangings. The tent has its history: it is loved, and every incident connected with it can be recalled and related: the long watches, the victories, the battles: it is a poem!

There was something of the East in the Christian camp. Our encampments are generally plain white erections, but those of the Middle Ages were full of colour, and very picturesque. Silks of all hues; red, green, blue, or varied as a peacock's tail, the golden balls glittering in sun-light: the flashing fluttering banners! Then the trumpets at daybreak and sunset lent a charm to the scene; the incessant movement of squires and grooms, the chaunts of the knights. At night-fall all the colour dies out: the dark groups of sentries march to their posts, and the watchmen exchange their calls in the silence of the night! Such is the scene in the Crusaders' camp. We need not embellish it by details of the vermin which swarmed around it—camp-followers and others, whom it is as difficult to exclude from the camp as it was to cleanse the Temple of money-changers and dealers.

Surrounded by a deep ditch, carefully guarded, the camp may have appeared impregnable, as it was well provisioned. But one has to reckon with the unforeseen, and sickness comes upon the army in want of fresh water; or perhaps the barges, laden with stores, have been sunk. Then no one is infallible, and mistakes are made; the communications are not sufficiently kept up—a very common fault in mediæval armies—with the base nor with the supports. This is a fatal error which has cost many lives of brave men by the enemy, by fever or disease. Sometimes the camp is quitted or struck, and the army marches blindly into the country : the hosts meet a skilled enemy, well acquainted with the district, who spies their weakness, and profits by their ignorance. The Christians can only retreat. Where are their provisions and water ? In the hand of the Infidel ! " Let us go and seize them ! Forward ! "

The striking of such a camp is no light affair, but it is accomplished more rapidly than one might suppose. The cords are detached, the pegs pulled up, the cloth falls against the tent-pole, and is rolled up, placed on the mule and carried onward. The favourite ruse of the enemy is to cut the tent-cords, and so the sleeping warriors are enveloped in the folds of the tent ! Thank Heaven, we are not within them.

Permit me now to sketch the army on the march. The host is rarely silent, the music plays, the ensigns are displayed, and if the king be present, the Oriflamme is at the head of the army. Skirmishers and scouts are in advance reconnoitring. This is all very well so far as it goes, but the interminable baggage-train, the mules laden with the tents, with the knights' trunks, their money, clothing, and so on; the long procession of camp-followers, the heavy carriages containing women : picture all these plunging across the Egyptian desert, and you have an ever-present source of danger, which has menaced and destroyed many armies.

It is necessary to halt occasionally ; sometimes for days, perhaps. The number of the sick is ever increasing. Dead bodies dot the route, and we cannot realise the horror of such a death as these have died. To fall in battle is noble, honourable, sudden ; but to fall in the desert half buried in the sand, and to lie alone—all alone—in the delirium of fever, with those terrible lucid intervals, in which home scenes and loved faces appear—the well-beloved Aëlis, the little Clémence, or Pierre ! Horrible ! Our Crusader nearly met such a death, but fortunately a camp-follower whose life he had saved during the disembarkation, passed by and rescued him. It is the story of the Good Samaritan over again ; there is nothing novel in it, but it is none the less touching.

So many men are " falling out " that the commanders determine to give battle now. But have they any clear plan—any decided strategy ? We must explain this clearly.

Generally in the eleventh and twelfth centuries there was no special strategy in small or great battles. The army was divided into battalions, or *échelles*, grouped as far as possible according to nationalities, and so calculated to give rise to the rivalry in battle which is always so desirable. An advance-guard, or attacking force, was placed in front of the main body. Behind it there was a rear-guard, a reserve in fact, which only came into action to check the retreat or to ensure the victory.

In the country during the campaign, the *fourriers*, or scouts, took the place of skirmishers. The same plan was adopted by the opposing army, and the two bodies awaited the signal to commence when they rushed upon each other, and many sanguinary duels ensued. At last the two commanders, or kings perhaps, encountered each other, and with the fall of one of them the battle was decided. The victors pursued the vanquished, who fled scattered, or mayhap in endeavouring to cross a river were drowned in numbers, or slain on the bank.

These were the ordinary "tactics," if we may apply the term to such plain advance and retreat. But some of our heroes, as Girard of Roussillon for instance, elaborated plans of campaign which they secretly communicated to their generals. The means most usually employed were ambuscades, which always succeeded and consequently always seemed novel. It is hardly necessary to say that the spy-system was also brought into use. But a good spy is not easy to find. He must be skilful in disguise, and be acquainted with many languages; he must be a pilgrim at times, and play the part of a dead man. He must be quick at organizing the pigeon-despatch, and send for assistance for the army with notes about a hundred birds' necks to obviate the risk of capture by the enemy's falcons.

Feints and reconnaissances were also employed, but rarely. The generals of the period were accustomed to employ machines which they could use in sieges or in the field. Carpenters were attached to the army to make these; and besides many *ruses* were employed. It was Godfrey who dressed his soldiers in different costumes, and passed them ten times in review before the astonished Infidels. Ogier made wooden soldiers and deceived Charles the Great. William penetrated into Nîmes in the disguise of a merchant, having previously very cleverly enclosed his knights in barrels.

Roland was carried into the Castle of Lanson on a bier—but we need not continue to cite examples. They were after all only childish deceits.

The best tactics displayed by our ancestors were those by which they employed certain classes of troops. It was not without some heart-burning that the knights had to confess that the battle was not delivered to the strong arm and the brave steed. They had to give the bowmen a trial, and they, somewhat unwillingly, had to utilize the Commons, from whom these most useful assistants were drawn. But only a certain proportion were admitted into the ranks—seven hundred archers amid fifteen or twenty thousand men-at-arms. The best archers were English, Brabantines, and Gascons. They could shoot very rapidly, and rarely missed at two hundred paces. The Norman archers decided the Battle of Hastings by firing high and striking the Saxons through their helmets and visors. Without knowing it, these archers made a great change in the world.

The cross-bowmen rendered the same service with their bolts as the long-bowmen did with their arrows. They were less mobile, however, and were particularly charged to facilitate approaches. The infantry, the foot soldiers properly so termed, had more trouble in assuming a position for themselves. To hear of one hundred thousand foot we must go back to the poems of the fourteenth century ; but these " geldons " had long a high reputation in England, and the future was all their own. The commercial militia were only " footmen," and occupied a very inferior position in feudal camps, but they behaved very well, and the poets seldom ridicule them. On the contrary, they are well spoken of.

These foot soldiers were compelled to render the greater service, inasmuch as they could not be always counted upon to devote themselves with the military punctuality of knights. What was to be done with men who only owed forty days' service ? This was the case with all vassals who did "simple" homage, and they were numerous. So, as early as the twelfth century, the "soudoyers," or mercenaries, were favourites in all armies. They were, in general, poor knights who took to a military career, and placed themselves at the disposal of kings or powerful barons. France supplied the world with them ! They were at first despised by the rich, but they ended in pardoning their poverty. *They could be depended on !*

But now our battle is about to commence; and will not present any novel conceptions. Manœuvres did not prevail much before the fourteenth century, though there are a few isolated cases.

The silence of the morning of the battle has been so well described by the great poets, that we will not essay to follow them. The silence is more solemn than lugubrious. Many thousands of knights are ready to charge, waiting silently the word, spear in hand. They await the order "Forward!" They have been to chapel with bare feet. They have emptied their alms-purses into the hands of the priests, for there are many monks present who will have plenty of occupation shortly. Every man has confessed, for each one thinks he may be dead ere nightfall. There were some true conversions—such as that of the old knight of Carcassonne. The "bachelors" renounce all their levity, and many repent in tears. In the midst of the valley altars have been erected, and the priests are chaunting mass. The holy men pass on, administering the Communion as all the knights kneel down before them. The sun shines upon the scene; it illuminates all; all rivalry and jealousy is put away; the kiss of peace is bestowed; the vow is taken—"If I survive I will never sin more;" "If I survive I will compose a fine song upon the battle." In fact they promise, if they do not subsequently perform, and they are signed with the Cross. Now to horse!

The call is sounded, the trumpets ring out. This is the time to speak to men who are about to die. "Barons," says the oldest of the priests, "you are on the brink of the battle which you have so desired. Remember the ills you have endured, and which this will put an end to. Your foes are numerous, but look up to Heaven, and remember that God will send you legions of Angels as He has done before. When you are in the battle, strike and spare not, till you have penetrated your enemy's ranks. Remember you are the soldiers of God! You have received absolution; let your penitence be shown in your striking down the Infidel. Go!"

Then after a pause—he continued gravely: "If by chance there be any amongst you who are afraid, let them depart. But remember, ere you go, that a place has been prepared for you in Heaven, and that those who die will to-night be with the Angels! Here is a relic which should give a whole heart to anyone who by chance is weak-spirited. It is a fragment of the spear which pierced the side of Jesus—I pronounce my blessing upon you with it!"

BEFORE THE BATTLE.—THE MASS.

This holy benediction falls o'er all the army! Thus it was at the great battle of Aspremont, when all the barons in the army of Charlemagne saluted the crucifix—a piece of the true cross—which Archbishop Turpin suddenly displayed, luminous, and which darted its rays into the middle of the *melée.* "Fear not Death," he cried; "but, for the honour of Him who suffered for you, seek it! Forward!"

Then the trumpets and horns sound the charge. More than once during the battle the rally is blown. God grant that the retreat be not sounded to-night! The shock of the battle is terrible: the enemy turns and charges in his turn!

The honour of "first blow" is eagerly sought, and to our baron falls the coveted distinction. No one refuses him the glory; he is so highly esteemed. He rides at the head of the advance-guard to strike, slay, or overturn all in his way. He kills the Saracen who first opposes him. The battle begins well for the Christians. The advance-guard is soon engaged with the Infidel, and then the whole of both armies mingle and fight like demons. Every man is drunk with the lust of slaughter; a thirst for blood seizes on everyone—a rage which, if it do not excuse, can account for so many atrocities. Our poets are very realistic and describe horrible scenes; heads arms, limbs, shorn off; bodies disembowelled, and other terrible scenes. The pennons are steeped in blood and flutter redly. What brutality—what savagery—what rage and grief are here displayed!

No one expects war to be gentle, but in the Middle Ages it was often positively atrocious. To the atrocities of the Pagans, Christians replied with others which they should have energetically condemned. When we think of the massacres perpetrated in Jerusalem by the early crusaders our blood runs cold. Can we recall the fact of the French converting the heads of their enemies into missiles at Antioch without a shudder; and I detest the horrible alternative offered to the Saracens—"Baptism or decapitation!" Twenty years ago I raised my voice against these past infamies; I do so now, and shall continue to do so!

The *melée* continues with all the usual accompaniments of battle, "the combatants resemble woodcutters in a forest," and some of our imaginative poets have compared the battle itself to a wood "in which all the flowers are points of steel." Wounded and dying turn

THE BENEDICTION AT ASPREMONT

[p. 482.

THE RESCUE OF THE ORIFLAME.

their eyes towards Jerusalem, while the fighting everywhere continues, and "this is a day when the brave are recognised." Our
baron perched on a rock, silently contends with twenty or thirty of
the enemy. Each corps shouts its war-cry *Montjoie* for France;
Rome is shouted by the soldiers of the Empire; *Bourgoigne* or
Avalon by the Burgundians; *Malo-Malo* by the Bretons; *Valée* by
the Angevins; *Biez* by the Gascons; *Dex Aie* by the Normans;
and *St. Sepulchre* by the true Crusaders. Each division has its
watchward and is proud of it. They died with these cries in their
mouths, and sometimes they could not utter the cry.

These battles continue for a long while and their episodes are
monotonous, but each has a rallying point—the flag—and this represents a grand idea, that of Religion or Country. The King of
France—the king *par excellence*—was not present at this particular
battle because his oriflamme was not there—nor was the Dragon:
but the barons of France rallied round a pure white banner on which
was emblazoned the figure of St. George. The standard-bearer
having been wounded, and on the point of quitting hold of his
precious charge, our baron hurries towards him, snatches the
standard from his failing grasp even as Ogier from Alori, and
rescued it. This exploit terminated the battle. The Infidels, vanquished on all sides, retreated and fled.

The Christians remained masters of the field, and lay there to
rest that night. The main body, however, pursued the flying
pagans, while the others guarded the camp. The latter are not
the most favoured, because the sight of the field is horrible and
revolting. The victory has been dearly purchased. The dead lie
thickly, the wounded are confided to the care of the priests and
monks. The men of peace have been spectators of the fight, but
now their turn has come, and they set about to succour and relieve
the wounded by the dying gleams of day. Litters and ambulances
are improvised: some ladies have accompanied their husbands, and
these go through the ranks assuaging thirst and assisting in
dressing the wounds, or consoling the sorrows of the men-at-arms.
In the centre of a little clump of trees the doctors have established
themselves. As soon as a wounded man is carried thither he is
tenderly disarmed and his hurts washed. White wine is also used
to cleanse his wounds, and then they are bandaged up, when
anointed with the unguents in vogue. That strange pharmacy

which only that very morning provoked the ridicule of the "bachelors," is now the means of saving them, and many are laid comfortably on the grass covered with a blanket and given sleeping draughts which render them insensible to pain.

But much more lugubrious is the office of the squires and grooms or their masters, who search torch in hand amid the dead in the valley for their friends or patrons. They discover only too many, and lay them out in a row on a small hill, where that morning the rear guard of the Infidels had been posted. Alas! there is no equality in the disposal of these dead. The mercenaries and the common soldiers are thrown into a pit, while the barons and the grandees are carefully laid out apart.

Some horrible scenes are witnessed. A soldier recognises his intimate friend, and stands regarding him with that mute expression of grief which is characteristic of soldiers of all countries and of all times. The ancient custom of the funeral prayer, which is consecrated to those who have fallen in battle, subsisted still at the time to which our description applies. To the end of time will be repeated the prayer which Charlemagne offered up for his nephew Roland in the vale of Roncesvalles. "Friend Roland, brave man, lovely youth, may God rest thy soul in holy flowers in Paradise, amongst the beautiful and glorified above."

But our field of battle is less illustrious if the hearts engaged are no less Christian and the address none the less military. Nevertheless, some abominable plunderers come across the field even while the knight and his priest are exchanging noble, heartfelt sentiments, and begin to pillage the dead! This is ever the case. These *hyænas* are always prowling round the field of battle. Two days have elapsed, during which the sweets of victory are enjoyed and tears for the dead are dried. A council of war is held, and the chiefs of the army decide to march direct upon the nearest town and at once besiege it. The march commences!

We have endeavoured to make our readers understand something of the "mechanism" of a battle in the twelfth and thirteenth centuries. We will now try to give an idea of the "mechanism" of a siege; but the wheels are complicated and the machinery intricate.

To invest a town the moat was first filled up, and immense

AFTER THE BATTLE.—"THE BARONS ARE CAREFULLY LAID OUT."

wooden erections, called *beffrois*, with ladders on wheels, were employed to approach the walls. These were as high as the battlements, and, unless burned by the besieged, permitted perhaps a thousand men to concentrate on a given spot. The number of men employed was always considerable, but art supplemented force. By proper distribution of men, and by strategem, the besiegers could strike terror into their enemies and give them exaggerated ideas of their strength. The bridging of the ditch was important, and for the purpose timber was used, and in well-wooded districts this was not difficult. But when timber trees were not available the besiegers broke up some of the ships, and then transported the material with much labour to the scene of action. But even under favourable conditions scarcely more than a hundred feet of the immense ditch or moat could be filled up. Yet this was sufficient to place the ladders in position, and then the question as to the first person to ascend was mooted. The unfortunate barons who made the attempt were certain to be slain by the enemy, and hurled headlong from the moveable ladders which had been wheeled up to the walls. Many brave men die; the balistas and catapults made no impression, the ladders are broken; the town seems to mock the assailants. The besieged with advantage hurl stones, boiling lead and oil, and other material on the besiegers, while clouds of arrows fly amongst those farther off. The town must be reduced by famine; but it is provisioned for a year! The besieged sally forth and prove themselves very much alive, and by no means the emaciated people their enemies had fancied them to be. The business must be concluded somehow.

If there is one person of more importance than another in the army now it is the engineer. He knows more of carpentry than the priests do of Latin, which is saying a good deal; and he gives himself airs in consequence, being, therefore, considered rather too proud of his service. But he is a power in the camp, and he is consulted as to what he is going to do. He will construct a *beffroi*—a moveable tower which will bring the assailants, under shelter, close up to the walls. Wood is found in about four days, and the immense scaffolding on wheels, having five stages capable of holding three hundred men-at-arms and fifty archers, is ready for action soon after.

The platform at the summit is level with the battlements of the

TENDING THE WOUNDED ON THE FIELD.

town and a kind of drawbridge, firmly fixed, and capable of sustaining fifty armed men, protrudes from the erection so as to reach the walls. The sides of the wooden tower are coated with fresh skins to obviate all danger of fire, and it is moved by ropes and pulleys, and drawn by horses right up to the wall where the ditch has been filled up by fascines, and boarded over. The besieged regard with terror this slowly, surely approaching machine, and attempt to check its approach with Greek fire. But the assailants manage to extinguish this with wet earth, ink, and vinegar, and though some lives are lost the tower is safe, and still moves on assisted by levers, while the horses pull steadily. The wheels revolve! Now is the time for the supreme effort.

From the level of the platform the archers and cross-bowmen discharge their missiles thickly, and so prevent the enemy from setting fire to the tower on which so many hopes are fixed. The machine still advances notwithstanding the rain of stones and arrows which welcome it. Behind the machine ladders are fixed, and its progress continues. To-morrow will be the crucial day. A large reward is offered to whosoever is the first man over the wall —the cry is raised "To the assault!" The "drawbridge" of the machine is lowered with a rattle of chains, a crowd of knights press on sword in hand; the archers take their places on the topmost staging, and the assault is delivered.

The besieged throng on the battlements, and a hand to hand conflict ensues. There are horrible, fearful wounds given and received. The fight becomes more and more fierce; more knights ascend to take the places of those slain or hurled into the ditch. "To the assault!" New shouts, new feuds—the town burns, men are roasted to death. Archers shoot, machines deliver deadly missiles. At length a tremendous shout goes up, and announces the victory of the Christian assailants; they are masters of the battlements and by immense audacity plant their standard on the Paynim stronghold. This is always a triumphant action, and appeals to the popular taste.

Our baron—whose career we have followed—is the knight who has this time triumphed. He has planted the banner of God on the walls of the Infidel. The *Te Deum* is heard in all directions. The town is taken!

CHAPTER XIX.

THE DEATH OF THE KNIGHT.

THE epic poems—our *chansons de geste*—German in their origin are Christian in their object. They are more—they are the most ancient popular poems which we can consult upon the doctrines of the Christian religion! No doubt they are not theological works, and their authors were not clerics, but they are spontaneous in the best sense of the word, and reveal to us exactly the lay belief during the early centuries of the Middle Ages. What ideas our fathers had of God, of man, and of the future life? No one can answer those questions so well as our old poets.

We know that they regarded God as a spirit and as the Creator (*Dex l'espirital, Dex li Creator*). These two epithets place their faith upon a far higher pedestal than that of Homer or Virgil. There is a great gulf between the polytheism of the Iliad and the simple faith of our knights!

It is the same as regards the future life. What did death leave to our Homeric heroes? A soul—a vain image—which, when life quitted it, dissolved, as a dream. In the realms of Pluto it was sometimes a soul, sometimes an image, but always without feeling.

But the Christian doctrine is altogether different as it is understood by our epic poets. Created in the image of God, the man was destined for Heaven, but the first man having sinned, all were condemned to hell. Jesus delivered us from this fate, and all men who do not die in mortal sin are saved and placed amidst "the flowers of Paradise," but destruction awaits the rest. This is the pith of the Treaty of Man in our theological epic.

It is true that we are here far from the splendid examples of St. Anselm, St. Bernard, and St. Thomas Aquinas, contemporaries of our poets, but it is only necessary to seek here for the popular expression of a popular doctrine, and that is what renders the testimony of our old poets so valuable. Nothing can replace it.

The ideas of hell were very material, and took the form of some vast gulf which was always ready to receive its victims. It was supposed to be situated in the centre of the earth, and was so represented in the, more than simple, maps. This hell was peopled with demons, nor were the *Mysteries* less delicate in their representations of the place of punishment. How terrified children were by this! There is no question of the eternity of the punishment. We read that it is everlasting. "*Diable emportent l'anme en enfer à tous dis!*" That is decisive!

Heaven was not understood by our poets as it is by theologians and divines; but it is also eternal in existence and in loveliness. The Paradise of our knights had nothing sensual about it. Certainly they did not speak of the blessed light, nor of the clear view of God, which is the essence of eternal felicity; but we find angels bending over all those slain in battle, receiving their souls, and bearing them away to share the glories of Paradise, while demons snatch away the pagans. Our poets have not embellished the idea of a future life; but they did not falsify it nor degrade it, and they accepted it willingly.

I am not surprised at the infrequent reference to Purgatory— our poets went to the extremes; but I am astonished that the doctrine of the resurrection of the body did not strike our simple reciters. On the other hand the judgment, considered by itself, dominates and alarms the whole Christian race. It has flourished on this wholesome terror, and has been saved by it. The idea was accepted by our poets, for we read that "if you (a certain king was in question) act in that manner the Saints, the Martyrs, the Apostles, and the Innocents will all rise up against you at the Day of Judgment!"

Such was the faith in which our baron lived, and in which he was to die.

He had always hoped to have ended his days near Jerusalem, or within the Holy City itself, his lips pressed to the tomb of Christ. If they could only avenge the disgrace of Tiberias. If! But no! The news became more and more disheartening. When he embarked for Egypt he had thought to die there. His ideal was to be slain by the Saracens, and he would rather have been roasted alive than deny his Master. Ah, welcome death! How often had he prayed for it!

Our baron's prayers were but half granted. He was about to die; but of wounds received during the Crusade, alas; prosaically, slowly in his bed! To be sure he has experienced the ineffable joy of meeting his wife and children again, but he rather regretted the East and an heroic ending. The day at length arrives when he can no longer get up, so he lies, supported by pillows, thinking of all that the minstrels had sung. The death of Roland is presented to him in a new light; he had never understood it so well before.

Angels carrying the souls of brave Knights up to Heaven.

He sees it all clearly now, and the grand simplicity of the death delights him. The whole scene comes vividly before him—the tears, the prayer, the gesture of submission to his sovereign; and the worthy baron is somewhat surprised that the angels do not appear to him and take him in their arms! He is delirious!

But there is another death which he prefers to that of Roland, viz., that of Orri of Bavaria, which is less known, but no less beautiful. Orri had been taken prisoner by the pagans in a sortie. He had to choose between his faith and his love. "Render up to us the palace and the tower, and we will give you your king, Orri," cried the infidels.

"Do not surrender!" cried the king; "I will die!"

He calmly prepared for death; it was a cruel martyrdom. He was shot to death with arrows, but he managed to kneel down and utter a prayer to God to receive his soul, as his body was no longer his own. And angels fluttered down to receive this pure spirit, as they had received Roland's.

Those and many others visit him in his dreams. His bed is surrounded by noble shades. Here are Vivien, Bérard, Fierabras, Ogier the Dane, whose later years were so well spent in works of mercy and chivalrous deeds. But, above all, Renaud de Montauban is there—he whose death causes our baron to weep. He possessed the rare combination of tenderness with force. He had engaged, almost unaided, with Charlemagne; he had delivered the Holy Sepulchre; he covered himself with glory, and having repented of the slaughter of so many men, he left home and became a workman at Cologne. He was killed, but his body arose and led the funeral procession, even to the place of sepulture. Truly our baron would prefer to imitate Renaud. Could he only quit his bed and travel, unknown, to Nôtre Dame de Paris, which was then being built!

But our knight is not always thus—it would not be natural if he were. He has his hours of tender thought, and moments of military aspiration! Sometimes he thinks of his charger, and becomes quiet excited, declaring that he must rise and slay! But those accustomed to invalids know how to regard these outbreaks, which do not last long. He soon calms down and asks pardon for his childishness. Every eight days he confesses. His mind is clear, his heart is brave; he loves God; he is ready!

One day his wounds re-opened, and everyone thought he would die. But the leech declared that the good baron would live just three months longer! The knight never quailed at the sentence.

Nothing could equal the serenity of the patient. He displayed all the self-possession of the Stoic, with the pride of the cult. "It will be well," he said, one morning, "if I make my will; let me disembarrass myself of all earthly considerations at once, for it is necessary that I look chiefly to my soul in future." He makes a disposition of his property, with every regard to circumstances and fairness. He provides for his unmarried daughter, and distributes

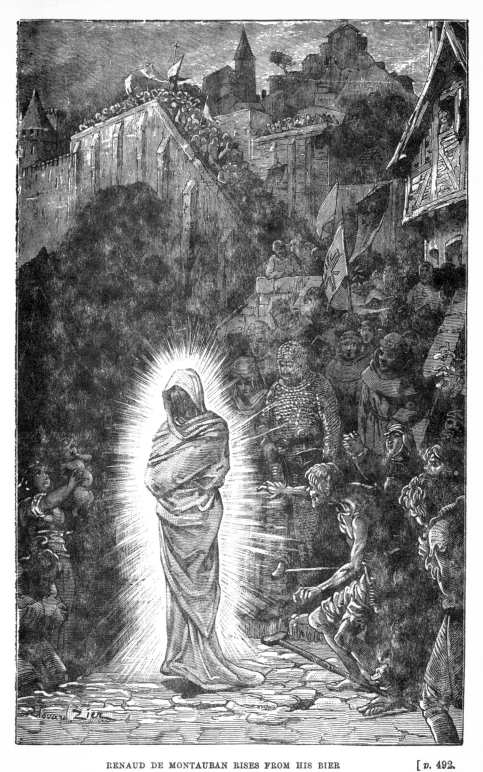

RENAUD DE MONTAUBAN RISES FROM HIS BIER [v. 492.

his goods with absolute fairness. He is somewhat fatigued after the will has been executed, but rallying, he requests his wife to proceed to Faye for two "silken-cloths," which she brings with her. These are of dark colour, and he destines them for his bier; if the day of his funeral should be wet he gives directions that they should be protected by other coverings. He goes into all these sad details without flinching, and as calmly as possible, while the attendants and his faithful spouse can but weep.

"Where would you prefer to be buried?" is the question which his eldest son puts to him next day, in a broken voice, and with a holy regard for his father—a sacred duty he considers it.

"I have loved the Templars so much that I would be laid in their chapel, and in exchange I will bequeath to them one of my manors."

It is scarcely necessary to add that he wishes—as was then usual—to be arrayed in monkish garments, and to die as a monk. With such a dress he will, he thinks, the more surely enter Heaven. But these last wishes and directions have greatly moved his attendants. They all are in tears, and a solemn silence reigns.

During the next few days the malady makes fatal progress. Death is drawing near, but the frame is so robust that it resists the approach of dissolution as an oak-tree resists the storm. Watchers, in parties of three, stand around. His son never quits the bedside.

The thought of his will occupies him very much, for, fearing it will not be perfectly in order, he has sent it to the bishop, and to the abbey of his beloved Cistercians, whom he has named as his executors. They attach their own seals to it, and return it. He holds it for a long while, gazing at the impressions on the wax; then, calling his wife, he says; "Embrace me now, for never more wilt thou embrace me." He falls into her arms as she supports him, and "they both weep," says the old poet: "*Il plora, et ele plora.*" His daughter had to be conveyed away.

As the illness continues, the priest takes an opportunity to enquire whether the baron's conscience is at rest, if the knight is at peace with all mankind, and if he has made restitution for any wrongs he may have committed. But the baron does not approve of this priestly interference, and, being of a hasty temperament, lets some hasty words escape him as to the presumption of the clerical visitor. But as the knight confesses every eighth day, no doubt he eased his conscience concerning this little outburst of anger, which was his last. His daughters then visited him, and were to him as "rays of sunshine."

All the people who have waited on invalids know that some days before death the patient enjoys a return of strength, which leads him to think that his end is not so near as he had feared. This is the case with our baron; he feels much better, and actually says that he feels inclined to sing! "And, truly," he adds, "for three years I have not felt this inclination." "Well then, sing," say his attendants, whose only desire is to please him. "No," he replied, "that were too ridiculous. Fetch my daughters hither, they shall sing to me and comfort me."

The ladies come in, Mahent and Jeanne by name, and seat themselves beside the bed. "Now, Mahent, do thou begin," he says. She is by no means inclined to do so, but her father's wishes are paramount, and, with sweet voice and simple tones, she sings the couplet of a *Chanson.* "Now it is your turn, Jeanne." The poor girl essays to obey, but her voice fails her, and the dying man at each false note gently chides her, and shows her how the song should be sung. Nothing more natural, nothing more touching, than this scene can be imagined; but it requires a powerful voice to do it justice, and our voice is, alas! like that of Jeanne!

The evening before his death the baron calls to him his eldest son, and says to him, "When I am buried you will be careful to be near the bier, and to give to the poor some of my goods. You must clothe fifty, and feed as many more." At length, feeling that his end is approaching, he apportions his last gifts to the monasteries, and particularly to those which had admitted him to their *societas* or *beneficum,* who had allowed him to participate in their good works, and in their prayers. He forgets nothing, and distributes the robes to his knights which he usually dispenses at Whitsuntide. But these latest efforts have visibly fatigued him. "Let him rest," they say. He sleeps; fever supervenes, delirium comes on. "There," he cries, "don't you see two men, two white men, one at each side!" To delirium succeeds pain, and the poor baron who has that morning confessed, is seized by the agonies of death. "Let the windows be opened; call his son, his wife, and all his relatives." They come in: the baron is leaning on the breast of his friend Jean. On his pale, yet darkening face, some rose-water

THE DYING BARON REQUESTS A SONG FROM HIS DAUGHTERS. [p. 494.

is sprinkled; this reanimates him for the moment. But he feels that the supreme moment is at hand. "I am dying, to God's care I commit you," he murmurs. Then he falls into his son's arms.

"Quick, quick, bring the cross!" The dying man sees it, adores and, leaning on his son, receives absolution and plenary indulgence in the name of the Pope. With a shudder his spirit escapes from earth: the baron is no more. Let us pray that his soul is with God—

> Prion Dieu qu'en sa sainte gloire—
> Le mete et en son Paradis!

Such are the incidents connected with the death of the knight as related by eye-witnesses. Some have been of more elevated piety—some have died in ardent faith; but there are few barons who did not die in the tenets of Christianity—soldiers of Christ.

The good knight is dead! He has been laid out by the women. The body is carefully opened by the leech in attendance; the heart, &c., are removed and conveyed, wrapped in thick stuffs (*paile*), to the neighbouring convent-church where they will be piously preserved. The body is sewn up, washed with wine and spices, and relaid upon the bed prepared for it. The body is then covered and the hands are crossed upon the ample chest. Some hours elapse, and then everyone enters to view the corpse and exclaim, "how little changed it is!"—"it is almost lifelike!" What singular consolations we devise for ourselves to compensate for the ravages of death!

The bier is ready; the body is carefully enwrapped in satin which is sewn on it and soon conceals the face. The remains are again folded in buck-skin which is also sewn over them, and this almost shapeless form is laid upon the bier. All the perfumes and aromatic herbs which can be procured are brought into use—and in these consist the only mode of embalming then known. The bier remains open, but over it are laid the famous silken materials which the baron had brought from the Holy Land, and which he had always intended for the purpose.

In honour of the dead and of the Holy Cross one hundred or two hundred candles are lighted around the bier. Twenty censers are burning in the chamber, and upon the carpet with which the marble floor has been covered are seated thirty or forty knights and servitors in tears. The brothers of the deceased and their wives now arrive to look for the last time upon their relative. The face-coverings are removed, and the spectators gaze long upon those features on which natural decay has already set its decomposing fingers. The widow begs the same favour; but the trial is too much for her, she faints away.

The next day the body is carried to the church when the " Vigils for the dead " are said in the presence of all the priests. Then the " death-watch " begins, and nothing is more striking than the appearance of the church, all in shadow save the chapel in which the bier rests in the blaze of many tapers. This is the same chapel in which the deceased baron formerly undertook his "armour-watch," and is dedicated to Saint Martin. But when day dawns it is not the cheerful Mass of the knightly "creation," but the solemn Requiem which echoes from its walls!

From the church to the cemetery is not far; the day is wet, and the handsome pall is shrouded by the cloth which had been pre-pared by the baron for such a contingency. Every tomb is of stone and is shaded by a tree. The body is laid in the ground, but it is hoped that a more worthy resting-place will soon be found for it beneath the great altar. The baron had often witnessed the desire of some of his contemporaries for magnificent tombs sculp-tured in effigy, and laid out with the feet of the figure on a lion, the head resting on a cushion, the hands joined! But to this truly Christian warrior a simple stone with a cross cut in the centre would suffice; yet the survivors might, without too great flattery, inscribe upon his tomb the truly chivalric legend—"*Ce fu li mieudres qui sor destrier sist.*" *

And while the dark clothed crowd quits the cemetery—while the disconsolate widow is giving orders to burn all her finery, while the poor body lies in the grave yonder—the soul of the good knight is in the " Holy Paradise " with the saints in glory!

* Roughly " He was one of the best knights who ever crossed a horse."

CHAPTER XX.

CONCLUSION.

WE have frequently had occasion to bring out the very consoling truth that will serve as a conclusion to this work, which we have compiled from the epic poems of the Middle Ages. This conclusion is "Truth is superior to Fiction." Herein, as elsewhere, *reality is* better than *imagination !*

The Charlemagne of history is superior to the Charles of legend ; and so with the greater number of the heroes of our *chansons de geste.* Those of our annals are of the highest "form."

Saint Louis in prison is a finer figure than William of Orange on the field of Aliscans ; Du Guesclin, "for whose ransom all the spinsters of France applied themselves to their distaffs," is greater than Renaud, the eldest of the sons of Aymon. Bayard is far superior to Ogier the Dane. But what are we to say of Joan of Arc ? As soon as that incomparable and charming figure appears all the others are eclipsed : in such a brilliant light the rest do not seem to shine.

We will go farther ; even if we provoke the disdain of those philosophers who delight in running down the human race, and in despising mankind. It is not necessary to believe that Chivalry belongs to any one epoch, or possesses any special character. The institution is dead, but its spirit lives, and there are knights under all the flags which have successively sheltered the honour of France —no matter what their colour !

We may add, to prevent disappointment, that it is quite possible for any one of the present day to become as chivalric as any knight of old time, and if anyone will conform to the ten commandments of the Code of Chivalry which we have enumerated, he will find this feasible, and actually true.

No doubt Feudalism has disappeared for ever, and this is no

longer a question of those duties which bound so strictly a vassal to his liege-lord. But the Church is weak, and this "august weakness" has more need than ever of an entire and living devotion. The doctrines of Islam are certainly no longer our hereditary opponents, but there are others against which true Chivalry will act more successfully than all the new pattern rifles, and the most murderous cannon.

Society is differently constituted now; it is no longer the same

St. Louis in Prison.

as it was eight or nine years ago, but there is still "Country," more united and better defined than formerly, and which has a right to count upon our intelligence as much as on our swords.

There is a numerous and influential "school," the members of which pretend that well-being is the aim-all and end-all of regenerated humanity. The sophists are under a gross misapprehension! A nation which loves luxury first is a nation lost! Such an one will be pushed aside, and obliterated by the more manly and vigorous race. It was—it is—Chivalry that saves nations! It is their very essence, and Chivalry disdains all those petty luxuries, and the ease of a nerveless life. It despises suffering: it is the old command put in action, *Esto Vir.*

The last commandment of the ancient Code appears to us to be more needed in the observance now. It is: *"Do not lie!"* Be truthful! I understand by that the feeling of horror of all the *finesse*, white lies, and petty insincerities, which in so many shades darken the vistas of our lives! Of all things here below Chivalry is most opposed to the "insinuation," to the shade of untruth! Chivalry would have us meet the daily danger with the most luminous frankness. We should never conceal our badge or banner. If we believe in Christ, let us, like those early martyrs, cry out: "I am a Christian!" Let us, with open brow, and transparent soul, learn, not only how to die for the truth, but learn also, what is much more difficult, how to live in it!

THE END.